PERSONNEL ADMINISTRATION IN LIBRARIES

Second Edition

Edited by
Sheila Creth
and
Frederick Duda

Neal-Schuman Publishers, Inc.
New York   London

Published by Neal-Schuman Publishers, Inc.
23 Leonard Street
New York, NY 10013

Printed and bound in the United States of America

Library of Congress Cataloging-in-Publication Data

Personnel administration in libraries.

   Bibliography: p.
   Includes index.
   1. Library personnel management.   I. Creth, Sheila D.
II. Duda, Frederick.
Z682.P394 1989   023   88-33048
ISBN 1-55570-036-5

Contents

Introduction   *Sheila D. Creth and Frederick Duda*   v

Chapter 1   Management and Personnel Administration
Frederick Duda   1

Chapter 2   The Legal Environment
Laura Gasaway and
Barbara B. Moran   13

Chapter 3   Staffing Patterns
Margaret Myers   40

Chapter 4   Personnel Planning and Utilization
Sheila D. Creth   64

Chapter 5   Recruitment and Selection
Billy R. Wilkinson   101

Chapter 6   Staff Development and Continuing Education
Sheila D. Creth   118

Chapter 7   Performance Appraisal: Purpose and
Techniques
Maxine Reneker and Virginia Steel   152

Chapter 8   Compensation Management
Frederick Duda   221

Chapter 9   Labor Relations
Frederick Duda   247

Appendix   Resources for Library Personnel
Administrators
Jeniece Guy   305

Index   333

Introduction

As stated in the introduction to the first edition of this work, the constantly evolving legal context within which personnel administration operates makes it imperative for personnel administrators to acquire a firsthand knowledge of a variety of complex, often confusing and sometimes conflicting federal, state, and local laws. These changes, coupled with the social revolution of the past two decades, major changes in the composition of the work force, the wide-spread computerization of work and the ongoing acceptance of varied life-styles, have presented new challenges and expanded the role of the personnel administrator significantly.

In the early 1970s, personnel administrators had already begun to assume responsibility for a broad range of complex functions, such as union contract negotiation and administration, affirmative action and equal employment implementation, training and development, job analysis and classification, wage and salary administration, and job counseling for all categories of staff. In the 1980s, we have seen the beginning of the end of mandatory retirement for most categories of positions, an increased attention to controlling benefits costs, major shifts in how work is accomplished, and the onset of challenges to affirmative action and civil rights laws enacted over the past quarter of a century. Although progress has been made in the area of equal pay, in the 1980s, there has been minor and limited progress on comparable worth. During the past decade women have made considerable progress and have gained acceptance in senior management positions in libraries, while minorities continue to be underrepresented at all levels of librarianship. In fact, social pressures will continue to have impact on employment legislation and on the function and significance of the role of the personnel administrator.

In any medium- to large-sized library, the duties of a personnel administrator are complicated. They not only have to include the staff in the decision-making process, but must make sure that substantive issues receive careful scrutiny from those directly responsible for library service activities, and provide staff with the opportunities to enrich their experience and attain job fulfillment. The importance of involving staff in the decision-making process is particularly acute in developing, implementing, and maintaining an effective personnel program, because the success of specific aspects of the program, such as revising the process for performance appraisal or the system for position classification, hinges on the staff's involvement and support.

The editors espouse the point of view that management is responsible for achieving organizational objectives through the effective utilization and involvement of staff. Although conceived from the point of view of the personnel administrator, *Personnel Administration in Libraries* is aimed at a broader audience of supervisors and managers in medium- to large-sized libraries, as well as those carrying full or partial responsibility for personnel functions. This book should also benefit those librarians who do not carry administrative or supervisory responsibilities because of its descriptions of the management process and their role in it.

The purpose of *Personnel Administration in Libraries* is to provide insight into the nature of the personnel function through an exploration of key areas of responsibility. Each chapter provides the background necessary to understand trends and development, summarizes differing points of view on key issues, offers guidance on techniques and procedures that have proved effective, and relates the issues to organizational objectives.

Two chapters have been added to this edition: "Management and Personnel Administration" and "Compensation Management." As in the first edition, communication and motivation are relevant to so many personnel concerns, they are not covered separately. Instead, they are integrated into the issues addressed in each chapter. Similarly, counseling, which most personnel administrators provide informally and which, owing to privacy issues and the need for specialist training, is a complex area, is treated in the chapters on performance appraisal and recruitment and selection. Few view counselling as a part of grievance administration and discipline, but it is integral to the correction of unsatisfactory organizational behavior and performance, and is another mechanism to address the development of staff at all levels of the organization. Areas not covered in the separate chapters include health and safety, records management and retrieval, and budget preparation and administration. References to a number of these areas can be found in the appendix.

In Chapter One, Frederick Duda, a personnel consultant, discusses the nature of personnel administration and its relationship to management. Management concepts and personnel objectives are covered with emphasis given to the importance of good line-staff relations in the

context of organizational objectives and the role of the chief administrator or librarian. The characteristics and qualifications considered essential for success as a personnel administrator are also covered.

In Chapter Two, Laura N. Gasaway, Law Librarian and Professor of Law, and Barbara B. Moran, Assistant Dean, School of Information and Library Sciences, University of North Carolina at Chapel Hill, discuss the legal framework governing employee-management relations from New Deal legislation through the aftermath of the Civil Rights movement and its myriad offspring. The topic is complex and compounded by variations from state to state and by evolving state case law. Despite the complexity of the legal framework, library personnel administrators need to attain a working knowledge of the issues.

In Chapter Three, Margaret Myers, Director of the Office for Library Personnel Resources, American Library Association, discusses the importance of proper staffing. It is inevitable that there will continue to be a wide range of methods and styles of staffing, but Myers notes the critical role of job descriptions and well-defined position classification systems in developing successful staffing patterns. The impact on staff of external and internal forces, such as technology, societal changes, increased costs, and participative management, is also considered.

Personnel planning and utilization and the relationship to recruitment, position classification and promotional systems, and compensation schemes are covered in Chapter Four by Sheila Creth, University Librarian, University of Iowa. The various components of a personnel planning and utilization program are reviewed and discussed, as are the elements necessary to conduct a meaningful job analysis. Creth emphasizes the human relations aspects of job analysis and evaluation, including the importance of maintaining effective communications with the staff throughout the process.

The recruitment and selection of library personnel is covered by Billy R. Wilkinson, Director of the Albin O. Kuhn Library and Gallery of the University of Maryland, Baltimore County in Chapter Five. The nature of the recruitment process is reviewed and the techniques and procedures of interviewing applicants for various types of library jobs are set forth.

In Chapter Six, Creth discusses the effective development of library staff. Distinctions between staff development and continuing education are explored, as are the elements necessary for effective programs in both areas. The crucial roles played by supervisors and personnel administrators in planning and evaluating staff development activities are discussed, as are the pitfalls to avoid.

Maxine Reneker, Deputy Director for Instructional and Research Services, The Stanford University Libraries, and Virginia Steel, Head of Access Services, University of California, San Diego, cover performance

appraisal from a developmental point of view in Chapter Seven. Many problems can be encountered in implementing or revising a performance appraisal program, but they can be minimized through careful planning and involving key library staff. In an effort to insure that the appraisal will be sound and based on relevant, accurate, and sufficiently complete information, the authors outline guidelines to follow.

The critical role played by the supervisor and the personnel administrator is highlighted. Too often supervisors view performance appraisals as necessary evils, and no one ever seems happy with the form in use or the process itself. The authors of this chapter provide a context for understanding how essential performance appraisal is in meeting organizational objectives while at the same time focusing on staff development and providing individuals with a sense that effort, improvement and contributions are recognized and appreciated.

Duda discusses compensation management in Chapter Eight, including the nature and objectives of compensation. Internal influences on compensation, both governmental and societal, are reviewed. Merit or performance-based reward systems are covered. The importance of benefits and other services are discussed. Timely and proper compensation administration is emphasized, as is salary equity analysis and computer applications.

The focus of Chapter Nine is management's role in labor relations. The aim of the chapter is to provide guidance to personnel administrators and library managers working in or about to work in a unionized library. Particular emphasis is given to contract negotiation and administration, including principles of resolving grievances and discipline and discharge. The latter topics should be of concern to personnel administrators and managers regardless of whether or not their libraries are unionized.

The appendix on sources in personnel administration was compiled by Jeniece Guy, Assistant Director, Office for Library Personnel Resources, ALA. It provides information on sources and opportunities available to maintain currency in the field. Experience alone does not provide an administrator or manager with guaranteed success on the job. Because we are living in a period of considerable change and technological evolution we must supplement our experiences by keeping abreast of new trends, developments, and points of view and by participating in staff development and continuing education activities.

Any work devoted to personnel administration in libraries should make some mention of library education. Since significant numbers of librarians assume supervisory and administrative responsibilities sometime in their careers, we hope this work will find an audience in library schools to contribute to future librarians' understanding of the complex and critical aspects of personnel administration.

The editors, as well as many chapter authors, have had direct involvement in a number of changes that significantly affected personnel administration over the past two decades. Although we may not have realized it at the time, we more often than not shared the point of view of Paul Pigors and Charles Myers, who for more than 35 years have stressed that "personnel administration is a *line responsibility* and a *staff function*" (*Personnel Administration: A Point of View and a Method*, 8th ed., New York: McGraw-Hill, 1977, p. 397).

Personnel administration is also in essence a *service*. Conflicts over authority and the proper role of personnel can generally be resolved to benefit the organization if the chief administrator and line management share these views. The personnel administrator should provide guidance in the recruitment and utilization of staff and in the development and implementation of policy. The personnel administrator should provide direction and guidance in all aspects of the personnel program but also should be an active member of the administrative team to contribute to the overall direction of the library. Contributions the personnel administrator can make to the library are presented in the chapters that follow. Success and satisfaction for the personnel administrator can best be achieved if he or she helps convey the sense of a "unity of purpose" within the organization and promotes a teamwork approach in resolving problems and dealing with issues of the organization.

Personnel administration, though at times stressful and frustrating, is an exciting and rewarding activity. The contributors to *Personnel Administration in Libraries* provide considerable background information on the many facets of personnel administration. Equally important are the perspectives set forth that offer opportunities for contributing directly to distinctive library service through the effective recruitment and utilization of human resources.

Sheila D. Creth
Frederick Duda

Editor's note: As this edition goes to press, several civil rights and affirmative action cases are pending in the Supreme Court. The Court unanimously refused to overturn a major civil rights precedent which gave minorities the right to use an 1866 Reconstruction-era law to sue for private acts of racial discrimination (commonly known as Section 1981 after its designation in the United States Code). At the same time, the Court ruled five to four to limit the statute's application in the employment area. The ruling means that a person can use the 1866 law to sue at the initial hiring stage, but not for racially discriminatory conditions on the job.

The rulings on Section 1981 are among several made by the Supreme Court in the first six months of 1989 that are being viewed by some as strengthening the constitutional principle of equal protection under the law, and by others as disastrous for affirmative action programs. Other responses to the Court's decisions include fear that government agencies that created affirmative action programs years ago can now be subject to challenges by non-protected employees, and predictions that civil rights leaders will exert pressure on Congress to enact legislation to restore what has been lost through the Court ruling. We are clearly entering a new era of political confrontation over affirmative action, which makes it imperative for personnel administrators to keep abreast of ongoing developments.

In addition to the ruling on Section 1981, other civil rights and affirmative action rulings by the Supreme Court during the first half of 1989 are: Richmond v. Croson (on January 23, the Court by a vote of six to three declared unconstitutional a Richmond, Virginia, ordinance setting aside 30 percent of public works contract spending for minority contractors); Price Waterhouse v. Hopkins (on May 1, the Court ruled six to three that in some cases alleging intentional discrimination, employers have the burden of proving that their refusal to hire or promote someone is based on legitimate and not discriminatory reasons); and Wards Cove v. Atonio (on June 5, the Court ruled by a vote of five to four that plaintiffs, not employers, have the burden of proving whether a job requirement that is shown statistically to screen out minorities or women is a "business necessity"; and Lorance v. A.T. & T. (on June 12, the Court ruled by a vote of five to four to place time limitations on the filing of lawsuits challenging seniority systems that are alleged to be discriminatory [within 300 days of the adoption of the system]). On June 12, the Court by a five to four vote ruled in Martin v. Wilk that court-approved affirmative action settlements are open to subsequent litigation by white workers, clearing the way for white fire fighters in Birmingham, Alabama, to challenge a court-approved settlement intended to increase the hiring and promotion of blacks (*New York Times,* June 13, 1989, p. 1).

1
Management and
Personnel Administration
Frederick Duda

Technology has liberated professional librarians from performing many of the routine and repetitive tasks associated with the practice of librarianship and it may well have changed the ratio of professional to clerical staff, but it has not had meaningful impact on the percentage of library budgets expended on personnel. Personnel costs have accounted for well more than half of library budgets for decades, and this ratio is not likely to change in the foreseeable future.

Library work is labor-intensive. This means that most librarian-managers only can accomplish their organizational objectives through the management of and interaction with *people*—whether they be a few part-time student assistants or a department of professionals. As Herbert White has stated, the manager's success will continue to depend on human relations skills:

> As practicing librarians know well, ours is not a book- or periodical-based profession; these are only the tools of the trade. Librarianship is a people profession, and we are only as successful as our ability to interact with others makes us.[1]

Librarians have to view themselves as managers of people and understand and accept the implications of getting work done through others. As William B. Werther, Jr., and Keith Davis have pointed out, "Among the resources available to an organization, none are more important than its people."[2]

The impact of technology on society requires special emphasis in any discussion of management and personnel administration. In a study of automation's affect on the workplace, Shoshana Zuboff observes that management has not responded with great vision to a new watershed in human history. Zuboff's comments on sound management approaches for dealing with technological change include:

> ... the requirements of an informating strategy support existing work-improvement efforts, such as the high commitment approach to work force management, with its emphasis on self-managing teams, participation, and decentralization. Organizations that are already pursuing this approach are more likely to have developed both the ideological context and the social skills necessary to plan and implement an informating strategy. . . . Challenges to the managerial role that can be unleashed by the informating process are likely to exacerbate the growing pains associated with participative management and to accelerate the need for positive change.[3]

MANAGEMENT CONCEPTS

Planning, innovation, coordination, administration, and control are generally accepted as the essence of management. But if there is a key word to describe management, according to Paul Pigors and Charles A. Myers, it is coordination:

> Coordination includes some decision-making: establishing broad objectives, initiating and approving changes in key personnel and in management organization, approving decisions of various matters in terms of the approver's interpretation of broad objectives, approving decisions on specific matters to avoid conflicts with other decisions.[4]

To expand on this concept, "management is organizational leadership, and one of its central tasks is effective coordination and development of available human and nonhuman resources to achieve the objectives of the organization."[5]

Organizational objectives can only be attained through the combined efforts of people. All managers have a personnel responsibility and a critical role to play in attaining objectives and influencing the organizational climate. Whether or not they articulate them all managers have personnel concepts which are based on a variety of assumptions about the way people behave in organizations, and they are generally reflective of different theories of management.

The Traditional Concept of Management

Douglas McGregor's "Theory X" provides the most succinct summary of the so-called traditional concept of management, namely management by centralized direction and control:

1. The average human being has an inherent dislike of work and will avoid it if he can.
2. Because of this human characteristic of dislike of work, most people must be coerced, controlled, directed, threatened with punishment to get them to put forth adequate effort toward the achievement of organizational objectives.
3. The average human being prefers to be directed, wishes to avoid responsibility, has relatively little ambition, wants security above all.[6]

This authoritarian concept of management continues to hold sway in many organizations. It involves clearly defined lines of authority or chains of command, with limited delegation of authority and full and detailed accountability up the line.[7]

The Personnel-Minded Concept of Management

The personnel-minded concept of management, based on the assumption that the best way to accomplish objectives is to work with rather than through people, is in direct contract to the authoritarian concept. McGregor calls this "Theory Y" and characterizes it as follows:

1. The expenditure of physical and mental effort in work is as natural as play or rest. The average human being does not inherently dislike work. Depending upon controllable conditions, work may be a source of satisfaction (and will be voluntarily performed) or a source of punishment (and will be avoided if possible).
2. External control and the threat of punishment are not the only means for bringing about effort toward organizational objectives. Man will exercise self-direction and self-control in the service of objectives to which he is committed.
3. Commitment to objectives is a function of the rewards associated with their achievement. The most significant of such rewards, e.g., the satisfaction of ego and self-actualization needs, can be direct products of effort directed toward organizational objectives.
4. The average human being learns, under proper conditions, not only to accept but to seek responsibility. Avoidance of responsibility, lack of ambition, and emphasis on security are generally consequences of experience, not inherent human characteristics.
5. The capacity to exercise a relatively high degree of imagination, ingenuity, and creativity in the solution of organizational problems is widely, not narrowly, distributed in the population.
6. Under the conditions of modern industrial life, the intellectual potentialities of the average human being are only partially utilized.[8]

McGregor's Theory X – Theory Y concept has had considerable impact on management thinking over the past thirty years. It was one of the bases for the participative management movement of the late 1960s, which is often misconstrued as an abrogation of managerial responsibility. As McGregor has noted, "participation is one of the most misunderstood ideas" to have emerged from the field of human relations.[9] He states further:

> The effective use of participation is a consequence of a managerial point of view which includes confidence in the potentialities of subordinates, awareness of management's dependency downwards, and a desire to avoid some of the negative consequences of emphasis on personal authority. . . . Since one of the major purposes of the use of participation is to encourage the growth of subordinates and their ability to accept responsibility, the superior will be concerned to pick appropriate problems or issues for discussion and decision. These will be matters of some significance to subordinates; otherwise they will see little point in their involvement.[10]

Behavioral Science Research

Behavioral research studies both support and question the general applicability of personnel-minded concepts of management, particularly in the causal relationship between job satisfaction and productivity. Stated very simply, the debates center on whether a satisfied employee is a higher performer *or* whether the higher performer is a more satisfied employee (Pigors and Myers, 8th ed., provide a good summary of the debates).[11]

We will continue to find examples of centralized control and direction (Theory X), but societal pressures and employee expectations, as well as findings of behavioral science research, tend to support management by participation in shared objectives. Individual management styles will vary from time to time for a variety of reasons, including personal attributes of incumbents and institutional goals, but as Pigors and Myers emphasize, "The essence of good management is getting effective results—not only in the short run, but also in the long run—through building and maintaining a productive human organization."[12]

Peter Drucker, who sees the debate over the validity of Theory X versus Theory Y as largely a "sham battle," offers the following perception:

> The basic fact—unpalatable but inescapable—is that the traditional Theory X approach to managing, that is, the carrot-and-stick way, no longer works. In developed countries, it does not even work for manual workers, and nowhere can it work for knowledge workers. The stick is no longer available to the manager, and the carrot is becoming less and less of an incentive.[13]

THE OBJECTIVES OF PERSONNEL ADMINISTRATION

Many libraries articulate their service objectives in staff handbooks or manuals, but it is rare to find a statement of an institution's personnel objective or philosophy. We can assume certain implicit objectives from statements on grievance procedures and affirmative action programs, but such policies are generally mandated by employment legislation or union contracts. An articulation of objectives of personnel administration should include a description of governance, staff development programs and opportunities, and staff involvement in the decision-making process.

All organizations have personnel objectives whether they are implicit or expressed in writing. They serve as guides for both personnel administrators and managers and form the basis of evaluating personnel actions. Werther and Davis state that "personnel objectives must recognize challenges from society, the organization, the personnel function, and the people who are affected."[14] Four objectives common to personnel administration are:

1. *Societal objective.* To be socially responsible to the needs and challenges of society while minimizing the negative impact of such demands upon the organization. The failure of organizations to use their resources for society's benefit may result in restrictions. For example, society might pass laws that limit personnel decisions.
2. *Organizational objective.* To recognize that personnel management exists to contribute to an organization's effectiveness. Personnel management is not an end in itself; it is only a means to assist the organization with its primary objectives. Simply stated, the personnel department exists to serve the rest of the organization.
3. *Functional objective.* To maintain the personnel management contribution at a level appropriate with the organization's needs. Resources are wasted when personnel management is more or less sophisticated than the organization demands. A personnel department's level of service must be appropriate for the organization it serves.
4. *Personal objective.* To assist employees in achieving their personal goals, at least insofar as these goals enhance the individual's contribution to the organization. Personal objectives of employees must be met if workers are to be maintained, retained, and motivated. Otherwise, employee performance and satisfaction may decline, and employees may leave the organization.[15]

PERSONNEL VIEWPOINTS

Contemporary viewpoints in personnel administration emphasize complementary themes that are critical to organizational success—and which are reflected throughout this book. They include:

1. *Human resource approach.* Personnel management is the management of human resources. The importance and dignity of human beings should not be ignored for the sake of expediency. Only through careful attention to the needs of employees do successful organizations grow and prosper.
2. *Management approach.* Personnel management is the responsibility of every manager. The personnel department exists to serve managers and employees through its expertise. So in the final analysis, the performance and well-being of each worker is the dual responsibility of that worker's immediate supervisor and the personnel department.
3. *Systems approach.* Personnel management takes place within a larger system: the organization. Therefore, personnel management must be evaluated with respect to the contribution it makes to the organization's productivity. In practice, experts must recognize that the personnel management model is an open system of interrelated parts. Each part affects the others and is influenced by the external environment. (Werther and Davis define an "open system" as one that is affected by the environment.)
4. *Proactive approach.* Personnel management can increase its contribution to employees, managers, and the organization by anticipating challenges before they arise. If efforts are reactive only, problems may be compounded and opportunities may be missed.[16]

Implicit in these viewpoints is the limitations of the role of the personnel administrator. Personnel administrators should influence the methods of operation of an organization and the treatment of employees, but they do not have the final say on either, a fact that can lead to conflict in an organization because of the differences between line and staff functions.

Despite the limitations faced by personnel administrators, it is clear that personnel management has moved from backstage to center stage in the last twenty years. Rosabeth Moss Kanter attributes this transformation to the growing recognition of human resources issues to organizational success. The issues Kanter cites to illustrate her point include:

> . . . compensation and incentives, dismissal, outplacement and resignation, employee counsel and appraisal, job analysis and satisfaction, employee rights, and a host of issues concerning labor, its costs, its productivity, and its turnover. There was also considerable attention to executive training in management development, affirmative-action issues in general, and women and minority groups in particular.[17]

LINE AND STAFF

O. Glenn Stahl's definition of line and staff, a relationship in organizational theory that "sometimes reaches the point of being a fetish," is appealingly succinct:

The functions for which the organization was created—carrying the mail, putting out fires, running a mental institution—are the "line" functions, and those existing *as the result of* creating the organization—personnel management, financial control, supply services—are "staff."[18]

Line-staff relationships assume the characteristics of a fetish when one begins to expand on their theoretical implications. Since the line functions are the raison d'etre and the staff *must serve* the line, it follows that the effectiveness of the staff depends on the degree to which it supports and satisfies the line. The logic begins to break down when one realizes that the legal framework governing personnel administration has changed dramatically during the past thirty years. Recent legislation in the areas of, for example, affirmative action and equal pay frequently prevents personnel administrators from fulfilling the real or imagined needs of line managers. The lack of clear interpretations of many aspects of recent employment legislation compounds the problem, creating conflicts between line and staff that often require resolution by "wise chief executives."

Stahl advises the "wise chief executive" not to worry about artificial distinctions between line and staff. Writing prior to the enactment of much of contemporary employment legislation, he emphasizes the validity of public concern about the employment and treatment of personnel:

It [the management of personnel] has indeed become almost an end in itself, ranking close in importance to the national defense, the management of communication and transportation, the conservation of resources, the conduct of public education, and the direction of foreign affairs because it is in and of all of these, and how it is done determines in large measure the very effectiveness of these most critical obligations of the modern State.[19]

The problems that develop between line and staff often intensify during periods of change, whether it be unionization or the introduction of new technology. Paul Pigors and Charles A. Myers, who point out that the staff function involves the element of "control" or "inspection," have observed that "staff control involves an information feedback to line managers, so that they can take corrective actions if they have not properly applied predetermined standards or policies."[20] Like Stahl, Pigors and Myers warn against the dangers of carrying line-staff distinctions to excess. In commenting on the degree of authority of the personnel administrator, Pigors and Myers make a number of points that both experienced personnel administrators and chief librarians will find particularly useful when conflicts over policy develop between the line and staff functions.[21] These tenets are summarized as follows:

1. It is an unwise personnel administrator who issues orders to managers or their subordinates. The personnel administrator should *advise* the chief executive and other top administrators on good personnel policies and on their consistent, uniform applications throughout the organization.
2. If the personnel administrator cannot persuade or convince a line manager that the advice is sound, he or she would be wise to suggest that they jointly report the disagreement to the appropriate top administrator. In this manner, the personnel administrator performs a control or inspection function, but it must be exercised sparingly in order to win the confidence and cooperation of line management.
3. If a personnel administrator has any authority, it is the authority of established personnel policies and procedures that he or she has helped to formulate and the authority of specialized knowledge, rather than the authority of the position.
4. A personnel administrator facing opposition from managers can succeed only if he or she is seen by managers as a source of help and not as a threat. [Although Pigors and Myers state that such help must be wanted, not imposed, experience would argue otherwise. It is not unusual for a personnel officer to *impose* a policy or procedure once it becomes official or required by law. The challenge is one of persuading or convincing managers of the justification for the action.]
5. The personnel administrator may be viewed as a "change agent," whose role is to help management think through the implications of decisions concerning the human organization, particularly on the capacity of that organization to change constructively with environmental or technological developments.
6. Although basic knowledge of behavioral science applications to management (i.e., assumptions found in McGregor's "Theory X") will enable the personnel administrator to become a more effective change agent, the kind of interpersonal skills required, which are discussed below, must go beyond an intellectual knowledge of the personnel field.

CHARACTERISTICS AND QUALIFICATIONS

The ideal characteristics and qualifications for a personnel administrator set forth by Pigors and Myers are:

1. A personality that makes both line and staff officers want to work with rather than against him or her;
2. The ability to help a manager develop the skills to handle future problems more effectively;
3. The ability to obtain results from staff in the personnel office and to develop subordinates (most personnel administrators have line responsibilities that provide them with opportunities to practice the theories they pass on to the line);
4. Patience, understanding, empathy, a willingness to listen first and talk afterward, and a professional knowledge of the personnel field.

5. Prior experience in a line position. The personnel administrator who trains as a specialist and enters an organization as a specialist is more likely to remain out of touch with the real personnel problems faced by the line managers.[22]

The characteristics considered ideal for a personnel administrator may not be restricted to beings on an endangered species list, but even those who inherently possess such characteristics will find themselves challenged because of the changing nature of librarianship and the need to adapt to the variety of approaches and attitudes represented by new members of the management team. Personnel administration will continue to involve change and the usual Sturm und Drang that it entails. Such an environment takes its toll on personnel administrators, but, under the right circumstances, it can increase an individual's commitment to the organization. This is most likely to occur when there is good communication between the personnel administrator and the chief executive and when there is a clearly articulated *unity of purpose* within the organization. The comments of Pigors and Myers are particularly relevant here:

> In an increasing number of companies and organizations line-staff conflicts in personnel administration are becoming less important because there is a "unity of purpose" among members of the management organization. Here both line and staff people appreciate the importance of human resources and of how they should be treated. In these situations, the personnel administrator can make decisions affecting the line without any apparent ill effects on the line; his ideas are more acceptable. In these organizations, there is a blurring of line-staff distinction because the managerial team includes people who perform *both* line and staff functions for the achievement of common organizational objectives.[23]

In an environment that has a strong sense of unity of purpose a personnel administrator is likely to place conflicts in their proper perspective. In such organizations, the personnel administrator and the line managers are more likely to reach a consensus and avoid conflicts that can compromise library objectives.

Discussing prior experience and training for personnel work, Pigors and Myers point out that in the United States there is no widely accepted professional training for personnel administrators as there is in Great Britain.[24] As mentioned earlier, they recommend prior experience in a line position before entering the personnel field. The nature of previous experience for a personnel administrator in libraries, as well as the other qualifications to seek, merits some comment. It is not unusual to receive an inquiry from a library seeking an opinion on whether the requirements for a library personnel administrator should include the

MLS, previous relevant experience in a library, an advanced degree in personnel administration, or some other type of experience and background. Perhaps the best response to such concerns is to make the requirements both as flexible and relevant as possible.

CHALLENGES TO MANAGEMENT

Changes in the composition of the work force, continued pressure for equal opportunity and salary equity, rapid changes in technology, and fiscal constraints will continue to affect library operations and objectives in the years to come. In dealing with these challenges, library managers and personnel administrators will continue to have varying degrees of success, regardless of good intentions and adherence to the most advanced concepts of management. Success is more likely when an organization subscribes to a personnel-minded concept of management, provided it is understood that participation in the decision-making process rightfully has limitations. As Rosabeth Moss Kanter points out:

> Participation would appear to work best when it is well managed. "Well managed" systems have these elements: a clearly assigned management structure and involvement of the appropriate line people; assignment of meaningful and manageable tasks with clear boundaries and parameters; a time frame, a set of accountability and reporting relationships, and standards that groups must meet; information and training for participants to help them make participation work effectively; a mechanism for involving all of those with a stake in the issue, to avoid the problems of power and to ensure for those who have input or interest a chance to get involved; a mechanism for providing visibility, recognition, and rewards for teams' efforts; and clearly understood processes for the formation of participative groups, their ending, and the transfer of the learning for them.[25]

References

1. Herbert S. White, *Library Personnel Management* (White Plains, N.Y.: Knowledge Industry, 1985), pp. v–vi.
2. William B. Werther, Jr., and Keith Davis, *Personnel Management and Human Resources,* 2nd ed. (New York: McGraw-Hill, 1985), p. 6.
3. Shoshana Zuboff, *In the Age of the Smart Machine: The Future of Work and Power* (New York: Basic Books, 1988), p. 413.
4. Paul Pigors and Charles A. Myers, *Personnel Administration: A Point of View and a Method,* 8th ed. (New York: McGraw-Hill, 1977), p. 6.
5. Ibid.

6. Douglas McGregor, *The Human Side of Enterprise* (New York: McGraw-Hill, 1960), pp. 33–34.
7. Pigors and Myers, 8th ed., p. 7.
8. McGregor, pp. 47–48.
9. Ibid., p. 124.
10. Ibid, pp. 125–26.
11. Pigors and Myers, 8th ed., pp. 10–18.
12. Ibid., pp. 22.
13. Peter Drucker, *Management: Tasks, Responsibilities, Practices* (New York: Harper & Row, 1974), pp. 232–35.
14. Werther and Davis, p. 9.
15. Ibid., pp. 9–10.
16. Ibid., p. 25.
17. Rosabeth Moss Kanter, *The Change Masters: Innovations for Productivity in the American Corporation* (New York: Simon and Schuster, 1983), p. 45.
18. O. Glenn Stahl, *Public Personnel Administration,* 5th ed. (New York: Harper & Row, 1962), p. 19.
19. Ibid., p. 21.
20. Pigors and Myers, p. 25.
21. Ibid., pp. 26–29.
22. Ibid.
23. Pigors and Myers, *Personnel Administration,* 7th ed. (New York: McGraw-Hill, 1973), pp. 31–32.
24. Pigors and Myers, 8th ed., p. 31.
25. Kanter, p. 275.

Bibliography

Drucker, Peter. *Management: Tasks, Responsibilities, Practices.* New York: Harper & Row, 1974.
Hendricks, Epsy Y. "The Role of Personnel Officers in University Libraries." Ph.D. dissertation, Indiana University, 1977.
Kanter, Rosabeth Moss. *The Change Masters: Innovations for Productivity in the American Corporation.* New York: Simon and Schuster, 1983.
McGregor, Douglas. *The Human Side of Enterprise.* New York: McGraw-Hill, 1960.
Pigors, Paul and Charles A. Myers. *Personnel Administration.* 7th ed. New York: McGraw-Hill, 1973.
————. *Personnel Administration: A Point of View and a Method.* 8th ed. New York: McGraw-Hill, 1977.
Stahl, O. Glenn. *Public Personnel Administration.* 5th ed. New York: Harper & Row, 1962.
Tichy, Noel M. and Mary Anne Devanna. *The Transformational Leader.* New York: John Wiley & Sons, 1986.
Werther, William B., Jr., and Keith Davis. *Personnel Management and Human Resources.* 2nd ed. New York: McGraw-Hill, 1985.

White, Herbert S. *Library Personnel Management.* White Plains, N.Y.: Knowledge Industry Publications, 1985.

Zuboff, Shoshana. *In the Age of the Smart Machine: The Future of Work and Power.* New York: Basic Books, 1988.

2
The Legal Environment

Laura N. Gasaway
Barbara B. Moran

The legal environment in which a personnel administrator must function has changed dramatically in the past few decades. The body of both federal and state law pertaining to personnel practices has expanded greatly and created both advantages and disadvantages. The major detriment is that a personnel administrator's freedom in such areas as employee selection, termination, conditions of employment, and collective bargaining is constrained by the continued growth in regulations and laws pertaining to the employer-employee relationship. On the other hand, this legislative framework, which was put in place largely because reliance on voluntary measures was not successful, has improved the working conditions of the average library employee. The laws relating to personnel practices have been instrumental in providing workers with a physically safe work environment, greater job security, privacy protection, and other employee rights and benefits. Additionally, such laws help insure that every individual, regardless of age, race, gender, religion, or national origin, has an equal access to any job for which he or she is qualified.

Familiarity with the laws and regulations governing employment is essential for library personnel administrators and managers. Although the reader must recognize that this discussion does not constitute legal advice, nor should it be relied upon in lieu of legal counsel, the importance of following the practices of the parent organization and seeking the advice of legal counsel when needed cannot be stressed too strongly.

The following discussion should provide library personnel administrators with an understanding of the basic elements of employment legislation. The legal framework for personnel matters in libraries consists of laws, administrative regulations, and executive orders at federal and state levels, municipal and other government ordinances and regulations, plus an enormous body of court decisions and arbitration agreements. Additionally, a seemingly infinite body of literature documenting and interpreting these laws and decisions exists.[1]

EQUAL EMPLOYMENT OPPORTUNITY

Equal employment legislation in the United States is of fairly recent vintage. Although there are antecedents prior to the 1960s, the first comprehensive anti-discrimination in employment statute was Title VII of the Civil Rights Act of 1964.[2] Commonly referred to as "Title VII," the primary aim of the statute is to make actionable overt discrimination in all phases of private employment. The act does not guarantee that women and minorities must be hired for vacant positions or promoted within a library, rather it requires that they be fairly considered and neither excluded nor hindered because of race, sex, religion, or national origin.[3] Employees who bring successful Title VII actions are entitled to back pay, and the court may order reinstatement or hiring and award attorneys' fees to the employee.[4] Although much progress has been made, Title VII's anti-discrimination promise has yet to be fully realized.

Title VII covers employers with fifteen or more employees engaged in interstate commerce. Today, almost all business enterprises are found to be engaged in interstate commerce; labor unions also are covered. Although the act originally excluded governmental units, it was amended in 1972 to include state and local governments with fifteen or more employees.[5] Title VII embraces all aspects of the employment process from recruitment, advertising, and hiring to salary, terminations, and retirement. The act created the Equall Employment Opportunity Commission (EEOC) to enforce its provisions.[6] Along with other agencies, the EEOC helped to develop the 1978 Uniform Guidelines on Employee Selection Procedures (generally referred to as the "Uniform Guidelines").[7] The Uniform Guidelines assist employers in understanding the provisions of the act and guide enforcement agencies.

The act's provisions clearly apply to most librarians and library workers. Virtually all libraries are covered by Title VII today: those in the for-profit sector are covered if the company has fifteen or more employees, public libraries are part of local government and the number of employees is aggregated for the local government unit, and academic libraries are included as a part of the parent institution.

Librarians responsible for personnel administration must be aware of the anti-discrimination requirements of Title VII and comply with its mandate. Frequently, parent organizations will have established procedures to ensure compliance and fairness in dealing with employees and applicants for positions.

Two of the act's protected categories require additional explanation: religion and sex. Under Title VII, an employer is required to make reasonable accommodation to the religious practices and beliefs of employees. This has been held to include the wearing of religious dress and working on religious holidays.[8] Courts continue to clarify what constitutes "reasonable accommodation" so the area is not static. Clearly, an employer may not accommodate one employee's religious preference to refrain from work on certain holidays observed by his or her religion if such accommodation unduly burdens other employees who must fill in for the observer.[9]

There are some unique issues in the area of sex discrimination: pregnancy and maternity, sexual harassment, and compensation. Additionally, there is a separate statute governing equal educational opportunity, which some litigants have attempted to use in employment discrimination suits against educational institutions.

Pregnancy and Maternity

Congress specifically amended Title VII to make it absolutely clear that discrimination on the basis of pregnancy is sex discrimination.[10] Thus, an employer may not refuse to hire a woman because she is pregnant or exclude only pregnancy from insurance coverage.[11] If an employer's health insurance provides benefits for pregnant employees, and if all medical conditions are covered for the spouses of female employees, then the insurance must offer pregnancy benefits for the spouses of male employees.[12] Further, an employer may not terminate a pregnant employee nor require or mandate a specified maternity leave period for employees.[13] On the other hand, some states offer increased benefits for pregnancy and maternity, specifically providing paid maternity leaves and guaranteeing that an employee on maternity leave may return to her job. The U.S. Supreme Court recently upheld this recognition of the uniqueness of pregnancy and maternity, thus allowing this special provision.[14]

Some forward-looking employers are beginning to offer employees of either sex parental leave regardless of whether the children involved are natural or adopted children. This leave is likely to become increasingly widespread as society recognizes the need of both parents to have some time at home with newborn or newly adopted children.

Sexual Harassment

Most people recognize that an employee should not be subjected to demands for sexual favors on the job, but only recently has the Supreme Court recognized sexual harassment as sex discrimination. It is precisely because of the person's sex that he or she is subjected to such treatment.[15] Conduct that qualifies as sexual harassment may range from offensive sexual innuendos to physical assault, and courts tend to consider a victim's response to such conduct in determining whether the conduct is sexual harassment. In other words, some employees enjoy and participate in sexual jokes while other workers would consider them harassment. Though not dispositive of the issue, whether the victim has participated in such workplace banter may be relevant to a court in determining if particular conduct constitutes sexual harassment in a given situation. The key issue in a sexual harassment complaint is whether an employer is liable to the employee for the harassing conduct of either supervisors or co-workers.

The EEOC promulgated guidelines which defined sexual harassment as unwelcome sexual advances, requests for sexual favors, and other verbal or physical conduct of a sexual nature occurring under any of three conditions: 1) where submission is either explicitly or implicitly a term or condition of employment, 2) where submission or rejection of the conduct forms the basis for an employment action, or 3) where the conduct has either the purpose or effect of substantially interfering with the individual's work performance or creating an intimidating, hostile, or offensive working environment.[16] Thus, any retaliatory action by a supervisor such as firing or denial of a promotion because of a refusal to submit to the sexual demands creates liability for the employer.

In *Meritor Savings Bank* v. *Vincent*[17] the Supreme Court endorsed the definitional portion of the EEOC guidelines, including the phrase "offensive or hostile work environment."[18] Clearly, in most situations an employer will be liable for actions of supervisory personnel. The EEOC guidelines impose strict liability on the employer regardless of whether the employer specifically prohibited harassing conduct or even knew about it and failed to take immediate and appropriate corrective action.[19]

The *Meritor* opinion does not go so far as to impose strict liability on employers for hostile work environment situations, but the Court does indicate that, in general, agency principles would apply in determining liability.[20] Liability for harassment of an employee by fellow employees was not addressed in *Monitor;* however, the EEOC guidelines state that the employer is liable for failure to take immediate and appropriate action if the employer knew or should have known of the co-worker conduct.[21]

The EEOC guidelines focus on voluntary action by the employer to publicize the seriousness with which the employer views sexual harassment. Employers are encouraged to make employees aware of the law and develop complaint and investigatory procedures for harassment complaints. Further, employers should educate management personnel about sexual harassment and its prevention.[22] The Supreme Court recognized the importance of such employer-initiated programs and indicated that employer liability might be lessened if such affirmative steps to stop sexual harassment were undertaken.[23] Not only to comply with the Court's reasoning, but also because it is sound practice, libraries should develop mechanisms for successfully handling harassment complaints. Educating supervisors and all employees about the fact that sexual harassment is illegal and that the library will take corrective disciplinary action will go a long way to eliminate harassment in a library.

Compensation

Title VII also covers compensation. There are, however, several issues affecting compensation that uniquely pertain to sex discrimination. Even prior to the 1964 Civil Rights Act, Congress passed the Equal Pay Act of 1963[24] which guaranteed equal pay for equal work. Subsequent cases and administrative interpretation determined that equal work meant substantial equality as opposed to absolute equality of work.[25] Jobs are compared on the basis of equal skill, equal effort, and equal responsibility, performed under similar working conditions.[26] The actual job duties are examined to judge equality of work and not just a written job description.[27]

In any event, to recover under the Equal Pay Act (EPA), a claimant must prove that an employee of the opposite sex is performing substantially equal work and receiving higher wages. Further, the reason for the pay differential must not be one of the statutory exceptions: a bona fide seniority system, a bona fide merit system, a piecework or quantity system, or any factor other than sex.[28] The EPA has been used successfully in eliminating pay bias in factory jobs, but it has been used less successfully for professional and managerial jobs.

Recognizing the failure of the EPA to eliminate salary inequities, library workers in recent years have pushed for pay parity. In American society, jobs that are predominantly occupied by females tend to receive lower pay and have less status than those jobs that are traditionally held by males. An examination of this problem in many states has led to comparable worth or salary parity studies which attempt to evaluate jobs on the basis of their value or worth to the employer. After eliminating a potential technical stumbling block to such cases under Title VII,[29] the U.S. Supreme Court has yet to hear a comparable worth or pay parity case. Some state governments have moved forward to implement pay parity, others have not.[30] The American Library Association (ALA) and various labor unions continue to push for salary equity by asking employers to study their jobs and eliminate sex bias in the evaluation and salary slotting of these jobs.

The result of salary equity studies in some states has been an increase in librarian and library workers salaries from 15 to 30 percent.[31] In other states librarians have been excluded from the study.[32] Library administrators should watch for future legislative and judicial activity in this area.

Employment in Education

The Equal Educational Opportunity Act of 1972[33] promotes equal opportunity in primary and secondary schools as well as in colleges and universities that receive federal funds. Employment is one of the activities included in the regulations.[34] Because the remedy for violations of the act is the withdrawal or denial of federal funds for the educational institution, individual employment discrimination cases in schools are referred to the EEOC under Title VII.[35] Thus, the act has little applicability in most school and academic library employment situations today.

Age Discrimination

Another class of employees is protected from discrimination under the Age Discrimination in Employment Act.[36] Although this is a separate statute, the prohibitions are quite similar to those found in Title VII. Basically, all employers with twenty or more employees are covered and all employment actions are included. Persons who have reached the age of 40 may not be discriminated against in hiring, promotion, termination, retirement, etc. Until recently, persons older than age 70 were excluded, but Congress now has removed the upper age-limit.[37] The primary effect of this recent amendment is that there no longer is a mandatory retirement age although until 1994 institutions of higher education may retain compulsory retirement at age seventy of tenured faculty.[38]

Discrimination Against the Handicapped

Handicapped persons are protected under two statutes: the Vocational Rehabilitation Act of 1973[39] and the Vietnam-Era Veterans Readjustment Act of 1974.[40] The Rehabilitation Act extends the basic Title VII protection and defines a handicapped individual as one who "has a physical or mental impairment which substantially limits one or more of life's major activities [or one who] has a record of such impairment. . . ." Institutions are required to make reasonable accommodation for a handicapped worker unless the employer can demonstrate that such accommodation would impose undue hardship.[41] Reasonable accommodation might include such things as improving facilities to accommodate mobility-impaired individuals and providing special tools, modified work schedules, or job restructuring.[42]

Institutions receiving federal funds must make special efforts to recruit and promote handicapped workers. Institutions with federal contracts of $50,000 or more and fifty or more employees must maintain written affirmative action plans for hiring disabled persons. The Vietnam-Era Act provides counselling and rehabilitative services for veterans and requires affirmative action plans for disabled veterans under the same requirements as the Rehabilitation Act.[43]

Antidiscrimination Executive Orders

Most of the antidiscrimination statutes do not apply to federal government employees. Instead, federal employees are covered under the provisions of various executive orders which apply the same prohibitions against discrimination. The primary one is E.O. 11478 under which federal agencies must maintain affirmative action plans.[44]

Another relevant executive order is 11246, which applies to federal government contractors and, as a part of the contract, requires an agreement not to discriminate on the basis of race, color, religion, sex, or national origin.[45] It covers contractors with a specified number of employees and contracts exceeding certain dollar limits. Remedies for discrimination under this order are the revocation or denial of government contracts. Individual employment discrimination complaints are forwarded to the EEOC for resolution. The most important requirement of E.O. 11246 is the maintenance of affirmative action plans.[46] Many libraries both in educational institutions and as parts of governmental units have federal contracts which require the maintenance of affirmative action plans.

AFFIRMATIVE ACTION

Affirmative action continues to be controversial despite its general acceptance in libraries. The controversy might well disappear if there were a better understanding of the various meanings of the law. In the area of employment discrimination, affirmative action describes three separate legal actions. First, affirmative action is used to define a remedial action that a court may order upon a finding of discrimination on the part of an employer. In other words, whenever an employer has been found to be in violation of various antidiscrimination statutes, the court may order the employer to take affirmative action to correct the problem.[47] Such action could include such things as recruitment and the hiring and promotion of minorities and women. It is perfectly proper for a court to order specific hiring or promotion goals as a part of this remedial action because a determination already has been made that the employer is guilty of employment discrimination.

Affirmative action also describes a voluntary program undertaken by an employer to achieve a more racially and sexually balanced work force in order to provide equal employment opportunity for women and minorities. Such voluntary affirmative action programs have been supported by the courts when challenged.[48] The third definition of affirmative action refers to the mandated maintenance of written affirmative action plans as required by certain executive orders. Each of the three types of affirmative action is appropriate, but while quotas are appropriate in the first, they are not in the other types. For purposes of this section of the chapter, the emphasis is on voluntary and mandated written affirmative action plans.

In its broadest sense, affirmative action refers to a plan in which specific personnel steps—including recruiting, hiring, and promotions—are taken for the purpose of eliminating the results of past discrimination. There is no requirement of a previous court determination of discrimination or an inference that an employer maintaining either a voluntary or mandated affirmative action plan is guilty of discrimination.

The most common reason for an employer's maintenance of a plan stems from Executive Order 11246,[49] which was issued by President Johnson in 1965 and amended by Executive Order 11375.[50] The order requires government contractors to have a written plan of affirmative action to remedy the efforts of past discrimination. The Office of Federal Contract Compliance Programs (OFCCP) administers the order.[51] Regulations under the order have been amended from time to time. Presently, any organization which has at least fifty employees and a nonconstruction contract of at least $50,000 is required to put its affirmative action plan in writing.[52] Thus, most large employers in the private sector as well as most academic institutions and many public libraries are legally mandated to maintain written affirmative action plans.

The OFCCP has defined affirmative action programs as:

> . . . a set of specific and result-oriented procedures to which a contractor commits himself to apply every good faith effort. The objective of those procedures plus such efforts is equal employment opportunity. Procedures without effort to make them work are meaningless, and effort, undirected by specific and meaningful procedures, is inadequate. An acceptable affirmative action program must include an analysis of areas within which the contractor is deficient in the utilization of minority groups and women, and further, goals and timetables to which the contractor's good faith efforts must be directed to correct the deficiencies, and thus, to increase materially the

utilization of minorities and women, at all levels and in all segments of his work force where deficiencies exist.[53]

Perhaps one of the least understood aspects of affirmative action programs is the establishment of hiring goals. Under the executive order, covered contractors are required to make a good faith effort to achieve a goal chosen by them which falls within the ranges acceptable to the government. Affirmative action does not require the employer to utilize unqualified individuals.[54]

Most large libraries have a written affirmative action plan. According to one study, academic libraries and large public libraries are likely to have been the most heavily involved with affirmative action because of the pressures exerted by centralized university and municipal affirmative action offices.[55] Most libraries are covered by the affirmative action plan of their parent institution.

The EEOC issued affirmative action guidelines in 1979, and other affirmative action guidelines have been issued by the OFCCP and the Office of Personnel Management.[56] These guidelines can assist the library administrator responsible for administering an affirmative action program. A successful program requires a substantial amount of data collection, review, and analysis and the guidelines provide assistance in performing these activities.

A number of steps are involved in drafting an effective affirmative action plan. The EEOC suggests the following eight steps:

1. Issue a written equal employment policy and affirmative action commitment.
2. Appoint a top official with responsibility and authority to direct and implement the program.
3. Publicize the policy and the affirmative action commitment internally to managers, supervisors, all employees and unions, and externally to sources and potential sources of recruitment, potential minority and female applicants, those with whom the organization does business, and the community at large.
4. Analyze the present work force to determine the number of females and minorities working in each department and each job classification, identifying the areas of concentration and underutilization. An area of concentration is one in which there is a significant number of minorities and females. Underutilization is defined as having fewer minorities or women in a particular job category than would be reasonably expected by their presence in the relevant job market.
5. Identify goals and timetables to improve utilization of minorities and females in each area where underutilization has been identified.
6. Develop and implement specific programs to achieve goals. This is the heart of the program. Review the entire employment system to identify barriers to equal employment opportunity; make needed changes to increase employ-

ment and advancement opportunities of minorities and females. These areas require review and action.

   a. Recruitment: All personnel procedures.

   b. Selection process: Job requirements; job descriptions, standards, and procedures; pre-employment inquiries; application forms; testing; interviewing.

   c. Upward mobility systems: Assignments, job progressions, transfers, seniority, promotions, training.

   d. Wage and salary system.

   e. Benefits and conditions of employment.

   f. Layoff, recall, termination, demotion, discharge, disciplinary action.

   g. Union contract provisions affecting above procedures.

7. Establish internal audit and reporting system to monitor and evaluate progress in each aspect of the program.

8. Develop supportive inhouse and community programs.[57]

As might be expected, some libraries have experienced difficulties in instituting affirmative action plans and guidelines. The literature of librarianship contains accounts of the problems encountered and hardships endured by some libraries in living with the affirmative action mandate. Libraries have reported that affirmative action laws have turned hiring into a long, rigid, expensive process which produces an adversary relationship between job seekers and employing libraries.[58] There also have been some complaints about "reverse discrimination"— the hardship that affirmative action might cause white male librarians.[59] Nonetheless, most library administrators recognize that affirmative action, despite its elements of bureaucratic intrusion, has been helpful in stimulating the reform of long-standing and discriminatory policies and procedures. Without a doubt, there are more women and minorities holding high-level positions in libraries now than there were before the advent of affirmative action.

Most people expected that the Reagan administration's antiregulation bias might seriously damage affirmative action; indeed, the Department of Justice has made a series of attempts to erode affirmative action requirements. In two recent decisions, however, the U.S. Supreme Court provided significant reinforcement to the concept of affirmative action. Considered in conjunction with related decisions issued a few years earlier, the Court has sent a message to employers about their responsibilities to free the workplace from the effects of present and past discrimination.

In *Johnson* v. *Transportation Agency, Santa Clara County*[60] and *U.S.* v. *Paradise*,[61] the Supreme Court was confronted with three questions left unanswered by previous decisions in this area: the legality of sex-conscious plans under Title VII, the factual basis necessary to support *voluntary* affirmative actions under Title VII, and the constitutionality of *court-ordered* numerical relief to remedy promotion discrimination.[62]

In *Johnson* the Court upheld the use of voluntary affirmative action plans which consider the sex of an applicant as one factor to be weighed in promotion cases. The Court affirmed that sex-conscious plans are entitled to the same protection under Title VII as are race-conscious plans.[63] In *Paradise,* the use of court-ordered numerical quotas for the promotion of members of minority groups was upheld after the trial court found a Title VII violation.[64]

These decisions have narrowed the terms of any future debate on affirmative action; however, in each of these cases the majority ruling in favor was small. Further changes in the composition of the Supreme Court might well weaken judicial support for affirmative action.

LABOR RELATIONS

Library employees long have formed "associations" within libraries to work for improved working conditions, status, and wages. These are not labor unions but represent attempts by library workers to create a mechanism for making their collective voices heard by management. Labor unions in libraries still are the exception rather than the rule, even though unionization problems in some libraries have received widespread attention.

There appears to be a growing tendency in academic institutions for librarians to affiliate with faculty unions and support staff to belong to various unions representing clerical employees. In some libraries, however, only the clerical staff is organized. The ALA officially has recognized collective bargaining as a method of conducting labor-management relations in libraries.[65] Collective bargaining is defined as an interactive process in which the rules that govern employment are negotiated by representatives of labor and management.[66]

In the early days of this country, an employer's right to deal with employees in whatever manner the employer saw fit was sacrosanct. This right remained unfettered for many years, reinforced by societal attitudes supporting noninterference in labor-management relations. Courts tended to enforce employer-sought injunctions against workers that prohibited strikes and union membership.[67]

The first industry to be affected by modern labor-management statutory control was the railroad industry through the Railway Labor Act of 1926[68], which created procedures for collective bargaining and settling disputes. In 1932, the Norris-LaGuardia Act[69] was enacted, likely as a result of the Depression. This act effectively restricted management in its dealing with labor unions and is based on the philosophy that government should refrain from interference in labor-management relations unless there is actual violence or damage to tangible property.[70]

The National Labor Relations Act,[71] commonly called the Wagner Act, went further by requiring that government take an active role to see that unionization was not hampered by acts of management. It established a procedure by which workers could select a union to represent their interests and enumerated activities forbidden to management.[72] Along with subsequent amendments,[73] these included interference with the right of workers to unionize, discrimination in employment, hiring and tenure in order to discourage or encourage union membership, the refusal to bargain collectively with a bargaining unit legitimately chosen, and giving financial support to an employee union.[74] Because of the one-sided nature of the Wagner Act, public support for it waned after World War II[75] and the result was the 1947 Taft-Hartley Act.[76]

Essentially an amendment to the Wagner Act, Taft-Hartley introduced a new concept: the neutral arbiter. Thus, the National Labor Relations Board (NLRB) was created to serve as an impartial umpire between labor and management. Employees could seek to be represented by a union or choose not to be so represented, and the government, through the NLRB, would support their choice. The collective bargaining contract negotiated between labor and management has the effect of law and is enforced by courts.[77]

Early on the difference between public and private employment regarding the right to unionize was recognized. Although federal law in this area does not apply to public employment, Executive Orders 10988[78] and 11491[79] created the basis for local, state, and federal employees to bargain collectively. Additionally, some state legislation recognizes the rights of public employees to bargain collectively, although other states continue to prohibit labor union membership for public employees.

Following the enactment of Taft-Hartley a series of court decisions considered whether, as professional employees, librarians in academic institutions could bargain collectively. The overall environment of the institution appears to be the critical factor in the decision.[80] In some instances, the NLRB included librarians and support staff in the same bargaining unit,[81] while in the *Yeshiva University* case[82] librarians had faculty status and the Board determined that faculty were managers and thus prohibited from engaging in collective bargaining.[83] The primary question in these cases appeared to be whether faculty had decision-making powers; for librarians, an additional question was whether the librarians had faculty status.

A wide variety of unions and associations represent librarians in the various types of libraries.[84] It is likely that labor organization activity in libraries will increase in the next decade.[85] Other aspects of labor relations, including grievances and arbitration, are covered in detail in Chapter Nine.

MISCELLANEOUS LAWS AFFECTING EMPLOYMENT

A variety of laws govern key aspects of employment, including compensation, overtime, on-the-job health and safety, and citizenship status. Although the parent organization oversees compliance with these laws, library personnel administrators must have a sound understanding of their implications. In addition, library personnel administrators have a responsibility to inform central offices of matters focusing on librarianship, such as challenges to the requirement for a Master's degree in library science (M.L.S.) for certain library positions.

Fair Labor Standards Act

The Fair Labor Standards Act (FLSA)[86] enacted in 1938 provides the basic wage and hour law for the United States. Originally aimed only at private employers, through subsequent amendments[87] schools, hospitals, and federal, state, and local agencies are included within the definition of employer.[88] The FLSA established the minimum wage provision and maximum number of hours that an employee may work without overtime pay. The hours of work provision contains an exemption for administrative, executive, and professional employees and thus excludes librarians as professional and administrative employees. The FLSA provisions clearly apply, however, to other library workers. State statutes also are applicable since under the act states may enact provisions to *raise* the minimum wage and *reduce* the maximum hours standard, as some have done.[89]

States have enacted child labor laws which set various limits on the number of hours, required breaks, and age limits for young people. Such laws certainly are applicable to libraries.

M.L.S. Validity

In the past, establishing hiring criteria for particular library jobs was fairly straightforward, especially for professional positions. Developments since the enactment of Title VII have called into question the requirement of an M.L.S. *Griggs* v. *Duke Power* [90] and subsequent EEOC guidelines prohibit the use of academic credentials as a requirement for hiring unless it can be shown that the academic credentials are related to actual job performance.[91] Thus, the indiscriminate requirement of an ALA-accredited M.L.S. or any other education requirement as a screening mechanism for hiring may violate federal and state laws.

When a library requires an ALA-accredited M.L.S. for a job, the institution must be prepared to show that the degree is a valid measurement of the particular skills required for the job.[92] Because validation of formal professional qualifications is an extremely technical and difficult procedure, some libraries have broadened their requirements for minimum qualifications for a professional-level position. Instead of requiring an M.L.S., these employers may also permit some combination of experience plus education as the basic requirement for a professional position.

A recent decision appears to have provided libraries that wish to require the M.L.S. a more substantive claim for doing so. In *Merwine* v. *Board of Trustees of State Institutions for Higher Learning,* [93] the plaintiff charged Mississippi State University with sex discrimination under Title VII for rejecting her job application for a library position later filled by a man. She further alleged that the university requirement of the ALA-accredited M.L.S. as an entry-level requirement for the position had an adverse impact upon women in violation of Title VII.[94]

In federal district court, the jury found sex discrimination and the plaintiff was awarded $10,000 in total damages. That action was tried before a magistrate who found that 80 percent of the ALA-M.L.S. degrees awarded over the past ten to twelve years had gone to women and that no reasonable jury would find the requirement of an ALA-M.L.S. degree a pretext for sex discrimination. Further, the magistrate found that the imposition of a degree requirement is a standard widely recognized in the profession. Thus, he rejected the jury finding and the damage award.[95]

Merwine appealed to the Fifth Circuit which upheld the magistrate's ruling. The court supported the magistrate's finding that the degree requirement was a widely recognized standard by academic and professional employers (including the U.S. Supreme Court library). The court found that "the uncontradicted evidence established that the ALA-M.L.S. is a legitimate, nondiscriminatory standard for hiring academic librarians."[96] The Supreme Court refused to hear the appeal and denied certiorari. Thus, the requirement of an ALA-accredited M.L.S. appears to be settled for academic libraries.

Although *Merwine* has been heralded as a victory by proponents of the ALA-M.L.S., some now believe that it may not have been so clear-cut. Despite its broad language, *Merwine* is limited in precedential value to the issue of whether the ALA-M.L.S. was a valid criterion for a single position at Mississippi State University.[97] Library administrators should be alert to further developments in this area. More needs to be done to identify basic competencies needed in librarianship and to determine whether these are met by M.L.S. programs or if they may also be acquired through some equivalent experience or combination of experience and other academic credentials.[98] Further, the part accreditation plays in determining the quality of competency training for librarians should be studied.

Safety and Health

The federal Occupational Safety and Health Act[99] was enacted to reduce worker accident and death in the workplace. The act gives the government authority to issue various safety and health rules and regulations through the Occupational Safety and Health Administration (OSHA).[100] Employers' work premises are subject to inspection by OSHA officials although enforcement of the act has been somewhat spotty. Many people criticize the act's focus on the physical conditions that cause accidents as opposed to the individual workers who have accidents.[101] With the exception of the removal of asbestos, OSHA has had little impact on libraries. The health implications of employees working on VDT's is of considerable interest to librarians.

Illegal Aliens

The Immigration Reform and Control Act of 1986[102] makes it unlawful for a person or other entity to hire, recruit, or refer for a fee any illegal alien for employment in the United States. The act permits employers to employ properly identified citizens of the United States as well as noncitizens who can document that they are lawfully authorized to work in this country. All employers are covered. Prior to hiring, employers must view and may copy original documents which establish the job applicant's identity and employment status. Upon request from the employer, applicants must submit copies of one of the following documents: United States passport, certificate of United States citizenship, certificate of naturalization, unexpired foreign passport, alien registration receipt card, temporary resident card, employment registration card, or Native American tribal document.[103]

If none of these documents are available certain combinations of other enumerated documents may be submitted by the applicant. Forms to be completed are supplied by the Department of Justice, Immigration and Naturalization Service, and must be retained by the employer as specified. Stiff penalties are imposed on employers who violate the act; such employers may be fined not less than $100 nor more than $1,000 for each individual with respect to whom such violation occurred. Employers with a pattern and practice of violating the act may be fined not more than $3,000 for each unauthorized alien for whom such violation occurs and imprisoned for not more than six months.[104]

PRIVACY OF PERSONNEL RECORDS

Over the years, interest in protecting the privacy of individuals has increased in all aspects of society. The constitutional right of privacy has been expanded in several ways, and has been important in the realm of personnel administration at least for the past decade. Privacy in the workplace includes a variety of issues ranging from the use of polygraph examinations, the collection of personal and work-related data on employees, and the disclosure of such information.[105] Additionally, mandatory alcohol and drug testing and screening for the AIDS virus are important current privacy-related employment topics.

Personnel Records

Employers maintain all sorts of personnel records on current and former employees for a variety of reasons. These records contain such information as positions held, past employment data, salary, performance reviews, disciplinary actions, medical records, etc. Until recent years, there was little restraint on the types of employee information an employer might retain, nor was there any guarantee that the employee have access to the data in the file. In fact, a supervisor's performance reviews might be written and the employee remain totally unaware of the content of the review or even that such a review of his or her work existed. Further, release of the data from files was unrestricted whether the inquiry came from a future potential employer or a credit-granting agency.

In 1974 the federal Privacy Act was enacted.[106] The act protects the privacy rights of federal government employees and focuses on the right of employees to control access to the data contained in their personnel records. Employees are guaranteed the right to review the contents of their files and an opportunity to correct erroneous factual information. Disclosure by the employer of information contained in the personnel records may constitute an invasion of the employee's right of privacy. Additionally, the act restricts the types of information that may be kept to that which is relevant and necessary.[107] Private employers are not covered by the Privacy Act, although there have been proposals for a new federal law that would include them as well.[108]

Several states have enacted statutes similar to the Privacy Act to protect state, county, and municipal employees under similar circumstances.[109] Critical to these statutes is the right of the employee to control access to the data and to respond to erroneous or unfair information contained in the files. Some states' statutes cover private employers as well as state and local government employers. An example of such a law is the Illinois Personnel Records Statute[110] which became effective in 1974. It covers all employers with five or more employees and closely follows the federal Privacy Act.[111]

Other federal statutes have applicability to this area, such as the Federal Fair Credit Reporting Act.[112] Although the act primarily regulates the activities of credit agencies, employers and applicants for employment are covered by the act. An employer using a consumer investigative report as a screening device must notify the employee that such a report is to be made, and, upon request by the employee, must disclose the results of the report.[113] Another example of a federal statute with some applicability to employee privacy is the Omnibus Crime Control and Safe Streets Act, which prohibits wiretapping and other interceptions of oral communications.[114]

With the conversion of personnel records to machine-readable form, many people fear an increased likelihood that confidential records may become available to unauthorized persons.[115] In fact, the trend to automate personnel records is the impetus behind many of the state laws governing the confidentiality of personnel records. Another concern for employers is that the release of unauthorized data from a personnel file could subject the employer to liability for defamation.

Mandatory Testing

The workplace privacy issues currently receiving the most media attention are involuntary drug and alcohol testing, the use of polygraph examinations as a prehiring screening device, and mandatory testing of employees for the AIDS virus. Not surprisingly, many employees object to lie detector examinations, citing the unreliability of polygraph results as well as the invasion of privacy issue for employment screening. Use of such tests already is prohibited by many states.[116] In response to criticisms of such tests, Congress enacted the Employee Polygraph Protection Act of 1988 which broadly prohibits the use of lie detector examinations in employment with exemptions for certain industries.[117]

Under the act employers may not directly or indirectly require or suggest that employees or potential employees submit to a lie detector test. Discharge, discipline, or discrimination against an employee or potential employee for refusing to take a polygraph examination is prohibited.[118] Exceptions include national defense employees, security personnel in facilities engaged in the production, transmission, or distribution of electric or nuclear power; public water supply facilities; shipment or storage of radioactive or toxic waste; public transportation;

and employees who have access to currency, negotiable instruments, precious commodities or instruments, or proprietary information.[119] Also exempted are employers authorized to manufacture, distribute, or dispense a controlled substance.[120] Use of polygraph examinations still is permitted in the course of an investigation regarding theft, embezzlement, or unlawful industrial espionage when the employee is one who has access to the property that is the subject of the investigation and the employer has a reasonable suspicion that the employee was involved in the matter under investigation.[121] The act establishes strict requirements for administering lie detector tests for these exceptions, including questions that may not be asked of examinees such as religious affiliation, personal sexual activity, political opinions regarding racial matters, and behavior involving lawful union activities.[122]

Mandatory drug and alcohol testing of employees by corporations has generated much debate. Concerns range from invasion of privacy to the degree of control an employer should be able to exercise over an employee's private life. Based on public safety concerns, however, it is likely that such mandatory testing will be allowed in some industries such as public transportation. It is possible that bookmobile drivers might come under similar restraints because of the public safety aspect of that particular job. This is far from a settled area, however; library employers should continue to monitor legal developments.

Mandatory testing for the AIDS virus is extremely controversial, especially since it appears unlikely that the virus is spread by casual contact. As fear of the spread of the disease rages, however, some employers have discussed mandatory screening to protect themselves and other employees and to limit insurance coverage. Not only is the screening likely to be unconstitutional, but any adverse employment action taken because of a positive result on an AIDS test likely is subject to challenge under either the federal or state handicapped discrimination statutes. Confidentiality of results of AIDS testing presents yet another serious privacy issue.

EMPLOYEE BENEFITS

As recognition of workers rights grew over the years, employers began to provide various benefits in addition to wages. Today, a wide variety of fringe benefits are provided by employers. The package of benefits offered to employees is determined by the individual library or the library's parent institution. Some benefits, however, are required by state and federal law, and, in unionized libraries, certain benefits are mandated by a collective bargaining agreement. The state and federal regulations regarding fringe benefits apply to almost all workers in the

United States. Among the benefits required by law are social security, unemployment insurance, and workers' compensation. Other benefits such as paid holidays and sick leave, group insurance, and leaves of absence may be voluntarily provided by an employer, required by state law, or mandated in a collective-bargaining contract.

Social Security

All fifty states now participate in the social security program which was enacted in 1935. Although a number of states continue to exclude state employees from the program, federal employees were recently phased into social security.[123] In contrast to unemployment insurance and workers' compensation payments which are funded entirely by employers' contributions, social security consists of equal contributions from both employer and employee. The amount of these contributions is based on a percentage of the employee's direct pay. The primary purpose of social security is to provide retirement income for employees. Employees may retire at age sixty-two with reduced benefits or at age sixty-five with full benefits.[124] The benefits paid to retirees have improved substantially since Congress linked them to the consumer price index in 1975.[125] This improvement, however, has resulted in increased costs to both employers and employees. The required contribution to social security has increased rapidly, rising from a combined employer-employee tax of 2 percent on a maximum of $3,000 in earnings in 1937 to a combined rate of 14.3 percent on a maximum of $42,600 in 1987.[126]

The financial stability of the social security fund has received much recent attention. When the members of the baby-boom generation reach retirement age, there will be far fewer workers providing contributions to the fund. To maintain the stability of social security some changes have been proposed, such as raising the retirement age, increasing the taxation on social security income, or again raising the amount of contribution required by employers and employees. It is likely that some modification of the program will be necessary in the future to insure its fiscal integrity.

Unemployment Insurance

Unemployment insurance also was created by the Social Security Act of 1935.[127] One of the act's provisions was a federal tax on payrolls, 90 percent of which was to be refunded to the states if they passed acceptable unemployment compensation legislation. Soon after enactment, all of the states and the District of Columbia had enacted such programs.[128]

The primary purpose of unemployment insurance is to provide

income to individuals while they search for new employment. To be eligible for payments, individuals usually must have lost a job through no fault of their own and be presently engaged in a search for suitable new employment.[129] Unemployment programs provided by state laws vary greatly. The benefit period ranges from twenty-six to fifty-two weeks, and the level of payment also varies from state to state. Although there have been numerous proposals for the federal government to intervene and establish standards for benefit levels, such proposals have not been adopted.[130]

Retirement Benefits

One of the major benefits provided most employees is a retirement program. In addition to social security, an organization may provide its employees with additional retirement benefits. These benefits can include options rarely found in libraries (for example, profit-sharing or stock-purchase options) as well as one found commonly in most libraries: a pension plan of some sort. Regardless of the type of program provided, the federal government now plays a major role in the regulation and control of private pension programs. The Employee Retirement Income Security Act (ERISA)[131] enacted in 1974 provides a number of protections and guarantees for the payment of benefits under private pension plans. ERISA does not require employers to provide pension plans. Instead, it governs provisions of private pension plans, if provided, by requiring minimum standards with regard to participation, coverage requirements, vesting, employer-contribution options, survivor annuities, and status disclosure reports.[132]

The law eliminates many of the inequities that previously existed and provides advantages to both employer and employee. Unfortunately, it also increases the amount of paperwork and reporting required of employers; ultimately, the costs of providing retirement plans also increased.[133]

Workers' Compensation

The purpose of workers' compensation is to provide payment for injuries sustained on the job. Currently, each of the fifty states as well as the District of Columbia and Puerto Rico has its own workers' compensation laws and administrative agency.[134] Workers' compensation programs are essentially insurance systems. Interestingly, workers' compensation was the first no-fault insurance in the United States. The benefits paid by the plan apply regardless of fault of injury.[135]

Since each state has its own plan, the benefits vary greatly. Most state plans provide benefits as a percentage of wages up to a maximum amount and for a specified period. Payments also are made for hospital expenses if necessary and for survivor benefits in case of death.[136] Workers' compensation plans typically cover only physical injury, however, some have been amended to include job-related mental and emotional illness.[137]

Employers pay premiums for workers' compensation to private insurance firms or to state-operated plans. The rate an organization pays is based upon its safety record.

Group Insurance

Insurance benefits offered as a portion of the compensation package for employees has become the rule rather than the exception. In most employee insurance plans the employer bears either the entire cost or at least a substantial portion and the employee pays the remaining costs. The modern trend is for employers to develop "cafeteria plans" which include a variety of benefit options for the employee; then, within certain limits, the employee selects those benefits which most nearly suit his or her needs. Regardless of the variety of benefits offered, employers may not offer them on a discriminatory basis since benefits are considered part of the compensation package and must comply with the mandates of Title VII and the Equal Pay Act. Additionally, the Supreme Court has held that employer-sponsored insurance benefits based on gender-based mortality tables violate the antidiscrimination provision of Title VII.[138]

The original reason for providing group insurance benefits was to increase employee satisfaction, although union demands also added impetus to increase benefits.[139] Insurance benefits commonly provided to library employees include group health, dental, life, and disability insurance. The amount of coverage included in employee health care insurance has increased steadily through the years. Most plans remain oriented toward hospital care and focus on acute care. Benefits may be limited in dollar amount and in services provided based on the policy.[140] Additionally, many employers now offer alternatives to traditional medical insurance in the form of health maintenance plans (HMOs). Although employers have been slow to offer HMOs, there is evidence that they reduce hospitalization utilization and costs. Most experts predict a continued trend toward employers offering employees a choice of health care insurance benefits.[141]

Disability insurance for income maintenance is a growing type of employee benefit offered first by Montgomery Ward Company in 1911. Now many states offer disability insurance for employees, and there is a developing trend for private employers to provide group disability coverage for employees.[142] Disability policies typically provide income benefits to replace lost wages due to accident or illness. The amount of the benefit varies with the particular plan offered and may include either full or partial wage replacement.[143] Additionally, plans generally include some incentive for returning to work, such as an automatic time limit or partial wage replacement as opposed to full replacement of wages lost due to disability.[144]

Group life insurance is another form of insurance likely to be offered by library employers. Most plans include both employer and employee contributions, with the employee contributions designed to be level throughout the work life of the employee. Benefits generally are determined by an established schedule.[145]

Holiday, Vacation, Sick Leave, and Leaves of Absence

The traditional reason that employers provided vacation leave was to reward employees for faithful service and to refresh them for future service.[146] Through the years it has been apparent that employees no longer think of vacation as a reward but as a right. Holiday and vacation leaves frequently are subjects for the collective bargaining contract, but most libraries offer such leave to employees regardless of the union situation. Leaves of this type are viewed as a part of the compensation package and are governed by the provisions of Title VII and the EPA.

Sick leave may also be included in the benefit package. Such leave must be granted for maternity leave if it is granted for all other types of illnesses or medical conditions.[147] Management clearly has a legitimate concern to see that sick leave claims are not abused and may establish reasonable rules for documenting illnesses.[148]

For both vacation or holiday leave and sick leave, it is important for employees to clearly understand when the right to these benefits are due them—vests. Most public employers and unionized libraries have policies that detail vesting. Whether these rights may be accrued and if there is a limit to accrual is of concern to management as well. Additionally, the library's employment policy should clearly state whether employees may receive pay for unused vacation, holiday, or sick leave at the time of termination.

Leaves of absence may be provided for specific purpose by library employers. Jury duty, voting, funerals, and union business are typical of brief leaves. Some, such as jury duty, may be mandated by state law. Employers also may grant leaves of absence for extended periods of time with or without pay. As a part of the benefit package provided, paid leaves may be offered for medical, maternity, or other personal reasons.[149] Professional librarians also may be granted leaves of absence for attending conferences, for professional development, and sabbaticals.[150]

CONCLUSION

The body of law relating to various minor employment issues is as enormous as the major law described. Additionally, statutes governing both public and private employment are amended frequently. Library managers should rely upon parent organizations for procedures and forms that have been developed to see that their organization complies with various federal, state, and local employment laws.

Factual details of any employment problem make generalizations about the law of limited value in settling particular issues. Thus, library managers should consult with legal counsel whenever a situation occurs that relates to whether the library has complied with statutory or regulatory mandates. In any event, good record keeping facilitates proof of compliance with laws and regulations and may be considered "preventative maintenance" in personnel management. Librarians have always been records managers, and personnel records should be added to the array of important records that receive attention. Contemporaneous written justifications for employment actions provide the documentation necessary to demonstrate that the library is complying with both the letter and spirit of the law of personnel administration.

References

1. Arthur Curley, "The Legal Framework of Personnel Administration," in *Personnel Administration in Libraries,* Sheila Creth, ed. (New York: Neal-Schuman, 1981).
2. 42 U.S.C. sec. 2000e et seq. (1964).
3. *Id.* at sec. 2000e–2(a)(1).
4. *Id.* at sec. 2000e–5(g).
5. 42 U.S.C. sec. 2000e, as amended (Supp. II 1972 & 1976 Supp. II 1978).
6. *Id.* at sec. 2000e–4(a).
7. 29 C.F.R. pt. 1607 (1979).
8. EEOC Guidelines on Discrimination Because of Religion, as revised, 29 C.F.R. sec. 1605.1–3 (1980).
9. *Id.* at sec. 1605.2.
10. 42 U.S.C. 2000e(k) (Supp. II 1978).
11. *Id.*
12. Newport News Shipbuilding & Dry Dock Co. v. EEOC, 462 U.S. 669 (1983).
13. Guidelines on Discrimination Because of Sex, 29 C.F.R. sec. 1604.10 (1979).
14. California Federal Savings & Loan Association v. Guerra, 479 U.S. 272 (1987).
15. Meritor Savings Bank v. Vinson, 477 U.S. 57 (1986).
16. 29 C.F.R. sec. 1604.11 (1980).

17. 477 U.S. 57 (1986).
18. *Id.* at 65–66.
19. 29 C.F.R. sec. 1604.11(c) (1980).
20. 477 U.S. 57, 71–72.
21. 29 C.F.R. 1604.11(d) (1980).
22. *Id.* at 1604.11(f).
23. 477 U.S. 57, 72–73 (1986).
24. 29 U.S.C. sec. 206(d) (1976).
25. 29 C.F.R. sec. 800.122 (1966).
26. *Id.* at sec. 800.125–.132.
27. *Id.* at sec. 800.121.1.
28. 29 U.S.C. sec. 206(d) (1976).
29. *See* County of Washington v. Gunther, 452 U.S. 161 (1981).
30. For example, the states of Minnesota, Wisconsin, and Iowa have implemented pay equity following statewide studies. After appropriating money for a pay parity study, the North Carolina legislature apparently had second thoughts and withdrew the funding early in 1985.
31. See "Pay Equity and the San Jose Strike: an Interview with Patt Curia," *Library Journal* 106 (1981): 2079 and "Job Evaluation Completed in Connecticut," *Library Journal* 110 (December 1985): 35.
32. In Minnesota university librarians have faculty status and thus were excluded from pay parity raises. Conversation with Gail Daily, Assistant Director, University of Minnesota Law Library, July 7, 1986.
33. 20 U.S.C. sec. 1681 (Supp. II 1972).
34. 34 C.F.R. sec. 106.51–.61 (1980).
35. 29 C.F.R. sec. 1691 (1983); 28 C.F.R. sec. 42.601–.13 (1983).
36. 29 U.S.C. sec. 621 et seq. (Supp. III 1965-57); (Supp. II 1978); 29 U.S.C.A. sec. 621 et seq. (West Supp. 1987).
37. 29 U.S.C.A. sec. 631(a) (West Supp. 1987).
38. 29 U.S.C.S. sec. 631(d) & note (Law. Co-op. Supp. 1987).
39. 29 U.S.C. sec. 701, et seq. (Supp. III 1973); 29 U.S.C.A. sec. 701 et seq. (West Supp. 1987).
40. 38 U.S.C. sec. 219 et seq. (Supp. IV 1974); 38 U.S.C.A. sec. 219 et seq. (West Supp. 1987).
41. 29 U.S.C. sec. 701 et seq. (1970 & Supp. III 1973).
42. 41 C.F.R. sec. 60-741.6(c)(1) (1980).
43. 38 U.S.C. sec. 2012 (1976 & Supp. III 1979).
44. Exec. Order No. 11478, 3 C.F.R. 803 (1966-70).
45. Exec. Order No. 11246, 3 C.F.R. 339 (1964-65).
46. *Id.*
47. 42 U.S.C. sec. 2000e(g) (1964).
48. *See* United Steelworkers of Am. v. Weber, 443 U.S. 193 (1979).
49. Exec. Order No. 11246, 3 C.F.R. 339 (1964-65).
50. Exec. Order No. 11375, 3 C.F.R. 803 (1966-70).
51. Exec. Order No. 11246, 3 C.F.R. 339 (1964-65).
52. 41 C.F.R. sec. 60-140 (1986).
53. 41 C.F.R. sec. 60-2.10 (1978).
54. Jones, "The Genesis and Present Status of Affirmative Action in Employ-

ment: Economic, Legal, and Political Realities," *Journal of Library Administration* (1986): 37.

55. James E. Dickinson and Margaret Myers, "Affirmative Action and American Librarianship," in 8 *Advances in Librarianship* 125 (Harris ed. 1978).
56. See generally, EEOC Guidelines 29 C.F.R. pt. 1608 (1979); OFCCP Guidelines, 41 C.F.R. pt. 60-4 (1978); OPM Guidelines, 5 C.F.R. pt. 720 (1979).
57. Equal Employment Opportunity Commission, 1 *Affirmative Action and Equal Employment, A Guidebook for Employers* 16 (1974).
58. *See, e.g.*, Christofferson, "The High Cost of Hiring," 102 *Libr. J.* 677 (1977); Caruthers & Demos, "Affirmative Action and the Hiring of Professional Librarians," 40 *Ky. Libr. A. Bull.* 5 (1976).
59. Nyren, "Affirmative Action and Charges of 'Reverse Bias'," 101 *Libr. J.* 985, 986–87 (1976).
60. 480 U.S. 616 (1987), 107 S.Ct. 1442.
61. 480 U.S. 149 (1987).
62. Levick, "Affirmative Action Cases Benefit Working Women," 9 *Nat'l L.J.*, Aug. 17, 1987, at S4.
63. 107 S.Ct. 1442, 1447 (1987).
64. 480 U.S. 149, 184–85 (1987).
65. American Library Association Policy Manual, Policy No. 54.11, *reprinted in* American Library Association, *ALA Handbook of Organization and Membership Directory* (1986).
66. Cruzat, "Collective Bargaining and the Library Manager, 7 *J. of Lib. Admin.* 67, 71 (1986).
67. Miner, *supra* note 71 at 121.
68. 45 U.S.C. sec. 151 et seq. (1928).
69. 29 U.S.C. sec. 101 et seq. (1934).
70. Miner, *supra* note 71 at 122.
71. 29 U.S.C., sec. 151 et seq. (Supp. V 1935-39)
72. *Id.* at sec. 151; Miner, *supra* note 64 at 123.
73. (1946 Supp. I), (1952), (1958), (Supp. V 1959-63), (Supp. IV 1974), (Supp. II 1978), (Supp. IV 1980), (1982); (Supp. II 1984).
74. Miner, *supra* note 71 at 122–23.
75. Curley, *supra* note 1 at 22.
76. 29 U.S.C., sec. 141, et seq. (1946 Supp. I).
77. Miner, *supra* note 71 at 123.
78. Exec. Order No. 10988, 3 C.F.R. 521 (1959-63).
79. Exec. Order No. 11491, 3 C.F.R. 861 (1966-70).
80. Cruzat, *supra* note 95 at 72.
81. *See* Long Island University, 189 NLRB No. 109, 77 *Lab. Rel. Ref. Manual* 1001 (1972).
82. Nat'l Labor Relations Bd. v. Yeshiva Univ., 444 U.S. 672 (1980).
83. *Id.* at 680-91.
84. *See* Cruzat, *supra* note 95 at 75.
85. *Id.* at 78-80.
86. 29 U.S.C. sec 201 et seq. (Supp. V 1935-39).
87. *Id.* (Supp. V 1959-63), (Supp. III 1965-67), (Supp. IV 1974), (Supp. I 1977); (Supp. III 1985).

88. *Id.*
89. Curley, *supra* note 1 at 8.
90. 401 U.S. 424 (1971).
91. *Id.* at 431–33.
92. Reed, "Employment Discrimination and Related Litigation in Libraries," 7 *J. of Libr. Ad.* 53, 57 (1986).
93. 754 F.2d 631 (5th Cir. 1985).
94. *Id.* at 632-33.
95. *Id.* at 633, 636, 640.
96. *Id.* at 638.
97. Reed, *supra* note 130 at 58-59.
98. *See* Cottam, "Minimum Qualifications and the Law: the Issue Ticks Away for Librarians," 11 *Am. Libr.* 280 (1980).
99. 29 U.S.C. sec. 651 et seq. (1970).
100. *Id.* at sec. 656.
101. Miner, *supra* note 71 at 118.
102. 8 U.S.C.A. sec. 1324(a) et seq. (West Supp. 1987).
103. *Id.* at (b).
104. *Id.* at (e)(4).
105. Duffy, et al., "Big Brother in the Workplace: Privacy Rights Versus Employer Needs," 9 *Indus. Rel. L.J.* 30, 31 (1987).
106. 5 U.S.C. sec. 522a (Supp. IV 1974).
107. *Id.*
108. Duff and Johnson, "A Renewed Employee Right to Privacy," 34 *Lab. L.J.* 747, 760-62 (1983).
109. *See generally,* N.C. Gen. Stat., sec. 126-22 et. seq. (1986); sec. 153a-98 et. seq. (1983); sec. 160a-168 et. seq. (1983).
110. Ill. Rev. Stat., ch.48, sec. 2001 et. seq. (1986).
111. *Id.*
112. 15 U.S.C. sec. 1681-1681t (1982 & Supp. III 1985).
113. *Id.* at sec. 1681(b); 1681(k).
114. 18 U.S.C. sec. 2510-20 (1982 & Supp. III 1985).
115. *See* Ledvinka, "Privacy Regulations and Employee Record Keeping," 7 *J. Libr. Ad.* 25, 25 (1986).
116. Miner, *supra* note 71 at 110.
117. H.R. 1524, 99th Cong., 1st Sess. (1986) passed the House. The Senate version, S. 1815, 99th Cong., 1st Sess. (1986) was not reported from committee. H.R. 1536, 100th Cong., 1st Sess. to amend the Fair Labor Standards Act to prevent denial of equal employment opportunity by prohibiting the use of lie detectors in employment was introduced on March 10, 1987; it is before the House Education and Labor Committee.
118. *Id.* at section 2002.
119. *Id.* at section 2006(e).
120. *Id.* at section 2006(f).
121. *Id.* at section 2006(d).
122. *Id.* at section 2007.
123. Social Security Act, 42 U.S.C. sec. 301 et seq. (1935 Supp. V), as amended.
124. *Id.*

125. *Id.* at sec. 1382f (Supp. V 1975).
126. *Statistical Abstract of the United States 1986,* 363 (1985).
127. 42 U.S.C. sec. 1104 (1935 Supp.).
128. J. Miner and M. Miner, *Personnel and Managerial Relations* 119 (4th ed. 1985).
129. *Id.*
130. *Id.* at 120.
131. 29 U.S.C. sec. 1001 et seq. (Supp. IV 1974); (Supp. II 1984); 29 U.S.C.A. 1001 et seq. (West Supp. 1987).
132. *Id.*
133. Miner, *supra* note 71 at 114.
134. W. Cascio & E. Awad, *Human Resources Management* 356 (1981).
135. *Id.* at 355.
136. Miner, *supra* note 71 at 117.
137. R. Middlemist, M. Hitt, and C. Greer, *Personnel Management* 336 (1983).
138. *See* Los Angeles Dept. of Water & Power v. Manhart, 435 U.S. 702 (1978) & Arizona Governing Committee for Tax Deferred Annuity and Deferred Compensation Plans v. Norris, 463 U.S. 1973 (1983).
139. Hall, "Designing Medical Care Expense Plans," in *The Handbook of Employee Benefits* 101–02 (J. Rosenbloom, ed. 1984).
140. Lipton, "Supplemental Major Medical and Comprehensive Plans," in *The Handbook of Employee Benefits* 163 (J. Rosenbloom, ed. 1984).
141. Hall, *supra* note 82 at 113–14.
142. Miller, "Group Disability Income Insurance," in *The Handbook of Employee Benefits* 231, 234 (J. Rosenbloom, ed. 1984).
143. *Id.* at 236.
144. *Id.* at 241.
145. Rabel, "Permanent Forms of Group Life Insurance," in *The Handbook of Employee Benefits* 77–79 (J. Rosenbloom, ed. 1984).
146. F. Elkouri and E. Elkouri, *How Arbitration Works* 731 (4th ed. 1985).
147. *See* Nashville Gas Co. v. Satty, 434 U.S. 136 (1977).
148. Elkouri, *supra* note 89 at 749.
149. Elkouri, *supra* note 89 at 756–60.
150. M. Martin, *Issues in Personnel Management in Academic Libraries* 150, 170 (1981).

3
Staffing Patterns
Margaret Myers

Library staffing patterns vary considerably depending on a wide variety of factors, such as type and size of institution, governance and funding patterns, and extent of automation. There has been considerable shifting in these patterns in the past decades in terms of the ratio of professionals to nonprofessionals, the definitions of duties and responsibilities, and the use of specialists. No doubt more shifts will occur as automation is increasingly used in even the smaller libraries. Declining resources and budget cuts coupled with increasing service demands and workloads have caused many libraries to look more carefully at the utilization of their human resources. Salaries can consume from 50 to 80 percent of the library budget. Since libraries are such labor-intensive organizations, the importance of proper staffing for maximum effectiveness needs to be recognized. Ultimately, the success of a library operation depends on the skills and abilities of people who make up the staff.

"Staffing" is not merely a synonym for "employment" but should be thought of as an integrated system for moving into, through, and eventually out of an organization.[1] It includes all methods of matching skills available with the tasks to be performed, through hiring, placement, promotion, transfer, job restructuring, and training. The theory of staffing is based on individual differences in abilities and interest.

Although there are a wide range of methods and styles of staffing, the prerequisites for a successful staffing pattern are clear; these are adequate job descriptions and a well-defined position classification system. Staff members should spend as much time as possible on tasks that require skills appropriate to their position classification and salary levels.

PERSONNEL UTILIZATION

Effect of Organizational Structure on Staffing

Staffing patterns in particular libraries depend greatly on the type of organizational structure that has evolved or been consciously created in a library. In *Organizational Structure of Libraries,* Martin describes in detail various types of organizations and their effect on staffing.[2] Organization can be by purpose, function, nature of material handled, geographical location, or clientele. Components of organizational structure, Martin maintains, are specialization and coordination, namely, dividing tasks into separate pieces of work to be done, but then putting the pieces together to achieve the purpose of the library.

Libraries are predominately organized by function (e.g., acquisitions, reference, circulation, cataloging), but organization by subject may be found in academic and larger public libraries. In these situations staff may be carrying out all the functions of selection, acquisition, cataloging, and reference within a specific subject area. In practice, these tend to be more expensive operations because of the duplication of some material and decentralization of staff.

Organizational structure determines how work, responsibility, and accountability will be distributed throughout the library. Sullivan and Ptacek consider the development of staffing tables to outline the appropriate size and kind of staff for units within a broad structure. How many employees and level of employees to be assigned need to be determined after considering unit functions, workloads, schedules, physical layout and size, complexity of tasks, and unique requirements.[3]

There is no one best structure; instead, an organization should be dynamic and change as needed. White indicates that most libraries are organized on a bureaucratic line-management model, but thinks they are moving toward more organic systems, with less rigidity in job definitions, greater dispersement and delegation of authority, and horizontal communication and cooperation.[4]

Levels of Staffing

The ratio of professionals to support staff in the libraries has varied through the years. In the 1930s and 40s, 50 to 60 percent of library staff were professionals. In a 1941 study of 37 public libraries, however, professionals were found to be spending an average of 35 percent of their time on routine clerical duties.[5] As efforts were made to clarify duties for the two groups, the proportional relationship of professional to support staff gradually shifted. The 1950s still found the ratio of two to one professional staff to support staff in some libraries although, by the 1960s, professionals in many libraries constituted 25 to 35 percent of the total.

In a study of staffing patterns and library growth at Association of Research Libraries (ARL) members over a twenty-year period, the number of professionals as a percentage of full-time staff members declined from a ratio of 41.6 percent professionals in 1962/63 to 32.6 percent in 1983/84.[6] Annual statistics published by the Association of Research Libraries and Association of College and Research Libraries (ACRL) provide data on the ratio of professional to support staff. The most recent figures for ARL (1985-86) show a median ratio of 0.5:1 professionals to support staff (excluding student assistants).[7] Professionals comprise a median of 25 percent of total staff; support staff constitute a median of 51 percent of staff, and student assistants are a median of 23 percent of staff.

The percentages vary widely, however, by individual library. Non-ARL library university data compiled by ACRL for the same year show slight variations with a median of 25 percent professional, 46 percent support staff, and 30 percent student assistant staff and a ratio of 0.6:1 professional-support staff. College libraries showed medians of 26, 42, and 27 percent of these same groups, while junior colleges showed more variation with medians of 31, 61, and 8 percent respectively for professional, support staff, and student assistant staff.[8]

The latest national data for public libraries (1982) reported 93,000 staff members of which 40.7 percent were professional; 53.6 percent were technical, clerical, and other; and 5.7 percent were plant operation and maintenance personnel. The ratios of staff, however, varied by size of institution. For those serving under 10,000 population, two-thirds were professional and 28 percent were support staff; the latter grew to 57 percent in libraries serving one million or more population.[9]

In school libraries, 82 percent of library media centers are administered by certified school library media specialists. Although most library media centers have clerks, 45 percent reported having no paid support staff in 1985-86. Only elementary schools are likely to have adult volunteers, and 33 percent report using no student volunteers. Twenty-one percent reported using from one to five student assistants.[10]

Although ratios vary considerably in practice, a ratio of one-third professional and two-thirds support staff is generally advocated in the library literature. As the ratios have changed through the years, many of the routine responsibilities that formerly were performed by professionals have shifted downward to the support-staff level, particularly when highly qualified paraprofessionals are available.

PROFESSIONAL/SUPPORT STAFF DUTIES

The distinctions between professional and support staff duties often have been blurred in practice even though efforts have been made to distinguish them in theory. Various local, state, and national groups have attempted to grapple with definitions. For example, as early as 1932 the California Library Association published a statement on professional versus support staff positions in libraries.[11] A list of professional and support staff duties in libraries was published by the American Library Association in 1948[12] and is still requested by individuals although it is now out of print and obviously does not take into account the new services and technologies since that time. The Library Association (Britain) defined professional/support staff duties by general functional areas in 1962 and updated this in 1974.[13] In 1968 a report entitled "Education and Manpower for Librarianship," by Lester E. Asheim,[14] provided the basis for an official policy statement, adopted by the American Library Association in 1970.[15] Five levels of personnel (two professional and three supportive) were recommended. Each level provided for library-related qualifications and nonlibrary qualifications, thus recognizing the importance of specialists with training in areas other than librarianship.

Another attempt to clarify duties was carried out by the Illinois Task Analysis Project (ILTAP), starting in 1969 and culminating in a final project publication that provided a list of library tasks, arranged by eight major subsystems and performance levels (e.g., professional, technical, and clerical).[16]

More work needs to be done by the profession in distinguishing between levels of duties in light of changes in staffing described later in this chapter.

Professionals

Librarians. The "Library Education and Personnel Utilization" policy states that "the title 'Librarian' carries with it the connotation of 'professional' in the sense that professional tasks are those which require a special background and education on the basis of which library needs are identified, problems are analyzed, goals are set, and original and creative solutions are formulated for them, integrating theory into practice, and planning, organizing, communicating, and administering successful programs of service to users of the library's materials and services. In defining services to users, the professional person recognizes potential users as well as current ones, and designs services which will reach all who could benefit from them."

It goes on to state that "the title 'Librarian' therefore should be used only to designate positions in libraries which utilize the qualifications and impose the responsibilities suggested above. Positions which are primarily devoted to the routine application of established rules and techniques, however useful and essential to the effective operation of a library's ongoing services, should not carry the word 'Librarian' in the job title."[17]

Although what are seen as professional duties may vary from one institution to the next, most will probably agree that professional responsibilities are those that require independent judgment and decision making, interpretation of rules and procedures, and analysis and solution of library problems. Neal Harlow defined professional responsibility as broad in scope; inherently intellectual; resting on a general body of knowledge, attitudes, and skills; and including integrity, competence, objectivity, initiative, and service.[18]

The *New Directions in Library and Information Science Education* project looked at professional competencies (knowledge, skills, and attitudes) and organized these by work setting, function performed, and professional level (entry, mid or senior level).[19]

Specialists

As libraries have grown in size and complexity, the use of nonlibrarian specialists has increased. These are usually either technical (in a specific subject area) or managerial specialists. A 1982 survey of specialist positions in ARL libraries had 60 libraries reporting 123 specialty positions, involving a wide range of activities. Personnel, budgeting, and automation specialists have been on large library staffs for some time, but newer areas include fund-raising, preservation, public relations, staff development, and library research.[20]

In a 1983 survey of 173 public libraries serving over 100,000 population, 49 libraries reported 110 individuals serving as specialists in either staff positions or in a support position to the library administrator. Most frequently, these persons dealt with personnel, general administration, community and public relations, systems analysis, and budget matters, with a few found in fund-raising, planning, research, or automation.[21]

In large special libraries, specialists may be involved as literature searchers, translators, abstractors and indexers, or information systems personnel. School library media centers may hire audiovisual experts who are not librarians, although in recent years media competency is usually a requirement for those interested in school librarianship.

Specialists are sometimes categorized within the position classification scheme for librarians, and in other institutions are found within a state or local civil service classification plan or a parent institution's nonlibrarian classification system. The ALA "Library Education and Personnel Utilization" policy recognizes that "skills other than those of librarianship may also have an important contribution to make to the achievement of superior library service . . . and there should be equal recognition in both the professional and supportive ranks for those individuals whose expertise contributes to the effective performance of the library."[22] A dual career lattice for librarians and specialists is suggested by this policy.

Support Staff

A wide variety of names have been used for support staff positions, including subprofessional, nonprofessional, paraprofessional, library assistant, library/media technical assistant, clerk, library aide, library associate, intern, and trainee. A number of personnel administrators have encountered difficulties with the term "nonprofessional" because of negative connotations, so many no longer use this terminology.

The staffing of support levels often depends on the definition given to the professional. The difficulty in reaching consensus on a definition of professional duties has complicated the analysis of supporting staff duties, since studies often have showed professionals performing functions that many consider clerical. A number of functions, such as descriptive cataloging and interlibrary loan, that were previously considered professional duties are now handled by paraprofessionals in some libraries. The role of support staff undoubtedly will continue to evolve as the librarian role expands or undergoes change owing to the impact of external and internal forces discussed later in the chapter.

The use of library/media technical assistants (LMTAs) as an intermediate level of staffing increased during the 1960s as some saw this type of position as an answer to the library "manpower" shortage. The number of formal two-year community college LMTA training programs increased during this period. The increase caused some concern among librarians who feared that employers would economize and see the LMTAs as less expensive substitutes for professionals. During the job shortage and budget cuts of the 1970s, LMTAs were sometimes considered a threat to professionals, who saw their jobs being eliminated or downgraded. In many instances, however, a more positive benefit occurred: a clearer delineation of roles emerged, resulting in more effective utilization of personnel according to their various levels of skills, knowledge, and abilities.

Many in LMTA positions have progressed through on-the-job training instead of through the formal educational programs. Therefore functions rather than training are more apt to characterize the LMTA. These functions usually are specified by regulations and routines and are carried out mostly under the direction of librarians. However, many LMTAs are supervising other support staff, such as clerks, pages, and student helpers. In some libraries they are supervising circulation departments, interlibrary loan operations, stacks, or various technical processing operations. As libraries increasingly use media, technicians are playing important roles in the production, organization, and retrieval of these materials, as well as becoming actively involved in automation procedures.

A category of personnel advocated by the ALA "Library Education and Personnel Utilization" policy is library associate. This provides for a class of personnel described as having "supportive responsibilities at a high level, normally working within established procedures and techniques, and with some supervision by a professional, but requiring judgment, and subject knowledge such as represented by a full, four-year college education culminating in the bachelor's degree."[23]

Library staff at this level are often called library assistants and can be found providing routine reference, readers advisory, and outreach services; assisting children's librarians; or administering small branch agencies, bookmobiles, or specialized subject departments where a broad background of librarianship is not considered necessary. In a study of library associates in large public libraries, no clear differentiation of duties between the lowest professional classification and the highest supporting staff level was found. Persons with a variety of backgrounds and experience at the library associate level were mentioned in the study as providing a good source of professional recruitment, a core of qualified flexible, part-time personnel, and the personnel needed to provide new services.[24]

Concern has been expressed about the lack of uniformity and standardization of the minimum level of competency required of those filling higher level supporting staff positions. A few states have developed procedures for certifying technicians for public libraries or school library media programs, but no national trend is apparent. Some city and state civil service departments have attempted to clarify these positions. Some library employers, however, have complained that often no attempt is made to spell out unique tasks in the library setting and library supporting staff are then lumped with other similar city or campus categories.

One attempt at defining subprofessional duties was made by ALA in a 1968 statement on "The Subprofessional or Technical Assistant."[25] The ALA "Criteria for Programs to Prepare Library Media Technical Assistants" provided guidelines for those establishing training programs for paraprofessionals.[26] Another attempt at defining paraprofessional tasks is ALA's *Paraprofessional Support Staff for School Library Media*

Programs—A Competency Statement, written in 1978 by the American Association of School Librarians.[27]

The Council on Library/Media Technical Assistants (COLT) has been actively involved since 1967 in clarifying paraprofessional roles and responsibilities through its conferences and publications. A 1985 COLT publication, *Job Descriptions for Library Support Personnel,* brings together samples from various types of libraries and shows a wide range of duties and responsibilities.[28] COLT is exploring the possibility of certification of library technical assistants.

Within individual library position classification systems, one often finds two to four different grade levels with increasing responsibilities for library assistant or associate titles, thus providing some career mobility, at least up to the professional level where additional formal education is then usually required (although a few libraries have examinations that paraprofessionals can take to attempt to qualify for professional positions). Some libraries are considering expansion of the number of grade levels to accommodate paraprofessionals who are supervising clerical staff in certain departments, or are actually in charge of such units as circulation, reserve, or interlibrary loan departments.

An important level of support staff in school and academic libraries is that of student assistants who work part-time, often under work-study programs. While student assistants often perform repetitive and more perfunctory work, given good training and adequate experience they can often perform at relatively skilled levels, and thus constitute an important segment of the library team.

Volunteers

The use of volunteers varies by type of library. School and public libraries are more apt to use volunteers than academic or special libraries, except for hospital libraries that rely heavily on volunteer help. Arguments, both pro and con, regarding the use of volunteers are found in the library literature. Some feel that volunteers lower the value of a service, weaken public support, are not cost effective, and are unreliable. Others argue that volunteers can be advocates for increased library support and recognition in the community, provide a good return on the investment, and can provide reliable service with good management.[29]

The amount of work performed by volunteers is modest in comparison with regular staff time expended. School library volunteers contribute the largest proportion of time; they assist primarily with routine duties such as circulation, processing, mending, and typing. Volunteers in public libraries often are able to strengthen links to the community through public relations, special projects, or extension of such services as delivering materials to hospitals or shut-ins and assisting summer reading clubs.

Most employers are conscientious in not using volunteers as a low-cost substitute for regular staff, although in places hit by budget cuts the use of volunteers often increases. The basic concept regarding the use of volunteers should be to provide supplemental and support services, never to replace library staff.

It is important to have a clear-cut policy on the use of volunteers and to match the skills, backgrounds, and abilities of the volunteers to the job as much as possible. For cost accounting purposes, time records of volunteers should be kept and regular personnel procedures for interviewing, training, and evaluating their performance should be carried out. In large libraries a volunteer coordinator is often a paid staff member.

An increasing number of organizations use contracts for volunteers. While it has no legal force, a written agreement usually outlines the number of hours and time period that the volunteer pledges to work, and outlines what the organization expects of the volunteer and what it will commit to training, guidance, supervision, and support. The basic purpose of a contract is to have clear communication regarding respective responsibilities. It can also provide the basis for a written record, evaluation, and letter of recommendation when a volunteer leaves a program.

STANDARDS, POLICIES, AND REGULATIONS

Through the years, many of the national and state library associations have issued a variety of guidelines and standards for library services, many of which have included sections on personnel. Generally, there has been a move from quantitative standards to qualitative definitions. Earlier standards and guidelines often dictated a certain number of staff per population served or volumes in the collection. Many statements now indicate that variations in the community served, philosophy of service, curriculum changes, or technology make it difficult to give precise recommendations in terms of level and size of staff.

The fact that no single model or formula can be provided easily in recommending optimum staff size or levels is reflected in the "Standards for University Libraries" adopted by the Association of Research Libraries and the Association of College and Research Libraries in 1979. While it is recommended that a library have "sufficient number and variety (of staff) to develop, organize and maintain collections and provide reference/information services to meet the university's need . . . size is determined by many factors, including number of physically separate units, number of service points requiring staff, number of service hours, number and special characteristics of items processed annually, the nature and quality of processing to which subjected, the size of collections and rate of circulation of collections—as well as interinstitutional cooperative arrangements which may also affect size."[30]

The "Standards for College Libraries" (1986) recommend a formula for the number of librarians based on a combination of student enrollment, collection size, and growth of the collection. However, other factors need to be considered, according to the Standards, such as services and programs, degrees offered, size of faculty and staff, and auxiliary programs. Examples of services and programs include reference and information services, bibliographic instruction, computer-based services, collection development, and collection organization. Auxiliary programs include extension efforts, community and continuing education, as well as size and configuration of facilities and hours of service. The Standards recommend that support staff shall be no less than 65 percent of the total library staff, not including student assistants.[31]

In comparing college libraries against the former standards published in 1979, Carpenter found that many colleges, particularly private undergraduate schools, fell short of the standards in terms of numbers of staff and ratio of professional to support staff.[32]

Other statements that have general sections on types of personnel for academic libraries include "Guidelines for Extended Campus Services," "Guidelines for Two-Year College Learning Resources Programs," and "The Mission of a University Undergraduate Library: Model Statement."[33]

School library/media standards long have advocated the concept of differentiated staffing that recognizes different levels of skills, training, and competencies depending on the tasks to be performed and the level of difficulty. The standards *Media Programs: District and School,* jointly prepared by the American Association of School Librarians and the Association for Educational Communications and Technology, were updated in 1988 (*Information Power: Guidelines for School Library Media Programs*). Both sets of standards recognize that the level and patterns of staffing depend on a number of variables, such as size of school, availability of funds, faculty/student expectations, the extent to which the library media program is integrated into the curriculum, physical plant, special student populations, and services provided by the district or regional program. The new standards indicate that all students and teachers deserve access to library media programs delivered by at least one full-time certified media specialist, with one full-time technical assistant or aide. Some programs and level of service may require more than one support staff person for each professional;

additional professional staff should be based on the specific components of the program.[34]

Earlier research generated by the ALA School Library Manpower Project, Jobs in Instructional Media Study, and others have produced a broad base of support for the development of competencies for school media personnel. In 1976 the American Association of School Librarians published professional level competencies in its *Certification Model for Professional School Media Personnel* and a complementary document on *Candidate Assessment Process for Professional School Library Media Personnel* was published in 1978.[35] These have been considered by some of the state certification agencies that set the qualifications for school library media personnel.

Although the Public Library Association's (PLA) *Minimum Standards for Public Library Systems, 1966* prescribed specific personnel requirements, in the 1970s the PLA moved away from these prescriptive national standards because of their failure to acknowledge differences in community needs and conditions. A *Planning Process for Public Libraries* provides guidelines for community-based planning and evaluation, so that staffing justifications will come from a local determination of programs and services needed.[36] Two new components of a Public Library Development Program include *Planning and Role Setting for Public Libraries: A Manual of Options and Procedures* and the second edition of *Output Measures for Public Libraries;* these continue the process of helping librarians with their planning and review of various service options. A design for a public library data service anticipates collection of selective data, including some staff information, from a number of public libraries that can be used for comparison and possible national norms in the future.[37]

The Medical Library Association's "Code for the Certification of Health Sciences Librarians" was developed to insure minimum levels of competence through establishing requirements for education and experience. The MLA *Minimum Standards for Health Science Libraries in Hospitals* indicates that all library services should be under the direction of a qualified medical librarian (a person with a graduate degree in library science from an ALA accredited program and certified by MLA, or with documented equivalent training and experience). If a qualified medical librarian cannot be employed, the hospital is to contract with a qualified library consultant or circuit librarian on a fee basis. The standards list minimum numbers of professionals and support staff for six sizes of hospitals, ranging from one part-time technical employee and a library consultant in the smallest library to three qualified medical librarians and four full-time support staff.[38]

The "Objectives and Standards for Special Libraries" outlines functions and qualifications for the special library administrator, duties and responsibilities for other staff members, including support staff and specialists who may not have a library education background. The standards state that a division of professional and support staff functions is necessary and that the special library must have at least one professionally qualified librarian and one clerical worker. The recommended ratio of support staff to professional staff is three to two.[39]

The Art Libraries Society of North America issued *Standards for Art Libraries and Fine Arts Slide Collections* in 1983 to update its 1977 document. The standards give a fairly detailed statement on the number and level of staff and ratio of professionals to support staff needed in relation to volumes, other institutional staff, hours open, annual acquisition statistics, and other factors. A ratio of 40 percent professionals to 60 percent support staff is generally recommended except in academic systems where technical services are provided by the centralized system; in the latter, the support staff recommendation is 75 percent. Another section of the standards addresses staffing for fine arts slide collections. Factors affecting staffing include circulation rate, accession rate, size of collection, and extent of services. Curatorial/professional, technical, and clerical/general staff categories are presented. These standards provide an example of fairly recent standards that do not follow the trend away from specific quantitative recommendations.[40]

Federal libraries still operate under the 1966 U.S. Civil Service Commission (now Office of Personnel Management) Position-Classification Standards. Attempts by OPM to rewrite these standards were fought by the library community in the early 1980s because of concern over the potential for downgrading positions. The proposed standards have not been issued, although the U.S. Office of Management and Budget Circular A-76 has affected staffing in some federal libraries, as agencies have determined what activities should be performed under contract with commercial sources or inhouse using government personnel. The ALA has expressed opposition to the wholesale contracting out of library services. A pilot project to allow certain federal agencies to determine their own classifications and salaries is a new development that may affect staffing patterns in the future.

At the state level, the third edition of the *Standards for Library Functions at the State Level* (1985) contains a short chapter on personnel. Specific number of personnel are not advocated but general qualifications and types of personnel are outlined.[41] Other examples of guidelines and regulations that affect staffing patterns can be found at the state and local level, wherever state library associations have recommended levels of staffing or where state and local civil service, certification, or personnel agencies exercise control in the development and implementation of classification systems and qualifications required for library personnel under their jurisdiction.

One attempt to develop staffing recommendations on the international level includes the "Standards for University Libraries" from the IFLA Section of University Libraries and other General Research Libraries. Here the variation in size of library and other factors is recognized by the general statement that the size and qualifications of staff "will be determined by many factors including size and scope of collections, number of separate library units, number of service points, number of service hours, rate of acquisition, rate of circulation, nature of processing, nature of service demand."[42]

VARIATIONS IN STAFFING PATTERNS

As suggested in the discussion on standards, variations in staffing patterns depend on many factors, such as type of library, type of function, and size of library. These factors all interrelate, making any generalizations about staffing requirements extremely difficult.

Type of Library

The Association of Research Libraries and its Task Force on Research Library Staffing has developed a set of organizational projections for assessing future research library staffing needs and prospects. Four options are derived from speculations about how universities and their libraries will address technological and other environmental developments. The models present variations for staff size, composition, skills and qualities, organization and classification, training and development depending on the university context, philosophy and role, and the extent to which the library centers around traditional functions or moves to discipline-oriented information services or a highly automated centralized academic information center.[43]

Public library staffing arrangements are influenced by the functional organization of the main library, the number of branches, outreach and bookmobile services, and whether the library is part of a larger county or multitype library system. In *Reorganization of the Public Library,* Webb presents case studies describing the steps taken by several libraries to respond to emerging community needs. Changes in service philosophy and, in some cases, financial reductions have resulted in organizational structures with different staff needs and patterns. In one example, Baltimore County Public Library's formula for staffing allocation of professional and clerical staff for each branch is based on service statistics for the previous year.[44]

In school/media libraries there are often two levels of staffing. At the district level one usually finds an administrator responsible for supervision and coordination of library programs in the district. Planning, in-service training, reporting, and consulting are all functions performed by the district librarian, who is a staff rather than line member. The district media director acts as the leader for heads of school media programs at the individual building level and determines priorities for the total media program.

Often school libraries are one-person operations; service to students and teachers, book selection, circulation, processing, and organization of materials all fall under this one person, although the employment of sufficient technical and clerical staff to work under the guidance of media professionals is essential to promote efficient and economical staffing.

In larger schools staff may be assigned to work with specified grade-level or age-level groups, with subject area specializations, specific blocks of instruction, or satellite subject resource centers.

Staff within special libraries are likely to need a strong subject background in the area of interest represented by the institution in which the library is located. The ability to provide a more intensive service through dissemination of information at a rapid pace is characteristic of many special libraries, which tend to have a more homogeneous library user. Library functions vary from literature searching, translating, and abstracting to indexing, editing, and providing current awareness services.

Type of Function

In a 1986 survey of ARL libraries, one-third cited major organizational changes due to the growing importance of specific functions over the last ten to fifteen years. Organizational charts of large universities often show the increasing importance of preservation, planning, collection management, and automation.[45] Academic librarians are spending more time in advising and teaching students and faculty on how to use the complexity of library resources more effectively.

In all types of libraries roles are shifting, particularly in distinctions between librarian and support staff duties. Paraprofessionals are taking over many of the responsibilities formerly performed by librarians, freeing librarians to spend more time on such administrative duties as planning and decision making, collection development, original cataloging, programming, etc. Although collection development has been a stable, traditional feature of libraries, there is increasing interest in moving from building collections to managing information resources.

Perhaps no other function currently shows as much diversity in reporting relationships as this function. In large academic libraries, for example, collection development functions might be fulfilled by a staff of full-time bibliographers with assignments by academic department, language, or subject area; a decentralized staff where a large number have collection development responsibilities as part of other duties; or a staff with a combination of some full-time bibliographers and part-time selectors. In smaller academic, public, and special libraries, selection duties may be included in the duties of the reference or acquisitions librarian or director. In some libraries a manager of collection development serves as a coordinator with few supervisory duties, and in others she or he may serve as a traditional department head with supervisory functions. Some librarians might have responsibilities for both acquisitions and collection development, while others may leave the acquisitions duties to a business manager.[46]

Considerable variation in reference desk staffing patterns is found, with public librarians working longer hours at the desk than academic librarians. Off-desk duties have increased with online searching and bibliographic instruction responsibilities. The use of support staff on the reference desk is a controversial issue for many librarians. Some managers do not use the on- and off-desk dichotomy as a concept in scheduling and assigning responsibilities, but instead think in terms of direct patron contact (including online searching) vs. noncontact duties. In many libraries it is common to supplement reference staff with part-time librarians, who tend to spend a larger proportion of their work week at the reference desk than full-time staff.[47]

Over the past ten to fifteen years the technical services area has been characterized by many changes in the organization, work flow, staffing patterns, and job responsibilities, primarily a result of automation and reliance on networks. In some libraries, copy cataloging operations with support staff can handle over 90 percent of the titles being acquired; in others it is less than two-thirds. The major pattern is generally more reliance on paraprofessionals with higher skills. Because of the accessibility of files in many places, staffing can be more flexible in terms of scheduling and work in off-peak hours. Administrative realignments in the cataloging and circulation departments have created variations in staffing needs as the distinction between technical and public services blurs.[48]

Size of Library

Although small libraries may operate in an informal manner, it is still important to look carefully at duties and responsibilities and define what is expected of each individual. With only a few staff members, there is a need for flexibility and the interchange of jobs or the performance of a wide variety of duties, but an attempt should still be made to assign major responsibilities to specific individuals based on their level of skill and knowledge.

In *Administration of the Small Public Library,* Sinclair has indicated that total specialization is rarely possible in a small staff. If the budget allows for three to four professionals, however, she proposes it is possible for public libraries to have an age-level specialist and one extension services person if the administrator can also handle some of the public or technical services.[49]

Separate career ladders for paraprofessionals are found almost exclusively in large public, university, and federal libraries. It is recognized that small staff-size limits upward mobility because there is little chance for advancement based either on specialization in a certain skill or added responsibilities in a supervisory role. Obviously, the larger the staff, the greater the specialization or differentiation possible. With a large staff, it is necessary to have clearly defined lines of authority and a chain of command that is spelled out through an organization chart. Generally speaking, while fifteen persons is probably the maximum number for which a supervisor should be responsible, this number varies depending on the nature of the responsibilities and the level of persons supervised.

In *Organizational Structure of Libraries,* Martin claims that size is a key factor in the management structure of a library. With up to twenty-five to thirty staff members, a director can usually do without an assistant director, but an assistant is desirable for a staff up to two or three times this size. In staffs of over one hundred there are often up to three general officers below the chief officer; the organizational structure will depend on the span of control that exists. A smaller span or fewer staff per supervisor, the larger the number of middle managers or assistant or associate directors. With a range of three to five subordinates on the average, only eighty to ninety staff can be accommodated in a four-tier structure (workers, department heads, assistant or associate directors, and director). With a range of seven or eight, four hundred staff members can fit into the same number of levels.[50]

In large academic libraries, the second echelon of administration is a comparatively recent pattern. With rapid expansion after World War II, many large libraries moved from having twelve to twenty department heads reporting to the chief librarian to the current general pattern with as many as five to six second-level appointments, with titles varying greatly (e.g., assistant university librarian, associate or assistant director, coordinator, officer, etc.). Responsibilities vary greatly and may include service department supervision, budgeting, planning, collection development, automation, personnel, and systems.[51]

CURRENT ISSUES

Impact of External Forces: Technological

In the early 1970s the application of the computer to library operations began to affect work flow and staffing needs. No matter where found in libraries, automation demands a closer analysis of work assignments. Each procedure needs to be examined to determine if it needs to continue or how it changes with automation. Changes in job content thus affect what level of staff should be used. The literature on library automation often discusses the need for a more integrated approach and greater need for cooperation and interrelationships between departments. As a result of automation, more and more librarians are considering reassigning functions previously performed by professionals to support staff.

There are little data on the impact of automation on staff. Some libraries have reported reductions in certain departments, but the total number of library workers has not been radically altered. Automation has resulted in employment of different types of personnel in many libraries, namely, data processing specialists, console operators, and programmers. Because of the need for increased standardization, accuracy, and upgrading of skills, automation often results in more intensive, formalized, structured, and centralized staff training. While some support staff are assuming some responsibilities, professionals are finding themselves involved with planning, administering, training, and vendor negotiating.[52]

Impact of External Forces: Societal

The knowledge explosion created the need for new patterns of library service, thus affecting staffing patterns. Changes in higher education in methods of scholarly communication, and variations in management and governance, have had an impact on academic libraries. Shifts in population patterns and growth trends have affected the staffing needs, particularly of public institutions. Student enrollments in public schools, colleges, and universities are having an impact on the size of library staff because the educational expenditures per student are often intertwined with the size of the collection and personnel. Public library staffing needs are changing as urban libraries in particular modify their traditional library services to reach new community groups. The role of school librarians also is shifting as individualized instruction and curricula reform result in a broader role as the school media center concept continues to take hold.

Impact of External Forces: Financial

With increased demands for service at the same time costs are escalating for materials and salaries, many libraries are having to determine whether professional skills are being used to best advantage. In some cases reduced public support is resulting in managers clarifying how support staff can be used more fully. With the increased trends toward accountability, particularly in the public sector, libraries are being forced to consider more carefully the appropriate staffing ratios and responsibilities for all levels. Cost analysis studies are not prevalent in the library field. Nevertheless, some analyses of labor costs are needed for purposes of budget preparation and justification, evaluation of yearly and seasonal changes, and impact of automation on procedures.

Impact of External Forces: Legal

There are a host of regulations affecting the staffing process, many of which are described in the chapter by Gasaway and Moran. Between the federal and state laws on fair employment and equal employment opportunity, collective bargaining agreements, and various civil service or certification regulations, few libraries are exempt from forces that influence who and what staff are recruited, hired, trained, promoted, and terminated. These legal requirements may result in more paper work and a longer time period for handling staffing procedures, but they are at the same time causing many libraries to look more carefully at their personnel practices, resulting in clearer written procedures and fairer management of human resources.

While some librarians have complained that laws and regulations hamstring their operations, others have been creative in working within the political arena and in devoting time to making certain that employees in personnel agencies and departments that are outside the library but still influence staffing procedures are fully aware of their libraries' functions and requirements. They have made certain that input from the library is heard and have engaged in a long-term educational effort regarding staffing needs so that unrealistic requirements are not imposed by the external agency.

Impact of Internal Forces

There are a number of internal pushes from within individual library staffs or within the profession at large impacting on library staffing. The library world has not been immune to the movement of participation in organizational decision-making, as employee groups have sought to influence the decision making about library operations and working conditions. Much has been written about participatory management that will not be repeated here, although it should be pointed out that an increased voice in the decision-making process can certainly affect staffing patterns; the traditional library hierarchy becomes much less rigid and increased flexibility in responsibilities will often result.

As more academic libraries have adopted the collegiate model of the teaching faculty, there has been a movement for academic librarians to be ranked on the basis of their professional achievements rather than by job function. Some academic personnel systems, however, do not follow the faculty status model. Because faculty status is a controversial issue in some places, there is a need to reconsider the meaning and impact of such status.

Another push has been for horizontal career ladders that recognize nonadministrative expertise and responsibilities on an equal footing with administrative duties. This resulted in a statement issued by ALA on comparable rewards or equal compensation for nonadministrative expertise. This policy states that wherever possible as many nonadministrative specialities as administrative staff should be assigned to the top classifications.[53]

There also is a movement to open up career ladders to supporting staff without formal education who wish to move into professional positions. In a few instances, experience or examination are routes to this upward mobility within an individual institution, although movement between libraries is more difficult. Employers must remember, however, that any "equivalent" qualifications to established practices cannot be set arbitrarily but must be based on a careful review of the job responsibilities and the skills, knowledge, and abilities needed.

Increasing constraints on the ability of management to shift personnel may come if unionization takes a greater hold in libraries, since certain types of redeployment may be precluded if job security concerns have been addressed in contract negotiation.

FUTURE CONSIDERATIONS

These trends and shifts in staffing patterns will undoubtedly continue. As the new technologies become more familiar, a clearer consensus might emerge as to how best to deploy staff. Nevertheless, there will be probably continue to be many variations since it is clear that a single pattern of staffing cannot be used in the wide variety of types and sizes of libraries. But, the tools of job analysis, job restructuring, cost analysis, and more sophisticated planning techniques can be of assistance to library administrators in determining the best pattern for their individual institutions.

References

1. Dale Yoder and Herbert Heneman, "Staffing Policies and Strategies," in *ASPA Handbook of Personnel and Industrial Relations* (Washington, D.C.: Bureau of National Affairs, 1974), I, p. 4-2.
2. Lowell A. Martin, *Organizational Structure of Libraries* (Metuchen, N.J.: Scarecrow, 1984).
3. Peggy Sullivan and William Ptacek, *Public Libraries: Smart Practices in Personnel* (Littleton, Colo.: Libraries Unlimited, 1982), p. 19.
4. Herbert S. White, *Library Personnel Management* (White Plains, N.Y.: Knowledge Industry, 1985), p. 29.
5. E.V. Baldwin and W.E. Marcus, *Library Costs and Budgets: A Study of Cost Accounting in Public Libraries* (New York: R.R. Bowker, 1941), p. 94.
6. Robert E. Molyneux, "Staffing Patterns and Library Growth at ARL Libraries, 1962/63 to 1983/84," *Journal of Academic Librarianship* 12 (November 1986): 296.
7. Association of Research Libraries, *ARL Statistics, 1985-86* (Washington, D.C.: ARL, 1987), p. 28.
8. Association of College and Research Libraries, *ACRL University Library Statistics 1985-86 & 1986 "100 Libraries" Statistical Survey* (Chicago: American Library Association, 1987), pp. 21, 59, 69.
9. Robert A. Heintze, "A Survey of Public Libraries 1982," *Public Libraries* 24 (Summer 1985): 58. See also "The NCES Survey of Public Libraries, 1982: Final Report," *The Bowker Annual of Library & Book Trade Information,* 31st ed. (New York: R.R. Bowker, 1986), pp. 346–52 and *Statistics of Public Libraries, 1981-82: Data Gathered by the National Center for Education Statistics, U.S. Dept. of Education* (Chicago: American Library Association, 1985).
10. Marilyn L. Miller and Barbara Moran, "Expenditures for Resources in School Library Media Centers 1985-86," *School Library Journal* 33 (June/July 1987): 44.
11. California Library Association, "Professional versus Nonprofessional Positions in Libraries," in *Handbook and Proceedings of the Annual Meeting 1932.* Publication no. 33, pp. 57–62.
12. American Library Association, Board on Personnel Administration, *Descriptive List of Professional and Non-professional Duties in Libraries* (Chicago: ALA, 1948).
13. Library Association, Research and Development Committee, *Professional and Non-Professional Duties in Libraries, A Descriptive List,* 2nd ed. (London: Library Association, 1974).
14. Lester E. Asheim, "Education and Manpower for Librarianship," *ALA Bulletin* 63 (October 1968): 1096–118.
15. American Library Association, "Library Education and Personnel Utiliza-

tion: A Statement of Policy Adopted by the Council of the ALA, June 30, 1970" (Chicago: ALA, 1970).

16. Myrl Ricking and Robert E. Booth, *Personnel Utilization in Libraries: A Systems Approach* (Chicago: ALA, 1974).

17. American Library Association, "Library Education and Personnel Utilization," p. 3.

18. Neal Harlow, "Misused Librarians," *Ontario Library Review* 49 (November 1965): 170–72.

19. Jose-Marie Griffiths and Donald W. King, *New Directions in Library and Information Science Education* (White Plains, N.Y.: Knowledge Industry for the American Society for Information Science, 1986).

20. Association of Research Libraries, *Specialty Positions in ARL Libraries,* SPEC Kit No. 80 (Washington, D.C.: ARL, 1982).

21. Barbara B. Moran and Peter Neenan, "The Public Library's Invisible Managers," *Library Journal* 112 (June 15, 1987): 27–29.

22. American Library Association, "Library Education and Personnel Utilization," p. 1.

23. Ibid., pp. 2, 5.

24. Charlotte Mugnier, *"Paraprofessionals and the Professional Job Structure"* (Chicago: ALA, 1980).

25. "The Subprofessional or Technical Assistant: A Statement of Definition," *ALA Bulletin* 62 (April 1968): 387–97.

26. American Library Association, "Criteria for Programs to Prepare Library/ Media Technical Assistants," rev. ed. (Chicago: ALA, 1979).

27. American Library Association, American Association of School Librarians, *Professional Support Staff for School Library Media Programs—A Competency Statement* (Chicago: ALA, 1978).

28. Richard L. Taylor and Raymond G. Roney, *Job Descriptions for Library Support Personnel* (Cleveland: Council on Library/Media Technicians, 1985).

29. Rashelle Schlessinger Karp, "Volunteers in Libraries," in *Advances in Library Administration and Organization,* ed. by Gerald B. McCabe and Bernard Kreissman, v. 5 (Greenwich, Conn.: JAI Press, 1986), pp. 15–31.

30. "Standards for University Libraries," *College and Research Libraries News* 40 (April 1979): 104. See also Kendon Stubbs, "University Libraries: Standards and Statistics," *College and Research Libraries* 42 (November 1981): 527–38.

31. "Standards for College Libraries, 1986," *College and Research Libraries News* 47 (March 1986): 194–95.

32. Ray L. Carpenter, "College Libraries: A Comparative Analysis in Terms of the ACRL Standards," *College and Research Libraries* 42 (January 1981): 7–18.

33. "Guidelines for Extended Campus Library Services," *College and Research Libraries News* 43 (March 1982): 87; "Guidelines for Two-Year College Learning Resources Programs (Revised)," *College and Research Libraries News* (February 1982): 45–46; "The Mission of a University Undergraduate Library: Model Statement," *College and Research Libraries News* 48 (October 1987): 544.

34. American Library Association, American Association of School Librarians, and Association for Educational Communications and Technology, *Media Programs: District and School* (Chicago: ALA, 1975); American Association of School Librarians and the Association for Educational Communications and Technology, *Information Power: Guidelines for School Library Media Programs* (Chicago: ALA, 1988).

35. American Library Association, American Association of School Librarians, *Certification Model for Professional School Media Personnel* (Chicago: ALA, 1976) and *Candidate Assessment Process for Professional School Library Personnel* (Chicago: ALA, 1978).

36. Vernon E. Palmour and Marcia Bellasai, *A Planning Process for Public Libraries* (Chicago: ALA, 1980).

37. Carolyn A. Anthony, "The Public Library Development Program: Options and Opportunities," *Public Libraries* 26 (Summer 1987): 55–57.

38. Medical Library Association, *Minimum Standards for Health Science Libraries in Hospitals* (Chicago: MLA, 1984).

39. Special Libraries Association, "Objectives for Special Libraries," *Special Libraries* 55 (December 1964): 672–74.

40. Art Libraries Society of North America, *Standards for Art Libraries and Fine Arts Slide Collections,* Occasional Papers No. 2 (Tucson, Ariz.: ARLIS/NA, 1983).

41. Association of Specialized and Cooperative Library Agencies, *Standards for Library Functions at the State Level,* 3rd ed. (Chicago: ALA, 1985), pp. 22–23.

42. Beverly Lynch, ed., "Standards for University Libraries," *IFLA Journal* 13, no. 2, 1987, pp. 123–124.

43. Association of Research Libraries, *Organizational Futures: Staffing Research Libraries in the 1990s: Minutes of the 105th Meeting, Oct. 24–25, 1984, Washington, D.C.* (Washington, D.C.: ARL, 1985), pp. 3–26.

44. T.D. Webb, *Reorganization in the Public Library* (Phoenix, Ariz.: Oryx, 1985).

45. Association of Research Libraries, *Organization Charts in ARL Libraries,* SPEC Kit No. 129 (Washington, D.C.: ARL, November/December 1986).

46. Association of Research Libraries, *Collection Development Organization and Staffing,* SPEC Kit No. 131 (Washington, D.C.: ARL, 1987); Bonita Bryant, "Allocation of Human Resources for Collection Development," *Library Resources and Technical Services* 30 (April/June 1986): 149–62; Bonita Bryant, "The Organizational Structure of Collection Development," *Library Resources and Technical Services* 31 (April/June 1987): 111–22; Thomas W. Leonhardt, "Collection Development and Acquisitions: The Divisions of Responsibility," *RTSD Newsletter* 9, no. 6, 1984, pp. 73–75; Jeanne Sohn, "Collection Development Organizational Patterns in ARL Libraries," *Library Resources and Technical Services* 31 (April/June 1987): 123–34.

47. Charles A. Bunge, "Reference Desk Staffing Patterns: Report of a Survey," *RQ* 27 (Winter 1986): 171–79. See also Martin P. Courtois and Lori A. Goetsch, "Use of Nonprofessionals at Reference Desks," *College and Research Libraries* 45 (September 1984): 385–95; Nancy J. Emmick and

Luella B. Davis, "A Survey of Academic Library Reference Services Practices: Preliminary Results," *RQ* 24 (Fall 1984): 67–81; John Montag, "Choosing How to Staff the Reference Desk," in *Personnel Issues in Reference Services,* ed. by Bill Katz and Ruth A. Fraley (New York: Haworth, 1986): 31–37.

48. Association of Research Libraries, *Managing Copy Cataloging in ARL Libraries,* SPEC Kit No. 136 (Washington, D.C., ARL, 1987); Malcolm Getz and Doug Phelps, "Labor Costs in the Technical Operation of Three Research Libraries," *Journal of Academic Librarianship* 10 (September 1984): 209–19; Ruth Hafter, *Academic Librarians and Cataloging Networks: Visibility, Quality Control and Professional Status* (New York: Greenwood, 1986); Karen L. Horny, "Fifteen Years of Automation: Evolution of Technical Services Staffing," *Library Resources and Technical Services* 31 (January/March 1987): 69–76; Karen L. Horny, "Quality Work, Quality Control in Technical Services," *Journal of Academic Librarianship* 11 (September 1985): 206–10; Joan M. Repp, "The Response of the Cataloger and the Catalog to Automation in the Academic Library Setting," in *Advances in Library Administration and Organization,* ed. by Gerard B. McCabe and Bernard Kreissman, v. 5 (Greenwich, Conn.: JAI, 1986), pp. 67–89.

49. Dorothy Sinclair, *Administration of the Small Public Library,* 2nd ed. (Chicago: ALA, 1979), pp. 71–89.

50. Martin, p. 233–236.

51. Allen B. Veaner, *The Assistant/Associate Director Position in ARL Libraries,* Occasional Paper No. 8 (Washington, D.C.: ARL, 1984), pp. 5–6.

52. Margaret Myers, "Personnel Considerations in Library Automation," in *Human Aspects of Library Automation: Helping Staff and Patrons Cope,* 22nd Annual Clinic on Library Applications of Data Processing, April 14–15, 1985), pp. 30–45.

53. David C. Weber and Tina Kass, "Comparable Rewards: The Case for Equal Compensation for Non-Administrative Expertise," *Library Journal* 103 (April 15, 1978): 824–27.

Bibliography

American Library Association Office for Library Personnel Resources. "Library Automation and Personnel Issues: A Selected Bibliography." Chicago: ALA, 1986.

———. *Library Personnel News,* v. 2, no. 1, Winter 1988 (Theme issue on the changing role of professionals and paraprofessionals). Atkinson, Hugh C. "The Impact of New Technology on Library Organization." In *The Bowker Annual of Library & Book Trade Information,* 29th ed. New York: R.R. Bowker, 1984, pp. 109–14.

Association of Research Libraries. *Job Analysis in ARL Libraries.* SPEC Kit No. 135. Washington, D.C.: ARL, 1987.

Atkinson, Hugh C. "The Impact of New Technology on Library Organization." In *The Bowker Annual of Library & Book Trade Information,* 29th ed. New York: R.R. Bowker, 1984, pp. 109–14.

Buck, Dayna. "Bringing Up an Automated Circulation System: Staffing Needs." *Wilson Library Bulletin* 60 (March 1986): 28–31.

Dakshinamurti, Ganga, "Automation's Effect on Library Personnel." *Canadian Library Journal* 42 (December 1985): 343–51.

Euster, Joanne R. "Changing Staffing Patterns in Academic Libraries." *Library Issues: Briefings for Faculty and Administrators* 7 (September 1986): 1–3.

Frank, Donald G. "Management of Student Assistants in a Public Services Setting of an Academic Library." *RQ* 24 (Fall 1984): 51–57.

Hoadley, Irene. "The World that Awaits Us: Libraries of Tomorrow." *Wilson Library Bulletin* 61 (October 1986): 22–25.

Stueart, Robert D. and Barbara B. Moran. *Library Management.* 3rd ed. Littleton, Colo.: Libraries Unlimited, 1987.

Veaner, Allen B. "Continuity or Discontinuity—A Persistent Personnel Issue in Academic Librarianship." In *Advances in Library Administration and Organization,* v. 1. Greenwich, Conn.: JAI, 1982, pp. 1–20.

4
Personnel Planning and Utilization
Sheila D. Creth

Library administrators are expected to perform a variety of functions: develop strategic planning, including financial planning; forecast service and program needs, and how these will be supported with shrinking resources and with an everchanging clientele or "market"; design library facilities; and develop the library's investment in both collections and human resources. All of these administrative activities are linked to effective and sound personnel planning.

The responsibility for identifying and forecasting personnel needs has been a requirement for library administrators for decades although it often has been handled informally. In addition, the attempt to identify personnel needs too often has been in response to a staffing problem; only when it becomes apparent that there are inadequate candidates for a particular type of position or that there are too many people employed for a specific function, is there a scramble to make adjustments in staffing patterns or job requirements.

In an organizational environment in which change is slow and limited in scope, an informal approach to personnel planning might have been tolerable if not always the most effective or efficient. The current library and information environment, though, requires an organized and comprehensive approach to personnel planning, as well as continual updating and exploring of different methodologies for effective planning.

The scope and pace of change in libraries is in considerable contrast to the past when change was measured in years, not in weeks and days—when change occurred in less dramatic, sweeping ways. Changes that are now affecting libraries are having and will continue to have a profound impact on the nature and concept of the library as a service organization. The organization of libraries, their services and operations, and, of course, the roles and responsibilities of staff will alter in reaction to these changes. The numbers of staff, the knowledge and experience of staff, the responsibilities and activities appropriate to different staff groups, indeed the entire context of the organization is likely to continue undergoing extensive change over the next decade or two.

It is vital for library administrators to recognize and understand the forces that are influencing the reshaping of library services so that planning anticipates the impact that such forces may have on the library organization. The shift from an industrial-based to an information-based economy suggests dramatic changes in the provision of information services. Information has always represented power but in an information-based society, with information as the commodity, this will intensify. There will be greater competition to acquire and provide access to information of all types and formats, and the value for free or low-cost access to information is likely to diminish. Traditional activities and services of libraries will no doubt require reconsideration in order to maintain a central role in the information society.

The computerization of information is another major force influencing library staffing. The automation of library operations should create not only efficiencies, but opportunities for new services. In addition, the application of new technologies to publishing will introduce a variety of formats not encountered previously, and national and international systems of telecommunications will introduce yet another powerful influence on the flow and exchange of information, both published and unpublished. In order for library services and activities to keep pace with the changes introduced by technology, there will likely be changes in the traditional hierarchical organization of libraries, and most assuredly of the responsibilities and job requirements for staff. The changes brought about by automation will affect libraries differently depending on a host of variables such as size and type of library, institutional commitment to computerization, and geographic location of the library.

At the same time that these technological changes are emerging, the users served by libraries continue to change, resulting in new expectations and demands for services. For example, university libraries must respond effectively to an increasing international student population, representing different experiences in the use of large libraries, disparate needs, as well as cultural and language differences. Similar changes in user groups are occurring in communities served by public libraries. Whatever the reason for shifts in user groups served by particular libraries, the library staff will be expected to anticipate and to realign services to meet the new needs.

Finally, like other organizations, libraries have legal and ethical responsibilities to insure a fair and equitable recruitment process and a salary compensation program. This requires an objective means of analyzing and evaluating the worth of the job to an organization. This process may become increasingly complex because of automation, which often results in greater diversity in job assignments, as well as an increased frequency in job changes.

The process of analyzing and responding to personnel needs, from recruitment and compensation to training and development, will become increasingly demanding and complex in the coming decades. It is important, therefore, that administrators consider the following questions during the planning process:

- How many staff are required?
- What are the appropriate staff groups or job families?
- What number and level of staff are required for each library operation and/or service?
- What requirements for knowledge, skill, and ability exist for each position?
- What are the best mechanisms for recruitment?
- What is a fair and equitable salary system for all job families and positions?
- What are the opportunities and requirements for staff to move laterally and upward to other library positions?
- Are we making the best use of the talent on the library staff? Are there opportunities for growth and development for staff?
- Are personnel dollars being used in the most effective and efficient way to deliver services?

Staff utilization and personnel planning require attention from all administrators and supervisors, not only because libraries continue to be labor-intensive, but because staffing costs continue to represent a significant segment of library budgets.

STAFF UTILIZATION

Administrators need to be able to anticipate the impact that changes will have on personnel requirements of the library rather than reacting once the change has occurred. There is no question that automation will bring about massive and sweeping changes to most libraries over the next decade, although it is likely to continue to be evolutionary in nature. In a context of gradual but constant change, a considerable amount of drift can occur if staffing needs are not continually assessed. As online catalogs are implemented and expanded to include order and receipt information and circulation transactions, certain job activities will be eliminated, others will be diminished, and new activities or services will emerge. It will be important not only to forecast what will be altered but to what extent. For instance, while it is clear that the automation of the online catalog will eliminate filing in the card catalog, what must be determined is the amount of staff time saved from this activity, what number and level of staff are involved in filing throughout the library system, and where this staff saving might be reallocated.

In addition to identifying those activities which may be eliminated, it is also important to identify activities which are likely to increase as a result of an online library system. For example, circulation use is likely to increase dramatically, an increased demand for reference services may occur, as will the demand for rush cataloging as users can see what has been received but not yet processed. Library administrators and managers, though, need to look beyond what impact automation will have on current activities and duties, and project what new services should emerge as a result of a fully automated environment.

In order to assess the full extent of staffing adjustments, library administrators need information on whether activities are being performed at the appropriate staff level, and whether the staff level for a job will alter with automation. In other words, how will automation qualitatively change an activity—will it become simpler or more complicated?

RECRUITMENT

Personnel planning has an important influence on recruitment because it requires focusing attention on the duties and qualifications of positions; reviewing labor market availability information; and maintaining current information on the skills, abilities, and interests of staff. Personnel planning focuses on an "analysis and forecasting of organizational needs as well as an assessment of the skills and abilities of the existing staff."[1] To understand organizational needs, the administrator should be able to answer questions such as:

- What is the turnover rate by job family for the library?
- Is the turnover rate different for the library than for other operations in the institution?
- Is there a considerable variance in turnover among library departments for the same or similar job?
- What are the reasons for staff resignations by job family, job level, and library department?
- What are the anticipated retirements for any particular year?

As recruitment policies and procedures are established for a library organization, legal guidelines provide the framework, including the identification of such "protected" groups as minorities, the physically and mentally handicapped, women, and Vietnam veterans. These legal requirements must be integrated into the recruitment policies and procedures of the library and considered part of personnel planning.

It is not sufficient, though, to simply identify the particular legal parameters that guide and direct recruitment because there is much about the laws and guidelines which require interpretation. Indeed, during the 1980s it has become obvious that interpretation of federal laws and regulations are at variance with interpretation and applications of previous administrations. Thus, the national political context influences the strength with which laws are applied and, more generally, affects society's response to the spirit of affirmative action and protection for certain groups of citizens. For instance, in the past decade there have been a series of lawsuits charging that the affirmative action plans of particular organizations result in reverse discrimination against white males. Even when these lawsuits are not successful, they can create a climate within an organization which diminishes the aggressiveness with which affirmative action is pursued, resulting in a decline in the hiring and promotion of minorities and other protected groups.

The complexities of interpreting and applying national and local recruitment guidelines will continue to demand close attention from administrators. Certainly a major challenge for libraries continues to be the recruitment of minorities for all job families—professional and support staff—so that libraries can adequately understand and meet the needs of diverse user groups.

In order to recruit the appropriate people for library positions, the personnel administrator has to be familiar with the labor pools on which the library draws. The labor pools for professional and support staff usually are defined differently, with librarians identified through a national pool and support staff recruited from the local labor market. Effective personnel planning requires the identification and projection of the numbers of people needed at all levels of the organization, the types of experience, knowledge, and ability that are required to perform these jobs, and to what extent people are available in the labor pool. This is essential for planning purposes in order to project difficulties in filling certain positions, to anticipate length of time to fill positions, and to identify knowledge and skills that may well have to be provided through on-the-job training because qualified people are lacking in the labor pool.

Collective bargaining agreements have a direct bearing on filling open positions in some libraries. This does not negate the need for planning, but places the focus on identifying the skills and abilities of the unionized staff and developing remedial methods through the library's staff development program when deficiencies are apparent. In other libraries, some or all employees may be governed by a civil service system (city, state, or federal) which may have testing and other requirements associated with recruitment. Again, this does not diminish the need for the personnel administrator to include these positions in a planning activity, but it entails different considerations in forecasting staffing needs.

All of these factors—equal employment and affirmative action, union contracts, civil service systems, market and labor factors, automation, the economy—contribute to the personnel planning process for both short- and long-range planning. Personnel planning is particularly critical when organizational change is underway. The development of new programs and additional services or a reduction of library programs and services always have an impact on staffing. It is imperative, therefore, that the personnel administrator be a member of the library administrative team so that staffing needs are considered at every stage of the library's planning and decision-making process.

POSITION CLASSIFICATION SCHEMES

The establishment and maintenance of an objective and fair classification scheme for positions is another aspect of library personnel administration which requires considerable attention. A position classification scheme is tied not only to recruitment but to the salary compensation program as well. It also is a mechanism by which promotional opportunities are identified for library staff. Again, civil service systems and collective bargaining agreements may impact on the degree of flexibility available to the library administration, but these factors do not negate the need for the library to insure that positions have been evaluated objectively and fairly in relation to an established scheme. As Wilkinson, Plate, and Lee observed, "nothing is more critical to the health of a library organization than the motivation of staff. Nothing is more detrimental to that motivation than an irrational position classification."[2]

The process of establishing a position classification scheme is a highly complex one, involving the evaluation of each position relative to all other positions in order both to develop a consistency within the library for job requirements among same or similar positions and to identify a hierarchy among positions relative to specific job factors. Once established for the appropriate categories of library positions (librarians, technical assistants, supervisors, clerical, and so forth), the scheme must be kept current so it can be used as a basis for determining levels for new positions, appointing new staff, and maintaining equity in salaries. A general guideline for maintaining a current position classification scheme is that it should be analyzed every five to seven years; this insures that any changes made over the years in job duties and requirements, as well as the addition of new positions and the deletion of others, have not affected adversely the overall fairness of the scheme. However, with the number of changes occurring in library organizations, particularly due to automation, this may be too long a time to insure a fair and equitable system. It may be necessary to review a classification scheme every three to five years.

PROMOTIONAL SYSTEMS

Library organizations frequently depend on the promotion of staff to fill positions requiring greater knowledge and skill. Promotional opportunities for library staff also are important in order to respond to needs that staff have to excel and achieve within the organization. Employees should know what opportunities do and do not exist for promotion and the requirements for such promotions.

The standard concept of promotion involves a person moving from one job to another job, usually at a higher level and salary. Since each internal promotion represents another open position and search, personnel administrators should become familiar with the annual number of internal promotions that occur on the average in order to project the effect these promotions will have on library services. Knowing the estimated number of internal promotions or transfers is also necessary for library staff who will want to know the number of opportunities that are likely to occur and in what jobs and departments.

In academic libraries there is frequently a second type of promotion available to librarians which is based on the faculty model and referred to as "promotion in rank." In this model a librarian promotes to a higher rank without a change in position or responsibilities. Instead, promotion in rank is based on an evaluation of the person's professional contributions as demonstrated through growth and development within a specific job assignment, as well as on contributions to the library profession. Since a promotion in rank usually results in a salary adjustment, the process has implications for salary administration.

SALARY COMPENSATION

The establishment of a salary compensation plan is one of the most critical aspects of an effective personnel program and one of the most problematic. There are two major components of a salary program: the determination of what positions will be worth in relation to one another, and the determination of how annual salary increases will be computed. In the first case, a salary compensation plan should be based on an evaluation of jobs using objective data such as complexity of the duties, degree of responsibility, supervision, accountability, and the like. Salary should be related to the demands of the job for knowledge, skill and ability, and standards of performance. Good personnel planning incorporates the process of establishing compensation plans with a sound methodology for evaluating jobs.

A salary compensation plan also needs a fair policy for salary increases awarded to individual employees for some period of performance review. As White has stated, "While appropriate salary policies do not necessarily build morale, the absence or perceived absence of fairness can lead to serious and sometimes irreversible morale problems."[3] Where salary increases are not dictated by union contracts or civil service guidelines, library administrators have to choose between an across-the-board system (reward everyone in the same way) or a merit system (reward individuals differentially based on the contribution they have made). Both systems have advantages and disadvantages.

An across-the-board system is far easier to administer; in fact, it involves only the computation of individual salaries once the amount of the increase is determined. It requires no justification or rationale from the administration since it is basically driven by available dollars, not library objectives or individual performance. Unfortunately, since it is a system in which the differences which do exist among staff in their achievements and contributions are not recognized, it can be demoralizing and discouraging. To administer a merit system, on the other hand, requires considerable attention. It is important to have stated criteria that will be used in evaluating individual performance and judging contributions and a clear process for determining the salary allocations. It is thus time-consuming for supervisors and administrators, and will not be well-received by all staff, particularly those individuals who are not perceived as contributing significantly to enjoy the benefits of a merit salary program.

PROFILING LIBRARY PERSONNEL

Library administrators should have a method of periodically acquiring information on library employees that includes their education and experience as well as their areas of competency and interest. This information is useful in determining how short-term staffing needs might be met through the transfer of personnel from one function to another, and how major changes in library activities can be met by existing staff. In addition, information on staff skills and abilities will help administrators identify the training and development needs of library staff.

Library managers and the personnel administrator also should know what interests individual employees have for long-term growth and career development. With this information they are better equipped to counsel employees about future opportunities within and outside the library and to help employees identify what preparation is needed to move into specific positions and/or levels of responsibility.

There are a number of ways that profile information can be obtained on employees' skills and abilities, for instance, through the annual performance evaluation. Or, some organizations have specific forms and procedures that encourage staff to submit on a periodic basis (usually annually) a description of their professional and continuing education activities.

Though both the annual evaluation and the activities form are very useful, neither one solicits information on what future opportunities the staff members are interested in, nor on the type of positions for which they would like to be considered. Without such information, poor utilization of personnel may result. Such information can be acquired by completing a skills inventory questionnaire that specifically focuses on employees' competencies and interests, rather than simply asking for a list of courses taken, workshops attended, and committees participated in. A skills inventory allows staff to update information on their acquired skills and abilities and relevant activities.

JOB ANALYSIS

Collecting objective data on job duties and requirements is a major component of an effective personnel planning system. In order to insure that staff are being utilized at the proper level, according to the needs and requirements of library positions, reliable data on job duties and requirements, work flow, and time allocated to activities needs to be obtained. Ficks and Suzansky suggest a systems design approach in organizational planning using standard techniques of job and task analysis giving consideration to "such factors as accountability, potential performance measures, minimal duplication, clear interfaces with other jobs, and job satisfaction."[4] They go on to state that if the organization is to be "maximally successful, the staffing (the number of people in each job) and the sizing (the number of times the organization will have to be replicated to accomplish the work assigned to a given geographical area) must be optimized."[5] They also point out the need to consider physical layout and space requirements in planning to meet staffing requirements.

These questions cannot be answered with only a superficial knowledge of library jobs; a systematic and objective methodology needs to be developed for analyzing library activities. The data collected in a job analysis can be used as the basis for job redesign, the development of a position classification system or the review of an existing one, the identification of job requirements to support recruitment activities and staff development needs, and the establishment of a compensation plan. Job analysis information also can provide departmental supervisors with useful information for analyzing work flow and procedures in order to improve operations.

The analysis and reassessment of job duties and requirements is not simply a one-shot study; it is an activity that should be continuous. Jobs change continually both because of the people who occupy positions and changes in the work environment. Even after a library undertakes a job analysis study in a formal manner there should be a mechanism established for reviewing jobs on an ongoing basis.

The personnel administrator should raise questions and explore the utilization of staff whenever positions become vacant in the library and certainly whenever reorganization or other change is being considered. Job data should reflect the duties performed and responsibilities exercised by the incumbent at the time of the study and not be based on assumptions, generalizations, tradition, or history. If discrepancies are identified between what duties the incumbent performs and what duties should be performed then this must be addressed by management to determine if a change is required. Job analysis should insure the acquisition of objective information. Hill and Watson have stated that "of all the tools available to the library manager for facilitating the library staffing process, no other tool is as valuable, indeed as critical, as job analysis."[6]

Conducting Job Analysis

Careful planning and organization is required when job analysis is conducted on a major scale involving all or a large segment of library positions. The responsibility for conducting such a study should rest with the personnel administrator, who has the basic knowledge of both job analysis and library activities and positions. Depending on the situation in each library, the personnel administrator may want to seek assistance in conducting the study. Since job analysis is a commitment of considerable staff time, it should be "discussed fully by the administrative staff before proceeding. There should be a complete understanding of the time and costs involved as well as the changes that may result from the findings. In particular, the library administration should be aware of the possibility of change, and be receptive to changes in certain library jobs and possible whole departments."[7] Once the approach and methodology for a job analysis is fully explored and agreed upon by the library administration, the personnel administrator can begin to implement the steps for the study.

A first consideration is to determine who will assist with the analysis and evaluation of library jobs. Appointing a committee to work with the personnel administrator will certainly provide adequate staffing for the study and bring together staff who offer different perspectives about library jobs. A staff committee also provides credibility that might not exist if the study were conducted solely by administrative staff.

The advantages of a committee must be considered in light of the possible disadvantages. Library staff who serve on a committee will continue to have as their priority their primary assignment, and consequently the job analysis may take longer to complete than originally anticipated. Secondly, as Wilkinson, Plate, and Lee have observed, committee members have to guard against a tendency to make decisions based on personal and subjective attitudes about library activities and staff that would affect the outcome of the analysis.[8]

Another difficulty that may be faced by a committee is the tendency for group members to want to reach consensus in the decision-making process. This can lead to poor decisions if the pressure to please all committee members overshadows the need to make the "right" decision. The personnel administrator can help prevent this situation by addressing potential problems in early discussions with the committee.

Another means for conducting a job analysis is through the services of a consultant who is a specialist in the field. Consultants can provide the expertise and knowledge about job analysis methodology, and they bring objectivity to the study. If a consultant is used a thorough orientation program should be offered to provide the essential background on the library's organization and operations and to insure that the consultant understands the dimensions of the project.

If a library staff committee is set up for the job analysis, the people involved should receive orientation and training covering the process of analysis, the purpose of the study, in-depth information on library jobs, and the procedures to be followed in the study. They also should receive training in the specific skills needed, such as interviewing techniques and interpersonal and analytical strategies.

The steps for the job analysis should be outlined in advance so that the tasks to be accomplished and the anticipated schedule are clearly understood. The library staff whose positions will be analyzed should be informed of both the purpose and the schedule for the job analysis study. In initiating a job analysis project, the purpose of the job analysis should be clearly identified and stated (from the purpose or objectives of the study, the specific goals and activities of the study can be identified), and a schedule should be prepared to outline the steps to be undertaken and the expected deadlines.

Communicating with staff about the job analysis is particularly important in order to create a positive environment and attitude toward the study. It is not unusual for employees to be fearful of job analysis. Time taken at the initial step in the job analysis process may minimize negative attitudes from staff that could result in defensive and uncooperative behavior. Specifically, library employees should be informed of the purpose and methodology of the study, and their role and responsibility. Staff should understand what process will exist to appeal any decision resulting from the job analysis that affects their job and/or status in the library. This understanding is particularly important when job analysis is being conducted in order to establish a position classification system or a salary compensation plan.

Several mediums can be used to communicate information to employees about the job analysis including the staff newsletter, a general memorandum, the immediate supervisor, or a general staff meeting. Because job analysis is very complex and sometimes difficult for staff to understand, it may be advisable to use more than one of these methods.

Job Analysis Methodology

There are several standard methodologies that can be used in gathering data on library jobs:

> . . . interviews with staff and supervisors; observation of staff in carrying out their duties; and distribution of a questionnaire to staff and supervisors. Most job analysis studies are focused on gathering data at the job level, though in recent years there has been increasing interest in focusing first on gathering information on tasks and then combining task information to study whole jobs.[9]

Since accomplishing job analysis in a thorough manner is a complex process, it is advisable to combine methodologies such as a questionnaire and interviews. Whatever the approach, the focus should be on obtaining objective data about library jobs: "The usefulness of job analysis depends entirely on the quality and quantity of data gathered. . . . The analysis should not only be thorough, it should be carried out in such a way as to provide the most objective data about the content and requirements of each job."[10]

Job Descriptions

In order to provide adequate data in a job analysis study, a comprehensive description of each job is essential. When an organization-wide study of jobs is undertaken, job descriptions are most often used in conjunction with one or two other methods, such as an interview, job questionnaire, or job audit. Job descriptions are relied on more heavily in situations where a well-articulated classification or compensation system already exists and job descriptions are the tool used for reviewing and updating positions.

Consistency in format and language is important in developing job descriptions. Because words can have a variety of meanings (for instance, terminology such as cataloging, bibliographic verification, and reference may have wide interpretation and application), it is helpful to develop a glossary of terms to establish the standard meanings for certain words.

The personnel administrator is responsible for developing the guidelines for writing job descriptions and for working with library managers to insure that accurate and comprehensive job descriptions are produced. The following information should be considered for inclusion in job descriptions:

- Job identification
- Job summary
- Duties performed
- Supervision received and given
- Relationship to other jobs and departments
- Tools, resources, and equipment used
- Skills and experience required

Job identification includes information on the payroll and job title (e.g., for payroll title: University Librarian II; for job title: reference librarian); the library department, and division if appropriate; and a code number for the position. The job summary section is a brief description of the responsibilities and reporting relationship of the job; it provides a general understanding of the job and then is followed by the more detailed section on duties performed.

The duties performed section is the most important item on the job description since it supplies specific information on what is being done and the purpose of each duty. Even though this section is more detailed than the job summary section, it is still brief and concise and usually stated in outline form. As Henderson points out, "This section is not meant to be all-inclusive, but rather to describe duties related to major performance requirements. Normally one sentence or one to three phrases in outline form may describe each major duty or responsibility and will assist the incumbent and his manager in identifying significant areas for goalsetting."[11] Duties performed should be listed in order of their importance, and each statement of a duty should begin with an action verb in the present tense (e.g., administer, advise, analyze, coordinate, delegate, design, monitor, perform, plan, select, supervise, train, and so forth). In addition, the percentage of time devoted to each duty should be indicated.

The next section of the job description should contain information on supervision received, including the degree and from whom, and supervision given, including the number and titles of positions that are supervised as well as the nature of the supervision.

The section on "relationship to other departments and/or positions" is important in defining both coordinating and working relationships that should be established and maintained by the job incumbent. In writing this section, some brief mention of the purpose of each relationship is useful.

The tools, resources, and equipment used section of a job description should provide an understanding of the type and complexity of materials and equipment used in carrying out specific duties.

The final section of the job description spells out the type and level of skills and experience required to perform the job duties in a satisfactory manner. It should cover both formal educational requirements or competencies and experience in terms of specific skills and abilities, including such human requirements as interpersonal skills. This section should reflect what is needed to perform the job duties and not be simply a reflection of the incumbent's education and experience.

Job descriptions should always be a primary product of a job analysis study, even when they are not used as the method for collecting the job data. Job descriptions are an essential tool for any organization since they provide basic documentation for personnel planning, particularly in recruitment and training. In addition, job descriptions provide the supervisor and employee with an understanding of the scope of the job.

Interviews

Interviews with library employees on specific aspects of their job responsibilities can provide useful information that is not readily observable or always clear in written documentation. Depending on the number of positions under review, all employees or a sampling of employees in like positions can be interviewed. For the interview to be successful in generating needed job information, several factors should be considered in advance.

First, there should be clear understanding of what is to be accomplished in the interview and what questions will be asked. The questions should be prepared in advance so that the important aspects of the job are investigated. The questions asked in the interview should not limit the opportunity for employees to raise their own questions or to discuss aspects of the job that have not been solicited by the interviewer.

The interviewer, however, has the responsibility to guide and control the discussion, and identifying questions in advance will make it easier to do so.

Interviewers also need to develop effective listening and interpersonal skills. They must be sensitive to the employee's feelings and demonstrate respect for the person and the job that is being performed. The interview should be scheduled at a time that is convenient for both employee and supervisor and in a place that provides privacy. At the beginning of the interview, the interviewer should be sure that the employee understands the purpose of the job analysis and that it is the job that is being evaluated, not the individual's performance. In addition, the interviewer should explain the interview process and what will occur after the interview has been completed. If personal or personnel matters are raised by the employee the interviewer should not comment but, instead, refer the employee to the immediate supervisor or the personnel administrator.

Job data obtained from interviews can provide meaningful, in-depth information on job duties and requirements, particularly the more intangible demands of the job. The disadvantage of the interview method is that it can be very time-consuming, and if the interviewers are not well trained, poor results can occur. The interview method is most effective when used in conjunction with written documentation, such as a questionnaire, and/or with observation of the job being performed.

Observation

Observing employees performing their job duties is useful when done in conjunction with another form of data gathering, for instance, with the interview. Observation will not suffice without some other means of identifying job duties and requirements. Not all employees included in the job study need to be observed, nor all tasks of a job; a sampling of jobs and tasks within specific functional areas may be sufficient to provide supplementary information. Also, not all jobs lend themselves to observation as an effective method of acquiring job data, either because of the intellectual nature of the job or because much of the work does not occur within an observable period of time.

Questionnaires

A job analysis questionnaire is the most common method used to obtain data on jobs. It provides a consistent format for obtaining information from a wide range of people and involves less time on the part of the job analyst than do the interview or observation methods.

There is a major drawback, however. There is too much reliance on the ability of the job incumbent to understand adequately the questions and to respond accurately. To combat this problem, the questionnaire requires clear terminology and directions. It should be designed with a heavy use of forced-choice questions, in order to standardize responses, rather than with open-ended questions that make it more difficult to analyze the data.

A poorly developed questionnaire is detrimental to obtaining the necessary information on jobs and may alienate staff who have to complete it. Since designing a questionnaire is a specialized task, the personnel administrator should seek out someone, in the library or elsewhere, who is knowledgeable in this activity.

It is equally important to hold orientation sessions for staff and supervisors who will complete the job questionnaire in order to review the purpose of the questionnaire and how to complete every section of it. This will do much to reduce confusion as well as inadequate and inaccurate responses.

Logs

One means of obtaining written information about library jobs at the task level is to have employees keep a daily log of work performed. The logs record what tasks are performed each day as they are performed, with a brief statement and the approximate amount of time spent on each task (i.e., answered directional question—3 minutes; opened mail—10 minutes). Daily logs are usually maintained for a period of one to two weeks in order to adequately represent the employee's total workload. Although it is a rather limited way to obtain adequate job data, because it lacks information on such factors as supervisory relationship, tools and resources used for each task, and other related factors, a daily log can be extremely helpful in identifying not only tasks performed and time spent on tasks and groups of tasks, but workflow as well. However, as a method for obtaining job information, the log should be supplemented with additional information provided by the employee and the supervisor.

Task Inventory

Analyzing jobs at the task level offers a more detailed approach than some other methods. Rather than obtaining information about jobs as a whole, the approach is to first identify all of the tasks that are performed and evaluate these tasks against some standard measurement. The tasks can then be combined back into jobs by having library employees identify those tasks that they perform and the percentage of time they spend on each.

Task analysis is a way to avoid focusing only on the general aspects of jobs. When evaluating jobs for degree of complexity and level and scope of responsibility, task analysis provides a more specific and detailed approach than other job analysis systems. A task inventory approach also provides a database that can be coded easily to develop a computer database with the information manipulated in various ways, depending on the needs for job redesign or operational reorganization. "When the analysis is made at the task level, with each task rated separately with respect to a variety of factors, it becomes possible to regroup or rearrange the tasks in accordance with a new combination of the factors involved."[12]

Task analysis is becoming more prevalent in organizations because it offers a quantitative methodology for evaluating jobs and thus a system that relies less on subjectivity or arbitrariness, and more on identifiable and measurable factors. Therefore, though the task approach, according to Ricking and Booth, has "historically been criticized as being more things-related than the more generalized methodologies, and thus less well suited to the analysis of professional work, contemporary usage demonstrates clearly that its applicability is not so limited."[13]

When a job analysis study is being considered for a library, choosing one or a combination of these methodologies should depend on ". . . the nature of the organization, its needs and problems, and the resources of both time and money it is able and willing to expend on the process. The primary determinant is, of course, the use to which the analysis is to be put. There is no value whatever in the most highly developed analysis if its objective and uses have not been determined before it is undertaken."[14]

JOB EVALUATION

Once data on jobs have been collected and organized, the next step is to evaluate the jobs. This process entails determining the worth of each job in relation to other jobs in the organization. Since job evaluation measures the "value" of a job in the organization, it is carried out when a salary compensation plan or a position classification system is being implemented. (If the sole purpose of a job analysis study is to identify jobs for job redesign, or to identify more clearly job requirements and standards for recruitment and/or training purposes, then job evaluation is not a necessary step.)

Job evaluation relies on the objective and thorough data obtained in the job analysis. The first step is to determine which employee groups will be included in a single evaluation system, since it is possible to have job families evaluated separately or against different criteria. It is important that the personnel administrator assures equitable treatment even though clerical employees may be evaluated by a different system than librarians.

The next step in the job evaluation process is to "sell" the idea of a systematic evaluation system to all participants—administrative staff, managers, and general staff and then determine how jobs will be evaluated and which evaluation system will be utilized.

Job Evaluation Systems

There are four standard approaches to job evaluation which fall into two general categories: nonquantitative and quantitative. The nonquantitative method is the simpler of the two approaches since it involves comparing whole jobs rather than specific factors within each job. The nonquantitative method uses simple ranking and grading, and relies on existing position grades or classification systems.

The quantitative system is a more detailed approach in which specific job factors are identified and then measured. As Ricking and Booth point out, "all quantitative methods involve a formal breakdown of a job or position into specific factors that contribute to its value, or weight, and the assignment of certain finite values, usually numerical, to these factors."[15] The two quantitative systems are the point system and the factor-comparison system.

Simple Ranking

This system establishes a hierarchy of jobs based on the "worth" of the jobs within the organization. It typically involves comparing all jobs using basic job descriptions and identified benchmark jobs. Benchmark jobs are those that clearly identify the top and bottom jobs in the organization against which all other jobs are compared and ranked. Simple ranking can be implemented with a minimum of time and cost if job descriptions already exist in the organization. Unfortunately, the simplicity which makes this system attractive is also its main disadvantage, particularly when more than a small number of positions are involved. Simple ranking is a crude system which makes it difficult to measure whole jobs, and there is no predetermined set of values or factors for job evaluators to use in measuring and comparing jobs. Instead, each evaluator uses his or her own set of criteria which affects the final ranking of positions. Depending on the size of the library, and the purpose of job evaluation, simple ranking can be used with success.

Job Grading

This approach utilizes job classes or grade descriptions and requirements against which all jobs are compared and fitted. Jobs are still measured as a whole unit without considering separately the specific factors of jobs. This approach is somewhat more refined than simple grading because jobs are compared against a set of already determined descriptions and general measurements.

The major drawback to the job-grading system is that broad definitions and statements are used to identify the differences in the grades. For instances, terms such as "direct supervision," "general supervision," and "general direction" may be all that exist to differentiate the degree to which a job requires independent decision making; and these general terms and definitions can be judged differently by the people evaluating the jobs. Quite often the classification and reclassification of jobs hinge on employees; ability to use the right key words in describing the job and not on a careful analysis of the differences between jobs.

Point System

The point system involves a quantitative approach to the measurement of job worth since specific job factors are identified to provide the bases for evaluation. The number and specific job factors to be used should be set by each library so that the factors reflect the reality of the particular library.

There are several major factors that appear in most job evaluation studies. They are referred to as "universal" factors and include such items as knowledge and skill, problem solving, decision making, and scope and impact of the job. Within each of these major factors there is usually a range of four to seven subfactors that provide the specific measurement.

After job factors are selected, a scale of values is constructed to measure each factor. In the point system it is first necessary to establish the total number of points that will be used and then to determine what percentage points will be allocated to each of the factors. This is the process of determining the value of each factor:

> In light of organization objectives, some factors are obviously more important than others. To account for this difference it is necessary to weight each factor in terms of its importance to organizational goals and objectives. This weighting or comparison process must be as exact as possible (recognizing that judgments are subjective even when made by experts). To date, the most exact method developed has been that of assigning points to each factor . . .

factors of unequal importance are assigned a different number of points to reflect the relative value of each.[16]

Once the total points have been defined for a given factor, then degrees for that factor can be established with the points distributed along a continuum. For instance, the following hypothetical situation demonstrates how education as a subfactor of knowledge and skills might be assigned a value for evaluating library jobs.

Points

10	20	30	40	50
high school or equivalency	2 yr. associate degree or equivalent	BA or equivalent	MLS or subject master's	MLS and second master's

In this scheme, education is assigned a total value of fifty points and distributed so that all library jobs can be measured against it.

As a scale is developed for all the factors and subfactors and applied to all jobs, a total numerical value is arrived at for each job. It is also possible to determine a numerical range for each job category in order to see whether specific jobs are fitting into the appropriate job category or family. For instance, a hypothetical scale in a library might be as follows:

Clerical	240–400
Library Associates	350–600
Librarians/Specialists	500–1,000

In developing the point system and scales, the specificity will be dictated by the purpose of the job evaluation. A major advantage of the point system is the stability of the scales, and the fact that as a quantitative system it lends itself to statistical analysis. But there are disadvantages. Canelas has summarized these as including the difficulty of developing the point-rating scale and the definition of factors and "each of their degrees precisely in a way that carries the same meaning for each of the raters. It is also difficult to weight each of the factors in accordance with their importance. Maintaining relative relationships between degrees of independence of performance and scope of responsibility is not easy ... [It] ... is time consuming. [And] ... finally, it is very technical, and not easy to explain the concepts to staff members."[17]

Others feel that the point system is too rigid, particularly when applied to professional positions in libraries. Research done by the Bureau of National Affairs, though, shows that the point system "is the most common method of job evaluation for all types of job evaluation plans . . . [and] frequently is combined with one of the other approaches . . . such as factor comparison, job classification, or market pricing."[18] The report also shows that the point system is used as frequently for exempt (or professional) positions as for nonexempt (clerical) positions.

Factor-Comparison System

This system relies on identifying "benchmark" or key jobs, which are compared to other jobs in terms of factors common to all. As with the point system, the first step is to identify job factors that reflect both common job dimensions and those considered of value by the organization. Though both the point and factor-comparison systems use specific factors, points or numeric values are not assigned in the latter system. This is a job-to-job type of comparison with a refinement over simple ranking because factors within each job are reviewed and compared.

The "benchmark" jobs are identified, according to Treiman, because "these are jobs about which consensus is presumed to exist regarding relative worth and the relative importance of the various factors determining worth."[19] The factor-comparison system requires that "benchmark" jobs be evaluated first against each of the factors, and this evaluation provides the scale to which other positions are compared. All positions are then "ranked and assigned a weight for each of the designated factors. If the salaries of the key positions are utilized as a benchmark, it is possible to deduce the appropriate salary level for the remainder of the positions."[20]

In libraries where the factor-comparison system is used for evaluating librarian positions, the system is used to establish the appropriate levels for positions and the level, in turn, indicates a salary range. An incumbent's salary is determined within this range based on the experience the person brings to the job. In this manner the job is evaluated to establish the job level and then appropriate salary range, and then the incumbent is evaluated in order to establish a salary within the established range.

Canelas states that the

> advantages of the factor-comparison method are that the position classification system is tailor-made for the library that develops it; there are excellent instructions available for implementing the system, and it's not difficult to train employees to use the method.[21]

Job evaluation is very complex and the results are of utmost importance to staff. There continues to be concern regarding the approach that is used and the influence that this choice has on the equity of salary administration. The study undertaken by Trieman[22] for the Equal

Employment Opportunity Commission in 1979 investigated the issue of the impact that job evaluation methodology had on creating a fair and unbiased system of job relationships and salary decisions. More recently, Madigan and Hoover have stated that

> universal norms of worth do not exist, therefore the concept of worth incorporated in different job evaluation plans is likely to vary. Relative job worth is likely to be a function of the method of job evaluation used; this likelihood has important legal and financial implications as well as implications for employee-management relations.[23]

JOB ANALYSIS AND EVALUATION IN LIBRARIES

Job analysis and evaluation studies are not new to library organizations. In some situations, they are undertaken by the parent institution to include jobs throughout the organization and so the library administrator may have minimal opportunity to influence the direction or selection of a methodology. The library administration is more likely to have control, or at least greater influence, when professional positions are being evaluated. What is important is that library administrators recognize the critical nature of job analysis and evaluation and take responsibility for orienting and educating nonlibrary personnel about the library's operations, terminology, and complexities whenever an organization-wide study is implemented.

Library administrators should also insure that library staff are informed about the importance of a study so that staff and supervisors can respond in a thorough and objective manner. In addition, it is important that the ongoing audit and review of library positions that occurs for individual positions be treated with a great deal of care and preparation. In every case where a position is to be audited, the personnel administrator should work with the supervisor to insure that job information is well organized for presentation to the auditor and that the position questionnaire is completed objectively and completely.

At the University of Iowa Libraries a major job analysis project was undertaken in 1988-89 to identify staffing requirements over a five-year period; both the library and the university central administration had agreed that the library was understaffed. In addition, the library was in the process of implementing an integrated online automated system which would have a considerable impact on job duties and assignments over several years, and it had implemented a strategic planning process which identified services and operations that needed strengthening and new initiatives for the library organization. It was clear that a thorough analysis of all departments and operations at all levels of staffing needed to be undertaken.

A methodology was developed to provide the following information for each job in the library system: current activities, estimated amount of time spent on each activity, a rating of how critical the activity is to the department, an estimate of how the activity will be affected with implementation of the online system (eliminated, reduced, not changed at all, unknown), and whether the activity is being performed at the appropriate job level (professional, clerical, student assistant). A list of over 500 library activities was compiled and the staff completed a questionnaire, indicating those activities or duties that they performed. The study was not intended to be a task analysis, but the level and scope of the study did, in fact, generate data at a level only slightly more general than tasks.

All of the data were coded so that they could be put into machine-readable form and to allow reports to be generated relating to position level and activities within a department and across the library system. Departmental supervisors completed an assessment of the information provided by the individual employee and projected staffing needs for a transitional period (of one to two years related to the demands of implementing the online system) and for ongoing recurring staffing needs.

The study generated considerable data to support subsequent staffing requests to the university administration. Equally important, it has made available information that can support decision making regarding reallocation of positions within the library as well as a review of operations for efficiency.

A similar study reported by Ferguson and Taylor was conducted with public service librarians to identify how time was being spent among four distinct groups of librarians: 1) subject specialists who worked at the reference desk and were involved in library orientation and collection development, 2) documents and maps librarians with similar duties but also involved in technical processing, 3) general reference librarians, and 4) one reserve collection librarian.[24] Librarians were asked to keep a daily log of all activities for five days using a form which listed forty-three separate activities from which they selected.

The authors indicate that the data allow an assessment of whether the public service librarians are allocating their time in support of the library's goals and objectives, and indeed feel the study provides evidence to this effect. In addition, they state that "cost benefit analysis is also possible with this type of data. . . . It is not enough to say a job is being done. Questions and answers need to be posed about the way an activity is being done and why it is being done."[25]

The University of Michigan Library implemented a position classification system in the mid-1960s, and in the intervening years the approach to analyzing jobs in order to maintain the classification system has been reevaluated and altered several times. Originally, the evaluation of professional positions was based on a point system, which required weighted values for the factors used in job evaluation. By 1975 a new process of evaluating professional positions was developed that used a factor-comparison approach instead. This change was made after several studies had been prepared and revisions considered by the classification evaluation committee and the library administration.

The basis for the new system was a factor-evaluation chart with two basic factors identified to govern the evaluation of professional positions: scope of assignment and level of responsibility. Each factor had a series of subfactors or elements. The scope of assignment factor covered difficulty of work performed, including guidance necessary and originality required; education and experience required to complete the assignment; and others. The level of responsibility factor had as elements the impact of the position beyond the functional unit, supervisory and managerial responsibility, and others. "Within each of these factors, three degrees of difficulty (A,C,E) were described in order of increasing complexity. Degrees B and D were not defined but would be used when a position fell between two defined degrees, or when a position compared with one degree in some respects and another degree in other respects."[26]

Data for this study were gathered in two ways: each librarian prepared a written job description which was supplemented by an interview to gain more information directly from the professional. After all of the job information was available, positions within the same unit were compared, and then benchmark positions were established for public services and for technical services for each of the four grade levels. Public services and technical services positions were then evaluated against these benchmark positions. When the evaluation was completed, the committee had to evaluate public and technical services positions at the same classification level in relation to one another. "The problem of providing equity when comparing positions with very different emphases and responsibilities presented a particularly difficult challenge to the committee."[27] The library classification evaluation committee concluded that "position classifications do not remain constant. The library and the library professional exist in an environment of continuing change."[28]

An example of an extensive job analysis and evaluation study based on factor-analysis is one undertaken in Illinois libraries. The study was a cooperative venture between the Illinois Library Association, the American Library Association, and the Illinois State Library. It was prompted by a belief that more effective utilization of personnel in libraries was essential in order to address growing staffing problems. In the first phase of the project, there were "1,615 tasks identified, performed by 116 individuals in 18 libraries of various types and sizes in Illinois. Each task was rated according to fifteen scales, producing some 400,000 bits of data."[29]

The job analysis methodology for this study was to establish a task inventory. The authors commented that "in all probability this is the first study that has attempted to apply the methods and techniques of functional job analysis to libraries. It provides a realistic description of work actually being done in public, school, academic, and special libraries. . . ."[30]

Once job information was acquired, factors and scales for measuring jobs were established. The major factors included in the study were job requirements (nature, extent, and level of knowledge and ability needed); difficulty of work (complexity and intricacy of work and mental demands such as judgment); responsibility (supervisory assistance and control and impact of work); personal relationships (skills required in work relationships and importance of such relationships). A final factor, labelled "other requirements," was used when appropriate and only for atypical positions.

The scales against which the factors were measured included performance standards (quality, kind, and nature of standards); task environment (setting in which task occurs); worker functions (dominant orientation of task-data, people, or things; general educational development (reasoning, mathematics, and languages); worker instructions (how explicit); training time (length of time to learn the task, including formal education). A system of appropriate factor weights and point values was established, while it was acknowledged that "each factor need not have equal weight or significance in measuring the relative worth of work."[31]

The resulting evaluation of all library tasks was used to determine the level at which tasks should be assigned among the library position categories of professional, technical, and clerical. The Illinois study is important because of the extensive nature of the study, the focus of the job analysis on tasks, and the use of an evaluation system combining factor analysis and point system.

A slightly different approach to task analysis was developed at the University of Connecticut Library. The first step involved acquiring information on all tasks performed in the library by functional unit or department (e.g., reference, circulation, serials). These tasks were described by departmental staff, though no one employee had to describe all the tasks of his or her job since there was a high percentage of shared tasks. The task descriptions included specific information on the process of each task, as well as information on the tools and resources used in completing the task and the frequency with which the tasks were performed.

Tasks were then evaluated against a standard measurement tool that contained specific factors such as education required; amount of specialized knowledge; level of skill required; degree of experience needed; analytical skill utilized; judgment exercised; problem solving exercised; and the degree to which general guidelines of specific instructions were followed. A Likert-type scale was designed so that the degree to which each factor was used for performing the task could be measured. The scale went from zero to four, and the numerical values for all factors were added, resulting in a score for the task.

Once all the tasks in a library department were evaluated and scores established, a computer-generated list was produced to show the departmental tasks in rank order from simplest to most complex. A cut-off score was identified to separate clerical and professional tasks. All library employees were then asked to identify which tasks they performed and the percentage of time spent on each using the list of tasks. This information was used to determine whether the staff were performing at the appropriate level based on the type of tasks performed and the percentage of time spent on the two categories of clerical and professional tasks; to identify jobs that required job redesign; and to analyze staffing patterns for a library department in relation to the number and kinds of departmental tasks that were clerical and professional, and the number and level of staff in that department.

The study was designed and conducted primarily to provide critical information in planning staffing for a new library building, but it was also useful for determining positions needing reclassification and for identifying certain training needs as well as requirements for recruitment. Like similar large-scale projects, the data from this study were coded so that computer-generated reports were possible making the data more useful for different management decisions.

Another approach to job analysis was developed by the University of Texas Medical School at San Antonio and Case Western Reserve University to study staff patterns in libraries in the health sector:

> In an attempt to investigate this area of manpower utilization, a Job Tasks Index was constructed. The index represents an abbreviated inventory of library-related job tasks, and is combined with a scale for recording the degree of involvement reported by respondents. Each item on the inventory . . . carries a value reflective of its degree of professionalism.[32]

The index was administered to a survey population of 4,000 professionals (employees with the MLS) and support staff (employees without the MLS) in health science libraries during 1969. The job-task index consisted of twenty-seven library-related tasks, with the index established so that a positive score indicated greater involvement in professional tasks and a negative score a greater involvement in nonprofessional tasks. Once a list had been developed of library tasks, ratings for degree of professionalism were assigned to each item by medical librarians.

There were actually four task groups: group-1 professional tasks and group-2 professional tasks, with group-1 requiring greater skill than group-2 tasks; and similarly for nonprofessional tasks with group-3 and group-4.

> A subject's degree of involvement with each task was recorded on two levels: primary and secondary. Weighted values were assigned to these two levels of involvement. For example, a subject reporting a primary involvement with a group-1 professional job task received a score of +4 for that item; a secondary involvement in a group-1 professional job task rated a score of +3, etc. Thus a nine-point scale was developed.[33]

A general conclusion arrived at from this study was that library employees are often utilized at job levels inconsistent with the position level, and this inconsistency is particularly true for librarians, who were found to be working below a professional level. Another conclusion reached in this study was that although the data indicated that the job-task index can differentiate among personnel groups (professional and supporting staff as defined in the study), "educational attainment when taken as the sole independent variable cannot predict job level."[34] The authors go on to state:

> This test of the index suggests that it will be a useful tool in the total study of manpower utilization in libraries. If a system of job descriptions and career guidelines for all levels of library personnel is developed to parallel the index, then any individual's performance could be measured and a judgment made as to the match among job involvement, educational attainment, income, and experience.[35]

These different systems for gathering job data and evaluating jobs have importance for libraries in enhancing the personnel planning process. Though each methodology can prove useful through its application and modification to the particular needs of the library, there is reason for personnel administrators to develop a greater familiarity with the quantitative methods reviewed earlier.

"The position-evaluation methodology long used by libraries has generally served its purpose fairly well, and it can be used just as objectively as a factor-analysis system. Even for purposes of position classification, however, the quantitative methods have certain advantages."[36] These advantages include reducing the possibility of overlooking some elements of jobs, or of basing evaluation on only one or more dominant factors, thereby failing to balance all factors; insuring that all tasks are measured by the same "yardstick" or scales, and eliminating intuitive judgments or bias on the part of those evaluating; and, most important, demonstrating to staff that an equitable system for purposes of compensation is being used.

Job Factors

Whether library jobs are evaluated using a system of ranking, grading, point, or factor analysis, or whether the evaluation is at the job or task level, it is important to identify to some degree those factors that form the basis for comparing and evaluating jobs. When either the point or factor-comparison system is used, the degree of specificity of job factors is more demanding.

Job factors can be described in three major categories: universal factors, subfactors, and degrees. "The first category, universal factors, contains descriptions applicable to elements or parts of each job in practically any organization. . . . Because of the broad nature of these universal factors, each is further defined through a second category, or series of subfactors. These subfactors permit the development of profile statements that more precisely define the work elements or specific attributes of a particular job. The breaking down of subfactors into degree forms the third category. It permits the reflection or measurement of the degree to which each subfactor is important in particular jobs."[37]

Depending on the purpose of job analysis and evaluation and the system used, it is possible to utilize only the universal factors and subfactors and not establish degrees. What is most important, though, in order to avoid duplication and overlap in measuring certain factors— as well as oversight of important job elements—is that the factors and subfactors are defined clearly and are thoroughly understood. The following criteria can be used in establishing job factors:

- Measures significant and distinct characteristics of work.
- Applicable to all positions but in varying degrees.
- Ratable in terms of recognizable and definable differences in level.
- Have a minimum of overlap between them.[38]

There is the need, then, to establish consistency in evaluating jobs and to develop factors that provide an adequate measurement. One means is to establish a controlled language which can reduce semantic problems by having all terms so well-defined that it is clear what is being measured, and by lessening the possibility of two factors measuring the same thing.

One approach to controlling language in job analysis is the scheme of job analysis:

- The scheme is based on the premise that tasks require a worker to utilize cognitive, interpersonal, and physical resources in varying degrees.
- Cognitive resources are directed at *date,* or information, ideas, facts, statistics.
- Interpersonal resources are directed at *people,* or clients, co-workers, customers.
- Physical resources are directed at *things,* or machines, equipment . . .
- Within each of these broad categories, moreover, are various levels of complexity against which tasks may be evaluated. These levels are regularly defined in a hierarchy . . .[39]

For each of these major areas—cognitive, interpersonal, and physical—specific factors can be established.

Hay Associates has organized factors in a somewhat different manner by identifying what they consider to be three basic elements or dimensions of any job: Know-How, Problem Solving, and Accountability. Each of these major factors has subfactors against which jobs are evaluated.

Know-How is the sum total of every kind of skill, however acquired, needed for acceptable job performance. Know-How has three dimensions:

- Specialized skills or technical knowledge required . . .
- Managerial Know-How.
- Human Relations skills required on the job.

Problem-Solving measures the intensity of the mental process: thinking required by the job for analyzing, evaluating, meeting, reasoning, arriving at and making conclusions. There are two basic dimensions to Problem-Solving:

- Thinking Challenge. How complex and unique are the problems normally faced in this position.
- Thinking Environment defines the degree to which the position is free to develop answers to the problems it faces.

Accountability measures the answerability for action and for the consequences of action, and it has three dimensions:

- Magnitude, or size of the area in which the job operates.
- Impact of the Job.
- Freedom to Act—the degree to which a person in the job can take action without consulting higher authority.[40]

Both of these methods for identifying and organizing job factors will include similar if not the same types of factors, and the result in evaluation will be much the same. What is important is that a system be devised and the language be clear and concise so that the factors to be measured are basic to the library conducting the study and will contribute to sound and objective results. In particular it is important to establish factors that measure the real elements of a job and not simply reflect the background of the current incumbent in a job. For instance, when measuring the factor of "knowledge" by type and level of education, incumbents indicate their own level of education, not necessarily what is really needed to perform the job.

HUMAN RELATIONS ASPECT OF JOB ANALYSIS AND EVALUATION

It is crucial not to lose sight of the human relations aspect when conducting a job analysis and evaluation. While the technical aspects of job evaluation, including the determination of values to be measured, is very complex and demanding, the human problems faced in implementing these systems is equally, if not more, complex. As indicated earlier, problems usually occur when employees do not understand or appreciate the process and purpose of job analysis and evaluation, or fear the impact that it will have on their status, earnings, or future promotional opportunities in the organization. In addition, employees may identify job variables or factors that they feel establish the worth of a job which are not necessarily the same as those identified by management. When this occurs it creates at the outset a conflict between employees and management regarding job evaluation.

In order to minimize conflicts and to demonstrate concern for the employees, library management should set a high priority on open and honest communication regarding the study. There are a number of options for communicating information to staff and these should be considered in relation to the library's specific needs and requirements.

Information can be communicated through staff meetings, an internal newsletter, formal memorandums, supervisors, or a combination of these. Written material providing a thorough explanation of the purpose of the study as well as the intended results should also be available to library employees. It is also important that library supervisors understand the job analysis and evaluation process so that they can help explain it to the staff and provide support to the program. A good approach to communicating information to staff is to develop written documentation and then to meet, first with the supervisors and then with all other staff, to present the particulars of the study and address questions and concerns of the staff.

Once a job analysis study has been completed, the personnel administrator should prepare policy and procedure statements regarding ongoing evaluation and reclassification, as well as information on compensation, promotional criteria, and position classification to be made available to supervisory staff and other employees. Policies that are well articulated on these sensitive topics and easily accessible to supervisors and staff alike will help to reduce confusion and minimize confrontation between supervisors and staff, and supervisors and the library administration.

It is particularly important that the staff understand that it is jobs that are being analyzed and evaluated, and not the individuals performing the jobs. "In job analysis, every effort is made to remove the human factor from the job. Although this is a difficult task, success requires as sterile an analysis of the job as possible (sterile meaning removal of the job-holder's personal influence). The important thing to focus on here is what the worker is doing, not how he is doing it."[41] If it is clear to library employees that it is not their individual performances that are being judged, there will be far less tension or resistance involved in the study.

Another human relations concern is the need for all the people involved in the study to be sensitive to employees' feelings about their worth in the organization and their pride in the work that they perform. The people conducting the study should focus on developing or improving their interpersonal skills so that they are able to establish a positive environment in which to conduct the study.

Grievance Process

In advance of the analysis and evaluation employees should be aware of what opportunity they will have for submitting a grievance, the bases for any grievance, to whom they may submit the grievance, who will hear the grievance, and who makes the final decision. Especially when the purpose of the study is position classification and/or a salary compensation plan, the personnel administrator and all others involved in the job analysis should be prepared to acknowledge that some of the recommendations they submit will not be accepted by staff and that grievances will follow. If the grievance process is clearly defined in advance it will help to minimize employees' concerns and establish a more cooperative attitude toward the process.

Red-Circle Rates

When the purpose of the job analysis and evaluation is to establish a salary compensation plan, the library administration should determine in advance how it will handle those situations where an employee's salary rate is above that defined for the job level or classification. Most often referred to as "red-circle rates," the problem can be handled in a variety of ways. Many organizations address it through normal turnover and adjust the salary when a new employee is hired. Another approach is to freeze the incumbent's salary. In still other organizations "red circle" positions are reviewed for job redesign in order to upgrade the responsibilities, or incumbents are transferred to positions with greater responsibilities in order to bring duties in line with salaries. These options are limited by the size of the organization and the level of turnover, as well as by the ability of the individual staff member to assume new and more complex duties.

Union Involvement

When staff are members of a union the library administration should determine in advance the degree to which the union will be informed and/or involved in the job analysis and evaluation project. To a large extent this depends on local conditions and the specifics of the labor contract. Certainly if the purpose of the job analysis is to establish a salary compensation plan, the union will have to be involved to a considerable degree, since compensation is clearly a negotiable issue. Whatever the requirements of the local environment, the job analysis should proceed in a manner that does not create antagonism with the union. And when possible, all attempts should be made to obtain the union's support.

Maintaining Job Analysis Data

A final consideration in job analysis is how to keep the information current and updated over time and how it will be used for analyzing jobs as the organization changes. The method used will depend to some extent on what methodology was used in gathering the data initially. If the approach to obtaining and codifying job data was by job descriptions then the following methods for updating information might be useful: 1) At the time of the annual performance evaluation, the individual's job description is reviewed and any changes noted and forwarded to the personnel administrator along with the performance evaluation; 2) A periodic review, based on an established timetable of all job descriptions by library supervisors and staff, is conducted, with changes forwarded to the personnel administrator; 3) Changes in a library department, such as reorganization, addition, or deletion of major activities, require the supervisor to submit a description of the staffing needs and job descriptions for each departmental position.

If the focus of the analysis was to obtain information on tasks, then a method is needed to update periodically information on tasks and add new tasks as they occur. This process keeps the task inventory information current and allows for a review of specific jobs as needed. Even if task data are maintained, updating job descriptions on a scheduled basis is still useful and should be established to insure that staff are working with a clear understanding of their job assignment.

If job analysis is to be an ongoing process in the library, there must be some way to maintain job information in a current and timely fashion to insure that it is being used for the purpose for which it was originally designed. It is the responsibility of the personnel administrator and library supervisors to continually analyze and evaluate information about library jobs and incorporate this information into recruitment plans, training activities, and recommendations on position classification and salary compensation.

References

1. Robert Lee and Charlene Swarthout Lee, "Personnel Planning for a Library Manpower System," *Library Trends* 20 (July 1971): 21.
2. John Wilkinson, Kenneth Plate, and Robert Lee, "A Matrix Approach to Position Classification," *College and Research Libraries* 36 (September 1975): 351.
3. Herbert S. White, *Library Personnel Management* (White Plains, N.Y.: Knowledge Industry, 1985), p. 139.
4. F.L. Ficks and J.W. Suzansky, "Work Systems as a Large-Scale Systems Design Process," in *Human Factors in Organizational Design and Management,* H.W. Hendrick and O. Brown, Jr. eds. (North Holland: Elsevier Science Publishers, 1984), p. 311.
5. Ibid., p. 311.
6. Virginia B. Hill and Tom G. Watson, "Job Analysis: Process and Benefits," *Advances in Library Administration and Organization* 3 (1984): 209.
7. Sheila Creth, "Cost Considerations in Personnel Management," in Ann E. Prentice, *Strategies for Survival: Library Financial Management Today* (New York: R.R. Bowker, 1978), p. 22.
8. Wilkinson, Plate, Lee, p. 362.
9. Creth, "Cost Considerations in Personnel Management," p. 21.
10. Ibid.
11. Richard Henderson, "Job Descriptions–Critical Documents, Versatile Tools, Part 4: Getting It on Paper," *Supervisory Management* 21 (February 1976): 17.

12. Myrl Ricking and Robert E. Booth, *Personnel Utilization in Libraries: A Systems Approach* (Chicago: American Library Association, 1974), p. 3.
13. Ibid.
14. Ibid., p. 5.
15. Ricking and Booth, p. 2.
16. Richard Henderson, "Job Descriptions–Critical Documents, Versatile Tools: Part 5: Compensable Factors," *Supervisory Management* 21 (March 1976): 32.
17. Dale B. Canelas, "Position Classification in Libraries and an Introduction to the Library Education and Personnel Utilization Policy." Paper presented at the American Library Association Preconference on Effective Personnel Utilization: LEPU Guidelines and Principles (Detroit, Michigan, June 16, 1977), p. 7.
18. *Job Evaluation Policies and Procedures, Personnel Policies Forum Survey* No. 113 (Washington, D.C.: Bureau of National Affairs, 1976), p. 2.
19. Donald J. Trieman, *Job Evaluation: An Analytic Review. Interim Report to the Equal Employment Opportunity Commission* (Washington, D.C.: National Academy of Sciences, 1979), p. 3.
20. Canelas, p. 7.
21. Ibid.
22. Trieman.
23. Robert M. Madigan and David J. Hoover, "Effects of Alternative Job Evaluation Methods on Decisions Involving Pay Equity," *Academy of Management Journal* 29.1 (1986): 85.
24. Anthony W. Ferguson and John R. Taylor, "What *Are* You Doing? An Analysis of Activities of Public Service Librarians at a Medium-Sized Research Library," *Journal of Academic Librarianship* 6.1 (1980): 24.
25. Ibid., p. 29.
26. "Position Classification at Michigan: Another Look," prepared by Members of the University of Michigan Library's Classification Committee for 1977-78, *College and Research Libraries* 40 (May 1979): 206.
27. Ibid., p. 209.
28. Ibid., p. 210.
29. Ricking and Booth, vi.
30. Ibid., p. vi.
31. Ibid., p. 104.
32. Leslie B. Rothenberg et al., "Job-Task Index for Evaluating Professional Utilization in Libraries," *Library Quarterly* 41 (October 1971): 321.
33. Ibid., p. 322.
34. Ibid., p. 326.
35. Ibid., p. 327.
36. Ricking and Booth., p. 2.
37. Henderson, "Job Descriptions–Critical Documents, Versatile Tools: Part 5," p. 28.
38. Ricking and Booth, p. 102.
39. Benjamin Roter, "An Integrated Framework for Personnel Utilization and Management," *Personnel Journal* 52, no. 12 (December 1973): 1033.
40. *Job Evaluation Policies and Procedures,* p. 27.

41. Richard Henderson, "Job Descriptions–Critical Documents, Versatile Tools, Part 2: Planning for Job Analysis," *Supervisory Management* 20 (December 1975): 19.

Bibliography

Basic Training Course in Position Classification: The Classification Process. Personnel Methods Series, no. 11. Part 2. U.S. Civil Service Commission. Washington, D.C.: Government Printing Office, 1965.

Chapman, Edward A., Paul L. St. Pierre, and John Lubans. *Library Systems Analysis Guidelines.* New York: John Wiley, 1970.

Clark, Philip M. *Personnel for Research Libraries: Qualification, Responsibilities and Use. Final Report.* New Brunswick, N.J.: Bureau of Library and Information Science Research, Graduate School of Library Service, Rutgers University, 1973. ERIC no. 072 836.

Cooper, Elizabeth A. and Gerald V. Barrett. "Equal Pay and Gender: Implications of Court Cases for Personnel Practices," *Academy of Management Review,* 9.1 (1984): 84-94.

Council on Library Resources, Inc. "Trends in Professional Employment," *CLR Reports,* 2.1., February 1988.

Creth, Sheila. *Manpower Planning: Job Analysis and Evaluation in Selected Academic Libraries and Private Industry.* Research Report to Council on Library Resources, Washington, D.C. 1980.

Crowe, William J. *Select Bibliography of Materials Relating to Position Classification in Libraries.* Prepared for the American Library Association Preconference on Effective Personnel Utilization, LEPU Guidelines and Principles, Detroit, Michigan, June 16, 1977.

De Cotiis, Thomas A. and Richard A. Morano. "Applying Job Analysis to Training." *Training and Development Journal* 31 (1977): 20–24.

Dowell, David R., ed. "Minimum Qualifications for Librarians. Papers from a Symposium." *North Carolina Libraries* (Spring 1980): 7–29.

Downs, Robert B. and Robert F. Delzell. "Professional Duties in University Libraries." *College and Research Libraries* 26 (1965): 30–39.

Duda, Frederick. "Columbia's Two-Track System." *College and Research Libraries* 41 (1980): 295–304.

Eason, K.D. and J.C. Gower. "Implications of New Technology on Work Organization: A Case Study." In *Human Factors in Organizational Design and Management,* H.W. Hendrick and O. Brown, Jr. eds. North Holland: Elsevier Science Publishers, 1984, 361–65.

Fine, Sidney A. "Functional Job Analysis: An Approach to a Technology for Manpower Planning." *Personnel Journal* 53 (November 1974): 813–18.

Gerczak, Anthony. *Library Selection Project: Job Analysis Report, Phase I.* Sacramento, Calif.: Selection Consulting Center, 1977.

———. *Library Selection Project: Selection Systems Design for Entry-Level Professional Librarians, Phase II.* Sacramento, Calif.: Selection Consulting Center, 1977.

Green, Samuel B. and Thomas Stutzman. "An Evaluation of Methods to Select

Respondents to Structured Job-Analysis Questionnaires." *Personnel Psychology* 39 (1986): 543–64.

Halachmi, Arie and Marc Holzer. "Merit Pay, Performance Targeting, and Productivity." *Review of Public Personnel Administration* 7.2 (Spring 1987): 80–91.

Henderson, Richard I. *Compensation Management: Rewarding Performance in the Modern Organization.* Reston, Va.: Reston Publishing Co., 1976.

———. "Job Descriptions, Critical Documents, Versatile Tools: Part 1. Structure and Uses." *Supervisory Management* 19 (November 1975): 2–10.

———. "Job Descriptions, Critical Documents, Versatile Tools: Part 3: Conducting a Job Analysis." *Supervisory Management* 21 (January 1976): 27–34.

Hestwood, Thomas. "Human Resource Planning and Compensation: A Marriage of Convenience." *Human Resource Planning* 7.3 (1984): 141–50.

Jensen, O.A. "An Analysis of Confusions and Misconceptions Surrounding Job Analysis, Job Evaluation, Position Classification, Employee Selection, and Content Validity." *Public Personnel Management* 7 (July-August 1978): 258–71.

Library Education and Personnel Utilization. A Statement of Policy Adopted by the Council of the American Library Association, June 30, 1970. Chicago: Office of Library Personnel Resources, American Library Association, 1970.

McCormick, Ernest J. *Job Analysis: Methods and Applications.* New York: AMACOM, 1979.

Prien, E.P. "The Function of Job Analysis Content Validation." *Personnel Psychology* 30 (Summer 1977): 167–74.

Rouleau, E.J. and B.F. Krain. "Using Job Analysis to Design Selection Procedures." *Public Personnel Management* 4 (September-October 1975): 300–04.

Rudary, R.F. and J.G. Ralls. "Manpower Planning for Reduction In-Force." *University of Michigan Business Review* 30 (November 1978): 1–7.

Schulman, Richard D. "Position Classification and Pay Plans: Important Instruments in Library Personnel Administration." *New Notes of California Libraries* 59 (Spring 1964): 277–80.

Smith, Michael J. "Job Evaluation Systems Fail to Meet Current Needs." *Managerial Planning* 32.4 (January-February 1984): 36–43.

Thayer, Frederick C. "Performance Appraisal and Merit Pay Systems: The Disasters Multiply." *Review of Public Personnel Administration* 7.2 (Spring 1987): 36–53.

Trieman, Donald J. *Job Evaluation: An Analytic Review. Interim Report to the Equal Employment Opportunity Commission.* Washington, D.C.: National Academy of Sciences, 1979.

Typical Class Specifications for Professional Positions in Public Libraries under Civil Service. New York: New York Library Association, February 1974. ERIC no. ED 100 330.

"Uniform Guidelines on Employee Selection Procedures (1978)." *Federal Register* 43 (166): 3829–3831.

van Rijn, Paul. *Job Analysis for Selection: An Overview.* Professional Series, 79–2. Washington, D.C.: Personnel Research and Development Center, Office of Personnel Management, August 1979.

Walker, C. Terrence. "The Use of Job Evaluation Plans in Salary Administration." *Personnel* 64.3 (March 1987): 28–31.

Zimmerman, Glen A. "Job Validation: The Library of Congress Experience." Paper presented at the Annual Meeting of the American Library Association. Chicago, June 27, 1978.

5
Recruitment and Selection
Billy R. Wilkinson

Attracting highly talented persons to librarianship always has been the most formidable—and crucial—task facing the profession. Seeking the best and the brightest as early as 1876, Melvil Dewey began discussions with his colleagues at the Philadelphia conference of librarians concerning the establishment of a school for librarians. Finally, he persuaded President Frederick A. P. Barnard and the Trustees of Columbia College to host the school.[1] Dewey immediately sought talented apprentices for the first class.

This priority should never change as librarianship continues to work to achieve first-class status among the learned professions and to have—and keep—a leading role in our knowledge-based world economy.

Over the last thirty years the recruitment pool of available and talented librarians has experienced its highs and lows. In the 1950s and 1960s the environment was such that each MLS recipient could choose from among ten or a dozen offers.[2] In order to fill open positions, all types of libraries—academic, public, research, school, and special— were hiring many who met only the minimum qualifications. Beginning in the mid-1970s the situation changed drastically: libraries could choose from a large number of applicants for every vacant professional position. A leading Eastern university library had some 70 applicants for a beginning reference position. A Midwestern public university library received 174 applications for two beginning general reference positions in 1978 and 128 applicants in 1979 for two similar jobs.

However, by the mid-1980s there was another swing of the pendulum. Library administrators were attending meetings entitled "Where are the librarians? Is there a shortage in the profession?"

Several fundamental questions should be answered: Are women, who once comprised the majority of the recruitment pool, entering other professions? Has librarianship failed to attract young people to the profession and are talented youth embracing the allied fields of computer science or information systems instead? Are capable students entering those professions perceived to be more financially rewarding? Even as the world economy grows more dependent on transmission of information, is our profession's very existence threatened?

As librarians seek to recruit the most talented persons they have to act as personnel experts, able to distinguish easily between the ordinary and the best; and they yet often have little or no personnel training or expertise in recruiting, interviewing, and selecting appropriate staff members. The personnel experience of some library administrators amounts to having hired a student assistant, and if it did not turn out too badly, continuing along, choosing others like the one who luckily worked out well. The result is that the standards of measurement and admission to librarianship have been very low.

If progress is to be made in the profession, we need to consider the standard practices and procedures by which libraries can recruit, screen, interview, and select the most highly talented staff members—from part-time student assistants to senior administrators, reference librarians, catalogers, and bibliographers—who are necessary to operate the nation's libraries.

THE RECRUITMENT PROCESS

Upon the resignation, transfer, promotion, retirement, dismissal, or death of a staff member, or the authorization of a new position, the costly process of recruitment begins. Although the nature of the recruitment effort depends on several factors, such as the size, complexity, and mission of the library, as well as the scope of the responsibilities and duties of the job in question, the employer should approach each vacancy as an important opportunity to increase the overall efficiency of the operation. If the vacancy is an entry-level professional position, concern should be given to an applicant's potential for advancement and growth. If the vacancy is for a part-time student assistant in technical services or is an assignment as a supporting staff member, the employer has different but equally important concerns.

In these years of budgetary constraints it is probable that the supervisor or department head is no longer automatically authorized to initiate the recruitment process, but must justify the continuation of the position to higher administrative levels. Often, the parent institution plans to reduce personnel costs through attrition and not all vacancies are filled. It also is not uncommon to find an unfilled professional position in one component of the library assigned to another unit or filled at a different level, perhaps as a part-time or supporting staff position. As part of the justification to fill a vacancy or as the first step in the recruitment process, the current job description should be reviewed and revised if necessary.

The employer is ready to develop a recruitment strategy appropriate to the vacancy in question upon 1) a review of the current job description in the context of the class specifications, if any, for the position series; 2) the final assignment of the appropriate classification, title, and salary grade by the library's personnel specialist and/or the parent institution's personnel office; and 3) the budgetary approval of the higher administrative line officer.

A perennial and perplexing question for all organizations is the dilemma of promotion from within versus importing special talent from outside. Rutherford D. Rogers and David C. Weber summarized the issue:

> There are very strong arguments in favor of internal promotions whenever possible. Such actions raise the hopes of younger employees that they, too, may be promoted if they stay and if they perform well. It is also true that one has a fairly accurate assessment of someone already on the staff, whereas one is likely to get favorable rather than unfavorable details in regard to a person at another institution. Furthermore, the person already on the staff knows procedures, persons, and policies, and this will shorten the time in the new assignment before he begins to make major contributions. Also, experience in one place in the university library system can produce extra dividends in other library assignments.
>
> Despite these several factors in favor of an internal candidate, the reasons for bringing in an outsider can be compelling. An outside candidate may offer truly superior qualifications; he may also bring collateral specialties that will prove useful on wider grounds than the immediate position. An internal candidate who is acceptable but not outstanding is often useful in an intermediate position but severely limited in more senior assignments. There is some danger of developing a monolithic staff when backgrounds of most employees have been built in one institution; even though such a situation may provide wider understanding derived from common experience, it suffers from the lack of diverse experience and ideas. There is no general prescription for any one appointment, but a mixture of internal and external appointments is probably healthy and is likely to be a natural consequence of a considered attempt to appoint the best available person in each instance. There are times when no suitable candidate appears to be available and the temptation is great to make an unwise compromise. Every appointment cannot be made with enthusiastic expectations, but this should be the objective. The writers are firmly convinced that the best policy is to postpone action before too quickly picking someone who seems a poor risk. . . .
>
> In canvassing internal candidates, there is always the question of the technique that will best produce the desired results. If the staff is not too large, the director or the personnel administrator may simply run through

the various possibilities and single out two or three candidates. The trouble with this method is that it doesn't give the person with an unexpressed interest a chance to make it known. For that reason, many libraries have adopted a posting system which lists vacancies and invites expressions of interest. . . .[3]

The temptation also is great for employers to select "la crème de la crème" of the institution's (or a neighboring) library school graduates because they wish to remain in the area, are so easily alerted to vacancies, and seem to have the potential to develop into excellent librarians. However, recruiters should be wary of developing a homogeneous staff lacking diverse experiences and ideas.

During recent years when affirmative action and equal employment opportunity programs have governed recruiting practices, many institutions more often go outside to hire qualified women, members of minorities, and others who are protected by the law, particularly for middle- and executive-level management positions. Also, during periods of financial exigencies (causing restructuring of units or complete reorganization of the library, which in turn requires lay-offs with recall rights, demotions, and reassignments), the various personnel programs, civil service systems, or union contracts under which the library operates have "bumping" and other detailed procedures that govern the emergency situation.

Strategies

Recruitment strategies vary greatly for differing library positions. For part-time student aides in academic libraries, the college or university usually has a central office for financial aid and student employment to which the library funnels its requirements for part-time employees. Many academic libraries also seek to supplement this by advertising part-time positions in prominent places in the library or in the student newspaper, setting up recruitment booths at freshman orientation or during class registration periods, and on an individual basis by personally asking bright student users if they would be interested in library employment.

Academic libraries are working successfully with campus cooperative education programs to employ students majoring in accounting, computer science, and other appropriate disciplines on a part-time basis in the library system. School libraries also recruit on a person-to-person basis through library clubs or student assistance programs. Public, research, and special libraries may attempt to attract both high school and college students from the area.

Strategies for attracting support staff may be as varied as the requirements of federal, state, or municipal civil service systems (where appointment must be made from the top three or five candidates according to scores on written tests) or as self-controlled as those of an independent research library. In most cases, however, the parent institution has a central employment office that assists in the recruitment of clerical positions.

Recruitment for professional positions is usually the exclusive province of libraries, with the exception of school libraries where the local or district office performs the hiring function for both teachers and librarians. Academic, public, research, and special libraries usually have much more discretion, since the standards and requirements are established by the library rather than the parent institution.

Libraries have greater freedom, and greater responsibility, in devising their recruitment strategies for professional positions than for nonprofessional. Some government agencies and institutions, as well as individuals in the profession, are questioning the validity of the MLS degree and have challenged it as the only entry factor necessary for a professional position.

The recruitment process for various positions in all types of libraries is complex and difficult. No effort can be spared in using older, proven methods, and in devising effective new ways to attract the best to positions in our libraries. For instance, during periods of tight markets for particular positions like skilled secretaries, using employment agencies may be the only way to secure an acceptable person for an open position. The substantial fee will seem minimal when compared to the costs of appointing an unqualified person or being forced to leave a vital position vacant.

Searches for student, support, or professional positions should invite recommendations from current employees. They can be an excellent source, eager to recommend persons who will meet the high standards of the library. Staff members may recommend members of their immediate families or more distant relatives. (Many institutions now have "enlightened nepotism" regulations that allow for the appointment of relatives; problems of morale are avoided by not permitting related persons to supervise each other.)

Libraries also have been singularly successful in recruiting their student assistants for part-time and full-time clerical or technical positions. The most talented student employees are soon recognized and may be nurtured and trained for more demanding duties. Promoting bright and hard-working students to support-staff positions often is the only way a library can make up for the central personnel office's inability to recruit enough qualified persons for the large number of such positions.

An innovative recruitment practice is to split one position into two part-time positions for persons who for various reasons (e.g., pursuit of an academic degree, family responsibilities, no need or desire for full-time employment) are attracted to part-time librarianship. One academic library recently appointed an outstanding and experienced reference librarian to a half-time position while she worked on a doctoral degree at a neighboring university. A subject division of a large public library employed part-time a leading authority in the discipline while she compiled and edited the guide to its literature. Such talent on a library's staff clearly outweighs any minor administrative inconveniences caused by part-time employment.

After a careful review of the various options for finding qualified candidates the final recruiting plan is adopted.

Affirmative Action and Recruitment

Employers can only seek and review candidates on the basis of their qualifications and abilities—not on their sex, age, or ethnicity; they also must make concerted efforts to include in the pool of applicants women, minorities, and others who are protected by law. Before a recruitment plan is implemented it should be forwarded for review and approval to the line officer in charge of that division of the library where the position is authorized, and to the library's affirmative action officer, if one serves in the local unit. The plan also should be forwarded to the institutional affirmative action committee or office. This will insure that the library's recruitment strategy includes the widest possible advertisement.

Advertising

In developing a recruitment plan, decisions have to be made about which media or channels to use for advertising. The choices—and costs—involved vary greatly, ranging from placing no ads or postings for students assigned to the library by the central academic office administering the federal work-study program to placing several ads costing thousands of dollars in the national media for senior professional or administrative positions.

Postings for both support staff and professional positions should appear inside the institution so that staff members are aware of promotional opportunities. In fact, this is a requirement of most affirmative action programs and union contracts. In unionized libraries, having internal postings before or concurrent with outside advertisement is often written into the first contract between management and the union. Such requirements generally present few problems for personnel administrators, unlike seniority clauses that mandate promotion from within of currently employed staff, provided that the staff member has the "skill and ability" to perform the duties of the position. Such seniority rules often make it impossible for the library to take affirmative action to recruit and appoint qualified women and members of minority groups, and they prevent the library from increasing the overall caliber and effectiveness of the staff. Although it is critical for morale to post vacancies internally, it is unwise to give "courtesy" interviews to internal candidates who do not meet the position requirements or whose work performance is less than fully satisfactory.

Whether or not to embark on a local or national search (particularly for professional positions) is not an easy decision to make. The decision often turns on the level of the position, or the requirements of an affirmative action program. There are other reasons for choosing to do a national search (e.g., the difficulty of attracting librarians with subject specialty backgrounds) or choosing not to (e.g., funds or the flexibility to bring candidates from distant places for interviews may not be available).

A number of media channels should be used, no matter the type of search. For instance, the local newspaper(s) should be used—particularly if the library is in a metropolitan area. The Sunday or special edition with the classified section is heavily consulted by prospective employees. Carefully monitoring the response rate will determine whether this should continue to be used.

Other local media and channels include city or state professional newsletters; employment "hot-lines"; campus, corporate, and other newsletters and information bulletins; bulletin boards and placement service publications of local and nearby library schools.

Even when conducting a national search it is appropriate to make use of local media and channels in addition to national newspapers, professional journals, and "hot-lines." The director or personnel administrator may also write to national ethnic and women's caucuses, to regional and national administrators (e.g., the directors of research libraries concerning a vacancy as deputy university librarian), and to those library schools accredited by the American Library Association. Some of the largest libraries, or a group of libraries, may send an officer to recruit at several of the leading library schools.

Several caveats are in order when conducting national recruitment: 1) the lead time to secure ad placement may add considerable time to the search process; 2) many national journals require ads to include the minimum salary or salary range.

SCREENING

In formal situations and in larger organizations, the screening process usually begins once the deadline for receipt of applications and/or nominations has passed and, after inquiries to nominees concerning their interest, the official pool of applicants is announced. In less formal circumstances, and in both small and large operations, the employer may casually and individually screen applicants as they come in to inquire about employment or from their letters of inquiry.

Sometimes large-volume interviewing is necessary where interviewers classify applicants only roughly, reserving for "later and fuller consideration those who survive the first coarse screening."[4] Completed applications are examined for bedrock qualifications such as hours available, educational level, necessary skills, and salary requirements. Applicants not meeting these qualifications are immediately excused. Those remaining might be invited to a short, highly structured interview. Later the most qualified and impressive persons are invited for additional interviews.

Various methods are used during the screening process to fill professional positions. In some instances, it is the personnel administrator who reviews the applications, résumés, nominations, and any other documents and decides who will be invited for interviews. This is the most efficient and time-saving procedure. Another approach has the director appoint a search-and-screen committee (or in the case of the position of director, the appropriate official or group appoints the committee). The committee may be asked to advise and make recommendations to the appointing officer on who should be interviewed, or it may be empowered to decide upon and invite those who will be interviewed. In such delegations of authority, the personnel administrator usually serves as staff to the committee, advising on correct procedures and overseeing much of the correspondence, recordkeeping, and other necessary work.

In either case the committee's charge should be in writing and sufficiently detailed to avoid misunderstandings that might occur during the process. Guidance on this matter, as well as on the formation of committees, use of the job description, advertising, ethical considerations, initial communication with nominators and applicants, selection and interview procedures, recommendations of candidates, advanced communications with candidates, extension of searches, announcement of appointment, and records of proceedings, was set forth in 1977 by the Board of Directors of the Association of College and Research Libraries of the American Library Association in the policy statement "Guidelines and Procedures for the Screening and Appointment of Academic Librarians."[5] Although they specifically address the academic environment, these excellent guidelines should be considered by public, school, and special librarians who are engaged in the search-and-screen process.

Search committee procedures vary greatly from institution to institution. The American Council on Education has described the committee's task,[6] as has the American Association for Higher Education,[7] and Richard Sommerfeld and Donna Nagely[8] have provided an operation manual. Many institutions develop their own written policy and procedure statements. In general, committees provide democratic means for the participation of staff and other concerned constituencies in the selection of personnel.

After the closing date for receipt of applications, committee members convene, discuss their charge, review the description of the position and the qualifications required, decide upon their own internal procedures if not already prescribed by the institution, devise their rating system for the review of the documents submitted by the applicants, and then actually begin the review process.

The two key documents given careful scrutiny during the screening process are the covering letter of application and the résumé. Despite the literature available on preparing résumés, the availability of commercial preparation services, and the considerable attention given to this topic by library school placement officers, too few librarians bother to take the time and make the effort to present themselves properly. Covering letters, which provide applicants with opportunities to supplement their résumés with additional information and demonstrate some degree of imagination concerning their suitability for a position, frequently contain grammatical and typographical errors. Too often, librarians merely list the titles of previous positions without giving clear indications of their responsibilities and accomplishments. Any librarian interested in applying for a position should demonstrate his or her seriousness of intent by presenting a clear and concise summary of responsibilities and accomplishments. (Several excellent guides to job hunting and career planning that include advice on résumé writing are available.)[9]

After the initial review of the documents submitted by the applicants, the committee usually decides to seek references for the most outstanding and qualified applicants. An inexperienced search committee may err at this point in being unwilling or unable to cut the group under serious consideration to an appropriately small number. Perhaps out of false kindness or a fear of being wrong, committees often ask too many referees for their evaluation of marginal or unqualified applicants. This is a disservice to both referee and candidate.

In times of shortage of excellent candidates, it is prudent to empower the chair or staff officer to notify finalists of the progress in the search. By apprising an applicant of the institution's continuing interest, good will is increased and early loss of a good candidate to another institution can be averted.

Search committees that are able to agree objectively by means of fair, consistent, and equitable processes may ask the chair or the staff officer to call the applicants' references and ask them a uniform list of questions devised by the committee. This method often gathers better and more specifically comparable information on the applicants than requesting letters, which tend to be glowing and general testimonials to unbelievable perfection. The calls should be summarized and reported to the committee. If the committee decides to ask persons other than those listed by the applicant about the applicant's performance or qualifications, particularly in searches for senior positions, the applicant, upon request, should be entitled to know who these are.

If letters of reference are requested, referees should be asked to address specific topics relevant to the position description. Again, this will improve the quality and consistency of information on the candidate.

It might seem obvious that references should be checked, but many committees fail to do so. Even if a jaded belief that one receives only "good notices" has developed, it is inexcusable not to check references. It should be the primary responsibility of the personnel administrator to perform this important task, which requires a certain level of sophistication to pick up the nuances in both written or verbal evaluations. It is also wise to have senior administrators or others check with colleagues at the candidate's institution, particularly if a doubt or specific question has arisen. It must be remembered, however, that "off-the-record" references are worthless and, if acted upon, subject to legal action by the candidate.

This discussion brings to the fore the problem of lack of candor in evaluations. Many supervisors find staff appraisal to be an extraordinarily onerous responsibility. Aside from giving deliberately false evaluations in order to rid a department or library of a problem staff member, supervisors for a variety of reasons—inexperience, the fear of not being backed by superiors, the wish to avoid possible allegations of discrimination, a distaste for confrontation—shy away from candor. It is an age-old human problem, but it can be addressed in librarianship through increased and better supervisory training to impart an understanding of the standards of performance and all the technical skills of performance appraisal.

After a reasonable period of time for the receipt of most references, the committee reviews additional information on the group of applicants being seriously considered and makes its final determination of those to be recommended for invitation to future interviews. At this point some search committees sometimes undergo a common feeling of depression. Perhaps the committee members may feel that, instead of picking winners (predicting candidates who will succeed if placed on the job and matching differences in the applicants to the differing job requirements), they have picked only losers. Or the recommended candidates may be perceived as threats to the general status quo or to particular committee members. The committee may be experiencing sheer boredom from a long, uneventful, or preordained process or exhaustion from a series of bitter and grueling battles between powerful constituencies on the committee.

Some observers of the elaborate committee process contend that considerable time and, therefore, money can be saved and as good, or even better, results achieved if a personnel or other administrator simply went through the letters of application and enclosed résumés and invited the best one or two persons for interviews. John F. Harvey and Mary Parr summarize this body of opinion:

> Many large libraries fill a dozen vacancies a year and typically are conducting several searches simultaneously. A library personnel adminis-
> trator can handle the details of these searches and narrow the choice skillfully and efficiently. The complexities of . . . searching . . . with federal and campus affirmative action, equal opportunity, and additional require-
> ments and voluminous correspondence and oral contacts, on campus and off, suggest that the burden of work and understanding will be much more onerous to a one-time-only search and screen committee chairperson than to a full-time personnel administrator already well acquainted with the poli-
> cies and routines involved.[10]

Another problem with the process is inexperienced staff who "delay the search by their unrealistic quest for the perfect candidate, even going so far as to abort the search by declaring none of the applicants qualified to meet the stated requirements of the position when several persons do qualify."[11] One veteran and respected educator believes that the "typical search committee ends up becoming more involved in placating the various interest groups on campus than in serving the best interests of the institution as a whole. Too many people get into the act. . . . And here it might be well to remember these anonymous words 'The greatest fool may ask more than the wisest man can answer.' "[12] And the chairman of the New York City Board of Higher Education, commenting on a news article concerning a presidential search, points out that the article's

> focus upon debate, sometimes highly personal, over the individual candi-
> dates may leave some readers with the impression that candidacy for a public office of this kind amounts to running a gauntlet of prying eyes and destruc-
> tive gossip. This is very far from the truth. At the final stage of an elaborate search process of this kind, the university's task is not to reject unqualified candidates, but to select from among several highly preferred and qualified individuals one whose qualities seem uniquely well suited to the task at hand.[13]

No matter how critical one is of the search-and-screen committee, the tremendous possibilities for the education of the staff who participate in them should not be dismissed. The library administration has an excellent opportunity to promulgate its plans and objectives to librarians, teaching faculty, and administrators when they serve on committees and convey to supervisors that they are considered an integral part of the management team. At the same time the process often lets staff and faculty communicate concerns that may not have been apparent to the administration.

Finally, search committees, although they can take up enormous energy and time, usually generate better recommendations than selections forced through by personnel or other administrators, provided of course that there are experienced staff on the search committee who guide the less experienced and less sophisticated.

Let us turn, then, to the last stage of the process—interviewing—when the committee, other participating staff members, and administrators attempt to "select from among several highly preferred and qualified individuals one whose qualities seem uniquely well suited to the task at hand."[14]

INTERVIEWING

One authority has posited three basic functions of the interview: to determine the relevance of the candidate's experience and training to the requirements of a specific job; to appraise his or her personality, motivation, and character; and to evaluate his or her intellectual abilities in terms of both quantity and quality.[15] Another authority points out that the interview is mutually informative:

> The truth is that the interview is indispensable, not only because of its information potential, which is considerable, but also because of its distinctly human aspects. No applicant wants to be judged for a position without an opportunity to discuss it face-to-face in a meeting with a company representative. The interview gives applicants the feeling that they matter, that they are being considered by another human being rather than a computer. The interview also gives them a chance to ask questions about the job, about the company, and about its salary and employment benefits. It also give you, the interviewer, an opportunity to do some selling if that is necessary, as it often is. Finally, because it gives applicants a chance to feel that they are the ones doing the deciding, it enables them to maintain their dignity in what can become a very impersonal process.[16]

This mutual benefit may apply more to those seeking professional or high-level positions than it does to the novice seeking a part-time or clerical job, but all finalists at the interview stage should be provided with meaningful background information about the job and the institution. For student or supporting staff candidates, this can be accomplished during the interview and supplemented by some general handouts describing the institution, the benefits, or other important matters. For professionals, more extensive documents (e.g., organization charts, departmental reports, etc.) should be sent to candidates in advance of interviews. For middle and executive positions, even more elaborate documents (e.g., institutional reports and surveys, budgets, etc.) should be furnished.

Basically, the interviewers should be looking for the one negative factor among many excellent ones, because the one may be all-important. According to Arthur A. Witkin:

> The applicant ranks high on analytical ability, understanding of people, detail handling, expression, self-confidence, mechanical comprehension, and forcefulness, but low on self-reliance. Which is the most important factor? The negative one, assuming it is relevant to the position being filled.
>
> The reason for this is that success on the job is a product of many factors, but failure can be the result of only one. Accordingly, it is easier to learn if the applicant has the characteristics for failure than if he or she has the characteristics for success.
>
> A sound selection procedure is, therefore, a search for the derogatory. It cannot be considered a meeting of the minds between employer and applicant to arrive at a hiring decision. Rather, it is an adversary proceeding, with the employer determined to learn of any factors that could inhibit success and the employee often determined to conceal them.[17]

Sheila Creth lists very important guidelines for interview preparation that too often are overlooked or ignored by library staff:

> Read the résumé or application carefully in advance. Review the requirements of the position prior to the interview, particularly if you are not a direct supervisor for the position and are not familiar with the job requirements.
>
> Organize an outline of the interview. This can be done by topic or by writing out a series of questions. An outline of what will be covered during the interviewing process is particularly important when several people will be interviewing a candidate separately or when a search committee will be talking with a candidate collectively. If this outline is not prepared in advance, the candidate will probably be asked the same questions repeatedly; this is not only boring for the candidate but means that important areas that should be explored may be overlooked.
>
> Review the questions that should not be asked in an interview (age, marital status, children, and others).
>
> Assure that the interview will not be interrupted or disturbed by phone calls or people dropping in.

The interviewer should also review the difficulties he/she may create in the interview situation, such as talking too much, interrupting the candidate, jumping to conclusions, suggesting the 'right' answers, and so forth. In addition, the interviewer should think through the kinds of problems that could arise in the interview due to an applicant's behavior. Situations that typically occur include: The candidate simply does not talk (yes or no answers are standard responses); the candidate talks a great deal but never provides substantive information; a candidate's personality does not appeal to the interviewer. There are others, of course, and interviewers should give some thought in advance to how they might handle these situations.[18]

Other sources on interview procedures include Richard A. Fear's *The Evaluation Interview* [19] and Felix M. Lopez's *Personnel Interviewing, Theory and Practice.*[20] David Peele has drawn from these two standard works and transferred them to a library context.[21] Academic librarians should also refer to the previously cited "Guidelines and Procedures for the Screening and Appointments of Academic Librarians" issued by the Association of College and Research Libraries. For an older, but detailed and excellent basic guide, see Anne F. Fenlason's *Essentials in Interviewing.*[22]

When all interviews have taken place the committee's recommendations are forwarded to the appropriate individual. The final determination may be as simple as the immediate supervisor and the personnel administrator meeting to discuss and decide on the finalist to whom an offer of appointment will be made. In most institutions, the policy is to permit the supervisor of the unit that has the vacancy to make the final decision as to who is hired, even though many studies on hiring decisions have found that "most supervisors frankly admitted that they did not have a clear idea or notion of what to look for" in a candidate and they "agreed that they turned down very few applicants, accepting approximately nine out of ten referred."[23]

Arriving at the final decision may be a very complex process, made only after long discussions by the search committee and concurrent discussions by other groups, such as members of the department in which the position exists, or a faculty executive committee if there is a library faculty governance structure; institutional units or offices, such as the personnel office, graduate college, or office of academic affairs if tenure is to be granted; and a host of individuals, such as the immediate supervisor, other supervisors, and co-workers.

Upon determining the finalist, the personnel administrator usually calls the candidate immediately, particularly if an outstanding person has been selected who may have offers from competing institutions. It is possible to have informal discussions with the finalist while his or her papers are being prepared and forwarded to the institutional affirmative action office or committee for approval, but the finalist must be clearly informed that an offer has not yet been made and cannot be made until final approval to offer the position is received.

Before a verbal offer is made important matters are negotiated, such as starting salary, effective date, type of appointment, and moving expenses. If final agreement is reached, a letter containing the formal offer of the position and describing the conditions of appointment is forwarded to the finalist. Upon receipt of written acceptance, appointment papers are completed and forwarded to the contract-issuing office. Only upon the final approval by the Board of Trustees and the issue of a contract is the appointment consummated; only then can the assumption of the position occur.

A word here on employment testing (performance or achievement, intelligence, aptitude, interest, or personality tests) and medical examinations is necessary. Recent court decisions have placed the onus on the institution to prove that any test used is predictive of job success. Properly developed and administered tests that are used with other selection tools can be a very important part of the selection process. The following guidelines are recommended for the effective use of tests:

1. Do not make tests the sole tool for selecting applicants.
2. Use the right tests for the job for which you are hiring.
3. Be sure that a test measures what you want to measure.
4. Try a test on present employees before adopting it.
5. Seek the advice of competent consultants in test selection.[24]

The chair of the search committee and the personnel administrator must retain the files of the search documents for a certain period of time after the conclusion of the search. Governmental monitoring, affirmative action regulations, and the possibility of lawsuits by unsuccessful applicants dictate maintaining these archives.

Selecting the best to become staff members is each library's means of providing the best possible service for its users. After the requirements of each position have been carefully established, a costly process begins to find persons who meet these requirements, with considerable attention paid to the educational and technical qualifications of the applicants, as well as personal characteristics, intellectual ability, and general suitability for the position involved. The recruitment process of advertising the vacant position has been fully described in this chapter. The screening of applicants, the interviewing of candidates, and the selecting of the finalist have also been discussed, with referrals made to the standard works.

In the serious business of operating a library, formal and systematic recruitment techniques are necessary. Candidates must be assessed as objectively, consistently, and independently as is humanly possible.

Warren G. Bennis has contributed a classic, and intimate, description of one well-known university's search for a president[25] and has researched another twenty presidential selections. He comments on our human ways and concludes that "in almost every case personal and political motives (very human impulses) insinuated themselves into the choice—in spite of the trappings of objectivity. Universities aren't unique in this. It is observable whenever personnel selection takes place from the naming of a church warden to the filling of a top-level managerial post.[26]

Stanley Marcus sums it all up in his *Quest for the Best:*

> I've watched many people in various lines of endeavor striving to attain the best, and I have tried to determine what qualities they had in common. Whether they were baseball pitchers trying for a no-hit game, runners attempting to break a world record, or grape growers intent on producing the finest wine in the world, they all had complete dedication to their goals. They displayed greater knowledge than their competitors; they were willing to put in the extra effort necessary to approach perfection; they never settled for second best. They exerted themselves to reach the heights of accomplishment for both financial reward and esteem of their peers or clients, and for their own satisfaction.[27]

It should only be the same for librarians selecting the ablest new staff member.

References

1. Ray Trautman, *A History of the School of Library Service, Columbia University.* (New York: Columbia University Press, 1954), pp. 7–12.
2. Kathleen B. Stebbins, *Personnel Administration in Libraries,* 2nd ed. rev. by Foster E. Mohrhardt (New York: Scarecrow Press, 1966), p. 36.
3. Rutherford D. Rogers and David C. Weber, *University Library Administration* (New York: H.W. Wilson, 1971), pp. 32–34.
4. Felix M. Lopez, *Personnel Interviewing: Theory and Practice,* 2nd ed. (New York: McGraw-Hill, 1975), p. 165.
5. "Guidelines and Procedures for the Screening and Appointment of Academic Librarians," *College & Research Libraries News* (September 1977): 231–33.
6. Richard A. Kaplowitz, *Selecting Academic Administrators: The Search Committee* (Washington, D.C.: American Council on Education).
7. Theodore J. Marchese, *The Search Committee Handbook: A Guide to Recruiting Administrators* (Washington, D.C.: American Association for Higher Education, 1987).
8. Richard Sommerfeld and Donna Nagely, "Seek and Ye Shall Find: The

Organization and Conduct of a Search Committee," *Journal of Higher Education* (April 1974): 239–52.

9. Juvenal L. Angel, *Why and How to Prepare an Effective Job Resume,* 5th ed. (New York: Simon & Schuster, 1972).

    J. I. Biegeleisen, *Job Resumes: How to Write Them, How to Present Them, Preparing for the Interview* (New York: Grosset and Dunlap, 1976).

    Richard N. Bolles, *What Color Is Your Parachute? A Practical Manual for Job Hunters and Career Changers* (Berkeley: Ten Speed Press, 1987).

    Burdette E. Bostwick, *Resume Writing: A Comprehensive How-to-do-it Guide,* 2nd ed. (New York: John Wiley, 1980).

    John P. Kotter, *Self-Assessment and Career Development* (Englewood Cliffs, N.J.: Prentice-Hall, 1978).

10. John F. Harvey and Mary Parr, "University Library Search and Screen Committees," *College & Research Libraries* 37 (July 1976): 348.

11. Billy R. Wilkinson, "The Plethora of Personnel Systems in Academic Libraries: A Phenomenon of the 1970s," *New Horizons for Academic Libraries, Papers Presented at the First National Conference of the Association of College and Research Libraries, Boston, Massachusetts, November 8-11, 1978,* Robert D. Stueart and Richard D. Johnson, eds. (New York: K.G. Saur, 1979), p. 141.

12. Paul C. Reinart, "The Problem With Search Committees," *College Management* (February 1974): 11.

13. Harold M. Jacobs, "City University's Search for a Brooklyn College President," Letter to the Editor, *New York Times,* 11 July 1979, p. 20.

14. Ibid.

15. Richard A. Fear, *The Evaluation Interview,* 3rd ed. (New York: McGraw-Hill, 1984), p. 88.

16. Lopez, p. 109.

17. Arthur A. Witkin, "Commonly Overlooked Dimensions of Employee Selection," *Personnel Journal* 59 (July 1980): 573.

18. Sheila Creth, "Conducting an Effective Employment Interview," *Journal of Academic Librarianship* 4 (November 1978): 357–58.

19. Fear, p. 24.

20. Lopez, p. 109.

21. David Peele, "Fear in the Library," *Journal of Academic Librarianship* 4 (November 1978): 361–65.

22. Anne F. Fenlason, *Essentials in Interviewing,* revised ed., Grace Beale Ferguson and Arthur C. Abrahamson revs. (New York: Harper, 1962).

23. Lopez, p. 163.

24. Lawrence A. Klatt, Robert G. Murdick, and Frederick E. Schuster, *Human Resources Management* (Columbus, Ohio: Charles E. Merrill, 1985), p. 211.

25. Warren G. Bennis, "Searching for the 'Perfect' University President," with editorial comment and discussion, *Atlantic* 227 (April 1971): 4, 39–44; (June 1971): 32–35.

26. Ibid., (April 1971), p. 4.

27. Stanley Marcus, *Quest for the Best* (New York: Viking, 1979), pp. 29–30.

6
Staff Development and Continuing Education
Sheila D. Creth

Unquestionably the quality of library service is dependent on the knowledge, skills, attitudes, and resourcefulness of staff. The range and scope of expectations for staff competencies and performance are expanding, though, due to the nature and complexity of library work. Libraries are now at the center of a fast-paced and rapidly changing global information environment that is influenced by the impact of computer technology on information access and delivery and is influencing the value of information.

In this environment libraries are becoming more visible than ever before to the public because of the role they play in providing access to information, and the funds they receive for collection development, the new information technology, and staff. With increased visibility comes increased risk. Many library users are going to expect fast and reliable service because timely access to information is critical to their activities. Others will expect to see major differences in library services as a result of the large amounts of funding that supports information technology.

These expectations by users for service will be met by staff, not by machines. And so staff with expertise in a wide range of subjects, operations, and management are required for today's complex library organizations. They also need to be clear thinkers and team players—able to work effectively not only within their own departments but across the organization as well as with diverse user groups. While recognizing that technology is the tool not the goal, staff also need to be technically astute in designing and using automated systems. In addition, libraries need people who can adapt quickly and see challenges, not barriers.

A major challenge for library administrators and supervisors in the next decade is to keep pace with new directions in library services that are emerging by addressing in a comprehensive way the training and development needs of staff. If libraries are to be effective in the future, allocation of resources is required to assure that staff acquire and update their knowledge and skills. Staff development and continuing education programs provide a framework to achieve the goal of a knowledgeable and competent staff.

Staff development incorporates a broad range of activities designed to provide staff with knowledge and skills that support their role and responsibilities in the organization. Staff development activities include, but are not limited to, orientation for new staff, on-the-job training, preparation of training materials, supervisory counselling, and seminars and workshops on topics as diverse as supervisory techniques, time management, performance evaluation, conflict resolution, communication skills, financial management, and teaching skills.

In contrast, *continuing education* focuses on the needs of the individual rather than the needs of the organization. The individual staff member has responsibility for selecting continuing education activities which are based on a personal interest rather than generated by job or organizational needs. Continuing education activities may be formal academic course work, seminars, and conferences, as well as more individualized and less structured activities such as reading and research. While continuing education is focused on the specific needs identified by the individual for additional learning, nonetheless the library is often the beneficiary. Therefore, the library administration should support continuing education to whatever extent is possible within available resources.

STAFF DEVELOPMENT

A program of staff development encompasses a range of learning activities, including those designed to teach specific skills, techniques, and procedures, and those that provide employees with an understanding of organizational objectives as well as the general knowledge, concepts, and attitudes necessary to insure effective performance. Only a multi-focused program will achieve the desired quality of staff performance. It is important to differentiate between a staff development program and a series of unconnected learning/training activities which may not reflect directions and priorities of the library. The program should be built on an understanding of the purpose and objectives of staff development so that it is clear what results are expected. From program objectives, goals can be developed which identify specific results, and within this framework, specific priorities can be set and activities selected and implemented.

A primary objective of any staff development effort should be to bring about a change—an increase in knowledge, the acquisition of a skill, and the development of confidence and good judgment. A goal might focus on the training of staff to implement an automated system and the activities required to accomplish this goal successfully.

Too often a library launches into presenting training activities without first identifying what it is they want to accomplish. Individual activities without the program structure may meet a short-term need but will not necessarily contribute to the overall direction of the library, and may indeed have a minimal impact even on the issue that was addressed.

When considering the support of a staff development program, it is important to recognize that there is not a choice as to whether or not to train and develop staff; there is only a choice of how to approach this responsibility. Regardless of whether or not a formal program exists or whether supervisors give the necessary attention to this function, training and development occur on a daily basis. In the absence of an organized approach to training, staff will try to seek the necessary information or skills independently through trial and error or by observing others or seeking assistance from co-workers. However, the process of learning by self-training, particularly for the person new to the assignment, may result in incorrect information and poor performance. Also, the possibility of learning a job adequately through an informal process is increasingly difficult in the more complicated automated environment of most libraries.

The failure to recognize the importance of staff development may result in higher costs to a library because of increased training time, the inability of employees to perform at acceptable levels or to maintain service standards, wasted work time due to errors, increased supervision, personnel problems, high turnover and low morale, and potentially a loss of credibility with the library's public.

On the other hand, a systematic and organized approach to the training and development of library staff benefits the library by:

- Increasing the quality and quantity of work,
- Eliminating the need for close and constant supervision, thus freeing supervisors to make more effective use of their own time,
- Improving staff morale and job satisfaction by developing independent and competent staff.
- Increasing organizational flexibility and stability by creating resourceful and adaptable staff.

The relationship between well-trained and knowledgeable employees and an efficient and effective library is obvious.

Responsibility for Staff Development

Without the full support and interest of all members of the staff, a staff development program will not succeed. Key members of the organization, though, assume major responsibility for its coordination, implementation, and support.

Supervisors. The supervisor's role is crucial since it is the supervisor who has primary responsibility for staff development. It is also the supervisor who most directly affects a staff member's attitudes toward the job and the library. The supervisor's views and opinions on the value of training and development will therefore make a difference as to whether employees feel encouraged to participate or become frustrated and stymied. Because of their key role supervisors should avoid the "tendency to rely on formal staff development activities, both in-house and external, to carry the bulk of training responsibilities. This tendency has negative attributes. Evidence strongly indicates that for training to have optimum effectiveness it must be job centered."[1]

The supervisor's role begins when an employee is first hired. The time and attention given to the planning of the initial training for a new employee indicates the value that the supervisor places on the work and the individual staff. Supervisors should evaluate their own job responsibilities and priorities to insure that they make the necessary commitment of time and energy to this important aspect of their jobs. Supervisors demonstrate a positive attitude toward employees' growth and development and success on the job by:

- Providing continual guidance and counselling to employees with regard to their overall job performance and potential
- Developing written training plans for initial orientation and training
- Encouraging employees to comment on and evaluate their training
- Providing opportunities for employees to assume greater responsibilities and different activities in order to test their acquired knowledge and skills
- Discussing with employees how they might improve their performance through participation in formal learning activities as well as personal efforts outside of structured activities
- Inviting employees' comments and suggestions regarding the supervisor's communication and leadership style
- Insuring that employees understand not only how a task is accomplished, but why it is important to the operation of the library

Supervisors also need to provide staff who have participated in learning activities to apply their newly acquired knowledge or skills since application is an important part of the learning process and the basis of staff development. If opportunities for testing newly acquired ideas and techniques are continually frustrated, the employee may develop a poor attitude toward learning, and possibly toward the job and the supervisor as well. Finally, employees should be given the responsibility for their work and the opportunity to learn from their mistakes as well as their successes.

Libraries Administrators. Through their leadership, commitment, and support of training and development activities administrators are a major key to the success of a staff development program. But although library administrators may articulate a commitment to training and development, they may be reluctant to devote the resources (funding and staff time) to this activity unless there are clear goals. As Snyder and Saunders note, administrators too often are

> presented with lofty ideals and only minimal cost justification for staff development programs; the staff development . . . program is perceived by both the staff and the administration as a self-contained unit or separate entity rather than as an integral part of library activities. . .[2]

It is essential that a staff development program is both realistic and relevant to library needs, not presented as a panacea for all that ails the library. Martell and Dougherty observe that "we often tend to expect too much from staff development. We overload it with expectations. Frequently we ask it to accomplish that for which it was never intended."[3]

The personnel administrator, or the administrator who functions in this capacity, has primary responsibility for developing and implementing an effective staff development program. This involves identifying staff development needs, implementing and coordinating library-wide activities such as workshops and seminars, establishing relevant policies and procedures, and insuring evaluation of both activities and the overall program.

The personnel administrator also should provide guidance and assistance to supervisors as they plan and develop orientation and job training activities within their departments, and should encourage and assist with the development of training materials such as audiovisual presentations or self-instructional guides. Such materials are helpful in standardizing the content and method of presenting job-related information and in reducing the time needed to instruct employees when relying completely on an individualized instruction process. In addition, the personnel administrator can act as a resource person by developing a collection of staff training materials from other libraries and organizations, by developing guidelines for training, and by maintaining a list of individuals within and outside of the library who might be called upon to develop or conduct learning activities. In these ways and by generally providing encouragement and standards for training, the personnel administrator can provide sound direction and a positive climate for staff development.

Advisory Committee. A personnel or staff development committee can play a vital role in establishing and maintaining a staff development program. It can provide valuable assistance to the personnel administrator in such functions as identifying staff development needs, coordinating and assisting with the presentation of library orientation as well as certain learning activities, assisting with the preparation of training and orientation materials, and advising on staff development policies and procedures. A committee also provides an important communication channel between library staff and the administration on concerns and interests in staff development. The committee should represent all staff groups in order to maximize the sharing of different staff viewpoints in the program design.

Staff. Library employees have a central role in staff development, for without their recognition of the importance of continued growth and development, learning activities will have a diminished impact. No employee should be exempt from staff development activities because of education, experience, position, or length of service. Employees who view training and development in a positive manner and who look forward to learning are more likely to be responsive to a changing library environment, and thus be able to provide the best library service on a consistent basis.

If library supervisors and administrators establish an environment that demonstrates to employees a strong commitment to the success of each person, employees are likely to respond in a positive manner to staff development opportunities.

Staff Development Program Components

A well-balanced staff development program includes a range of formal and informal activities that focus on three components: orientation, on-the-job training, and development. Formal activities are those for which there is a specific plan and structure, such as a training plan for a new employee or a workshop on supervisory skills. Informal activities, such as discussions with the supervisor regarding performance strengths and weaknesses, personal reading, and research, have no definite structure but nonetheless contribute to an employee's learning. The following discussion of staff development focuses on the formal learning activities that might be organized by a library though those activities which are informal in nature should not be overlooked by supervisors and staff.

Orientation. Orientation familiarizes an employee with basic information regarding policy and procedures as well as the philosophy and values of the organization. It occurs in several phases: orientation to the specific job and work environment, to the library organization, and to the parent institution. Job and departmental orientation consists of general information about job requirements and duties, departmental procedures and policies, location and use of equipment and facilities, and introduction to co-workers. The immediate supervisor is responsible for planning and coordinating orientation at this level though other members of the department may assist in handling specific portions. Involving co-workers in both orientation and job training helps build a commitment to an employee's success and establishes a foundation for good working relationships among staff.

The employee should receive an introduction to library policies and procedures. In larger libraries this may be handled by someone in the personnel office or through a formal orientation session, otherwise the supervisor assumes responsibility for this as well. Finally, for those libraries that exist within a larger organization, information about the parent institution is also needed.

Because there is so much for an employee to learn, particularly one new to the library, a useful tool for supervisors is an "orientation checklist," which lists the variety of information that typically should be available to a new employee during the first few days of employment. Supervisors can use the checklist to insure that all relevant topics have been covered even if they are not ultimately the ones to provide the information.

While supervisors and others responsible for staff development may provide basic information such as work schedules, time reporting, and vacation and sick leave policies and procedures, what is often overlooked is the need to educate the individual to the intangible aspects of the library organization.

All organizations are social settings with specific requirements for behavior, communication, roles, and responsibilities. This aspect of an organization is most often referred to as the "corporate culture." Drake characterizes the corporate culture as representing a "set of values and beliefs shared by people working in an organization. It represents employees' collective judgments about the future based on past corporate rewards and punishments, heroes, villains, myths, successes and failures." She goes on to say that

> understanding the corporate culture and acting in accordance with the culture often determines a person's success or failure on the job. A qualified

ORIENTATION CHECKLIST

Staff Member's Name _____ Date Hired _____

Department _____

A. THE JOB
_____1. Position description/overall purpose of position
_____2. Outline/schedule for training
_____3. Goals and objectives for the department
_____4. Departmental organization
_____5. Work of others in the department
Other:
_____
_____

B. PHYSICAL SURROUNDINGS
_____1. Introduction to co-workers
_____2. Work area
_____3. Location of equipment/supplies
_____4. Location of restrooms
_____5. Location of bulletin boards
_____6. Location of eating facilities

C. RELEVANT MATERIALS
_____1. Packet of materials for new employees
_____2. Union contract

D. HOURS OF WORK
_____1. Work week & hours
_____2. Explanation of flexible scheduling
_____3. Meals/rest periods
_____4. Medical appointments & the like

_____5. Taking university courses

E. LEAVE
_____1. Vacation
_____2. Sick leave
_____3. Holidays
_____4. PL days
_____5. Leaves without pay

F. COMPENSATION
_____1. Where, when, and how often paid
_____2. Rate of pay
_____3. Raises
_____4. Compensatory time/overtime pay
_____5. Probationary reviews
_____6. Tuition reimbursement

G. MEDICAL BENEFITS/ RETIREMENT
_____1. Meeting scheduled with university personnel

H. RIGHTS AND RESPONSIBILITIES
_____1. Attendance
_____2. Punctuality
_____3. Attitude desired
_____4. Conduct/appearance
_____5. Safety
_____6. Grievance procedures

and competent employee may fail because he or she doesn't fit in, while a less competent person who understands the culture has a higher probability of success.[4]

An important aspect of orientation is for the person to learn and adapt to the corporate culture of the library. Referred to as *socialization,* this process represents how each of us learns how to behave in a particular environment, what the values and philosophy are of the people and the organization, what formal and informal guidelines exist for acceptable behavior, what the rewards and punishments are for behavior, and what the accepted roles and relationships are among members of the organization. Socialization is the process by which we learn about the world around us without having a rule book; instead we learn by listening, watching, and absorbing.

The process of socialization occurs whenever we enter a new social setting. The quality of this process determines largely whether new employees will succeed or fail. Therefore, supervisors and others involved in orientation should find ways to transfer this understanding of the organization to staff, to respond to the needs of individuals to understand the environment in which they work and interact with others. Equally important as knowledge and skills is the feeling that an individual employee has of belonging and contributing to the organization.

Job Training. Job training focuses on the knowledge, skills, and abilities that the person needs to acquire to perform effectively. It is central to a staff development program because it addresses the fundamental need for an employee to meet performance expectations. Job training should bring about a change; it is not successful unless the person can do something new or different, or demonstrate a change in behavior.

Job training should be structured to consist of both formal and informal activities that address each of three dimensions—knowledge, skill, and ability. And the goals of training should be clear enough so that the trainee understands what outcomes or behavior are desired. Typically job training has focused rather narrowly on providing instruction in specific information, procedures, or equipment required in the performance of job tasks. While these aspects of training will always be essential, the results will be inadequate to meet library needs if a broader context is not provided and if the needs of the individual employee are ignored.

While the majority of job training still occurs within a department under the direction of the supervisor, in the future we are likely to see an increase in centralized training due to automation. But even when training occurs outside of the employee's department, the supervisor still is responsible for insuring that the application of what has been learned is achieved at the desired level.

Although job training should be viewed as a continuous process, not as a series of separate or unrelated incidents in a person's work life, there are situations that require specific attention and an organized approach to training. Though these training situations have a great deal in common, it is helpful for supervisors to recognize the distinct differences in their contexts and requirements. Specific training situations exist for the new employee, performance improvement, and operational problems or changes. As the supervisor plans for job training, it is important to identify and respond to the differences in each of these situations.

Job training is expensive. If training results in desired performance, then the investment of time and energy has been worth it. If training is ineffective, then the dollars associated with training are wasted, and additional funds must be spent to retrain the same employee or to train another employee. Therefore, the supervisor benefits by planning for training rather than approaching it haphazardly or casually.

Initial planning requires a commitment of time and effort from the supervisor that may not have been devoted to this activity in the past; but once completed, it will be possible to modify and update what already has been developed for the same position when subsequent training is required. In addition, supervisors' skills in planning for training will be strengthened with practice, thus reducing the amount of time demanded for planning future training efforts.

The planning effort for job training should result in a *training plan*, a plan that is built on a careful analysis of job duties, and performance standards or expectations. A training plan should include objectives (i.e., what results are expected and in what time frame), the content of the training, the sequence, the names and titles of the trainers, and the location of training if it varies. All staff involved in the training process, including the trainee, should receive a copy of the training plan. A copy of the training plan also should be placed in the staff member's personnel file so that there is a record of the training provided. When writing training plans:

- Be specific in describing what will occur in training and the results desired,
- Use action verbs in describing training and the desired results,
- Provide background information in separate handouts,
- Describe activities in positive terms rather than negative ones,
- Consider how to address desired attributes or behaviors that will not be covered formally in training, such as working as part of a team, taking initiative, and working cooperatively with co-workers.

When developing a training plan, supervisors should determine if there are other staff in the department (or in another department) who might assist with the training process because of their knowledge, skills, training abilities, and positive attitude. When job training is for new employees, the supervisor should build into the plan regular meetings with the person in order to monitor training progress. Weekly meetings with the employee allow the supervisor to provide support and encouragement and to discuss openly any problems the person may be having.

The supervisor also should hold regular meetings with trainers to assess the progress the trainee is making and generally how the training plan is working.

Training plans have limitations; they do not, in and of themselves, guarantee quality results in job training. First, a training plan cannot be all-inclusive, though all major aspects of the person's assignment certainly should be addressed. It is simply not possible to write down everything about all facets of a job. Additionally, if the training plan is used in an inflexible manner it can become a liability. The plan should be used as a guide, but one that will need to be reviewed, updated, and altered as circumstances dictate. Changes may occur because of situations in the department, the trainee's learning pace, or time constraints. If the plan is used appropriately and as a dynamic document, it should not limit or inhibit creativity on the part of a trainer or trainee in accomplishing the learning required.

Finally, a trainee, particularly a new employee with little work experience, may be overwhelmed by a training plan and have reservations about his/her ability to accomplish everything that is described. To minimize the employee's concern the supervisor should review the training plan at the start, explaining the purpose of the plan, the flexibility of the plan, and the schedule for reviewing with the trainee his/her progress and concerns.

Success of job training depends primarily on the willingness of the immediate supervisor to invest time in planning, implementing, and evaluating the training. The orientation and training process, particularly for a new employee, is critical to success since work habits and attitudes are being developed at the same time that the person is acquiring skills and knowledge. An organized approach to training is much more likely to produce a high level of performance and positive attitudes than one that is poorly planned and implemented. A well-planned job training process also should provide the supervisor with objective information with which to conduct a probationary evaluation.

Job training is a process that requires continual attention. It is not a "one-time short-term cycle of activity that occurs only during the first phase of an employee's career or only during the initial hiring period."[5] And so training does not end after the probationary period; supervisors will need to recognize and address additional training needs in a thoughtful and organized manner in order to insure sustained quality performance by employees. Additional training may be necessary for a number of reasons. Employees may still lack certain skills; infrequently used skills or knowledge may be forgotten; policies, procedures, and equipment may be altered; and new services may require new knowledge or skills.

Quality job training should be a basic aspect of any staff development program for without quality training at this level other program activities will not be fruitful. Job training requires time and effort, but effective training is an investment for the future through staff.

Developmental activities are broader in scope and content than job training, and usually address concepts and general techniques. Management training, introduction to statistics or automation, teaching techniques for user education, and time management are just a few examples of developmental activities. Library employees typically participate in developmental activities when familiarity with different techniques and approaches or new knowledge becomes essential for effective performance. Developmental activities are aimed also at encouraging staff members to seek new approaches and solutions to problems, to reassess their familiar patterns of thinking and acting.

Since developmental activities tend to be broader in scope than skills training, and usually are concerned with applications of the behavioral sciences and management theory, as well as other organizational concepts, they often are conducted by experts outside the library. The personnel administrator has primary responsibility for coordinating the implementation of development activities, though supervisors and individual employees must assist in identifying the needs that exist, as well as possible ways in which to meet these developmental needs.

Staff Development Materials

A staff development program should encourage the use of training and educational technology and the expertise of media and educational learning specialist. For instance, programmed instruction in shelving the collection can be used effectively to train a large number of staff, often widely dispersed, for routine or basic informational activities.

Libraries have effectively used a variety of materials to instruct patrons in the use of library resources and bibliographic tools, such as self-instructional materials, audiovisual shows, and filmstrips. Yet these same techniques are minimally used for training and instructing library staff even though their use would reduce costs and improve the effectiveness of the training process.

In fact, there are a number of formats and techniques that can be used in training materials—singly or in combination—including audiovisual aids (slide/tape, filmstrip, video) and written aids (programmed or self-instructional). Materials can be developed in segments or modules to allow brief and focused presentations and the flexibility for an employee to review or learn a small portion of information at a time. For example, rather than developing a half-hour slide-tape show on the library's classification schemes, a more effective approach would be to develop individual contained segments on each classification system.

Developing training materials in alternative formats not only allows for an improvement in the quality of training but also permits employees to use the materials independently and at their own pace, thus creating an environment more conducive to adult learning, At the same time, it frees the supervisor and other staff from having to rely exclusively on the standard time-consuming individualized instruction.

The Planning Process

The success of a staff development program depends on how relevant the activities are to staff and organizational needs. Staff development has to be approached in a systematic way in order to insure that it is integrated into the activities and operations of the library, and to avoid the kinds of staff frustrations that are inevitable when priorities are not clearly articulated. The temptation to offer faddish or popular activities is more likely to occur when there is no plan and no agreement on priorities.

There are several key components to the planning process: establishing program goals and objectives, identifying needs, setting priorities, identifying resources, and evaluating the learning activities and the program. The major elements for effective planning for staff development—as with other library planning activities—are that objectives are clearly understood, information needed to make decisions is available, different viewpoints and ideas are considered, and critical thinking takes place.

The first step in implementing a staff development program is to define the scope and function of the program. Therefore, a well-defined set of objectives and goals should be developed that in turn provides the framework for activities to be implemented, funds to be requested, and policies to be developed. As Snyder and Saunders have stated, the objectives of the staff development program should be

> action-oriented and achievable in concrete terms. The program should touch on every aspect of the educational maintenance activities of the staff and should be aimed at building a climate for constant awareness of the potential for learning and growth in even the most mundane daily activity.[6]

The next step in planning is the process of identifying training and developmental needs for all categories and levels of library staff. A needs-assessment process should be undertaken so that the efforts invested for staff learning will create the desired result. The staff undertaking needs assessment should consider the following:

- What specific information is wanted?
- What are the sources for this information?
- What method(s) will be used to obtain the information?

Katz suggests that the value of a needs assessment is found in one or more of the following:[7]

- Identification of organization and individual needs and priorities
- Identification of attitudes concerning new subjects, skills, or technologies required for performance
- Identification of possible causes of performance problems and whether they are training related
- Identification of performance gaps, or when performance does not meet desired expectations or standards

The needs assessment process should focus on both the immediate and long-term in order to support library objectives and goals, departmental and job needs, and the needs of the individual employees.

Staff development needs at the department and job level include three dimensions necessary for effective performance: knowledge, skill, and ability.

Knowledge refers to the information that is needed to perform a set of activities efficiently and effectively. Examples are knowledge of reference tools, cataloging practices, collection development policies, automated circulation system protocols, call numbers, and management guidelines.

Skill refers to the techniques, the approaches, and the styles of translating knowledge into action or practice. For instance, librarians need the skills to conduct a reference interview, to interpret cataloging rules in relation to the intellectual content of the material, and to evaluate staff performance.

Ability refers to the intangible qualities or characteristics that are necessary for performance and are often referred to under the rubric of "motivation" or "attitude." Abilities needed by library staff include flexibility, cooperation, service attitude, and leadership.

Staff development needs that support organizational objectives focus on services that need to be improved as well as plans for change such as reorganization, automation, new services, policies, or procedures. It is the library administrators who are likely to provide the long-range and organizational view of staff development needs. Supervisors and staff should provide the assessment of training and development needs for the job level.

All library staff (supervisors, librarians, technical and support staff), or a representative sample, should be included in the needs assessment process in order to obtain a full range of ideas and viewpoints. While this initial contact with employees is valuable, it is important for the planners to realize that at the outset of establishing a staff development program employees may have little understanding of the purpose and scope of the program. This will minimize their ability to respond constructively to a needs assessment. Another potential problem is that staff expectations with regard to the types of activities and the potential rewards of staff development may be unrealistic, resulting in disappointment and frustration. These potential problems can be minimized if clear definition of the purpose and scope of staff development is articulated throughout the planning and needs-assessment process.

In addition to the library staff, other major sources of information for needs assessment are the records and statistics maintained by the personnel office. Quite often the valuable information that is maintained by the library personnel office is overlooked when a staff development needs assessment is conducted. This oversight is a mistake, since these records provide factual data that may give an important perspective on staff development needs. Information on the following topics should be obtained and used when analyzing staff development needs:

- All job titles and the number of employees in each
- Job requirements for all positions
- Knowledge and skills most lacking in new employees
- Turnover rates and patterns (numbers and percentage of openings by job titles and department)
- Performance problems or weaknesses identified through the performance evaluation process or disciplinary actions

Prior to implementing needs assessment it is necessary to determine how the information will be obtained and organized for analysis. The following factors should be considered when determining what approach will be used to gather the data:

- Time available to conduct the needs assessment
- Size of the staff
- Physical location and accessibility of staff
- Ability to design an effective questionnaire
- Availability of staff with good interviewing skills

The standard means for gathering information are questionnaires and interviews, or a combination of both. Before reviewing the advantages and disadvantages of these methods, it might be worthwhile initially to consider a different approach to identifying staff development needs. Since the personnel administrator has responsibility for coordinating this activity, he or she might develop—with the assistance of a committee—a tentative program statement and plan for staff development. This would include a statement of objectives and a list of potential learning activities in the areas of orientation, skills training, and development. The proposal can be developed by working with data available from the personnel records as well as the knowledge of the personnel administrator and committee members. The tentative proposal would be reviewed first with the administrative staff and revised as necessary and then reviewed with other staff in group sessions or by using a questionnaire format to solicit suggestions for additions, deletions, or revisions.

This approach to developing a program plan avoids a costly survey of staff when initially there may be little understanding of the scope and purpose of such a program. By presenting a tentative program proposal, administrators and staff have a tangible set of objectives and activities to which to respond and therefore their responses are more likely to be pertinent and constructive. This approach does require that the planners be open to changes in the proposed program so that suggestions made by staff are given serious consideration.

If it is decided to conduct a general survey of staff in order to identify staff development needs, then careful planning is necessary. A questionnaire has to be well designed; and if interviews are to be conducted, they must be well organized with specific topics identified for discussion.

A questionnaire obviously provides advantages because information can be requested on a number of topics and materials can be organized in several different formats (e.g., open-ended questions or structured questions requiring multiple choice or single response). In addition, a questionnaire allows for a large number of employees to be canvassed in a timely manner.

Questionnaires are difficult to design, though. The results from a questionnaire may not be useful if questions are vague or if the writing skills of staff are relied on too extensively by the use of "essay" questions. On the other hand, a questionnaire that relies exclusively on a checklist of topics is restrictive and minimizes the quality of the responses.

Interviews, particularly group interviews, may overcome some of the problems inherent in using a questionnaire, provided that they are well organized and conducted by skilled interviewers. The major advantages to the interview are that it allows for immediate clarification or expansion on a specific need identified by a staff member, encourages an exchange among employees on staff development issues, and provides an opportunity for selling staff development to employees while determining their interests and commitments. The time spent on well-planned interviews with staff may not be any greater than that spent on designing and analyzing a questionnaire.

If time permits, it is beneficial to consider using both the questionnaire and interview to take advantage of the positive aspects of each method. In using either method, though, planners should avoid providing a laundry list of topics or subjects to which staff are asked to respond. The tendency to provide a list of topics or subjects tends to produce inconclusive data on what staff actually see as needs and what they view as priorities. For instance, topics such as supervisory training, communication skills, and searching techniques will have different meanings to different employees; thus, planners will have an inadequate understanding of how to develop and focus learning activities to meet staff needs.

There are several ways to structure the data gathering (whether a questionnaire or interviews) in order to obtain a more effective response. One approach is to ask supervisors and staff to identify "the type of training that might be appropriate before beginning their particular job assignment, the training needs that arise as a result of on-the-job changes and demands, and future demands and challenges likely to require substantial development."[8]

Still another approach is to ask supervisors to consider the organization and operation of their units and determine "what factors in the environment affect the effectiveness and efficiency of their unit."[9] This encourages supervisors to look at more than individual jobs or employee performance and consider the functioning of the unit in order to assess both immediate and long-range implications for staff development.

A more specific and detailed approach would be to develop a list of knowledge and skills needed in various jobs in the library. This list can be compiled by identifying a sample group of staff to provide suggestions and/or by reviewing job descriptions or job analysis data. It can be refined to reflect no more than fifty or sixty items and then distributed to all staff, with a request that they identify the ten most critical knowledge and skill competencies necessary for their own performance. In addition, supervisors should be asked to identify the ten most important competencies needed by employees they supervise, and staff can be asked to identify the competencies needed by their supervisors. The responses can be compiled and organized (by departments, by jobs) so that a ranking is established for those knowledge and skill competencies most frequently identified as critical to performance. The data can be analyzed to identify staff development activities that would be appropriate to support the effective performance of staff. In his article on surveying supervisory training needs Bellman describes a similar approach.[10] He suggests developing a list of questions related to supervisory responsibilities, as in the following examples.

Motivation
1. How do I get my people to take a real interest in their jobs?
2. What do I do with the employee who knows how but doesn't do a good job?

Performance
1. How do I set work standards for my people?
2. How can I evaluate my people's performance fairly?

Time
1. How do I get my people to make better use of their time?
2. What can I do about excessive demands upon my time by other people?

A list of questions such as the above can be compiled by using a sample group of supervisors to review typical responsibilities and related problems. A questionnaire could be developed listing the questions and asking each supervisor to identify the questions for which knowledge and skill would be most critical to their performance. The responses are analyzed by frequency as well as the weight (degree of importance) that each supervisor assigns to the questions. As Bellman states, with this technique the planner "will be able to point out areas of greatest felt need and recommend appropriate actions including, but not limited to, training."[11] Used by Bellman for identifying supervisory training needs, this approach can be used for other job functions as well.

At least at the outset of planning for staff development there are advantages to using several different techniques if a survey is going to be conducted. It is important though to avoid getting bogged down in the techniques or spending too much time in preparing complicated questionnaires or lengthy reports; the needs assessment process should not become the priority.

Once staff development needs have been identified and analyzed, a number of different actions may result, such as the implementation of specific learning activities, identification of training materials to be developed, development of policies related to staff development, and acquisition of source materials to assist supervisors in the implementation of effective job training. Since there is so much that will need to be accomplished in staff development, and since realistic constraints of staff time and budget exist, library administrators have to establish criteria to aid in identifying priorities for the staff development program. Establishing priorities is particularly important to insure that emphasis is given to the activities most critical to current needs and that learning activities do not conflict with operational demands on library departments. As Snyder and Saunders say,

> the program should be carefully planned, timed and spaced so that periods of major activity will not coincide with peak periods of operational activity and so that there will not be too many activities going on simultaneously.[12]

The planning, development, and implementation of a staff development program can create a level of enthusiasm among the staff that can have meaningful influences on staff development results. The enthusiasm should be tempered, however, by an understanding that there will be limitations on the number and types of activities because of time and budget constraints, and that a staff development program must be based on a logical assessment of organizational and staff needs.

Resources for Staff Development

The next consideration in planning for staff development is to identify the resources necessary to meet those needs requiring specific learning activities and/or the development of training materials. There are a number of resources available, including library staff, consultants, staff of the parent institution, programs in higher education, professional associations, and commercial organizations. In addition to these resources, library staff should explore ways to share resources with other libraries in their city, state, or region. Resource sharing might include joint sponsorship of a workshop, asking staff from a neighboring library to attend an inhouse training activity, and sharing of training materials developed for library staff.

Mechanisms for implementing and improving staff development activities have not been sufficiently explored. One group that has emphasized and benefited from resource sharing is the ALA/ACRL Personnel Administrators and Staff Development Officers Discussion Group. They maintain an information exchange system to encourage and facilitate the sharing of information on each library's staff development activities, of training materials that have been designed for library training, and of evaluations of commercially produced programs, films, and other materials. The exchange contributes to an awareness of what is occurring in other libraries and allows individual libraries to benefit from what others have already accomplished in staff development.

The advantages and disadvantages of the available resources should be evaluated. The following are factors that might be considered in this process:

1. *How specialized is the material to be covered?* If the content of learning activity is specific to the procedures and policies of the library, then resources outside of the library are unlikely to be appropriate. On the other hand, if the content is general and conceptual or standard to other libraries, then the focus of the learning does not have to be on the specific organization, and outside resources might be appropriate.
2. *Are there library staff with the knowledge and ability to design and conduct the learning activity?* The components of both knowledge and ability to train should be available within the staff in order to insure a quality activity; otherwise resources outside of the library should be identified.

3. *How quickly must the learning occur?* If there is an immediate need, the decision must be made as to whether resources within or outside of the library can respond in a more timely manner.
4. *How many employees need to be trained immediately and in the future?* If there are a number of employees to be trained initially as well as over a period of time, it may be more cost-effective to have someone in the library assume responsibility for the learning activity on an ongoing basis.
5. *To what extent is the activity intended to address attitudes as well as skills and knowledge?* When the objective of the learning activity is to introduce new attitudes and behavior, participants may view a trainer from outside the library as more objective and less judgmental and, therefore, be more receptive to the learning environment.
6. *Is exposure to different viewpoints and ideas important to the learning experience?* If this is an objective, then having staff attend an activity outside the library may be most effective since they will be exposed to the experiences and ideas of the other participants as well as to those of the trainer. Specifically, when broad topics such as supervisory or managerial training are to be presented, it may be effective to have library staff participate in activities that include nonlibrary staff in order to learn from experiences representative of other work environments.
7. *What amount of funding is available?* Obviously, if funding is minimal or lacking, the ability to take advantage of outside resources also will be limited and the staff development needs will have to be addressed as effectively as possible within the library. Most important, though, is the need to establish priorities within the staff development program so that whatever funding is available is used wisely.
8. *How accessible are resources outside the library?* Libraries that are located in urban areas or within a reasonable distance to these areas may have no difficulty in utilizing programs offered by other associations and organizations. For those libraries that do not have easy access to such resources, the matter of travel time and expenses will have to be weighed when considering using nonlibrary resources.

A series of factors should be considered since no one factor typically is sufficient for decision making. Determining the appropriate means for meeting staff development needs is never simple, since there are advantages and disadvantages in either the use of internal or external resources.

When external resources are to be used, all elements of the activity should be carefully reviewed by the individual employee and the immediate supervisor. In particular, the objectives, content, and methods of instruction for the activity should be evaluated to determine its potential effectiveness as well as appropriateness to the person's assignment. Library staff should never hesitate to ask for additional information on an activity if they feel that they have incomplete information on which to base a decision.

When it is determined that library staff will be responsible for developing and conducting a learning activity, the personnel administrator should work with the trainer(s) to insure that the activity is well planned. The trainer must first begin by identifying the specific objectives for the activity. Once training objectives are identified they act as the criteria for outlining content, selecting materials, and determining instructional techniques and methods of evaluation. In the absence of objectives for the training activity, learning is often unfocused for both the trainer and the trainee.

Training Methods. The library trainer should become more knowledgeable about learning principles that focus on motivation, feedback, reinforcement, practice, and span of attention. Trainers should also explore different methods and techniques that can be used effectively in a learning activity. The following options should all be considered depending on the content and focus of the training activity.

Demonstration is the method that is most often used in job training. It involves a trainer explaining specific procedures, equipment, and routines to the trainee by demonstrating how a task is carried out or how to respond in a specific situation. Demonstration is a valid training method and is most effective when it is used first by the trainer to show how something is done and then by the trainee to show that he or she has understood and mastered the technique. This is a highly personalized, individual-focused approach to training; it also requires a high degree of instructor skill to be effective.

Lecture format should be used when a great deal of background information is required or to train a large group of people in specific procedures. While the lecture format can be useful when training a large number of people, there are disadvantages which should limit its use except when used in combination with other training techniques. The primary disadvantage is that trainees are passive during a lecture; they listen, take notes, and possibly ask an occasional question. Another disadvantage is that the lecture method is not very adaptable to the various levels of knowledge or learning that exist among the trainees.

Discussion format is especially valuable when the trainees are learning about concepts or principles and their application. Discussion can be structure or unstructured. In a structured discussion, the trainer outlines the content and determines the issues to be covered. Although the trainee is an active participant, it is the trainer who determines the focus and course of the discussion. The unstructured discussion format is more directed or influenced by the trainee. This method uses more of a conference approach, whereby the trainees identify the topics or issues and the trainer facilitates the discussion and provides clarification if necessary. This type of training format is most appropriate when judgment has to be exercised regularly; for instance when the trainee is exploring alternatives for responding to situations.

Programmed instruction is an option that is not used much in libraries though there are many job tasks that could be effectively presented in this format. Programmed instruction provides information to trainees in small segments and allows them to check their progress in learning against self-tests that are part of the packaged materials. The trainee can review and repeat the materials multiple times until the desired learning or behavior has been achieved. Programmed instruction can be in written format or computer assisted materials. Libraries that are becoming increasingly automated should be exploring ways to transfer certain types of training to the computer format.

Role play can be used both in workshops and for job training. It allows the trainer to establish a "drama" to depict a real-life situation that the trainee is likely to encounter. This assists trainees in anticipating situations and in developing appropriate behaviors to respond effectively. While there is a cost associated with developing useful role play materials, there are also sources in the library literature that can be drawn on by trainers.[13]

Case study method is similar to the role play except the trainee does not act out the role. Instead, the trainee is expected to take all of the material presented, analyze the information, and present a recommendation for action. This approach allows the trainee to work independently on a problem, to draw on his or her resources, and to practice dealing with complex situations that typify what will be encountered on the job. As with the role play materials, sources are available in the literature to draw upon in developing case studies.

Other methods and formats that can be used in learning activities include job rotation, field trips, and seminars. It is not unusual to combine several methods. For instance, a supervisory training activity focused on developing employment interviewing skills might involve the following methods: 1) lecture by an expert on affirmative action and employment interviewing guidelines and techniques; 2) film or videotape to reinforce material presented in the lecture; 3) discussion among participants and trainer; 4) role-play materials that allow participants to test their own understanding and skills. When planning on-the-job training, a supervisor might typically use a number of methods, including job instruction, a slide-tape presentation, programmed instruction, lecture(s), job rotation, and coaching to supplement and reinforce the other methods.

The following criteria should be considered when determining which methods or approaches would be appropriate: the objectives of the training activity, the requirement for trainee involvement and demonstration of knowledge and/or skill during training, the complexity of the content to be presented, the frequency with which the same training session will be offered, the skill level of the trainer, the adaptability to differences among trainees, and the costs.

Selecting and Training Trainers. Since a great deal of training in libraries, including workshops and seminars, is presented by library staff, it is important to focus on the characteristics and skills of effective trainers. While an excellent trainer can do much to overcome a poorly organized training program, a poor trainer cannot create success even from a well-organized training program. The trainer needs to be knowledgeable on the subject to be covered but also effective in presenting the information. Characteristics needed for trainers to be successful include the following:

- Ability to teach knowledge and skill to another person
- Enjoyment of interacting and sharing knowledge with others
- Openness to new ideas and suggestions
- Ability to assess performance of trainees
- Possession of a positive and constructive attitude toward the work, the department, the library, the supervisor and co-workers

Therefore, the most knowledgeable employee on a particular topic may not be the most capable trainer if the other abilities are not present. Guidelines for trainers should be developed to clarify expectations and as a means by which to measure successful trainer performance. These guidelines should focus on the trainer's ability to:

- Take an interest in the trainee
- Create enthusiasm
- Keep morale high
- Communicate clearly
- Listen
- Provide feedback in a timely and supportive manner
- Recognize the importance of self-confidence and self-esteem in the learning process
- Understand adult learning principles
- Recognize the value of learning from mistakes

A priority in a staff development program should be to develop quality trainers within the library.

Evaluation. One of the most critical aspects of a staff development program is evaluation. Unfortunately, however, evaluation of the program and the specific activities which constitute the program is not always given appropriate attention. Conroy states that evaluation can accomplish many of the following:

- Furnish accurate information to assist further planning, to improve decision making, and to document achievements
- Determine to what extent a program and/or activity is accomplishing its goals and objectives, and what impacts are occurring
- Identify program strengths and weaknesses and the reasons for specific successes and failures
- Assure most consistent quality in learning activities and efforts
- Reinforce learning and develop an awareness of growth and change
- Determine the cost and benefits of the program and its activities
- Justify the investment and answer demands for accountability
- Produce documentation that allows information to be shared with others[14]

Obviously, evaluation of learning activities must occur if a staff development program is to be effective. Consistent evaluation of staff development activities is necessary to insure that policies, planning, implementation, staff participation, and funding are adequate and realistic. Moreover, the effect of staff development on employees' performance and morale as well as the library's ability to meet its objectives should be considered as part of the evaluation process. A thorough approach to the evaluation of activities and the program will contribute toward continued support for staff development.

Typically, trainees are asked to evaluate a staff development activity at the conclusion of the activity. The evaluation may focus on a number of dimensions, including the trainer, content, training methods, and materials used in the activity. It is the opinion of the trainee that is sought on each of these dimensions, and there are several approaches to acquiring this information. The trainer may choose to have a discussion among trainees at the conclusion of the training session to gain immediate feedback. The advantage to this approach is that it is immediate, includes all trainees, and allows an opportunity to explore specific comments or suggestions of the participants, The disadvantages are that trainees may be reluctant to be critical in the presence of the trainer, and it may be too immediate for the trainees to have gained a perspective on the learning activity and its application to their job responsibilities.

A more standard approach is to use a questionnaire that trainees can complete, usually anonymously, either immediately before leaving the training session or after they have returned to their work environment. Different formats should be considered when designing an evaluative questionnaire, not only to obtain specific information, but also to encourage trainees to expand on their suggestions or criticisms. For instance, both open-ended questions and ranking scales can be incorporated into a questionnaire. The following example demonstrates this approach:

To what extent do you feel the role-play situations were effective? (circle one)

$$1 \qquad 2 \qquad 3 \qquad 4 \qquad 5$$
(ineffective)   (effective)

What specific suggestions do you have for improving the role-play materials?

The advantages of using a questionnaire are that the responses are recorded and can be reviewed and compiled at a later date. It also requires that the trainee be specific in evaluating the learning activity on a number of dimensions, and, because it is anonymous, people may be more critical in their evaluation. On the other hand, it is sometimes difficult to obtain questionnaires after a trainee has left the training environment; more importantly, even a well-designed questionnaire has limitations to the amount of information that can be acquired. Despite the limitations in obtaining participants' evaluations, their opinions of specific learning activities are worthwhile and should be given consideration. A trainer or administrator should not be discouraged when contradictory evaluations are received, because people come to a learning activity with different sets of needs and expectations, and this diversity naturally influences their learning and thus their evaluation of the experience.

Participants' evaluations are only one aspect of the evaluation process. As Pratt points out, evaluation

> has predominantly focused on variables which deal with the actual process of training, including the instructor's style and technique, effectiveness of resources, and the student-instructor's interaction. Often left unaddressed is the impact of training on practice and, ultimately, on the 'system' in which the learner operates.[15]

There is no doubt that evaluating the impact of training on the work environment is difficult, but it is important to explore ways in which it might be accomplished. Different approaches to evaluating "impact" should be considered based on the content and objectives of the activity and the background and experience of the participants. Approaches to impact evaluation rely on observation, interviews, and questionnaires. When specific skills or procedures are the focus of the training, it might be appropriate, for example, for the trainer to observe the trainee in the work environment. Other approaches might include a follow-up questionnaire to both the trainee and the immediate supervisor asking for an evaluation of the training based on specific examples of performance improvements or changes. The same information might be obtained through an interview with the trainee and the supervisor.

Factors that may be used as measurements for evaluating the

impact of learning activities include a reduction in error rates, a decrease in the number of staff needed to accomplish specific work, an increase in efficiency, a decrease in backlogs, a decrease in user complaints, and an increase in job satisfaction expressed by employees. In addition to direct follow-up through interviews or questionnaires, the performance evaluation process should be used as a source of evaluation of staff development activities, and the exit interview process should also provide information on how terminating employees viewed their training and development.

As Pratt states,

> impact evaluation examines the effect of some intervention (in this case training) on the ultimate objective of the . . . [employee]. In some kinds of training the impact on practice is relatively clear. We can see the results of training when someone moves from not knowing how to do something to doing it. Technical skills often afford this kind of obvious impact evaluation.[16]

In those situations where the learning activity is not focusing on obvious skills or techniques, but on providing employees with new ideas or behaviors, it will be necessary to consider alternative means for evaluating the impact. In certain situations the impact on performance is not expected to occur immediately but is more likely to be gradual. Accordingly, evaluation of the learning activity has to be structured over time.

The personnel administrator should work with trainers (both library staff and consultants hired by the library) to establish methods for evaluating internal training activities. The evaluation of staff development activities should not be restricted to those conducted in the library. Whenever an employee is scheduled to participate in a staff development activity outside the library it should be with the understanding that an evaluative report will be prepared at the conclusion of the activity. The evaluation of outside activities should focus on the same dimensions mentioned earlier: objectives and content, instructor's style and methods, and materials used. The evaluation report should be submitted to the immediate supervisor and the personnel administrator so that information is available for determining the appropriateness of the specific activity for future library staff participation.

The personnel administrator or personnel committee must, in turn, review all learning activities and other components of the staff development program against the stated program objectives. The evaluation of the program provides the justification for continuing or discontinuing present learning activities, identifying additional activities, revising or developing policies, and requesting funding support. It is through a process of evaluation that the administrative and managerial support for staff development will be built and sustained.

Budget

An integral part of a staff development program is the availability of funds to support activities. There are various costs associated with staff development, including the rental or purchase price of training materials and/or equipment, the duplication cost of written materials and the production cost of slides and transparencies, fees for consultants, and registration fees, and other costs associated with staff participation in staff development activities outside of the library. It is difficult to forecast the budgetary needs of a staff development program, but records of costs should be maintained and itemized for future budget requests. In those libraries that do not wish to provide a set budget for staff development but instead absorb the costs into other accounts, records should still be maintained in order to demonstrate the cost associated with staff development.

Certainly the foundation for any ongoing library program or activity is funding. Therefore, all efforts should be made to secure funding for the staff development program. A budget also requires accountability and therefore encourages a staff development program that is practical and realistic relative to library needs.

It takes several years to establish a fully functioning and effective staff development program. The time and effort are necessary, though, if a sound program that will support the library's ongoing activities and operations is to be established.

CONTINUING EDUCATION

Though there are similarities between staff development and continuing education, a sufficiently different focus exists to warrant a separate discussion. Whereas staff development supports the objectives of the library through job and organization-related activities, continuing education is broader in scope and addresses primarily the needs of the individual and only secondarily those of the library.

Because the focus is on individual needs, continuing education is by and large a self-directed process, with the person assuming responsibility for his or her continued growth and development in order to avoid obsolescence, to plan for future job and career opportunities, and for solely personal satisfaction. In determining what continuing education and professional activities to pursue or what new avenues to explore, it is the individual who must develop a plan for ongoing development.

In some cases, the continuing education activities identified by the employee may also meet needs of the library, but library administrators and staff must recognize that this is not always the case. Martell and

Dougherty state, "All that benefits the library does not necessarily benefit the individual and vice versa. Each manager should be aware of the constant tug between these two demands. The need to balance costs and benefits related to the individual employee in the context of the organization must be kept in mind."[17]

Continuing education activities typically include formal coursework; attendance at workshops, seminars, and conferences; research leave; and job exchange or internships at another institution. What distinguishes any of these activities as continuing education and not staff development is the need that will be met. For instance, a librarian who decides to take business administration courses in order to strengthen his or her future career opportunities would be participating in a continuing education activity. On the other hand, the librarian who is expected to strengthen his or her subject knowledge in business in order to act as the business reference librarian would be participating in a staff development activity when taking business administration courses.

Even when activities cannot be related directly to library effectiveness they serve an important purpose since staff actively involved in learning and development contribute to the vitality of the organization. All staff need to be encouraged to seek out appropriate continuing education activities in order to maintain currency in their particular field of expertise and to provide a stimulating environment for themselves. Professional staff in particular should be involved in a range of continuing education activities and programs as part of their commitment to the field of librarianship. In this context, libraries benefit from the continuing education activities of their staff.

Martell and Dougherty indicate that continuing education "can be viewed from two perspectives. First and rather pragmatically, it is a fringe benefit to the employee. Some employees would use coursework to improve career opportunities. Others would use it to develop new opportunities and new aptitudes. The second perspective suggests that continuing education can be selectively used by the administrator and the employee in a consultative process, the purpose of which is to further organizational role and job-centered aspirations."[18]

The role of library administrators is not to develop a specific continuing education plan for each employee, but to establish an environment in which continued growth and development is valued by all employees. The degree to which such activities can be supported by the library with funding and release time has to be determined by each library based on considerations such as staffing levels, service commitments and priorities, and budget priorities. While libraries have a responsibility to encourage a wide range of activities for library staff, they must be sure that there is not a headlong rush into such activities at the expense of the library user. The concern with staff growth and development must be balanced against the needs and objectives of the library organization to meet its commitment to the public.

The personnel administrator should coordinate the library's continuing education program primarily by insuring the articulation of policies and procedures to all staff and by seeking ways to make known to staff the various opportunities for continuing education activities. The following factors are important in defining a continuing education program.

1. Guidelines for participation in activities, release time, responsibility for reporting on activities, and evaluation of activities.
2. Funding available for continuing education activities with specific identification of what activities will receive priority in funding allocations, and the procedures for applying for funds.
3. Definition of recognition and reward that will operate for participation in continuing education activities.

Library staff need general guidelines in order to understand clearly the expectations that exist for participation as well as the limitations that exist. For instance, different expectations for participation in continuing education and professional activities typically exist for professional and support staff; as a result, these two groups of staff may receive different degrees of support for such activities. Such expectations, as well as anticipated support for both funds and release time, should be clearly spelled out for staff.

Certainly each library needs to determine whether the amount of release time granted individuals from their work schedule to participate in continuing education activities needs to be defined specifically or whether a flexible policy can operate, leaving the judgment up to the individual employee and the supervisor. In many libraries specific policies exist, for instance, with regard to release time for academic coursework, while in others a specific number of days are granted for professional and continuing education activities. When possible, library administrators should maintain an open policy where the merits of the particular activity can be weighed against the needs of the individual and the library. What would be helpful in most libraries are general guidelines to assist staff in setting realistic commitments and goals for such activities such as committees, special projects, workshops, and academic coursework.

Library staff need to give more thought to what continuing education activities have relevance to them and not proceed, as Stueart has characterized, in a "frenzied rush to update credentials, to acquire new skills, and to gain new knowledge . . . [taking] any continuing education offering we can get our hands on, just for the sake of participating in continuing education." Stueart goes on to say that

> instead of a group of isolated, unplanned, and unintegrated learning experiences, we must move to the point where we can experience sequential modules of learning that will have a continuous and cumulative impact on our individual career development.[19]

Most specifically, it is necessary for library administrators to decide whether continuing education activities will be supported with release time and funds based strictly on job-relatedness, or whether a broader interpretation will be used. In many situations library administrators must follow the policies established by the parent institution, but where there are no policies the administration should establish them. Well-defined policies and procedures provide an environment in which staff are encouraged to be active and self-motivated and, at the same time, minimize potential disagreements between administrators and staff regarding limitations on continuing education and professional activities. When establishing such policies, library administrators should also decide whether formal or informal reporting of activities will be expected and who will have authority for granting time for participation in activities.

The allocation of funds is a major issue in continuing education. Even though institutional guidelines will apply with regard to defining legitimate expenses, the library administration usually retains discretion regarding what type of activities will be supported and the amount of support to both activities and individual staff members. Policies should be stated so that staff are informed of priorities for allocating funds and the manner in which funds are to be requested. For example, some libraries allocate funds for conference attendance based on committee membership in the specific association. The difficulty with this criterion is that it may not encourage the new staff member to explore activities and opportunities within the profession because of a lack of financial support. Libraries should establish criteria that will support those activities of the greatest benefit to the individual and the library.

Decision making regarding allocation may depend not only on the parent institution's guidelines but also on the existence of a collective bargaining unit. In some libraries, funds allocation is solely an administration decision; in others a staff review committee recommends allocations to the administrative staff.

The third major aspect of a continuing education program is the question of recognition or reward. As interest and concern for continuing education and for professional activities within the library field increase so will the pressure for direct reward for participation in such activities. Library administrators, though, should guard against rewarding staff for participation specifically and instead should continue to focus on a reward system (including merit increments, promotion in rank, promotion to vacant position) that is based on demonstrated job performance and/or demonstrated contributions to the library field.

> There is a danger that as continuing education becomes more prominent in the field, emphasis will move away from a system of recognition and reward based on demonstrated job competency to a system based on participation in activities. Though participation in continuing education activities should enhance someone's ability to contribute to their job and library, it is conceivable for someone to participate in such activities without any improvement in performance or contribution of new ideas or approaches. Therefore, recognition and reward should always be focused on . . . performance and not on the single fact of participation in certain activities.[20]

What libraries need are not specific policies on recognition and reward for continuing education but well-defined criteria explaining how personal growth, development, and contributions as demonstrated through job performance will be recognized and rewarded in the library.

Continuing education should be viewed as complementary to staff development. There should be a clear understanding of the manner and extent to which the library will support continuing education, as well as of the role that supervisors will play in providing support and direction to employees as they develop a plan for their continued growth and development. As Martell and Dougherty observe:

> Since continuing education is often used for strictly personal objectives, library administrators may feel dubious about the organizational benefits. This feeling should not be allowed to obscure the indirect benefits—the inner satisfaction employees hold toward the library—as a result of a responsive staff program. Any manager wishing to promote a creative, dynamic library environment should look to continuing education programs as an integral link. Once employees have sensed an explicit managerial concern for their personal growth and well-being, they may begin to seek a more direct correlation between . . . [continuing education activities] and library work. Without this possibility, employees will find their life satisfaction in areas external to their library role.[21]

References

1. Charles R. Martell and Richard M. Dougherty, "The Role of Continuing Education and Training in Human Resources Development: An Administrator's Viewpoint," *Journal of Academic Librarianship* 4, no. 3 (July 1978): 153.
2. Carolyn A. Snyder and Nancy P. Saunders, "Continuing Education and Staff Development: Needs Assessment, Comprehensive Program Planning, and Evaluation," *Journal of Academic Librarianship* 4, no. 3 (July 1978): 114.
3. Martell and Dougherty, p. 155.
4. Miriam Drake, "Managing Innovation in Academic Libraries," *College and Research Libraries* 40 (Nov. 1979): 504.
5. Martell and Dougherty, p. 153.
6. Snyder and Saunders, p. 144.
7. Charles E. Kratz, "How to Know Your Staff's Needs," *Staff Development: A Practical Guide,* ed. Anne Grodzins Lipow, American Library Association/ Library Administration and Management Association, 1988.
8. Douglas L. Zweizig, "Organizational Assessment of Staff Development Needs: A Model and a Case Study," in *The Evaluation of Continuing Education for Professionals: A Systems View,* ed. Preston LeBreton et al. (Seattle, Wash.: The University of Washington, 1979), p. 181.
9. Ibid.
10. Geoffrey Bellman, "Surveying Your Supervisor Training Needs," *Training and Development Journal* 29 (February 1975): 32.
11. Ibid., p. 32.
12. Snyder and Saunders, p. 146.
13. Mildred H. Lowell, *Library Management Cases* (Metuchen, N.J.: Scarecrow Press, 1975); Mildred H. Lowell, *The Management of Libraries and Information Centers* (Metuchen, N.J.: Scarecrow Press, 1968); Thomas J. Galvin, *The Case Method in Library Education and In-Service Training* (Metuchen, N.J.: Scarecrow Press, 1973).
14. Barbara Conroy, *Library Staff Development and Continuing Education: Principles and Practices* (Littleton, Colo.: Libraries Unlimited, Inc., 1978), p. 191.
15. Clara C. Pratt, "Evaluating the Impact of Training on the World of Practice," in *The Evaluation of Continuing Education for Professionals.,* ed. Preston LeBreton et al. (Seattle, Wash.: The University of Washington, 1979), p. 350.
16. Ibid.
17. Martell and Dougherty, p. 153.
18. Ibid.
19. Robert D. Stueart, "Career Goals Achieved through Continuing Education," *College and Research Libraries NEWS* 41, no. 5 (May 1980): 140.
20. Sheila D. Creth, "Continuing Education—III," *College and Research Libraries NEWS* 39, no. 3 (June 1978): p. 160.
21. Martell and Dougherty, p. 154.

Bibliography

Abella, Kay Tyler. *Building Successful Training Programs: A Step-by-Step Guide*. Reading, Mass: Addison-Wesley, 1986.

Association of Research Libraries, Office of Management Studies, Systems and Procedures Exchange Center. SPEC Kits and FLYERS. Number 75. *Staff Development*. 1981.

Birnbrauer, Herman and Lynne A. Tyson. "How to Analyze Needs," *Training and Development Journal* 39 (August 1985): 53–58.

Breiting, Amelia, Marcia Dorey, and Deirdre Sockbeson. "Staff Development in College and University Libraries." *Special Libraries* 67 (July 1976): 305–10.

Brinkerhoff, Robert O. "Expanding Needs Analysis," *Training and Development Journal* 40: (February 1986): 64–65.

Cost Considerations in Continuing Education and Staff Development: A Bibliography. Chicago, Ill.: Library Education Division, Continuing Education Committee of the American Library Association, 1977.

Creth, Sheila D. *Effective on the Job Training: Developing Library Human Resources*. Chicago: American Library Association, 1986.

Jones, Noragh and Peter Jordon. "Staff Training and Development," in *Staff Management in Library and Information Work*. Hampshire, England: Gower, 1982.

Kearsley, Greg. *Cost, Benefits and Productivity in Training Systems* (Reading, Mass.: Addison-Wesley, 1982).

Knowles, Malcolm S. *The Adult Learner: A Neglected Species*, 3rd ed. (Houston: Gulf Publishing, 1984).

Mager, Robert F. *Preparing Instructional Objectives*, 2nd ed. (Belmont, Calif.: Pitman Learning, 1975).

Malinconico, S. Michael. "Technology, Change and People: Hearing the Resistance," *Library Journal* 108 (January 15, 1983): 112–

Mitchell, Betty Jo. "In-House Training of Supervisory Library Assistants in a Large Academic Library." *College and Research Libraries* 34 (March 1973): 144–49.

Prytherch, Ray. *Handbook of Library Training Practices*. Hants, England: Gower, 1986.

Rosenberg, Jane A. *Resource Notebook on Staff Development*. Washington, D.C.: Office of Management Studies, Association of Research Libraries, 1983.

Sheldon, Brooke E., ed. *Planning and Evaluating Library Training Programs. A Guide for Library Leaders, Staffs and Advisory Groups*. Tallahassee, Fla.: The Leadership Training Institute, School of Library Science, Florida State University, 1973.

Sokol, Ellen and John C. Bulyk. "The Truth About Training," *Journal of Information Systems Management* 2 (Fall 1985).

Staff Development in Libraries. A Directory of Organizations and Activities with a Staff Development Bibliography. Chicago, Ill.: Library Administration Division, Personnel Administration Section, American Library Association, 1978. 33pp.

Stueart, Robert D. "Preparing Libraries for Change," *Library Journal* 109 (September 15, 1984): 1724–1726.

Tracey, William R. *Designing Training and Development Systems*. New York: American Management Association, 1971.

Varlejs, Jana. "Cost Models for Staff Development in Academic Libraries," *Journal of Academic Librarianship* 12 (January 1987): 359–364.

Warncke, Ruth. *Planning Library Workshops and Institutes*. Chicago, Ill.: American Library Association, 1976.

Wehrenberg, Stephen B. "Supervisors as Trainers: The Long Term Gains of OJT," *Personnel Journal* 66, no. 4 (April 1987): 48–51.

Zemke, Ron, Linda Standke, and Philip Jones. *Designing and Delivering Cost Effective Training and Measuring the Results*. Minneapolis, MN: Lakewood Publications, 1981.

7
Performance Appraisal: Purpose and Techniques

Maxine Reneker
Virginia Steel

Since the perfect performance appraisal has yet to be devised, the topic continues to be covered in both library and management literature. Questions about its relevance and importance have extended into discussions of techniques used to select employees and to monitor their effectiveness in many different job responsibilities. Noteworthy articles on the theory and application of performance appraisal, often with an emphasis on the evaluation of managers, have appeared in the *Harvard Business Review*. In recent years *Personnel Journal and Personnel* have included many useful articles on performance appraisal, with practical advice to supervisors and managers.

Library personnel administrators and students of performance appraisal in libraries should read these especially to enhance their understanding of the subject:

1. McGregor, Douglas. "An Uneasy Look at Performance Appraisal," *Harvard Business Review* 50 (September-October 1972): 133–138.

2. *Performance Appraisal: Research and Practice*, edited by Thomas L. Whisler and Shirley F. Harper. New York: Holt, Rinehart and Winston, 1962.

3. Kellogg, Marion S. *What to Do About Performance Appraisal*. New York: American Management Association, 1965.

4. Johnson, Marjorie. "Performance Appraisal of Librarians—A Survey," *College and Research Libraries* 33 (September 1972): 359–367.

5. Yarbrough, Larry N. "Performance Appraisal in Academic and Research Libraries," *ARL Management Supplement* 3, May 1975.

6. Rader, Jennette. *Performance Evaluation: A Selected Bibliography*. Compiled for ALA OLPR, 1967, and its Supplement, May 1979.

7. *Personnel Performance Appraisal—A Guide for Libraries*. ALA LAMA PAS Staff Development Committee, June 1979.

8. *Performance Appraisal: An Annotated Bibliography*. Compiled by Berna L. Leyman. Reproduced in ALA ACRL College Libraries Section Continuing Education Committee CLIP Notes: College Library Information Packets, 1–80 Performance Appraisal, 1980.

9. *Performance Evaluation: A Management Basic for Librarians*. Edited by Jonathan A. Lindsey. Phoenix: Oryx Press, 1986.

The need for an in-depth knowledge of performance appraisal in libraries is usually triggered by the desire to evaluate the present system in use in one's organization with the objective of implementing it more effectively or developing a new system. The decision to develop a new system might follow on dissatisfaction with the present system or as the result of the introduction of the concept of merit pay or pay for performance. The identification of other types of appraisal systems that promise to be more effective may also occasion a hard look at the present system. Effectiveness of performance appraisal is judged by the ability of the system to provide the types of information regarding employee performance needed by the organization to achieve its objectives.

Performance appraisal, as used in this chapter, may be regarded as referring to comparatively formal, systematic programs of the evaluation of employee performance, developed to improve the quality of judgment applied to that performance and to insure frequent and timely assessments.[1] The aim of this chapter is to provide library managers and employees with information on the purpose of appraisals, the different methods and instruments in current use, and the advantages and disadvantages of each as well as techniques that will contribute to an effective implementation of an appraisal system. Throughout the chapter, references to business and library literature will be intermingled, but wherever possible, it will emphasize the specific problems concerning the evaluation of library employees and the characteristics relating to the performance of library tasks and functions.

IMPORTANCE OF THE APPRAISAL PROCESS

The importance of an effective performance appraisal system in an organization cannot be over-emphasized. The appraisal of an individual's performance on the job occurs continually in an organization, just as it occurs in all facets of an individual's life. Peers appraise each other's work, employees evaluate their supervisor's effectiveness in performing his or her job, and supervisors rate their subordinates' performance. If the appraisals are done well, they will provide the evaluator with an accurate and complete picture of the performance of the people being rated. These evaluations can then be used to assist the appraised individuals to do a better job in meeting organizational goals and objectives, to develop employees' potential to assume jobs requiring higher level qualifications, to alert them to areas of performance that are marginal or unsatisfactory, and to allow the organization to reward those individuals who contribute to achieving its objectives.

Evans and Rugaas[2] have identified sixteen "specific beliefs about the nature and function of" performance appraisal systems:

1. The process is essential to good management.
2. The process is natural or normal.
3. The process is the only reasonable method available for assuring at least minimal performance.
4. The process is the only valid basis for granting or withdrawing employee economic benefits.
5. The process is the primary means of maintaining control of staff productivity.
6. The process is essential for growth and well-being of the individual employee.
7. The process is an important element in an effective system of motivation.
8. The process is essential in work orientation programs.
9. The process is or can be an objective assessment of an individual's strengths and weaknesses.
10. The process is primarily directed toward the subordinate.
11. The process is continuous and reflects a careful analysis of the individual's daily performance.
12. The process is equally effective whether carried out by the supervisor or the employee's peers.
13. The process is concerned with all aspects of an individual's work, not just the performance of the assigned duties.
14. The process is useful in assessing an employee's future and potential progress in the organization.
15. The process is essential in planning organizational personnel needs for the present and the immediate future.
16. The process is important in counseling and suggesting areas of improvement that the individual should achieve if the individual hopes to gain more responsible positions either in the organization or outside it.

If appraisals are handled badly, they can be extremely harmful to the organization and greatly undermine the esteem of both the employee being evaluated and the supervisor.[3] Poor appraisals can be very costly to the organization when they result in poor production or service or the failure to improve poor service. Other costs include absenteeism and turnover, the promotion of an employee who does not have the abilities to handle a higher-level position, and the failure to encourage employees with good potential to develop that potential and to apply for promotions.

John Rizzo underscores the importance of the appraisal process in the introduction to his chapter on employee appraisal:

It is a fact of organizational life that employees will be evaluated and conclusions will be drawn about their value to the organization. These conclusions will affect each employee in different ways. Destinies will be shaped in their current work roles. Careers could be affected beyond the confines of their current job. In these ways evaluation is a serious matter and represents a critical managerial function.[4]

Just as the importance of the process needs to be emphasized, so does the difficulty of implementing an effective system. In an often-quoted article, Douglas McGregor cites the resistance of supervisors to performing their function as evaluators.[5] Beatty and Schneier expand on the problem: "There is probably no program as difficult for many in personnel to implement effectively as performance appraisal. Whether it be the uneasiness resulting from judging others, the hesitation to confront workers with poor performance or the failure to remove one's biases from the rating process, performance appraisal systems are frequently troublesome."[6]

From 1975 to 1982, Evans conducted an informal survey of librarians' attitudes towards performance appraisal which asked the following questions and elicited the subsequent responses:[7]

1. Is formal performance appraisal necessary for good supervision?
2. Do you feel confident and "comfortable" in conducting a performance appraisal?
3. Do you think the system provides a factual assessment of the employee's job performance?
4. Do you think the process has a positive influence on the employee's job performance?
5. Do you think the process can help improve or correct an employee's job performance?

	% Yes	% No
Question 1	90.6	9.4
Question 2	16.7	83.3
Question 3	47.1	52.9
Question 4	13.0	87.0
Question 5	2.7	97.3

As Evans notes, "it appears that this group of 407 persons, although predominantly feeling that performance appraisal is important, seems to have little or no confidence in the value of the process."[8]

Creth specifies the following reasons for the failure of appraisal systems:

Problems with performance evaluation are numerous but can be generally put into the following categories:

1. Supervisor lacks objective information on which to evaluate.
2. Supervisor has not determined the basis for the evaluation in advance.
3. Supervisor is poorly prepared and/or trained to conduct an evaluation. . . .

Too often evaluation interviews and the written evaluations become meaningless because nothing substantive is being said by either the supervisor or the employee.[9]

The alternative to formal, systematic evaluations are informal judgments of supervisors or seniority.[10] Despite the difficulties of implementing formal systems, certainly the advantages of regular feedback to employees concerning their contributions to the organization and areas of needed improvement are of sufficient value to warrant the formal program. Few managers would agree that seniority alone should form the basis for salary and promotion decisions in libraries. Informal evaluation systems also may be suspect legally due to their inherent inconsistencies and lack of peer involvement.

APPRAISAL IS A LINE FUNCTION

The evaluation of an individual employee's performance on the job is a primary responsibility of the person's supervisor. It is the supervisor who analyzes the job to be done, trains the employee to do it, sets the job performance standards, and measures the work of the employee against them. These functions may be performed in conjunction with others, particularly with the employee, who may participate in setting his or her performance goals and standards, and with peers who evaluate performance for promotion, merit pay, and tenure decisions. But ultimately it is the supervisor who has the responsibility for seeing that the work of the department is performed. In addition, supervisors as line managers have an obligation to let employees know what level of performance is expected of them and to provide them with frequent feedback on how they are measuring up to these expectations.

Performance appraisal is therefore ultimately a line responsibility.[11] The function of the personnel administrator is to provide the supervisor with assistance in the performance of this function. The personnel department of the library or the parent organization provides expertise to the library's management team when it considers establishing a new system, or reviews the implementation of the current system for effectiveness or compliance with new laws or executive orders. It may monitor the fairness of ratings across departments. It provides training to the supervisors and raters in evaluating validly and reliably and to employees in writing effective goals and self appraisal statements. In addition, it may maintain the files of appraisals, alert supervisors when it is time to perform them, and compile composite evaluations if multiple raters are involved in the appraisal process.

PURPOSE OF PERFORMANCE APPRAISAL

Improve Performance of the Organization

"A library's performance appraisal system has the broad purpose of improving the library's performance of its organizational service goals. . . ."[12] This statement is taken from the introduction to the staff performance evaluation program at McGill University Libraries. In its document, "Personnel Performance Appraisal—A Guide for Libraries" the Staff Development Committee of the Personnel Administration Section of the Library Administration and Management Association of ALA states the same principle as follows:

> Personnel appraisal is an integral part of supervision and should be used as a means toward the realization of organizational goals in three principal ways:
> 1. human resources within the library are inventoried for utilization and development;
> 2. communication is stimulated;
> 3. individual employees are motivated to improve their performance and to work toward organizational goals.[13]

Libraries, as service organizations, are heavily labor-intensive. In order to accomplish such goals as the provision of books and other sources of information to their clients, they must have library staff members who perform their duties at the highest levels possible. To perform at this level, employees must understand what the organization is attempting to accomplish, how their tasks relate to organizational goals, exactly what is expected from them so that they might perform those tasks well, and any areas of their performance that need improvement.

Some performance appraisal systems are designed to address directly the definition of organizational goals. In addition, they assist employees in relating the goals of the organization to their perception of their individual role in the organization. These systems may be characterized as goals-based evaluation systems.

The literature on strategic planning reinforces the idea that goals-based performance appraisal systems must be tied to the formalized goals of the organization. In implementing such an evaluation system one of the primary responsibilities of library directors and other members of the library's management team is to analyze the informational and service needs of the institution or communities they serve and then translate these needs into goals for the organization. Employees at all levels in the organization may contribute to the setting of these goals, but it is ultimately the responsibility of the library managers to see that the goals are valid and realistic. Odiorne warns that if management cannot define organizational goals, then subordinates cannot help the organization meet its goals.[14]

Once these overall organizational goals have been established, division and unit goals flow from them, translated by middle management and supervisors into jobs and tasks designed to achieve them. At this point in the goal-setting process, individual employees are involved in establishing the goals for performance of their responsibilities for the next evaluation period. The review of job duties, the mutual setting of goals conducted by the employee and the supervisor, and the communication and explicit statement of mutual expectations contributes greatly to the ability of the employee to achieve the objectives. He or she must, however, have a clear understanding of how these objectives can be reached.

The University of Connecticut Library has implemented a performance appraisal system for professional employees in which written performance appraisal goals are related, in a narrative evaluation format, to job responsibilities. Quantified standards for the measurement of successful achievement are provided when possible. The appraisal process includes not only evaluation of performance in meeting the goals, but suggestions for addressing the developmental needs of the employee and estimating the employee's potential to develop skills and abilities within the context of the present job assignment.[15]

Stanford University Libraries implements a similar "Annual Career Development Review" for its academic and career staff, including a statement of specific goals to be worked on during the coming year. The supervisors' instructions issued with the program note that the employees' performance should be described in terms of how well the employee carries out the responsibilities in his or her job description in terms of: "a. levels of competence, b. productivity, c. contributions to the objectives of the Library, and the University, d. individual potential and career development, and e. communications."[16] A list of goals is proposed separately by the supervisor and librarian and discussed in the evaluation conference. The goals instruction paragraph indicates that the goals should "relate to the goals and objectives of the department and to the position description of the employee."[17]

McGill's staff performance evaluation program gives full definitions of library objectives, departmental goals, unit goals, unit performance standards, individual goals, and individual performance standards. It has sections on the formulation of these goals and standards, with guidelines for the periodic review of unit goals and standards and periodic evaluation of individual performance. It links activities with observable results, and goals with performance standards.[18]

Improve Individual Performance

Improvement of the individual's performance is one of the most important components of the goals-based systems. This component tends to be lost in the grandiose discussion of meeting organizational goals. Nevertheless, one of the most effective ways of improving organizational performance, or effectiveness, is to improve the performance, or production, of the individual employee. A good performance appraisal system identifies areas of performance that are weak and provides a mechanism for determining precisely how performance can be improved. A good system stresses the areas of performance that are critical to the successful functioning of the employee in his or her particular position and will place less emphasis on less critical areas. It will stimulate the supervisor to suggest specific approaches for achieving better performance, and most importantly, it will assist in motivating the employee to improve.

Jeffrey Gardner has noted that "most librarians have a desire to achieve a high standard of performance as an element of self-image. This is merely saying that librarians, like most individuals, want to perform well. Related to this is the motivational factor of the need for recognition from within the organization: good performance must be perceived, understood, and formally recognized if it is to be reinforced."[19]

The improvement of performance implies a change in behavior to effect the improvement. Howard Smith and Paul Brouwer write, "Any appraisal and development system makes assumptions about motivations and behavior. . . . An organization gets better performance from people when it operates on the expectation that people want meaningful involvement in work and want to contribute to the achievement of organizational goals."[20]

It is clear that not all employees have high achievement needs that can be directed to increasing their performance level. However, many of the professional and support staff in libraries are what has been described as high-growth need employees[21] and do demonstrate the strong needs for personal accomplishment, for learning and developing, and for being stimulated and challenged. Research has shown that opening feedback channels is one way to produce high levels of internal work motivation, quality work performance, and job satisfaction, as well as low absenteeism and turnover. Such feedback includes knowledge of results of employees' work, both directly from performance measures as they do the job and from recognition by the organization, their supervisor, and their peers that they are performing effectively.[22]

John Rizzo cites the controlling of current performance as one of four purposes of appraisals. In his view, "concerns about current performance lie at the heart of the superior-subordinate relationship and at the heart of the organizational process."[23] He sees in the various techniques of participative planning, work planning and review, management by objectives, job analysis, delegation and job design, the means to develop performance by defining it, monitoring it, providing feedback, administering rewards, and developing skills.[24] James Michalko sees performance improvement coming from "increased commitment through participation in goal setting, communication with supervisors, accurate feedback, and a sense of direct responsibility."[25]

Larry Yarbrough also discusses performance improvement at length in the *ARL Management Supplement* devoted to performance appraisal in academic and research libraries. He broadens the traditional concept of performance improvement that results from judgment on the individual's actions by including three other variables affecting a person's performance: the job itself, the supervisor, and the organizational environment.

According to Yarbrough, taking these into account enlarges the potential for significant improvement by using job enrichment; job redesign; reordering of job priorities; redefinition of the supervisor's role; determination of what the supervisor might do, stop doing, or do differently to help the subordinate; clarification of the supervisor's expectations; changes in the nature and quality of communications; redefinition of organizational priorities; and restructuring of the organization.[26] Although these factors go beyond the scope of performance appraisal, it can identify the need for them.

How does the old-time concept of the performance review as a time for the supervisor to distribute praise and a little criticism for the past year's performance fit into the new conceptual picture? According to Cederblom, "evidence suggests that praise by the supervisors may improve interview outcomes, but only if presented effectively . . . criticism from superior to subordinate tends to function ineffectively or negatively."[27] Criticism was shown to have a negative effect on performance in a widely cited study at General Electric.[28] Criticism does serve the function of pointing out the fact that an employee is not performing at the level expected by his supervisor; however, it does not motivate the employee to improve her or his performance, or show the employee ways in which to meet expectations.[29]

Thomas Wilson wrote a useful article on "Making Negative Feed-back Work." He talks about the need for the employee's understanding and acceptance of the feedback. The article points out, "To be useful, negative feedback must be intended to help the recipient—not to 'unload' on the person."[30]

There are also positive and negative aspects to the distribution of praise. In certain circumstances it can be interpreted as an indication that earlier performance was unsatisfactory, or as a means of establishing the supervisor in a superior position by condescending to praise the subordinate. Most of us would say from our own experience that praise from someone whose opinion we value does motivate us to continue the behavior for which we received the praise.

The question as posed in current research is whether the praise itself, or the knowledge of the results of behavior that produced the praise, is the significant motivator. Praise in this context is seen as a "specific type of feedback cue that is evaluative in nature . . . external to the receiver, and . . . is based on knowledge of results concerning the employee's present performance as it relates to the goal set or the employee's previous level of performance."[31] Praise, used in conjunction with goal setting, does seem to enhance performance, perhaps by enabling employees to accept the goals and by supporting their efforts to continue to attain them.[32]

Before we leave the subject of the use of appraisal to improve individual performance, it is important to emphasize that an employee must know what kinds of results and what kinds of behaviors are expected of him to perform a job well. In DeProspo's succinct statement, "Evaluation then can only succeed, by definition, when it differentiates performance."[33] To differentiate good from poor performance requires job descriptions written in terms of both the specific behaviors required and the results which the behaviors[34] will generate under a specific set of circumstances. A system of appraisal that not only establishes goals for good future performance but also identifies the kinds of behavior that are most likely to lead to their achievement will best assist the employee to improve his or her performance.

In order to be legally defensible, Hodge recommends that "performance expected of employees is communicated and goals and objectives of the ratee's job are made clear in terms of behavior and the results to be achieved.[35] Although one hopes never to have to defend personnel actions in court, it is nevertheless good personnel practice for the organization, supervisors, and subordinates to clearly communicate performance expectations and anticipated results and accurately document how well an employee has met the expectations and results.

Appraisal for Employee Development

The use of performance appraisal to assess an employee's potential to perform in other, presumably high-level positions, has two purposes. The first is to identify particular strengths of the individual on which he or she can build or, alternately, areas of weakness that need correction. The employee can correct these deficiencies either by experience or formal study to then be qualified to assume other positions.

The second purpose of such a program is to identify individuals in the organization who can assume positions as they become vacant.[36] Although Sheila Creth's study of manpower planning in libraries reveals a very low state of the art,[37] libraries do have career ladders, formally or informally defined. Also, library personnel administrators and managers have specific concepts of skills, abilities, and training that individuals need to possess to be qualified to hold these positions. An appraisal system that ignores the possibility of using the assessment of an employee's performance and his or her abilities and skills misses the most logical opportunity an organization has to gather this data.

The Stanford University Instructions for Performance appraisal form instructs the supervisor to address an employee's "individual potential and career development." It also instructs the employee "to identify areas in which the libraries can help by providing opportunities for further professional growth."[38] Rizzo recommends that these appraisals be conducted at a different time so that this function is kept a separate and critical one. He notes the appropriate role of personnel administrators "or other relevant specialists" in the process to identify training needs and maintain succession and manpower plans.[39]

The United States Office of Personnel Management *Guide for Improving Performance Appraisal: A Handbook* also addresses the problems of the use of the same system for appraising current performance and future potential. In the section on merit promotion, the guide states, "A supervisory appraisal of performance in the present job is a part of assessing an employee's qualifications for another position. The more similar the duties of the two positions are, the more valid is past performance in predicting future performance.[40]

Supervisors and personnel administrators must be aware of the risk to individuals in appointing them to positions in which they need to grow in order to succeed. They also need to be aware of the two types of error latent in the assessment for promotion: the rejection of candidates who would have succeeded, and the selection of those who will fail.[41]

The third purpose of using performance appraisal for employee development is to provide continuing nonmonetary motivation for good performance. Although Rothstein[42] presents a gloomy picture of a "greying" library work force that will not change significantly in the near future, through performance evaluation and discussion it is possible to enlarge and enrich employees' jobs so that they will remain interested and not feel that they have plateaued. Career planning may be tied to this discussion in order to assist employees in deciding how they would like to develop their careers and "where they might like to go from here."

For employees whose future plans include aspirations for higher-level positions, moving to another geographic location, or leaving the job market temporarily to rear children, the appraisal review is a good time to assess their current level of education and experience and to plan realistic job-hunting strategies, or to pursue additional academic and/or continuing education programs.

Performance Appraisal as a Basis for Salary Allocation

The issue of the relationship of salary distribution to appraisal is a complex one involving several components. One must first question whether the knowledge that salary monies are riding on an appraisal works against the purpose of performance improvement. Some writers believe that employees are so concerned with the dollars related to the evaluation that the emphasis of the appraisal interview becomes a justification of supervisory action and past performance, rather than a means of further improvement.[43] On the other hand, those employees who do perform in a superior manner should have their higher contribution to organizational effectiveness recognized, not only by words on a form, but by higher salary.[44]

Many businesses and libraries do attempt to relate salary increases directly to evaluation decisions. "Pay for performance" is a concept that is gaining increasing support as a means of linking performance with compensation. Some organizations, however, particularly those with civil service systems, do not have the potential for relating variations in performance to differentials in salary. Often these systems require an evaluation for the purpose of justifying a set increase by movement into the next step of the salary scale.[45] If the appraisal indicates that the performance is unsatisfactory, then the increase is withheld, and corrective or disciplinary action instituted.

Occasionally civil service systems will also have the potential for granting larger increases as a reward for superior performance. In Arizona, the Board of Regents establishes general parameters for salary increases. Each state university then sets percentages or levels of merit that individuals may receive. If an individual is recommended for more than the top merit level, the Board of Regents must approve the action. Krull recommends a merit plan for public libraries that relates position of the current salary within the salary range for a position to levels of overall performance as assessed by a written performance appraisal.[46]

In most libraries salary increases come from a specific allocation of funds in a fixed amount. Therefore, a larger increase to one individual will mean a lower increase for another individual. For obvious reasons this zero-sum aspect of merit increases should not be emphasized. Paul Thompson and Gene Dalton describe the consequences of a system in which high performers were given raises earlier in the year and in a more visible manner than lower performers, in an attempt to reward good performers and stimulate performance improvement. The system backfired for several reasons: high-rated employees were unhappy when they discovered others received raises before them, employees rated average were unhappy with this designation, and poor performers became insecure and reluctant to leave the organization because they were afraid they could not succeed elsewhere.[47]

Salary increases should be greater for employees who perform better. Libraries cannot, however, tie salary directly to results, like sales organizations or factories paying workers on a by-piece rate. Although there may be some merit (no pun intended) in paying catalogers for the number of titles cataloged or shelvers for correctly shelved books, such systems based entirely on quantitative standards without regard for quality are not likely to be implemented in the near future. Therefore, appraisal systems that distinguish between five to ten levels of performance and tie salary increases to these ratings, discretely and from goal-setting or performance-improvement sessions, appear to combine the advantages of reward for superior performance with a deemphasis on pitting one employee against another for dollars in the salary pot.

The University of Chicago Library distributes its pool of dollars available for salary increases based on the recommendation of department and division heads. Each division head allocates the pool for his or her group of employees. The distribution of monies is based on supervisory ratings in a range of four categories based upon a performance evaluation, with a written justification required of the supervisor to substantiate his or her rating. The pool of monies available to the division head is based on the percentage which the salaries in each division constitute of the total salary expenditure for the library.[48]

Other libraries may include a review by a committee of peers in the process of the distribution of salary monies. At the University of Colorado, the supervisor assigns up to four points in the merit distribution process. Up to another full point is based on an assessment of professional activities; this assessment is performed by the libraries' Review Committee.[49]

At institutions where employees are represented by collective-bargaining agents, salary raises may be specified in the contract negotiated at particular intervals. For example, members of the University of Connecticut Professional Employees' Association are evaluated on a goals-based system. Salary increases also include a cost of living component as well as an annual increment for longevity tied to satisfactory job performance. There is, however, a small pool of additional monies available for merit increases tied to a separate evaluation and recommendation process.[50]

At Kent State University annual performance reviews are used as documentation for merit money distribution within the Collective Bargaining Agreement. Library Administration Faculty wishing to be considered for merit must make written application to the Director of Libraries and furnish appropriate documentation, including the annual performance evaluation, personnel folder items, and a summary of activities in the merit evaluation period.[51]

Appraisal for Promotion in Rank and Tenure

An area of appraisal unique to academic libraries is evaluation for promotion in academic rank and for decisions relating to tenure. These appraisals are conducted at institutions where the professional library staff are on faculty or academic staff appointments, as well as in institutions having systems of professional rank instead of, or in addition to, differing levels of positions determined by a job evaluation structure. Often, the performance evaluations conducted for the purposes of improving organizational and individual performance serve as important components of the evaluation process for promotion in rank.

In many university libraries, for example, Arizona State University Libraries, the criteria for promotion, and the equivalent of tenure, continuing appointment, closely follow the three criteria for similar personnel actions for the faculty: job performance, professional development, and service. At the University of California at Riverside, four criteria are used: professional competence and quality of service within the library, professional activity outside the library, community and public activity, research and other creative activity.[52] In both of these systems the performance appraisal provides information which assists evaluators to determine whether the criteria have been met.

Appraisal for Disciplinary Action and Termination

Most organizations have a set of procedures to follow when an employee's performance is so poor that his or her supervisor begins to consider the necessity of involuntary termination. These procedures are designed for two purposes: to establish a series of actions by which an employee is informed that he or she is not performing up to expected standards and is in jeopardy of disciplinary action or termination, and to provide the employee with clearly stated standards or expectations which he or she must meet to avoid the action.

This type of appraisal differs in emphasis from a regular appraisal for improvement because it begins with evidence or an assumption that standards are not being met. The employee is told in very specific terms what he or she has to do in a specific time period, which is shorter than, or on a different schedule from, the regular appraisal process.

Allan and Reynolds provide a model for identifying, analyzing, and solving performance problems. Although they do not discuss the use of performance appraisal instruments in their article, their model relies upon the continual evaluation of performance and feedback between supervisor and employee inherent in the performance appraisal process in order to reach an acceptable conclusion to these types of personnel problems.[53]

During appraisal for disciplinary action, the supervisor is required to document specifically what standards, performance areas, or behaviors are not being met; often this requires documentation of specific incidents or failures for some time previous to the action. Where employees are covered by collective bargaining agreements or civil service regulations the procedures governing these actions, and the documentation required to implement them, are often elaborate. The rules are written with the point of view of protecting the employee in his or her position. That is, the employee is viewed as having a "right" to a position or job until the supervisor and employer can demonstrate clearly that the employee has violated specific rules.

Marion Kellogg outlines the following seven steps for termination appraisal and action. The manager

1. Makes a formal appraisal and documents it
2. Communicates the appraisal to the employee
3. Determines the reasons for poor performance and makes constructive suggestions for improvement
4. Establishes a probationary period and develops work plans
5. Provides adequate coaching and support during the probationary period
6. Summarizes and documents his appraisal of performance during this period
7. Communicates the final decision to the employee[54]

Often these steps are undertaken with the guidance of the personnel officer or policies of the library or parent institution, with a view to protecting the supervisors and the institution from the expense of justifying the actions to an executive or judiciary body.

In an enlightening article on performance appraisal and terminations, Barrett and Kernan review court decisions examining cases in which terminations were defended on the basis of performance appraisals. In those cases in which employers successfully defended their termination decisions, three major themes were identified:

1. Courts do not wish to decide if performance appraisal systems are just or unfair or whether they conform in all respects to accepted professional standards. They only wish to rule on whether or not performance appraisals discriminate. That is, does the organization treat similarly situated individuals differently?
2. Courts seem to look favorably on the use of a review system by upper-level personnel to prevent individual bias.
3. Courts also react favorably to the use of performance counseling designed to help employees improve substandard performance.[55]

Appraisal for Validation of Selection Techniques

Personnel management practices regarding the use of performance appraisal to test the effectiveness of other personnel-related decisions has come a long way since 1975 when Alan Patz wrote, "Virtually no analyses of performance appraisal are performed to test the efficacy of more complex manpower policies and practices such as job rotation or hiring."[56]

The "Guidelines on Employee Selection Procedures" first published in 1970 states:

> The work behaviors or other criteria of employee adequacy which the test is intended to predict or identify must be fully described ... the appraisal form(s) and instructions to the rater(s) must be included as part of the validation evidence. Such criteria may include measures other than actual work proficiency, such as ... supervisory ratings. ... Whatever criteria are used they must represent major or critical work as revealed by careful job analyses.
>
> In view of the possibility of bias inherent in subjective evaluations, supervisory rating techniques should be closely examined for evidence of bias. ... The general point is that all criteria need to be examined to insure freedom from factors which would unfairly depress the scores of minority groups.[57]

The 1970 Guidelines were initially directed toward selection procedures. Subsequent court decisions have held that the same principles apply to performance appraisal systems. The "New Uniform Guidelines on Employee Selection Procedures," which became effective June 1, 1978, reflect these decisions, applying to "tests and other selection procedures which are used as a basis for any employment decision.

Employment decisions include but are not limited to hiring, promotion, demotion . . . , referral, retention." According to this definition, performance appraisal is a selection procedure and as such may be examined by the courts.[58]

Performance appraisals are logical tools to use to validate the organization's selection decisions. Do the employees we hire perform better than those who were screened out by our selection processes? If not, we should use other tools. If so, do we wish to use these tools even if they are found to have "adverse impact" on members of minority groups protected by Title VII of the Civil Rights Act and Executive Orders 11246, 11375, and 11758? If adverse impact exists, the burden of proof shifts to the employer to demonstrate that the procedure used is related to job performance. If the test of job relatedness cannot be demonstrated to the court's satisfaction, the employer is liable.[59]

In order to use performance appraisals as valid measures for justifying the validity of selection procedures, the appraisals themselves now have to have demonstrated validity. Richard Beatty and Craig Schneier list the following criteria that performance appraisal objectives must meet to validate selection techniques:

1. Job relatedness, comprehensive list of dimensions tapping the behavioral domain of the job and/or
2. Systematic job analysis to derive criteria; and/or
3. Assessment of inter-rater reliability; and/or
4. Professional, objective administration of format; and/or
5. Daily continual observation of ratee performance by raters.[60]

Two other aspects of appraisal that must be guarded against for potential review by the courts are listed by William Holley and Herbert Feild:

1. Ratings (that) have been based on rater's evaluations of subjective or vague factors;
2. Racial, sexual, etc. biases of raters (that) may have influenced the ratings given to ratees.[61]

Beatty and Schneier stress that the use of behaviorally anchored rating scales is the most effective appraisal technique for satisfying the criteria needed to validate selection.[62] These scales are discussed in more detail later in the chapter.

Holley and Feild also recommend systems based on MBO (Management by Objective) or output measures as potentially acceptable under the framework of the Equal Opportunity Commission and court requirements.[63]

Research done under the Library Selection Project by the Selection Consulting Center, with funds administered by the California State Library, attempted to validate selection criteria of entry-level professionals in libraries in California. The object of Phase III of the project was to statistically link performance on key job dimensions to an index of promotability to higher-level positions. It is noteworthy that the measures of candidates' knowledge and ability necessary for successful performance in the entry-level librarian positions were rated during the pre-employment selection process on five-point, behaviorally anchored rating scales. However, because of changes in priorities and funding problems the Library Selection Project has not been implemented.[64]

Appraisal at the End of Probationary Periods

Close monitoring of performance during an employee's probationary period is a critical supervisory function. During the period of training the employee is particularly receptive to suggestions for improvements in the way he or she is performing, because the tasks and tools of the position are still being learned. The supervisor needs to set up specific review dates and expected standards of performance. Too often supervisors neglect those periodic reviews during probation, then come to the end of the period not having a clear idea of whether or not the employee can do the job. Because there is no clear basis for recommending termination, the supervisor gives the marginal employee a satisfactory evaluation, only to discover several months later that the employee is not performing successfully and probably will never do well. At best, this situation leads into the review for disciplinary action and termination. At worst, if the employee is represented by a collective bargaining contract or civil service regulations, termination on the basis of inadequate performance may be a difficult and lengthy process.[65]

USE OF APPRAISAL SYSTEMS

How prevalent is the use of formal appraisal systems in libraries, and what types of systems are used more than others? Several surveys provide a general indication of trends in libraries' use of performance appraisals.

In 1962 Marjorie Johnson reported on a survey of responses from 138 university libraries with more than fifteen librarians on the staff. Almost 95 percent had some form of appraisal, ranging from casual observation with no written records to lengthy interviews based on results recorded on a form. The forms used were categorized as follows: 35 (25%) rating sheet types; 17 (12%) teaching faculty evaluation types;

and 22 (16%) based on special competencies of librarians. Forty-three respondents indicated they were considering revising their present techniques.[66]

In a 1980 survey of thirteen hundred public libraries and over one thousand academic libraries, Nancy Patton Van Zant reports the following results based on the responses of 510 public libraries and 416 academic libraries. The three tables on page 171 are from *Personnel Policies in Libraries*.[67] Unfortunately Van Zant reports no results relating to the type of appraisal methods used.

A 1987 survey by the Association of Research Libraries yielded information about the system in use in seventy-one academic research libraries.[68] The survey results show heavy reliance on qualitative judgment with a few libraries associating weighted or unweighted numerical scores with criteria to derive a total score for ranking purposes. It is clear that the performance appraisal systems in those libraries that responded are undergoing change. In forty-seven libraries the criteria in use have undergone revision or are being revised, fifty-six of the libraries reported revision to the procedures either in progress or occurring within the past five years.

Several surveys on the use of performance appraisals in the corporate world in the past decade have been published in the business literature. In 1983 Hewitt Associates surveyed 625 employers across the U.S. and found that 88 percent had formal performance appraisals of which 38 percent used MBO, 24 percent factor-rating scale, 19 percent combination, 9 percent trait rating scale, 8 percent essay, 1 percent critical incident, 1 percent BARS, and less than 1 percent paired comparison.[69]

In the mid-1970s two other surveys of performance appraisal usage were published in *Personnel Journal*. Of 216 responses from organizations belonging to the Personnel and Industrial Relations Association, Los Angeles, 57 percent used a rating scale, 25 percent essay, 12 percent MBO, and other types 6 percent. In 98 percent of the organizations, the immediate supervisor was involved in making the appraisals; in 78 percent the supervisor had sole responsibility for them.[70]

Robert Zawacki and Robert Taylor surveyed 130 firms throughout the United States with a view to determining if organizational satisfaction with the system was related to a dichotomy of traditional versus collaborative techniques. Results from forty-six responses show that although firms anticipating changing their systems were going from traditional to more results-oriented collaborative approaches, firms using those approaches were no more satisfied than those using traditional methods.[71]

Finally, Kenneth Teel reports on the results of a recent survey of corporations with headquarters in California: 78 percent use both

TABLE 1. Are Library employees given performance evaluations?

	Yes	No
Public libraries serving population of less than 20,000	34	29
Public libraries serving population of 20,000 to 99,999	196	58
Public libraries serving population of 100,000 and up	180	17
Academic libraries: four-year colleges	143	35
Academic libraries: universities	217	21

TABLE 2. How are these evaluations used?

	Reappointments, Promotions	Tenure	Demotion	Self-Improvement	Salary Raises	Dismissal
Public libraries serving population of less than 20,000	9	0	2	23	22	13
Public libraries serving population of 20,000 to 99,999	50	32	46	153	155	100
Public libraries serving population of 100,000 and up	79	44	82	136	129	130
Academic libraries: four-year colleges	98	62	9	98	96	70
Academic libraries: universities	170	147	49	191	188	156

TABLE 3. Who conducts performance evaluations?

	Supervisors	Supervisors and Peers	Peers	Supervisors and Subordinates	Peers and Subordinates	Supervisors, Peers and Subordinates	Self and Others
Public libraries serving population of less than 20,000	22	1			1		3
Public libraries serving population of 20,000 to 99,999	187	2		3		3	6
Public libraries serving population of 100,000 and up	171	6					3
Academic libraries: four-year colleges	111	23	11			14	
Academic libraries: universities	135	39		4	1	14	6

narrative approaches and ratings, while only 17 percent use narrative forms alone. He reports a definite trend toward frequent modification in the systems, though he describes the changes as evolutionary rather than revolutionary. A common change is the addition of sections asking for statements of employee achievements, objectives, and plans.[72]

TYPES OF APPRAISAL SYSTEMS

In discussing the types of appraisal systems, four separate categorizations must be kept in mind. Too often when supervisors or managers are asked to describe the type of system in use in their library they resort to a discussion of the form that is used. The form is only the paper-and-pencil tool of the type of appraisal system, which in itself is only a tool to measure performance. Thus, a rating scale, a paired comparison, or a critical incident technique can be used, separately or in conjunction with each other, to measure performance.

Almost any standard text on personnel administration will include a description of appraisal methods. The looseleaf service *Employment Coordinator* gives a brief but comprehensive overview of performance appraisal techniques.[73] Rizzo[74] has an excellent discussion in *Management for Librarians*, though unfortunately he does not include descriptions specifically oriented to work in libraries.

When considering appraisal systems, it is important to keep in mind not only the purposes for which the system is designed, but what we are attempting to evaluate or measure, what techniques or formats we will use to make the measurements, against whom or what the measurements are made, and who will make them.

In answering the first question, it is useful to adopt Beatty and Schneier's[75] distinctions between behavior, performance, and effectiveness:

1. Behavior is simply activity or what people do on the job
2. Performance is behavior evaluated for desirability or efficacy on the job
3. Effectiveness refers to the outcomes or results of varying degrees of performance.

In measuring behavior, performance, or effectiveness, what techniques or formats do we use?

1. Open-ended essays written on an overall or global basis or broken down into specific aspects
2. Ratings on a scale, either in a checklist or graphic form
3. Choices among people or statements of behavior or performance
4. Measures of output
5. Tests of proficiency

When we take the measurements, against whom or what do we take them?

1. Traits
2. Other employees doing the same or similar work
3. Standards of performance
4. Specific behaviors defining levels of performance
5. Goals established by the organization, individual, supervisor
6. A combination of measures

There are numbers of combinations of possible evaluators to answer the fourth question: the immediate supervisor, supplementary evaluators who rate specific aspects of a person's performance, the supervisor's supervisor, self, peers, and a combination of supervisor(s), self, and peers.

WHAT THE APPRAISAL SYSTEM MEASURES

Several things must be kept in mind when discussing the concept of performance. The first is to recognize that our measurement of perform-ance, i.e., behavior evaluated for desirability or efficacy, is a construct, or mental picture, of an ideal; our objective in the appraisal system is to "make the measure conform as closely as possible to the definition of the construct."[76]

If we picture the construct as one circle, and the measure as another, we are trying to create complete overlap between the two circles. In the portion of the circle representing measurement that does not overlap, we have measurement contamination—elements in the measure that are not in the construct, for instancy supervisory bias. In the portions of the circle representing the construct that do not overlap, we have measurement deficiency.

Cummings and Schwab suggest the example of a deficient measure is one that accounts only for quantity of output, but excludes quality. We must realize that our measures do not, and probably cannot, accurately and completely represent the desired behavior or results of behavior. We can only try to maximize the overlap—construct validity.[77]

The Fournies and Associates *Performance Appraisal Design Manual* states:

It is absolutely necessary to perceive the differences between individual abilities, personality characteristics, strategies of performance, goals, responsibilities, and the actual behaviors of each job. If we cannot accurately describe what is to be measured, perhaps we are measuring something we are unable to observe, or cannot be changed, or is irrelevant.[78]

Rizzo points out that multiple measures of performance can increase the area of the construct circle covered by the various measures. He is also correct in indicating that if two such measures are highly correlated, it is probably not reasonable to use them both. The appraisal system, including its criteria, must be practical—not excessive or time-consuming—and acceptable to those who use it.[79]

The system must also be reliable, that is, it must produce ratings that are consistent. Ratings of the same employee by the same rater at relatively close points in time (assuming there are no sudden or erratic performance changes) should be the same or very similar; this phenomenon is called intra-rater reliability. In addition, ratings by different raters who have the same knowledge or perspectives of the ratee's performance should also be consistent; the term for this is inter-rater reliability. If a performance criterion or appraisal system produces differing ratings of either type, the validity of the entire system is diminished. A system can be no more valid than the square of its reliability coefficients.

It should be noted that the more knowledge librarians have about what performance is; what influences it; and how individuals, supervisors, and organizations can manage it, the better library appraisal systems will be. The complexity of the concept of performance, of both individuals and organizations, is discussed at length by Hannabus.[80]

An understanding of the integrated model of the determinants of performance developed by Cummings and Schwab is helpful in this process of conceptualization. Performance is seen most directly as a consequence of the employee's ability and his or her motivations to perform. It displays graphically the interrelationship of organizational variables, ability, motivation, satisfaction, goal aspiration, and performance. It is useful in illustrating the complexity of the determinants of performance. "Both experimental research and field research strongly support the notion that account must be taken of a variety of variables often connected in complex ways if performance is going to be adequately predicted."[81]

Yarbrough listed the variables relevant to performance, which were cited earlier in the chapter.[82] The distinction between behavior, performance, and effectiveness emphasized by Beatty and Schneier is useful not only in sharpening our perceptions of what we are measuring, but also in categorizing the techniques and types of measures available to be used as components of appraisal systems.

TECHNIQUES FOR MEASURING PERFORMANCE

Open-ended Essays

Open-ended questions or narrative formats are popular because they allow one form or set of questions to be applied to many types of jobs. The open-ended format also allows the appraiser a great deal of freedom to record important incidents and examples of performance, and to explain in as brief or complete a manner as he or she feels necessary. Teel states that this format is better (than ratings) for work planning and review as well as documenting critical incidents.[83]

Schneier and Beatty categorize the global, single-question format as poor for feedback and development, however, [84] and suggest that it is very difficult to keep rater error from biasing the appraisal. When a number of different raters evaluate different groups of employees in an institution, it may also be difficult to compare performance based on these loosely structured essays. Open-ended essays are also time-consuming to prepare and may require more time than a supervisor is prepared to spend in order to provide a thorough evaluation of an employee's performance. The supervisor's writing skills may often unduly influence the outcome of a narrative performance evaluation.

Open-ended essays are frequently used in rating the performance of professional librarians in academic libraries. Often the instructions to the supervisors and employees writing these narratives include specific criteria to be addressed in the essays and, in those libraries using goals-based systems, discussions of the success in meeting specific goals is also a part of the essay.

Ratings on a Scale

Rating on a scale is a popular technique that has gained recent publicity and favor with the application of behavioral anchors to the scale. This type of evaluation system does not require a great deal of time to complete, and scores are easily translated into numerical ratings that can be used as the basis for salary adjustments. Rizzo[85] and Cummings and Schwab[86] provide a concise discussion of these graphic scales. Schneier and Beatty's second article in the three-part series in *Personnel Administrator* is devoted to the subject of developing Behaviorally-Anchored Rating Scales.[87] Hodge also discusses the development of a similar system in a library.[88] The evaluation forms from Oakland University reprinted in the College Library Information Packet I-80 provide examples of three kinds of these scales, used to rate probationary employees, administrative-professional employees, and students.[89]

Choices Among People or Statements of Behavior

The techniques of choices among people or forced choice among statements of behavior seem to be on the wane in current appraisal systems. Miner has a good explanation of the method by which each employee is compared with every other employee in a group.[90] Miner[91] and Rizzo[92] describe the "forced-choice" procedure, a technique designed to counteract rater-bias by disguising in a group of behavior descriptions those statements that were found to discriminate good versus poor performance when measured against external performance criteria. Raters choose one favorable and one unfavorable statement in each group of four statements. The selected statements that discriminate good from poor performance contribute to an overall performance score, while the "neutral" statements do not. No example of this type of comparison technique, nor of paired comparisons, has been identified in the research in library literature undertaken for this chapter. The technique is time-consuming to develop, and provides no feedback potential because the supervisors do not know which behavior statements are related to good performance.

Cummings and Schwab describe the weighted checklist technique, in which a rater chooses among statements of behavior determined to be related to successful or unsuccessful job performance. The rater is not forced to choose a statement, but simply indicates whether or not an appraisee engages in the bahavior. A total score is determined by summing the scores of the items checked.[93]

Measures of Output

Measures of output or other direct measures of performance indicate whether or not previously determined standards are met. Techniques such as Management by Objective, which normally include quantitative performance measures, flourish. Performance standards which justify ratings to give to catalogers and which emphasize the quantity and quality of titles cataloged are being implemented at the Library of Congress and the Center for Research Libraries.

At the National Library of Medicine performance standards are also being implemented; quantitative indexing standards distinguish less difficult, medium difficult, and most difficult articles, with rates of indexing varying from 4.0 to 5.0 articles per hour and a production range of 105 to 355 articles per month.[94]

Managers can easily be judged by whether or not they stay within or exceed certain budgets under their control. As program budgeting comes to libraries, measures such as interlibrary loan (ILL) transactions filled within a specified time or number of guides developed to assist in the use of key reference tools may be identified for inclusion in appraisal programs.

Tests of Proficiency

Two other techniques of appraisal deserve mention. In appraising an employee's knowledge, skills, and potential for promotion, proficiency tests, work simulations such as in-basket tests, leaderless group discussions, conflict resolution exercises, and budget analyses may be used in addition to evaluation of performance in the candidate's current job.

Assessment centers in particular have received much attention as techniques for selecting supervisors and managers in private industry.[95] The University of Washington Career Development and Assessment Center assessed eighty-nine librarians in a three-year experiment that proved the usefulness of applying assessment center technology to libraries.[96] The Association of Research Libraries Office of Management Studies workshops use similar techniques to train library managers.

AGAINST WHOM OR WHAT ARE THE MEASUREMENTS MADE?

We have discussed the concept of the construct of performance and how various measures of it may be deficient or contaminated. In what ways do appraisal systems typically attempt to measure the ideal of performance?

Trait-based Systems

We are all familiar with the trait-based systems that are currently in great disrepute. David Peele wrote feelingly concerning their potential abuse[97] and violation of "librarians' rights." Abstractions such as dependability, cooperativeness, judgment, and initiative still appear on many library appraisal forms. Yarbrough accurately states, "Despite the most careful definitions of the traits, some remain ambiguous or inappropriate when they are used to evaluate performance in a particular job."[98] For example, what does cooperativeness imply when related to a card filer's job? That the filer accepts his or her assignment eagerly? That the filer allows patrons access to the drawers in which he or she is filing? Or that the filer trades assignments with coworkers when asked?

What we have done, and what a rater must do, is to define the trait in terms of some behavior, job-related or not. If the filer does any or all of the three interpretations of cooperativeness listed above, is he or she a good filer? Is the filer performing the job better than an uncooperative filer, who will not trade work assignments or always looks disgusted at the amount of cards in the box? If it is an important job-related behavior to trade work assignments, wouldn't we be better off telling the filer that we value this behavior, and focusing the supervisor's attention on it when the appraisal is made, rather than risking significant potential contamination in a rating from a supervisor who really likes eager employees?

David Dowell reports on the results of a 1974 workshop on performance standards for librarians in which a trait-based form was used as the basis for an appraisal exercise. The inter-rater reliability of the seventy ratings is appalling, covering the range from excellent to unsatisfactory. Dowell reports, "In only seven of the nineteen (trait) categories was there even a 51 percent majority consensus as to what the rating should be."[99] Furthermore, the "eight raters who gave . . . an overall rating of one hundred were no more in agreement with each other on individual traits than were the seventy raters taken as a whole."[100]

It is clear that trait-based systems not only leave an organization open to EEOC charges that the system is invalid and not job-related, but such a system also does a poor job of serving the purposes of performance improvement, furthering organizational goals, and identifying potential, in fact, all the purposes for which appraisal is done.

Comparison of Employees with Each Other

A second type of performance measurement is comparison of employees with each other. Employees may be ranked in a number of different ways, in a straight ranking from highest to lowest on the criteria of overall job performance or promotability or on specific traits or criteria. The raters may select first the highest, then the lowest, then the next highest, and the next lowest, and so forth until all employees in a unit have been compared.[101] A third type of ranking is called paired comparison, in which each employee is ranked against another employee in a unit. Miner provides an example of a rating form that can be used with this method, and mentions a fourth variation of ranking, forced choice, where raters place employees in percentile categories according to predetermined proportions. He also discusses the advantages of ranking systems in overcoming errors of central tendency, halo effect, and use of different standards among raters.[102] This technique may result in a ranking that is useful when determining salary adjustments, if one assumes that the range and distribution of performance between all groups is the same. However, this method does not provide useful feedback data for performance improvement. No examples of the use of these systems in libraries have been found.

Standards

A third method of measurement is against absolute standards or criteria related to specific job functions. The question of the appropriateness of performance standards for librarians is one that is being asked with increasing frequency. As early as 1974 Joyce Veenstra discussed this issue in a paper called "Performance Standards for Librarians, Are They Coming or Not?[103] Veenstra offers some useful insights into the question of the feasibility of establishing standards for professionals. Citing Columbia University Libraries' experience with attempting to implement an MBO program, she writes,

> What we all ultimately agreed upon was that performance standards for librarians are definitely worthwhile, even though extremely difficult to write. . . . We realized how difficult it is to write measurable and meaningful performance objectives, especially in an area like reference—and yet the objectives exist in the mind of the head of the department as well as in the minds of the reference librarians—for themselves and in judging their peers. What we are attempting to do is to articulate together what those objectives are.[104]

Finally, taking these internalized objectives outside the institutional context, she continues, "Professional specialists . . . seemingly derive their rewards from inward standards of excellence, from the intrinsic satisfaction of their task. In fact, they are committed to the task, not the job; to their standards, not their boss."[105]

Performance standards should be statements of expected behavior, output, or accomplishment that apply to all employees engaged in similar work. They are intended to be applied as evaluation criteria for an indefinite length of time and are not created to be used solely in one individual employee's evaluation. In addition, such standards are set by a group of supervisors, subordinates, managers, or personnel specialists, rather than by an individual supervisor and employee for evaluating an individual employee's performance.

In order to meet legal requirements, employees engaged in the tasks for which the standards are set should participate in establishing the standards; the standards will then be consistently applied across a category of positions.

Following the enactment of the Civil Service Reform Act of 1978 the Library Operations Division of the National Library of Medicine (NLM) established performance standards for all of its professional and support staff positions. Library supervisors, often in conjunction with staff members who perform the tasks, established task-specific standards for the major responsibilities of each position; these standards relate to a combination of critical and noncritical elements in the position. The nonperformance of any critical element is sufficient grounds for personnel actions, for example, reprimands, suspensions, and withholding of salary increases.

An example of the type and format of the standards is a matrix linking the difficulty of the articles to be indexed for inclusion in Index Medicus with quantity standards for the production of indexing in each category of difficulty.[106]

In the reference section at NLM, the librarians are finding that creating standards for reference service is hard. Early efforts resulted in the traditional trait descriptions such as tact and courtesy. The traits are now being revised in an attempt to translate these concepts into statements addressed to specific job elements comprising the various positions in the reference section. For example, the job elements such as "Provides reference service to both patrons and staff of NLM in person, at the Reference Desk, Learning Resource Center and in the Section via telephone and through correspondence," has paragraphs describing when the objectives of the element are partially met, fully met, and exceeded. To exceed the objectives on this element, the librarian:

> shows initiative in understanding and interpreting patron requests, always probing the most specific level of the requestor's inquiry, responses are invariably accurate, and seldom has difficulty in handling stressful situations or dealing with demanding patrons; takes initiative in gaining knowledge and understanding of NLM collections; not only reviews and quickly assimilates the use of new reference tools but also may suggest additional tools for acquisition, and displays a good ability to instruct patrons in their use; takes initiative in learning and understanding of relevant information resources outside of NLM and conveys this understanding well to patrons; takes the initiative in learning of database capabilities and incorporating their use into reference work and possesses an excellent knowledge of the formal search service and refers patrons appropriately; not only possesses a good knowledge of reference policy and procedures and reports activities and statistics promptly and accurately but also suggests appropriate changes/ improvements and works well within the deadlines set; not only possesses a good knowledge of section administrative procedures but also makes appropriate suggestions for changes/improvements and takes the initiative in calling potential problem areas to the attention of the supervisor.[107]

The Civil Service Reform Act of 1978 decreed that all federal employees must be under a system of performance standards by 1981. According to Fred Thayer, "the reform's viability is almost wholly dependent upon periodic performance appraisals of career administrators, based solely upon "merit" and "competence."[108] Thayer believes that performance appraisal systems cannot work to achieve this purpose. Thayer's reasoning leads him to the conclusion that "since superiors cannot possess the requisite 'performance-based' knowledge, they have no alternative but to retreat to the use of 'person-based' factors."[109]

Although his article is useful in calling attention to the possible abuses of appraisal systems, particularly within the framework of the Civil Service System, his arguments are not valid, at least in relation to evaluation of personnel in federal libraries. In order to be effective managers, supervisors must have adequate comprehension of the knowledge, skills, and abilities required in their subordinates' positions, and can set measurable and attainable standards.

Beaulieu, also writing in the context of the performance appraisals mandated by the Reform Act, takes "an easier look at performance appraisal" than Thayer. He dismisses the assumption that performance standards must be completely measurable by quantifiable yardsticks, suggesting that the issue is verification of accomplishments, not quantification of standards. He describes accomplishments as the worthy things visible after an employee goes home; these should form the basis of job standards, and they are far easier to arrive at than rigidly quantifiable measurements. He determines a list of accomplishments by asking the question, "If we had ideal people populating the place, what would we see them accomplish during a twelve-month period?"[110]

Mellenhoff also disagrees with the comments that work performed by professionals can't be measured. He describes an evaluation system for highly trained professionals in a state government agency providing technical assistance to local government officials. His work-measurement system developed specific performance indicators for key result areas, and like Beaulieu, it strives "for a standard that a competent and diligent employee could reach most of the time with reasonable effort."[111]

Specific Behaviors Defining Levels of Performance

The concept of employment as a behavioral rental agreement, the importance of understanding jobs in terms of specific behaviors, and steps to improve performance by managing behavior are described in the Fournier *Performance Appraisal Design Handbook*.[112]

Measures of performance may be taken against specific behaviors required in a job which are graphed in such a way as to clearly state what behaviors will be rated excellent, what behaviors indicate average performance, and what behaviors will be considered poor. Under the Library Selection Project in California, BARS were developed for use in selection interviews for entry level positions on such job dimensions as oral communication, instructional/training ability, and community awareness/interest.[113] BARS have been established for managerial and technical positions as well as for manufacturing and clerical ones. They are time-consuming to develop, but once in place offer excellent guides to employees for improving performance and identifying what specific actions will be recognized with a good appraisal.

In 1983 Pfister and Towle called for the development of BARS covering the major job dimensions of school library media specialists in order to increase understanding of their roles in school media centers.[114] Vincelette and Pfister describe a process followed in Sarasota County for school library media specialists to develop model performance appraisal instruments, and they recommend using an accompanying statement of resources to accomplish each job duty and behavioral anchors or examples to overcome the problem of judging the level of goal accomplishment.[115]

Earlier, the School Library Manpower Project, administered by the ASSL Division of ALA, compiled a list of competency-based job functions and task statements for school library media personnel. This *Behavioral Requirements Analysis Checklist* lists "approximately 700 statements that collectively describe most of the tasks which encompass three professional job positions: school library media specialist; school library head, media center; and district school library media director."[116] These task statements could be used as the basis for job dimensions from which BARS could be prepared for school media personnel.

There are many jobs in libraries that are essentially the same from library to library: shelving positions, circulation desk attendants, catalogers, personnel administrators, and systems analysts. Although a BARS appraisal system, like any other system, needs to be tailored to an individual organization, and, to gain maximum acceptance from the library staff, developed with input from staff members, BARS established in one library could be adapted for use in similar libraries with similar positions. Such adaptation could significantly reduce the time needed to develop the individual BARS for each group of positions. For example the Arizona State University Libraries uses a performance appraisal form for classified personnel that defines the behaviors related to five dimensions of performance ranging from unsatisfactory to outstanding on specific components of an individual's performance. Figure 1 displays the range of behavior on the factor, "Relations with personnel from other departments and/or the general public."

Goals-based Systems

An individual's performance can also be measured against goals, performance-rating elements, standards, targets, or other terms used to describe a measure established by a supervisor and/or individual

FIGURE 1. Arizona State University Libraries performance appraisal form.

RELATIONS WITH PERSONNEL FROM
OTHER DEPARTMENTS AND/OR THE GENERAL PUBLIC

Take into account the employee's interaction with patrons, employees from other departments, and/or the public either in person or on the phone. Consider willingness to cooperate and ability to communicate. Consider also tactfulness, courtesy, and helpfulness, and how these factors influence ability to work effectively.

Note: For these purposes courteous means polite, considerate means respectful of the rights and feelings of others, and thoughtful means anticipates the wants and needs of others.

Unsatisfactory Is often discourteous and/or uncooperative with patrons or other university employees; often communicates inappropriately or unclearly; avoids assisting patrons or other university employees.

Marginal Is sometimes discourteous and/or uncooperative; sometimes communicates inappropriately or unclearly; sometimes avoids assisting patrons or other university employees.

Satisfactory Is generally courteous and cooperative; usually communicates clearly; assists patrons and other university employees as necessary.

Very Good Assists patrons and other university employees willingly; is usually courteous, considerate, and cooperative; communicates clearly and concisely.

Outstanding Assists patrons and other university employees willingly; suggests and implements methods to improve department's interaction with patrons and other university employees; is consistently courteous, considerate, thoughtful, and cooperative; communicates clearly and concisely.

employee for a specific position and used for a specific appraisal period. Ideally the individual's goals are established subsequent to the effort of an entire library to establish objectives. From the organization's objectives follow the setting of department and unit objectives; finally, within the framework of the unit objectives, goals are developed for each individual staff member.

According to Kin and Hammer,[117] support for the effect of goal setting on performance and satisfaction has been well documented in laboratory settings. DeProspo gives an excellent concise description of what he calls the goals method approach.[118] Berkner presents a brief overview of articles discussing applications of goals-based systems in libraries.[119] Finally, Michalko's lengthy article on management by objectives discusses its conceptual foundations and the claims of its proponents; he concludes that MBO is, after all, a style and not a set of techniques. As a style, some of its central concepts may be profitably integrated with existing practices. . . ."[120] Kane and Freeman disagree, however, and define some of the problems of MBO as it is applied to performance evaluation.[121]

Most MBO programs involve three separate phases: first, the goals are established jointly by the supervisor and subordinates; second, action plans are developed to enable the subordinate to meet the goals; and third, performance is reviewed to ascertain if the goals were met during the performance period.

In the process of goal setting, the present level of performance for each objective may be stated, the future target level established, and a target date set. The objectives may be expressed as a quantity measure, a quality measure, and a cost measure.[122] However, as Creth emphasizes, all goals should be results-oriented, measurable, and realistic.[123] Creth also suggests that individuals divide goals into four general categories: maintenance, problem solving, innovative, and developmental.[124] When writing goals, she recommends that the majority be considered as maintenance goals while a fewer number are drawn from the other three categories. Her recommendation is based on the greater level of difficulty associated with the achievement of problem solving and innovative goals.

McConkie emphasizes that though MBO is more easily described than defined, it is

> a managerial process whereby organization purposes are diagnosed and met by joining supervisors and subordinates in the pursuit of mutually agreed upon goals and objectives, which are specific, measurable, time bounded, and joined into an action plan; progress and goal attainment are measured and maintained in appraisal sessions which center on mutually determined objective standards of performance.[125]

A variation on measuring performance against individual goals is the concept of a performance contract form in which an individual employee "contracts" to achieve certain objectives in the time period covered by the contract. The supervisor also contracts to provide specific assistance in attaining these objectives.[126]

An important observation should be made in relation to effectiveness measures as a basis for evaluating performance. These measures should be linked as closely as possible to the measures of effectiveness of the library as a service organization.[127] Evaluation of ways to meet primary user needs; of the success of the library in meeting standards external to the institution, or internally set; and of the library's success in contributing to the provision of information needs in a network or consortial context will be done on specific quantity or quality measures. The more closely these measures are tied to objectives of the organization and its individual units, and indirectly to performance goals of individual employees, the more effective the organization will be in directing the efforts of its staff toward organizational goals and motivating and assisting employees to achieve them.

Lancaster states this idea bluntly when he writes:

> There seem to be two major qualitative measures of success as applied to information services:
>
> 1. Does the user get it or not?
> 2. How completely and/or accurately does he [or she] get it?
>
> All of the public services of an information center must be evaluated according to time, cost, and quality criteria. The technical services, however, should be evaluated on the basis of both internal efficiency, including time and cost factors, and the effect of these technical services on the public services of the library (i.e., effects on quality).[128]

Performance measures related to the quantity of a cataloger's errors in establishing access points, the number of possible citations not identified in a search of an online database, or a targeted decrease in the number of unfilled interlibrary loan transactions are measures of an individual's effectiveness which can be directly linked to the library's goals and the measures of effectiveness the library has defined for itself.

In a paper delivered to a symposium conducted by the Syracuse School of Library Science, Richard Dougherty addresses measuring library effectiveness and makes two points relevant to the linking of individual and organizational effort. First, he defines effectiveness as "the capacity of an organization to maximize the employment of its human resources ... the proportion of individuals who are able to perform tasks which both simulate (sic) them and require the full use of their talents and capabilities. Stated in today's vernacular, maximum effectiveness results when the organization's objectives are furthered by each person doing his own thing."[129] Secondly, Dougherty suggests that measures of effectiveness should focus on the performance of work groups such as departments, rather than on the output of individuals.[130]

Relating Dougherty's suggestions to cataloging standards, for example, such standards might more comprehensively measure the effectiveness of the department's effort to achieve bibliographic control if the quantity standards combined the production of individual catalogers with others in a team or unit, or even the whole department. This composite score could represent a portion of the individual cataloger's appraisal. It would address that part of the construct of performance that individual quantity and quality measures do not touch. It might include such factors as ability to work effectively with others; ability to perceive and define the unit's goals in relation to those of the library; and contribution to the development of new concepts of bibliographic control as the physical formats of catalogs change.

WHO PERFORMS THE EVALUATIONS?

Immediate Supervisor

Traditionally, an employee's immediate supervisor performs the evaluation of his or her work. Although Johnson's survey showed that only in six percent of the responses was the immediate supervisor alone involved in the appraisal,[131] she indicates that the supervisor was usually consulted even if not responsible for the appraisal. In Van Zant's survey (see the tables in the section Use of Appraisal Systems in Libraries), only 21 of the 926 responses were in categories that did not include the supervisor.

The evaluation of subordinates is one of the functions attributed to supervisors in most discussions of supervisory responsibility. Beyond the simple expectation that evaluation is part of a supervisor's job is the belief, Thayer to the contrary, that a supervisor is in one of the best positions, if not the best, to know what an employee is expected to do to fulfill his or her job responsibilities and how well he or she meets these expectations. Even under the collegial arrangements of library faculty in some academic libraries, where performance evaluation is assigned to a committee, the supervisor's evaluation is usually given heavy weight. In some libraries the supervisor comments not only on performance of job duties, but on the subordinate's professional contributions and service to the university and community as well.

The evaluation of volunteers, student employees, and support staff will best be performed primarily by the immediate supervisor. Under certain conditions, where support staff (as well as professionals) perform responsibilities involving a great deal of patron contact or extending broadly throughout the library or its parent institution, evaluation by other supervisors, professionals, or support staff may be appropriate to obtain a more complete picture of the employee's achievements.

Supplementary Evaluators

Evaluation by additional raters should be restricted to specific performance areas of which the rater has direct knowledge. Evaluation criteria may be weighted to reflect the importance of the performance area to the ratee's entire range of job responsibilities. For example, an interlibrary loan assistant handling the verification and transmittal of ILL requests from branch libraries might be rated by branch librarians or peers in other branch libraries on the timeliness of referral, accuracy of verification, or hit rate. The evaluations by these multiple raters do not supersede the evaluation of the supervisor, but rather complement it and provide the supervisor with direct knowledge about the subordinate's performance in key job areas. It is the supervisor's responsibility to provide the subordinate with the feedback from the multiple raters and to assist the subordinate in improving in those areas of responsibility which the appraisal shows are not being fully met or in which targets have not been reached.

One of the results of the increasing use of the model of combining reference responsibilities, collection development, bibliographic instruction, and online computer searching subject specialist positions is the increasing need for "supplementary" evaluators who assess the performance of the librarian in these areas. If the librarian's primary responsibility is to provide effective reference service while also handling these additional duties, the reference department head will serve as a "primary evaluator" who will need input from colleagues possessing expertise in each area in order to fully evaluate the librarian's performance in all areas of responsibility.

An example of an evaluation program where supplementary evaluations are provided to the primary supervisor is in use at the University Libraries at the University of Notre Dame. The library implements a system in which "activity supervisors," department heads, and major committee and task force chairs provide written input to the direct supervisor as part of the annual review.[132]

Supervisor's Supervisor

Appraisals are often reviewed by the supervisor of the rater either before or after they are discussed with the subordinate. As Peter McGuire points out, there is a danger that knowledge of this higher-level review may cause the supervisor to emphasize comparative rank of the ratee in relation to other employees and to provide justification of negative remarks at the expense of suggestions for ways to improve performance.[133] This review is useful, however, because it provides the second-level supervisor with knowledge not only of the performance of subordinates in units under his or her direction, but also of the ability of first-line supervisors to effectively manage the human resources in their units by developing the skills and abilities of their subordinates and by solving performance-related problems. In libraries where low ratings may be appealed, it is important to alert the supervisor to potential appeals and for both supervisors to feel that the rating is fully documented as well as justified.

This review by a higher administrative level is also important in ensuring that evaluations are done consistently within the division and is viewed favorably by the courts as a measure to prevent supervisory discrimination against an individual employee.

The Texas A&M University Library's evaluation process requires that each faculty member be evaluated by the appropriate division head and assistant director in addition to the supervisor. These evaluations may be oral or in writing.[134]

Self-ratings

All employees approach an evaluation interview, and read the results of their performance appraisal, with their own concept of how they have performed in the interval since the last appraisal. The technique of self-rating allows the employee to participate more actively in the process by bringing out this self-conception early in the appraisal process, either independently of other raters by filling out a separate appraisal form, or by providing a statement of accomplishments that form the basis of the appraisal process.

Statements in the literature regarding the validity of self-ratings are contradictory. According to some writers, their experience with self-ratings indicates employees appraise their own performance accurately[135] and in some cases, too leniently. Kenneth Teel gives a rationale for such leniency: "By underrating their performance, subordinates structure the situation so that the supervisor is more likely to praise than to criticize them . . . overrating one's self invites criticism."[136]

On the other hand, Lloyd Baird found in a study of self and superior ratings that high self-esteem/low performance subgroup members exhibited the highest level of disagreement with superiors, with their self ratings significantly higher.[137] Thus, those employees whose performance is in most need of improvement are the very ones who perceive it least accurately, and to whom a supervisor will have to defend his or her rating most strongly.

Rizzo specifies three positive results associated with self-appraisal: more satisfying and constructive interviews, less defensiveness on the part of the employee regarding the interview, and improved job performance.[138] In addition to these benefits it is clear that the knowledge that a self-appraisal will be required forces the employee to focus more specifically on the evaluation criteria and his or her performance in relation to them during the evaluation period.

Hopefully, this increased attention to criteria will direct the employee's efforts to the specific performance areas which will be self-rated and rated by others, and overall performance in them will be improved. Instead of being a passive participant in the appraisal interview, the employee is thus engaged in an active discussion of the factors and considerations leading to the self-ratings, which are then compared with those of the supervisors, and perhaps those of other evaluators. The tone of the evaluation interview can be one of mutual problem-solving, rather than simply a justification of the supervisor's rating.

Peer Evaluations

In 1973 Johnson's survey reported that 29 percent of the responding libraries involved committees, councils, or peer groups in the appraisal process.[139] In Van Zant's survey, 115 of the 626 respondents included peers, either alone or in combination with other raters (see table seven Who Conducts Performance Evaluations). The results of the 1987 ARL survey reveal that 21 of 71 of the institutions responding use some type of peer review, although in the documentation provided by the University of Kansas it can be seen that the use of peer review at that institution has been somewhat controversial.[140]

The use of a committee of professional peers to evaluate professional achievements and competence has developed in academic libraries in line with the ACRL Standards for Faculty Status for College and University Librarians. Two sections of this statement are particularly relevant:

1. Professional responsibilities and self-determination:
Each librarian should be assigned general responsibilities within his particular area of competence. . . . The degree to which he has fulfilled them

should be regularly and rigorously reviewed. A necessary element of this review must be appraisal by a committee of peers who have access to all available evidence.

2. Promotion:
Librarians should be promoted through ranks and steps on the basis of their academic proficiency and professional effectiveness. A peer review system similar to that used by other faculty is the primary basis of judgment in the promotion process for academic librarians.[141]

Many appraisal processes in academic libraries integrate evaluation by supervisors with evaluation by peers. Decisions regarding promotion in rank or receipt of tenure, or appointment to positions without limit of time, are normally made by the peer review process. In some libraries the supervisor's statement regarding the performance of job responsibilities forms a key part of the documentation considered by the committee. In other processes, the faculty member provides a statement of accomplishments, upon which the supervisor comments before forwarding it to the committee of peers. Yeh, one of the early proponents in print of the peer review process, describes a system in which a personnel committee evaluates librarians' working effectiveness, scholarship and productivity, special services to library and college, and professional activities on the basis of a statement provided by the librarians. The dean of the library forwards an independent recommendation to the president.[142]

In some of the evaluation processes conducted by peer review committees, the areas of emphasis receiving primary consideration are professional activities such as participation in professional meetings, service on library and university committees, research and publications. To some extent this emphasis reflects the institutional conception of the primary role of the librarian as a researcher contributing to a body of professional knowledge or as an educator of students and faculty in the techniques of accessing the library's storehouse of knowledge. It is also evidence of the conceptual dichotomy[143] of librarians as professionals with basic allegiance to professional goals, interests, and clients, versus librarians as employees of an organization. Where the concept of the librarian as an employee in a hierarchical organization is emphasized, so is the right of the library managers and supervisors to define specific job responsibilities and to appraise the librarian first and foremost on the performance of those functions.

There is an alternate side to the use of the peer review process to evaluate professional activities. It reflects that the peer review committee is more comfortable assessing professional areas of competence, and less so with evaluating competence in such specific areas of job responsibility as providing reference service or cataloging the library's media and collections. Unless members of the committee have a unique knowledge of the librarian's performance in these areas, they must rely on the supervisor's evaluations. To the extent they do so, their function becomes one that is traditionally delegated to the personnel office of an organization, that is, review of the evaluations to counteract tendencies of harshness or leniency on the part of individual supervisors—to insure consistency or ratings throughout the library. Review by a peer committee also encourages a diversity of input and introduces a broader perspective into the evaluation than could be given by the supervisor alone.[144]

Columbia University Libraries' system of splitting the evaluation functions into supervisory appraisal of the performance of job responsibilities for the purposes of performance improvement and salary determination, and peer evaluation for promotion in rank seems to most efficiently utilize the unique knowledge of the raters in the evaluation process for two differing purposes.[145] The peer committee makes the recommendation for promotion on the basis of quality of service on library committees, library instructional activities, professional activities outside the library, research and academic achievement, and participation in university affairs. The Columbia system emphasizes that "the intent of the system [is] to foster the professional development of the individual through external activities and the pursuit of advanced degrees in conjunction with, but not at the expense of, fulfillment of responsibilities to the Columbia libraries. . . . High quality job performance is one criterion which must be met for any promotion."[146]

The University of Illinois at Urbana-Champaign also uses peer review in the performance appraisal of librarians. A committee is selected when a librarian is hired, and the committee members continue to serve until the librarian has been evaluated for promotion and tenure, which often takes six years. The visiting committee is composed as follows:[147]

> For each untenured faculty member of Departmental Library Services and each tenured faculty member seeking promotion within the following academic year, two tenured members of the faculty are asked by the Director to serve as a visiting evaluation committee. Ideally, such a committee includes at least one person from the council to which the candidate's library is affiliated. The committee never includes a faculty member from the same library unit in which the candidate undergoing review is employed, nor is input sought from individuals who work under the direct supervision of the candidate under evaluation.

The visiting committee seeks information on which to base its evaluation largely through personal or telephone interviews with faculty, students, other library clients, and professional colleagues, in the course of which comments are solicited which may facilitate promotion and/or the achievement of tenure by faculty who are undergoing evaluation. The procedure provides for obtaining detailed information on various specific areas of responsibility, as well as evaluating job performance in general terms. The process is personally supportive, and provides opportunities for informal discussion and for forwarding positive comments as well as recommendations for improving job performance.[148]

Wallace describes the appraisal system at Northern Colorado University, in which a single instrument is used to evaluate both teaching and library faculty. Although the department chairs make the initial rating, the evaluation must be reviewed by the next level, usually the dean. Any difference in evaluation requires review by the University Advisory Committee. During the first year of use of the evaluation system one quarter of the evaluations required the review of the Committee, composed of selected faculty, two chairs or deans, and one student.[149]

There are difficulties with the peer review process. Roland Person is accurate in his statement that ". . . we have not yet developed, thoroughly tested, nor adequately applied techniques for judging the quality of our peers' performance."[150] In their 1987 article, McEvoy and Buller review a number of reasons employees lack confidence in peer review systems: 1) peer reviews may be popularity contests, 2) managers may not believe there is any reason to include peers in performance appraisals, 3) peer reviews may be biased because of interpersonal relationships, and 4) employees who receive low ratings from their peers may in turn give low ratings to the people who rated them.[151] McEvoy and Buller also found that more highly educated employees tend to mistrust peer review to a greater degree. "So that if that finding were to be true for the population of all employees, college faculty would clearly be among the most educated and, hence, potentially the most hostile to the use of peer appraisals."[152]

Reifler, reporting on a one-year experiment in the use of peer evaluation at Washington State University, states that the experiment failed there because the peer evaluation system was an adjunct to, rather than an integrated part of, the library administrative evaluation process, which made for time-consuming duplication of effort and because of the lack of familiarity on the part of the members of the Peer Evaluation Committee with the work of those being evaluated. However, she credits the experiment with improving the criteria in rating the faculty and with enabling broader peer input to be solicited as part of the administrative evaluation process.[153]

One apparent difficulty of the peer review process as it is implemented in many libraries is that the judgmental role of the committee dominates the process. The developmental role of improvement in performance is made difficult by the need to preserve the confidentiality of references and by the lack of an appraisal interview not only explaining the basis of the decision, but offering concrete suggestions for performance improvement.[154] The most effective kind of appraisal for developmental purposes is ongoing evaluation with frequent feedback; usually, it is the supervisor who provides it.

Perhaps the strongest reason for use of the peer review process is the need for acceptance of the evaluation decisions by all members of the library and university professional staff. This acceptance is critical when librarians must function as members of a work team, with good communication, coordination of effort, shared goals, and task interdependencies.[155] Where acceptance of the decision is critical, organizations are well advised to allow participation in the decision-making process. Given strong, ongoing supervisory evaluation and feedback in relation to performance of job responsibilities, the peer process can lead to high-quality decisions concerning the librarian's professional stature, accomplishments, and ability to function as a member of the library faculty or professional workgroup.

MULTIPLE RATERS AND TECHNIQUES

In any evaluation, not all the potential evaluators can appropriately make an appraisal using each of the techniques, nor would they be familiar with all aspects of the performance to be measured. But many combinations of techniques, measures, and raters are possible, and library personnel designing appraisal systems will do well to consider possible combinations. Regarding the raters, Schneier presents a strong case for the use of multiple rater groups,[156] citing the advantages of the generation of a larger database, identification of out-of-line ratings, multiple perspectives, evidence of inter-rater reliability, and increased commitment to the appraisal system from the wider participation. Beatty and Schneier discuss the advantages of combining MBO (effectiveness-based) and behaviorally based systems in the final article of their three-part series in *Personnel Administrator*.[157]

Stinson and Stokes report on a managerial appraisal system successfully used at Gulf Oil that combines multiple techniques and multiple raters. The techniques used include an overall assessment of job performance (linked to merit payments), an analysis of managerial effectiveness against a seven-factor, empirically based model developed from careful job analysis techniques, and a narrative evaluation elaborating on the analysis.[158] This system is also notable because the ratees themselves selected five to eight raters each to do the appraisals, as well as making self-assessments. The supervisor takes the summary feedback form compiled by the company's Human Resources Department and is responsible for communicating the results of the appraisal to each ratee. He also monitors performance improvement.

Rizzo points out that different rating or evaluation methods can be constructed to fit different jobs.[159] Certainly, different methods are appropriate for use with differing groups of library employees.

Holleman described an evaluation system for community college librarians which combines a criterion-referenced trait-rating form which supervisors and/or peers can use to assess personal characteristics and factors related to job performance; a self-evaluation form consisting of open-ended questions; an MBO component [with] ... short- and long-range goals for individual and unit growth and development; and a specific follow-up for identified professional improvement activities.[160]

Cummings and Schwab suggest differing systems for use with employees at differing levels of performance. They propose a developmental appraisal program for high-performing employees demonstrating potential for continued growth; a maintenance action program for the average, acceptable performer with low promotion potential; and a remedial action program for below-standard performers.[161]

Corey and Steel report on the use of a multiple-rater technique called "TE*MS" (Team Evaluation and Management System) used to evaluate librarians at Arizona State University for merit. As it was applied, TE*MS combined an anonymous peer evaluation with the supervisor's assessment of the success the librarian had in meeting previously established performance goals. Like many evaluation systems, the implementation of TE*MS had mixed results. It produced a numerical score for each librarian which could be used to determine the amount of merit the librarian would receive, and TE*MS was less time-consuming to complete than performance evaluations requiring narrative statements. However, participants in the TE*MS experiment at Arizona State questioned the validity of the scores, and the supervisors felt that they were not able to explain and interpret the scores that the peer reviewers had given.[162]

Whether or not the library chooses the option of different techniques, measures, or rater groups, it is important to know which methods have been demonstrated to provide the best data for the specific purposes for which the appraisal is made. Several writers have attempted to relate techniques to purpose graphically. Beatty and Schneier[163] present the most comprehensive table describing the relative ability of PA methods to attain the objectives of validation, promotion potential, measurement accuracy, development, assessing training needs, and rewards allocation. They rate the use of behaviorally anchored rating scales and MBO far higher than personal trait scales, dimensionalized scales (both not behaviorally anchored), and adjective or numerically anchored global scales.

McMillan and Doyel[164] evaluate three common appraisal methods: trait checklist, MBO, and free-form, and a fourth "responsibility rating" against characteristics that include purpose, error, job-relatedness, and ease of administration. They choose the responsibility rating for the purpose of salary administration; this method emphasizes job-specific rating factors and performance planning and review techniques. Cummings and Schwab[165] also have created a table outlining the procedures most appropriate to their three-pronged appraisal approach (developmental, maintenance, and remedial). Their table includes the types of errors most likely to occur with each method, mechanisms for prevention of the errors, and brief statements addressed to implementation questions. It is noteworthy that behaviorally anchored rating scales and/or critical incidents are recommended, along with some other methods, for each of their "programs."

DESIGN AND IMPLEMENTATION

The first consideration in the development or revision of an appraisal system is the purpose for which the appraisals are conducted. Is the emphasis to be on judgment or evaluation of past performance—for the purpose of salary distribution or promotion in rank, or is the emphasis on the improvement of performance? A system that attempts to achieve too many objectives is likely to fail to achieve any of them. Systems emphasizing evaluation for salary or promotion require a numerical rating for direct comparison with other employees; systems designed to improve performance require statements of the kinds of behaviors or outputs needed to demonstrate improvement.

For a system to be most effective, the supervisors and employees must accept it as valid and be committed to utilize it for its stated purpose. Articles discussing the implementation of MBO stress the need for top management to participate in setting organizational objectives as well as publicly advocating the system's implementation in the organization.[166] It is clear that the involvement of supervisors, raters, and the employees themselves in the development of the task descriptions, performance criteria, and behavioral anchors is very important. Not only does this involvement facilitate the inclusion of job-specific elements into the system, but it also commits the supervisors and raters to a system in whose development they have participated and makes the system more easily defended in the courts.

System design should begin with the task statements and/or job descriptions to be included in it. The performance evaluation programs described by Benedict and Gherman and by Hall are good examples of systems where performance expectations and standards relate directly to the task statements of individual positions.[167] The system of evaluation for tenure and promotion at the University of Illinois at Urbana-Champaign is notable for the use of standard questions relating to areas of responsibility such as reference and information service, collection development, and management and administration, used by the evaluation committee in soliciting appraisals from library clients, departmental faculty, department library committee chairs, and executive officers of academic departments or colleges, as appropriate to the responsibility.[168]

Systems that relate measurement criteria directly to the job responsibilities of positions or develop goals for the performance of individual employees are most likely to be defensible on the grounds of evaluation on objective, job-related criteria. Library managers must be aware that the design of these job-specific systems are costly and time-consuming, especially when numbers of supervisors and employees are involved in the development of the criteria or goals. The time required to develop behaviorally anchored rating scales for one position or group of positions has been estimated at approximately fifteen hours per each participant, plus additional time to compute scale values, arrange the anchors, and do the final editing.[169] Anyone who has participated in the design of a system for review of professional performance, or who has served as a member of the professional review committee performing the evaluation, knows the cost in time and energy involved.

Supervisors and other supplementary evaluators who consistently participate in the process as raters are the key to effective implementation of any appraisal system. They must be trained to observe behavior on an ongoing basis; to consider the coaching and evaluation of subordinates an important responsibility; to be aware of such rater errors as central tendency, leniency, and halo effect; and to provide constant feedback on how an employee is performing. Supervisors must overcome their natural resistance to communicate poor performance and to evaluate with a view to justifying the rating rather than providing the information needed to facilitate performance improvement. They must know that only by experience with the evaluation process can they expect to become proficient in it. They must learn to integrate the management style they have developed with their appraisal techniques.

Finally, even systems that include measures of output and behaviorally based task statements require that supervisors exercise an element of subjective judgment. Management must make clear the supervisor's rights in the appraisal process, particularly when appraisals are grievable. Supervisors need to be aware of the documentation required—and the procedures they must follow—to justify appraisals resulting in job actions, demotions, or termination.

IMPLEMENTATION OF A POORLY DESIGNED SYSTEM

Most libraries function within the institutional setting of a parent organization. In some circumstances the library is mandated to use the performance appraisal system of the larger organization. Occasionally these systems may be poorly designed, emphasizing only the judgmental aspects of performance on the basis of traits or global statements of performance.

A library that must use a poorly designed system may be in a position to modify it either by supplementing the forms required by the parent organization with its own forms, or by holding informal goal-setting conferences between supervisors and subordinates. It may expand on the criteria or factors that are inadequately defined and may even be able to run parallel appraisal systems, with the mandated forms returned to the parent organization and the library's or department's forms kept within the unit.

Since performance appraisal is a process, its effectiveness relies on continual communication between the supervisor and the employee and the clear understanding of expected behaviors and outputs. Such communication and clearly stated expectations can improve the effectiveness of any system—no matter how poor.

CONDUCTING THE APPRAISAL

The appraisal process is a structure within which communication—or feedback on performance—takes place, with a view to improving that performance, relating it to organizational goals, and assisting the organization in rewarding excellent performers and removing unsatisfactory ones.

Both the raters and the employee play a critical role in the process. Employees, as well as raters, should be trained to actively participate in it. As Lynch states, "training in this essential component of the supervisor's job is critical to the successful conduct of it."[170] When goals-based systems in particular are implemented, all participants must have a clear idea of what goals are, how they may be linked to their job responsibilities, and how to develop realistic, clear, and measurable ones.

An effective appraisal:

1. Evaluates performance on the basis of goals, standards, or behaviors which are clearly stated at the beginning of the evaluation period
2. Is scheduled well in advance to allow both the raters and the ratee plenty of time to review performance since the last appraisal and to prepare required documentation
3. Is discussed in an appraisal interview that is private, unhurried, and allows both the rater and the employee being evaluated to effectively speak his mind and present his views
4. Is confidential and conducted with a seriousness which emphasizes its importance to the supervisor, the employee, all additional raters, including peers, and the organization
5. Often emphasizes a problem-solving, rather than a judgmental, approach[171]

The appraisal interview itself is a crucial part of the appraisal process. Stevenson has gathered together relevant citations and developed a helpful set of guidelines for conducting appraisal interviews in libraries.[172]

DIFFERENT SYSTEMS AND CRITERIA

Student and Part-time Employees

Student employees, volunteers, and other categories of part-time staff with rapid turnover are most efficiently evaluated under a simple system that emphasizes a few critical performance areas and provides an answer to the question of whether the rater recommends rehiring the employee.

The appraisal must still relate to important elements of the job being performed, but there is more justification for a single form relating to broad classifications of positions. Important criteria include adherence to schedules, willingness to perform a wide variety of duties, and speed and accuracy in filing or shelving books. A supervisor is often required to do a large number of evaluations at the end of a semester or academic year. Therefore, the forms should be simple, though most successful ones will allow the inclusion of job-specific behaviors or output measures. These employees must have a clear knowledge of the supervisor's expectations of what constitutes satisfactory performance, however, and they should be given continual feedback on their performance, as other employees are.

Support Staff

Appraisal systems for support staff should be designed to emphasize critical tasks or job elements. If possible, representatives of the staff should be involved in selecting these elements and the developing behavioral anchors or standards. It is clearly management's prerogative to set standards and establish acceptable levels of output. Often, however, groups of employees may be involved, either in the development of the criteria, the negotiation of the standards, or the schedule for their implementation.

As library budgets tighten and professional librarians devote more time to meeting increasing demands for high-level reference service or struggle to contain technical processing backlogs of uncataloged material, responsibilities in some support-staff positions are expanding. They include provision of basic reference service, cataloging with copy, and supervision of large numbers of student employees or of other support staff. It is crucial that clear statements of expected performance level, and assistance in meeting them, be available to these staff members through an effective appraisal system. Futhermore, the time has passed in most libraries when ineffective staff members could be carried in the library's budget. Library supervisors must be able to identify poor performance and utilize effective techniques to bring about improvement in it.

Implementation of MBO systems has typically been restricted to managerial and professional employees. Lewis, however, has reported using MBO in the acquisitions section of a serials unit with five full-time library assistants.[173] The experiment yielded mixed results in terms of reduction in errors and job satisfaction, but it may open the way to increased use of such participative, effective-based systems with the support staff in other libraries.

Evaluation of Supervisors

Supervisory responsibilities form a large part of the job duties of many librarians, support staff, and even, to some extent, student employees. The evaluation of this portion of a supervisor's performance is critical, especially since most library employees learn how to perform these functions on the job, with little formal training. Feedback through an appraisal system is an important element in this learning process. Jaffe and Ives are accurate in stating, "Many librarians attain supervisory positions primarily on their expertise in collection development, programming, grantsmanship, cataloging, etc., without even being assessed on their ability to manage people." They have developed a supervisory development instrument with twenty questions measuring leadership abilities, communication skills, organizational climate, and human relations within the library to facilitate the supervisory development process.[174]

There are two obvious raters with knowledge of a supervisor's performance of his or her supervisory duties: the superior and the subordinates. The superior can utilize feedback from the appraisal of subordinates to improve supervisory skills. In addition, the supervisor's superior can incorporate these evaluations into appraisal of the subordinates' success in performing their supervisory functions.

The University of New Mexico has implemented a system that uses the following set of guidelines for both evaluators and supervisors:

—Performance of supervisory functions
  (keeping you informed, giving clear work assignments, accessibility . . .
  making his/her expectations clear. . . .)
—Development of innovative library procedures
—Promotion of good public relations within the library
—Creation and maintenance of an atmosphere that encourages staff creativity
—Knowledge of the process of his/her own department
—Work habits[175]

The evaluations based on these guidelines are incorporated into the annual evaluations of the supervisor. At the completion of the evaluation process, all written evaluations, and any notes taken during oral evaluations, are destroyed.

The system of department head evaluation at Virginia Polytechnic Institute and State University has been described by Linkins, while Lorna Peterson reports that evaluation by subordinates was a "positive, innovative, and useful management tool" when implemented at Iowa State University.[176]

Professional Librarians

"The librarian, who was to be in holy orders, should once a year hand over to the chancellor and proctors the keys of the library: If after visitation he was found to be fit in morals, fidelity, and ability he received them back."[177] This statement, from a 1412 code of statutes respecting administration of the first University Library (Cobhan's Library) at Oxford, represents an early statement of performance criteria. One wonders if the visitation was more dreaded than evaluation interviews can be in our times, and what specific abilities the librarian was to demonstrate.

McAnally gives a more recent statement of evaluation criteria which emphasizes the obligations of librarians who are members of the faculty: success in teaching, research and creative work, professional competence and activity, university and public service, and administrative service.[178]

Libraries are service organizations with the primary goal of the provision of material and information to the library's various groups of clientele: researchers, students, faculty, and members of the community. Given this stated organizational goal, the performance appraisal system for the library's professional staff should direct each librarian's efforts toward it through a process that places primary emphasis on the key responsibilities of the individual librarian's position. Success in teaching, research, and creative work should be emphasized, as these skills facilitate the performance of the key job responsibilities.

The *ARL SPEC Flyer* #140, reviewing the changes in the use of performance appraisal systems in ARL libraries, notes that in 1979 a previous survey reported several encouraging trends: "New approaches to performance review are oriented toward contributing to organizational goals, opening lines of communication between the supervisors and employees, and developing staff members."[179] Results from the present survey reveal "research libraries treat performance appraisal as an important, formal communication process, and they expect strenuous effort to devise processes that are open, multidirectional, and designed to encourage rather than dishearten."[180]

The focusing of attention on key responsibilities may be done most effectively by function. Reference librarians should be evaluated on such criteria as effectiveness in providing information requested by patrons, measured by unobtrusive tests, opinions of user service,[181] or opinions of peers; librarian-initiated student contracts; development of library in-service instructional programs; one-on-one teaching of students and other library patrons in the use of the card catalog, reference collection, or the general collection.[182]

Schwartz and Eakin describe a process of developing an evaluation checklist of reference skills such as attitude and demeanor; interviewing, listening, referring, search strategy; knowledge of resources and collections; and knowledge of services and policies from a preliminary list of qualities associated with good reference service.[183] Young also advocates focussing on behavior: what reference librarians do and how they do it.[184]

The fall/winter 1984 issue of *Reference Librarian* addressed the topic of evaluation of reference services. In it, Weech summarizes the variable of staff characteristics and concludes, "Research results seem to confirm the need to go beyond the paper credentials of education and experience and the subjective assessment of personality to properly predict and evaluate the performance of individual reference staff." He recommends the use of interviews, questionnaires, tests, and observations to facilitate the evaluation.[185]

In the same issue, Adams and Judd describe a process of goal analysis that leads to a list of desired "performances" divided into various levels. For example, the goal, "Reference librarians should relate positively to patrons," has as two (of six) performances: appears approachable to patrons by smiling, in maintaining eye contact, . . . listening carefully and reassures the unskilled, unsure patron.[186]

Catalogers may be evaluated on quantity and quality measures. Additional evaluation criteria might include success in learning to catalog in new online systems, undertaking assignments in subject areas outside the cataloger's primary specialty, and development of a collection of cataloging tools.[187]

Many professional librarians hold responsibilities that require subject or technical expertise in areas other than library science. Personnel librarians may be rated on their knowledge of federal, state, and local personnel practices, rules, and regulations and their awareness of current developments in the field, for instance, interpretations of federal guidelines on affirmative action or sexual harassment. Though it is difficult for evaluators to assess such technical competence,[188] they do know if other libraries are using programs or systems that reflect a later state of the art. They are also aware of failures on the part of the specialist to avoid arbitration hearings or claims of noncompliance or discrimination.

Librarians with responsibilities for developing collections may be rated on such criteria as knowledge of the specific subject area in which they have collection development and assessment responsibilities; knowledge and responsiveness to target audiences within the library mission; knowledge and use of review media and publishing sources; knowledge of the resources of area libraries and the community; and knowledge of established selection procedures. The Phoenix Public Library has developed an appraisal system using these six criteria, each of which are broken into components used in developing a subject specialist self-development plan and a self-evaluation at the end of the appraisal period.[189]

At the University of Illinois at Urbana-Champaign factors addressed in interviews with evaluators include keeping abreast of research and current developments in the field of expertise, identification and acquisition of materials in the field, responsiveness to faculty, user suggestions for material for acquisition, and appropriateness of items purchased within the limits of budgets and collection development policies.[190]

Professionals with administrative responsibilities must be evaluated on their performance in these responsibilities. Charles McClure has written, "Library managers must become managers first and librarians second."[191] He suggests such critical performance areas as increased utilization of human resources, involvement in the way actual decisions are made in the library, library planning, and the application of basic research and statistical skills to find out what is happening in the library.[192]

Berkner suggests some additional performance criteria taken from Charles Gibbons's "marks of a mature manager": ability to make decisions, act on them, and accept responsibility for them; ability to delegate and to depend on subordinates; and ability to maintain good relationships with others.[193]

Paul Metz's survey of the role of the academic library director found moderate to heavy involvement in the following functions from which performance criteria could evolve: making policy, supervising staff, making up budgets, determining user needs, getting money and other resources, and interpreting library programs.[194]

Weingand and Ryan used a list of fifteen administrative competences and a set of managerial skills to survey top-level managers in libraries in the United States and Canada serving a population base of 100,000 or greater, the study attempted to determine whether these directors and their assistants or deputies had acquired these skills using self-assessments and assessments of the director by the head of the library's governing board. Weingand and Ryan report that the directors feel they are well above average in their managerial abilities.[195]

The Dupage Library System, a multitype library system, uses a goals-based system for evaluating its executive director in six goals-based areas which include fiscal, physical plant, personnel/staff, relations with member and affiliate libraries, the board, and professional and legal relationship with other organizations.[196]

Middle managers at the University of Nebraska at Omaha Library are evaluated by subordinates on twenty-nine factors including vision to see possibility for constructive change, effective use of resources, delegates/shares responsibility for decision making in a meaningful way, and works effectively to promote a high-level of morale.[197]

Price lists thirteen qualities or job-related factors that should be provided by administrators for the best possible employee-employer relationship which include stability, responsibility, meaning in the position, leadership, flexibility, support by administration, and growth opportunities.[198]

Special librarians have a distinct set of criteria, identified by Bess Walford, which includes short- and long-term planning for space, equipment, and utilization of new technologies; supervision; provision of budgeting and accounting information; indexing, classification, and cataloging to retrieve material for the user; and knowledge of specialized information sources outside the parent organization.[199]

The Value of Performance Appraisals

We have come a long way in librarianship from performance systems emphasizing morals, fidelity, and as a third priority, undefined abilities. As resources supporting libraries become less abundant, and service demands, output of information, and inflationary pressures increase, libraries will be able to meet their service goals only with maximum utilization of their human resources. Effective performance appraisal systems are a key element in the ability of libraries to effectively use and actively increase the knowledge, skills, and abilities of members of their staff. Yet, they are time-consuming to develop, the evaluation process itself is a difficult task for supervisors and raters, and the search for improvement in both system and process leads organizations to change their programs frequently in an attempt to improve them. Given these costs and problems, there is need for continuing research to facilitate this improvement and to provide evidence that conducting appraisals through a formal evaluation process is directly related to maintaining or improving an individual's contribution to the library.

Evans and Rugaas list four areas of potential research to gather evidence about: the effectiveness of performance appraisal practices; the influence of performance appraisal on work relationships (superior/subordinate and peer); the relationship between performance appraisal and productivity; and the cost-benefit of conducting performance appraisals.[200] Results of the research in these areas will be welcomed by administrators, librarians, and other members of library staffs as they work to improve their contribution of the performance appraisal system to the service programs of the libraries.

References

1. This definition has been adapted from Dale Yoder, *Personnel Principles and Policies: Modern Manpower Management,* 2nd ed. (Englewood Cliffs, N.J.: Prentice-Hall, 1959), p. 323.
2. G. Edward Evans and Benedict Rugaas, "Another Look at Performance Appraisals in Libraries," *Journal of Library Administration* 3 (Summer 1982): 62–63.
3. Paul H. Thompson and Gene W. Dalton, "Performance Appraisal: Managers Beware," *Harvard Business Review* 48 (January-February 1970): 159.
4. John Rizzo, *Management for Librarians: Fundamentals and Issues* (Westport, Conn.: Greenwood Press, 1980), p. 223.
5. Douglas MacGregor, "An Uneasy Look at Performance Appraisal," *Harvard Business Review* 50 (September-October 1972): 133–38.

6. Craig Eric Schneier and Richard W. Beatty, *Personnel Administration Today: Readings and Commentary* (Reading, Mass.: Addison-Wesley, 1978), p. 109.
7. Evans and Rugaas, pp. 65–66.
8. Ibid., p. 66.
9. Sheila Creth, *Performance Evaluation: A Goals Based Approach.* CE 106 (Chicago: American Library Association, 1982), p. 2.
10. Paul Pigors and Charles A. Myers, *Personnel Administration: A Point of View and a Method,* 8th ed. (New York: McGraw-Hill, 1977), p. 273.
11. Ibid., p. 272.
12. Association of Research Libraries Office of University Library Management Studies and McGill University Libraries, *Staff Performance Evaluation Program at the McGill University Libraries* (Washington, D.C.: ARL, 1976), p. 2.
13. Reprinted in *CLIP Notes: College Library Information Packets. #1-80: Performance Appraisal* (Chicago: Continuing Education Committee, College Libraries Section, Association of College and Research Libraries, American Library Association, 1980), p. 127.
14. George S. Odiorne, *Guide to Successful Goal Setting* (Westfield, Mass.: MBO, Inc., 1980), p. 7.
15. Information supplied by Susan Lee, Associate Director for Administrative Services, University of Connecticut Libraries.
16. Association of Research Libraries, *SPEC Kit 140: Performance Appraisal in Research Libraries* (Washington, D.C.: ARL, 1988), p. 73.
17. Ibid.
18. Association of Research Libraries, Office of University Library Management Studies, and McGill University Libraries, pp. 4–17. As this chapter is being prepared for publication, the staff performance evaluation system at McGill is under review.
19. Jeffrey J. Gardner, "Performance Evaluation in Libraries," in *Personnel Development in Libraries,* ed. R. Kay Maloney. (New Brunswick, N.J.: Bureau of Library and Information Science Research, Rutgers University Graduate School of Library Service, 1976), p. 3.
20. Howard P. Smith, with the assistance of Paul J. Brouwer, *Performance Appraisal and Human Development: A Practical Guide to Effective Managing* (Reading, Mass.: Addison-Wesley, 1977), p. 9.
21. J. Richard Hackman et al., "A New Strategy for Job Enrichment," *California Management Review* 17 (October 1970): 57–71.
22. For a discussion of the relationship between job satisfactions and performance (i.e., does performance lead to satisfaction or satisfaction to performance) see Donald P. Schwab and L.L. Cummings, "Theories of Performance and Satisfaction: A Review," *Industrial Relations* 9 (October 1970): 408–30.
23. Rizzo, p. 227.
24. Ibid., pp. 227–28.
25. James Michalko, "Management by Objectives and the Academic Library: A Critical Overview," *Library Quarterly* 45 (July 1975): 237.
26. Larry Yarbrough, "Performance Appraisal in Academic and Research

Libraries," *Association of Research Libraries Management Supplement 3* (May 1975): 2–3.

27. Douglas Cederblom, "The Performance Appraisal Interview: a Review, Implications, and Suggestions," *Journal of Library Administration* 4 (Summer 1983): 111, reprinted from *Academy of Management Review* 7 (1982): 219–27.

28. Herbert Meyer, Emanuel Kay, and John R.P. French, Jr., "Split Roles in Performance Appraisal," *Harvard Business Review* 43 (January-February 1965): 123–29.

29. Howard P. Smith, p. 17.

30. Thomas B. Wilson, "Making Negative Feedback Work," *Personnel Journal* 57 (December 1978): 681–82.

31. Jay S. Kim and W. Clay Hammer, "Effect of Performance Feedback and Goal Setting on Productivity and Satisfaction in an Organizational Setting," *Journal of Applied Psychology* 61 (February 1976): 48.

32. Ibid., p. 56.

33. Ernest R. DeProspo, "Personnel Evaluation as the Impetus to Growth," *Library Trends* 20 (July 1971): 65.

34. See Harry Levinson, "Appraisal of What Performance?," *Harvard Business Review* 54 (July-August 1976): 30, for an evaluation program emphasizing behavior as well as results.

35. Stanley P. Hodge, "Performance Appraisals: Developing a Sound Legal and Managerial System," *College and Research Libraries* 44 (July 1983): 238.

36. Alva F. Kendall and James Gatza, "Positive Program for Performance Appraisal," *Harvard Business Review* 41 (November-December 1963): 153–66, describes a program that emphasizes the development of potential.

37. Sheila D. Creth, *Manpower Planning, Job Analysis and Job Evaluation,* Council on Library Resources Fellowship Report, November, 1980.

38. Association of Research Libraries, *ARL SPEC Kit #140,* p. 73.

39. Rizzo, p. 231.

40. *Guide for Improving Performance Appraisal: A Handbook,* prepared by Priscilla Levinson (Washington, D.C.: U.S. Office of Personnel Management, revised 1980), p. 6.

41. Michael Day, "Performance Appraisal," in *Administration of Personnel Policies,* ed. Rachel Naylor and Derek Torrington (Epping: Gower Press, 1974), pp. 136–37.

42. Samuel Rothstein, "Professional Staff in Canadian University Libraries," *Library Journal* 111 (1 November 1986): 31–34.

43. Richard J. Mayer, "Keys to Effective Appraisal," *Management Review* 69 (June 1980): 60; and Meyer, Kay, and French, Jr., pp. 124, 129.

44. See Thomas A. Basnight, "Designing Master, or 'Ideal', Pay Performance Matrices," *Compensation Review* 12 (Fourth Quarter 1980): 44–50, for a technical discussion of how to design pay matrices linking performance and salary levels.

45. Levinson, p. 5.

46. Jeffrey R. Krull, "A Merit Pay Plan for Public Libraries," *Library Journal* 112 (15 June 1987): 36.

47. Thompson and Dalton, p. 149.
48. Information supplied by Gerald Munoff, University of Chicago Library, Assistant Director for Administration and Development.
49. Information supplied by Joan McConkey, Assistant Director for Administration, University of Colorado Libraries.
50. Information supplied by Susan Lee, Associate Director for Administrative Services, University of Connecticut Library.
51. Association of Research Libraries, *ARL SPEC Kit #140*, pp. 95–96.
52. Ibid., pp. 54–61.
53. Ann Allan and Kathy J. Reynolds, "Performance Problems: A Model for Analysis and Resolution," *Journal of Academic Librarianship* 9 (1983): 83–88.
54. Marion S. Kellogg, *What to Do About Performance Appraisal* (New York: American Management Association, 1965), pp. 117–26.
55. Gerald V. Barrett and Mary C. Kernan, "Performance Appraisal and Terminations: A Review of Court Decisions since Brito v. Zia with Implications for Personnel Practices," *Personnel Psychology* 40 (1987): 496.
56. Alan L. Patz, "Performance Appraisals: Useful but Still Resisted," Harvard Business Review 53 (May-June 1975): 74.
57. U.S. Government, "Guidelines on Employee Selection Procedures," *Federal Register* 35 (August 1, 1970): 12334 as cited in William H. Holley and Hubert S. Field, "Performance Appraisal and the Law," *Labor Law Journal* 26 (July 1975): 422–29. This article, along with Dena Schneier's cited below, provides a good review of the court decisions interpreting the guidelines.
58. Dena B. Schneier, "The Impact of EEO Legislation of Performance Appraisal," *Personnel* 55 (July-August 1978): 25.
59. Ibid., p. 27.
60. Richard W. Beatty and Craig Eric Schneier, *Personnel Administrator: An Experiential/Skill Building Approach* (Reading, Mass.: Addison-Wesley, 1977), p. 81.
61. Holley and Feild, p. 428.
62. Beatty and Schneier, p. 81.
63. Holley and Feild, p. 429.
64. Nancy Percy, Assistant State Librarian, California, may be contacted for further information on the third phase of this project.
65. See Nancy Patton Van Zant, ed., *Personnel Policies in Libraries* (New York: Neal-Schuman, 1980), pp. 174–96, for both public and academic library policies covering evaluation during the probationary period.
66. Johnson, pp. 359–60.
67. Van Zant, p. xix, xxi.
68. Association of Research Libraries, *ARL SPEC Kit* #140, p. 1.
69. Hewitt Associates, *Employment Coordinator,* RIA section PM-14, 055, n.d.
70. Alan H. Locher and Kenneth S. Teel, "Performance Appraisal: A Survey of Current Practices," *Personnel Journal* 56 (May 1977): 245.
71. Robert A. Zawacki and Robert L. Taylor, "A View of Performance Apprais-

al from Organizations Using It," *Personnel Journal* 55 (June 1976): 291–92.

72. Kenneth S. Teel, "Performance Appraisal: Current Trends Persistent Progress," *Personnel Journal* (April 1980): 297–301.
73. Hewitt Associates, *Employment Coordinator,* RIA, section P.M.-14,051–14,070, looseleaf.
74. Rizzo, pp. 143–274.
75. Craig Eric Schneier and Richard W. Beatty, "Integrating Behaviorally-based and Effectiveness-based Methods," *Personnel Administrator* 24 (July 1979): 66.
76. Cummings and Schwab, p. 71.
77. Ibid., pp. 72–73.
78. *Performance Appraisal Design Manual,* 2nd printing. Bridgewater, N.J.: F. Fournies and Associates, Inc., 1983 looseleaf, pp. 3-11–12.
79. Rizzo, pp. 233–36.
80. Stuart Hannabus, "The Concept of Performance: A Semantic Review," *ASLIB Proceedings* 39 (May 1987): 149–58.
81. Cummings and Schwab, p. 71.
82. Yarbrough, p. 2.
83. Teel, p. 297.
84. Schneier and Beatty, "Integrating Behaviorally-based and Effectiveness-based Methods," p. 68.
85. Rizzo, pp. 246–48.
86. Cummings and Schwab, pp. 91–93.
87. Craig Eric Schneier and Richard W. Beatty, "Developing Behaviorally-Anchored Rating Scales (BARS)," *Personnel Administrator* 24 (August 1979): 59–68.
88. Hodge, pp. 238–41.
89. *CLIP Notes: College Library Information Packets, #1-80,* pp. 43–52.
90. Miner, pp. 216–19.
91. Ibid., pp. 194–96.
92. Rizzo, p. 245.
93. Cummings and Schwab, p. 86.
94. Information supplied by Pamela Meredith, Head, Reference Section, PSD/LO National Library of Medicine. Indexing standards related to the elements in specific positions in the Indexing Section are included in the section's Employee Performance Management System. For additional information about EPMS elements, see the section on Standards.
95. See *Personnel Administrator* 25 (February 1980) for a series of articles on assessment centers.
96. Peter Hiatt, "Should Professionals be Managers?" *Journal of Library Administration* 4 (Spring 1983): 21–39.
97. David Peele, "Performance Ratings and Librarians' Rights," *American Libraries* 1 (June 1970): 595.
98. Yarbrough, p. 3.
99. David Dowell, "How Would You Rate Joe Benson?," *Southeastern Librarian* 27 (Summer 1977): 72.
100. Ibid., p. 73.

101. See Yoder, p. 333, figure 18:1, for an example of this type of ranking.
102. Miner, pp. 212–13, 214–19.
103. Joyce D. Veenstra, Performance Standards for Librarians: Are They Coming or Not? Ed 096 956. Paper presented at the American Library Association Annual Conference, New York, 1974.
104. Ibid., p. 7.
105. Ibid., p. 8.
106. The information on the standards established at the National Library of Medicine was provided by Pamela Meredith, Head, Reference Section, PSD/LO, National Library of Medicine. The Indexing Section Employee Performance Management System.
107. National Library of Medicine. Reference Section, *Employee Performance Management System Elements,* Calendar year 1987, p. 134.
108. Fred C. Thayer, "Civil Service Reform and Performance Appraisal: A Policy Disaster," *Public Personnel Management Journal* 10 (1981): 20.
109. Ibid.
110. Rod Beaulieu, "An Easier Look at Performance Appraisal," *Training and Development Journal* 34 (October 1980): 56–58.
111. David J. Mollenhoff, "How to Measure Work by Professionals," *Management Review* 66 (November 1977): 41.
112. F. Fournier and Associates, pp. 7-1–7-13.
113. One example of the interview rating form was published in *Library Selection Project: Selection System Design for Entry-Level Librarian-Phase II* (Sacramento, Calif.: Selection Consulting Center, 1978), p. 41.
114. Fred C. Pfister and Nelson Towle, "A Practical Model for a Developmental Appraisal Program for School Library Media Specialists," *School Library Media Quarterly* (Winter 1983): 119.
115. Joyce P. Vincelette and Fred C. Pfister, "Improving Performance Appraisal in Libraries," *LISR* 6 (1984): 191–203. See also Fred C. Pfister, "Competences Essential for School Media Specialists," *Journal of Education for Librarianship* 23 (Summer 1982): 29–42.
116. Robert N. Case, *Behavioral Requirements Analysis Checklist: Information Resulting from Phase II of the School Library Manpower Project* (Chicago: American Library Association, 1976), p. ix.
117. Kim and Hammer, p. 48.
118. DeProspo, pp. 66–68.
119. Dimity Berkner, "Library Staff Development through Performance Appraisal," *College and Research Libraries* 40 (June 1979): 377–8.
120. Michalko, p. 250.
121. Jeffrey S. Kane and Kimberly A. Freeman, "MBO and Performance Appraisal: A Mixture That Is Not a Solution, Part 2," *Personnel* (February 1987): 26–32.
122. See Craig Eric Schneier and Richard W. Beatty, "Combining BARS and MBO: Using an Appraisal System to Diagnose Performance Problems," *Personnel Administrator* 24 (September 1979): 53.
123. Sheila Creth, *Performance Evaluation: A Goals-Based Approach,* p. 9.
124. Ibid., pp. 11–14.
125. Mark L. McConkie, "A Classification of the Goal Setting and Appraisal

Process," *Academy of Management Review* 4 (1979): 29–40, reprinted in *Journal of Library Administration* 2 (Spring 1981): 71–86.

126. "Contract 'Evaluation' Form," *The Unabashed Librarian* 23 (1977): 7.

127. Neal K. Kaske, "Personnel and Employment: Performance Appraisal," in *ALA Yearbook 1978: Review of Library Events, 1977* (Chicago: American Library Association, 1978), p. 229.

128. F.W. Lancaster, "The Evaluation of Library and Information Services," in F.W. Lancaster and C.W. Cleverdon, *Evaluation and Scientific Management of Libraries and Information Centres* (Leyden: Noordhoff, 1977), p. 9.

129. Richard M. Dougherty, "The Human Side of Library Effectiveness," in Allan F. Hershfield and Morell D. Boone, eds., *Approaches to Measuring Library Effectiveness: A Symposium* (Syracuse, N.Y.: Syracuse University School of Library Science, 1972), p. 42.

130. Ibid., p. 46.

131. Johnson, p. 364.

132. Association of Research Libraries, *ARL SPEC Kit* #140, p. 19.

133. Peter J. McGuire, "Why Performance Appraisals Fail," *Personnel Journal* 59 (September 1980): 745.

134. Association of Research Libraries, *ARL SPEC Kit* #140, p. 5.

135. Dowell, p. 77.

136. Kenneth Teel, "Self-Appraisal Revisited," *Personnel Journal* 57 (July 1978): 366.

137. Lloyd Baird, "Self and Superior Ratings of Performance: As Related to Self-Esteem and Job Satisfaction with Supervision," *Academy of Management Journal* 20 (June 1977): 291–300.

138. Rizzo, p. 106.

139. Johnson, p. 364.

140. Association of Research Libraries, *ARL SPEC Kit* #140, p. 43–49.

141. *College and Research Libraries News* 8 (September 1972): 210–11.

142. Thomas Yen-Ran Yeh, "Library Peer Evaluation for Promotions and Merit Increase: How It Works," *College and Research Libraries* 34 (July 1973): 270–74.

143. Mary Lee Bundy and Paul Wasserman, "Professionalism Reconsidered," *College and Research Libraries* 29 (January 1968): 16; and David G.E. Sparks, "Academic Librarianship: Professional Strivings and Political Reality," *College and Research Libraries* 41 (September 1980): 419.

144. Gardner, pp. 9–10.

145. Frederick Duda, "Columbia's Two-Track System," *College and Research Libraries* 41 (July 1980): 298.

146. Ibid.

147. Association of Research Libraries, *ARL SPEC Kit* #140, p. 34.

148. Ibid.

149. Patricia M. Wallace, "Performance Evaluation: The Use of a Single Instrument for University Librarian and Teaching Faculty," *Journal of Academic Librarianship* 12 (November 1986): 284–90.

150. Roland Person, "Library Faculty Evaluation: An Idea Whose Time Continues to Come," *Journal of Academic Librarianship* 5 (July 1979): 143.

151. Allen M. McEvoy and Paul F. Buller, "User Acceptance of Peer Appraisals in an Industrial Setting," *Personnel Psychology* 40 (1987): 185–86.
152. Ibid., p. 795.
153. Henrietta Reifler, "Peer Evaluation at Washington State University Libraries: A Two-Year Experiment," *Journal of Library Administration* 4 (1983): 51–73.
154. At the University of Illinois at Urbana-Champaign the visiting committee is charged with meeting with the candidate for tenure or promotion with instructions that "praise and helpful suggestions may be offered as appropriate. Information obtained via interviews may be summarized for candiate (sic) but confidentiality of sources must be maintained." Association of Research Libraries, *ARL SPEC Kit* #140, p. 40.
155. Rizzo, p. 105.
156. Schneier, "Multiple Rater Groups and Performance Appraisal," *Public Personnel Management* 6 (January-February 1977): 14.
157. Schneier, "Combining BARS and MBO," pp. 51–60.
158. John Stinson and John Stokes, "How to Multi-Appraise," *Management Today* (June 1980): 43–53.
159. Rizzo, p. 237.
160. Peggy Holleman, "Evaluating Community College Faculty Librarians," *Community and Junior College Libraries* 2 (Fall 1983): 69.
161. Cummings and Schwab, pp. 119–26.
162. Constance Corey and Virginia Steel, "Pay for Performance: The TE*MS Experiment," in *Energies for Transition; Proceedings of the 4th ACRL National Conference,* ed. by Danuta Nitecki (Chicago: Association of College and Research Libraries, 1986), pp. 122–29.
163. Beatty and Schneier, *Personnel Administrator,* pp. 81–82.
164. John D. McMillan and Hoyt W. Doyel, "Performance Appraisal: Match the Tool to the Task," *Personnel* 57 (July-August 1980): 17.
165. Cummings and Schwab, pp. 124–25.
166. H.S.J. Carroll, Jr., and H.L. Tosi, "Implementation of MBO: Some Organizational Considerations," reprinted in Craig Eric Schneier and Richard W. Beatty, *Personnel Administration Today: Readings and Commentary* (Reading, Mass.: Addison-Wesley, 1978), pp. 145, 147.
167. Forest C. Benedict and Paul M. Gherman, "Implementing an Integrated Personnel System," *Journal of Academic Librarianship* 6 (September 1980): 212–13, and Mary A. Hall, "A Funny Thing Happened on the Way to . . . a Performance Appraisal Form," *Public Libraries* 171 (Spring 1978): 13–14.
168. University of Illinois at Urbana-Champaign, *Visiting Committee Procedures: Evaluation of Job Performance of Departmental Library Services Faculty.* Appendix B. Typewritten pp. 1–4.
169. Schneier and Beatty, "Developing Behaviorally-Anchored Ratings Scales (BARS)," p. 62.
170. Beverly Lynch, "Supervisory Training in Libraries: Performance Appraisal Communication, Decision-Making, and Motivation," *Journal of Library Administration* 1 (Fall 1980): 36.
171. Norman R.F. Maier has written a classic volume on types of appraisal

interviews: *The Appraisal Interview: Three Basic Approaches* (La Jolla, Calif.: University Associates, 1976).

172. Sally Stevenson, *Performance Appraisal for Librarians: A Guided Self Study Approach* (Albany, N.Y.: State University of New York, 1984): 31–38. ED234-804.

173. Martha Lewis, "Management by Objectives: Review, Application, and Relationship with Job Satisfaction and Performance," *Journal of Academic Librarianship* 5 (January 1980): 329–34.

174. Martin Elliott Jaffe and Sheila Ives, "They Shoot Supervisors, Don't They," *Library Journal* 112 (15 February 1987): 116–18.

175. The system was first described in a memorandum from Paul Vassallo to: All Library Employees; Subject: Evaluation of Supervisors, dated February 12, 1981 and continues in use, supplemented by an evaluation of department heads by other department heads.

176. Germaine C. Linkins, "Department Head Evaluations: The Virginia Tech Library Experience," *Journal of Library Administration* 5 (Winter 1984): 53–60, and Lorna Peterson, "The Pecking Order Reversed: A Description of Administrative Review at the William Robert Parks and Eleu Sorge Parks Library," *Journal of Education Media and Library Sciences* 22 (Spring 1985): 241.

177. Strickland Gibson, *Some Oxford Libraries* (London: Oxford University Press, 1914), p. 8.

178. Arthur M. McAnally, "Privileges and Obligations of Academic Status," *College and Research Libraries* 24 (March 1963): 103.

179. Association of Research Libraries, SPEC Flyer #140 *Performance Appraisal.* January 1988. Washington, D.C.: ARL, 1988.

180. Ibid.

181. Charles A. Bunge, "Approaches to the Evaluation of Library Reference Services," in Lancaster and Cleverdon, p. 53.

182. John W. Ellison and Deborah B. Lazeration, "Personnel Accountability Form for Academic Reference Librarians: A Model," *RQ* 16 (Winter 1976): 145.

183. Diane G. Schwartz and Dottie Eakin, "Reference Standards, Performance Criteria, and Evaluation, *Journal of Academic Librarianship* 12 (March 1986): 4–8.

184. William F. Young, "Methods of Evaluating Reference Desk Performance," *RQ* 25. (Fall 1985): 69–75. Young criticizes the use of MBO in evaluating reference librarians and writes, "The argument may be made that MBO as a tool of personnel evaluation has had a detrimental impact on traditional reference service . . . the emphasis on MBO has, moreover, caused us to neglect traditional reference service and to focus on more measurable factors such as 'personal development activities,' 'initiated faculty consultations,' professional associations . . . 'librarian-initiated student contacts,' etc."

185. Terry Weech, "Who's Giving All Those Wrong Answers? Direct Service and Reference Personnel Evaluation," *Reference Librarian* 11 (Fall/Winter 1984): 115, 117.

186. Mignon S. Adams and Blanche Judd, "Evaluating Reference Librarians:

Using Goal Analysis as a First Step," *Reference Librarian* II (Fall/Winter 1984): 139.

187. Laura Cummings, former Chief, Bibliographic Control Division, Columbia University Libraries, suggested some of these evaluation factors as appropriate supplements to quantity and quality standards.

188. See "Appraising Experts Out of Your Field," *Research Institute Personal Report for the Executive* (December 2, 1980), pp. 5–6, for techniques on establishing criteria for their performance.

189. "Six Broadly Defined Selection Characteristics Central to Quality Subject Selection with Lists of What an Excellent Collection Developer Does," Phoenix Public Library, Phoenix, Arizona, typewritten, 3 p.

190. University of Illinois at Urbana-Champaign, *Visiting Committee Procedures,* Appendix B, p. 2.

191. Charles R. McClure, "Library Managers: Can They Manage: Will They Lead?" *Library Journal* 105 (15 November 1980): 183–85.

192. Ibid.

193. Berkner, p. 339.

194. Paul Metz, "The Role of the Academic Library Director," *Journal of Academic Librarianship* 5 (July 1979): 151.

195. Darlene E. Weingard and Noel Ryan, "Managerial Competencies and Skills: A Joint Study in the United States and Canada," *Journal of Library Administration* 6 (Spring 1985): 23–44.

196. "A Goals and Objectives Evaluation for an Executive Director," *Library Personnel News* 1 (Fall 1987): 30.

197. Joseph A. Starratt and Thomas A. Tollman, "Upward Evaluation of Library Middle Managers," material distributed at ALA Poster Session, Chicago, 1985.

198. Cheryl A. Price, "What Professional Librarians Expect from Administrators: One Librarian's View," *College and Research Libraries* 48 (September 1987): 408–12.

199. Bess P. Walford, "The Evaluation of Special Librarians," Special Libraries 65 (December 1974): 489–91.

200. Evans and Rugaas, p. 68.

Bibliography

Adams, Mignon S. and Blanch Judd. "Evaluating Reference Librarians: Using Goal Analysis as a First Step." *Reference Librarian* 11 (Fall/Winter 1984): 131–45.

Allan, Ann and Kathy J. Reynolds. "Performance Problems: A Model for Analysis and Resolution." *Journal of Academic Librarianship* 9 (1983): 83–88.

"Appraising Experts Out of Your Field," *Research Institute Personal Report for the Executive.* (December 2, 1980), pp. 5–6.

Association of Research Libraries. *SPEC Flyer* #140: January 1988: *Performance Appraisal.* Washington, D.C.: ARL, 1988.

Association of Research Libraries. *SPEC Kit #140: Performance Appraisal in Research Libraries*. Washington, D.C.: ARL, 1988.

Association of Research Libraries, Office of University Library Management Studies, and McGill University Libraries. *Staff Performance Evaluation Program at the McGill University Libraries*. Washington, D.C.: ARL, 1976.

Baird, Lloyd. "Self and Superior Ratings of Performance: As Related to Self Esteem and Job Satisfaction with Supervision." *Academy of Management Journal* 20 (June 1977): 291–300.

Barrett, Gerald V. and Mary C. Kernan. "Performance Appraisal and Terminations: A Review of Court Decisions Since Brito V. Zia with Implications for Personnel Priorities." *Personnel Psychology* 40 (1987): 489–503.

Basnight, Thomas A. "Designing Master, or 'Ideal' Pay Performance Matrices," *Compensation Review* 12 (Fourth Quarter 1980): 44–50.

Beatty, Richard W. and Craig Eric Schneier. *Personnel Administrator: An Experiential/Skill Building Approach*. Reading, Mass.: Addison-Wesley, 1977.

Beaulieu, Rod. "An Easier Look at Performance Appraisal." *Training and Development Journal* 34 (October 1980): 56–58.

Beer, Michael, and Robert A. Ruh. "Employee Growth through Performance Management," *Harvard Business Review* 54 (July-August 1976): 59–66.

Benedict, Forest, and Paul Gherman. "Implementing an Integrated Personnel System." *Journal of Academic Librarianship* 6 (September 1980): 210–14.

Berkner, Dimity. "Library Staff Development through Performance Appraisal," *College and Research Libraries* 40 (June 1979): 335–44.

Bundy, Mary Lee, and Paul Wasserman. "Professionalism Reconsidered." *College and Research Libraries* 29 (January 1968): 5–26.

Bunge, Charles, A. "Approaches to the Evaluation of Library Reference Services," in F.W. Lancaster and C.W. Cleverdon, *Evaluation and Scientific Management of Libraries and Information Centres*. Leyden: Noordoff, 1977.

Burke, Ronald J., William Weitzel, and Tamara Weir. "Characteristics of Effective Employee Performance Review and Development Interviews: Replication and Extension." *Personnel Psychology* 78 (Winter 1978): 903–19.

Carroll, H.S.J., Jr. and H.L. Tosi. "Implementation of MBO: Some Organizational Considerations," reprinted in Schneier, Craig Eric, and Richard W. Beatty, *Personnel Administration Today: Readings and Commentary*. Reading, Mass.: Addison-Wesley, 1978.

Case, Robert N. *Behavioral Requirements Analysis Checklist*. Chicago: American Library Association, 1976.

Cederblom, Douglas. "The Performance Appraisal Interview: A Review, Implications, and Suggestions," *Journal of Library Administration* 4 (Summer 1983): 101–15, reprinted from *Academy of Management Review* 7 (1982): 219–27.

CLIP Notes: College Library Information Packets. #1-80: Performance Appraisal. Chicago: Continuing Education Committee, College Libraries Section, Association of College and Research Libraries, American Library Association, 1980.

"Contract Evaluation Form." *The Unabashed Librarian* 23 (1977): 7.

Corey, Constance and Virginia Steel. "Pay for Performance: The TE*MS Experiment," in *Energies for Transition: Proceedings of the 4th ARL National Conference,* edited by Danuta Nitecki; pp. 122–129. Chicago: Association of College and Research Libraries, 1986.

Creth, Sheila D. *Manpower Planning, Job Analysis and Job Evaluation.* Council on Library Resources Fellowship Report, November 1980.

——. *Performance Evaluation: A Goals Based Approach.* CE 106. Chicago: American Library Association, 1982.

Cummings, L.L. and Donald P. Schwab. "Designing Appraisal Systems for Information Yield." *California Management Review* 20 (Summer 1978): 18–25.

——. *Performance in Organizations: Determinants and Appraisal.* Glenview, Ill.: Scott Foresman, 1973.

Day, Michael. "Performance Appraisal." In *Administration of Personnel Policies,* Rachel Naylor and Derek Torrington, eds. Epping: Gower Press, 1974.

DeProspo, Ernest R. "Personnel Evaluation as an Impetus to Growth," *Library Trends* 20 (July 1971): 60–70.

Dougherty, Richard. "The Human Side of Library Effectiveness." In Hershfield, Allan F., and Morell D. Boone, eds. *Approaches to Measuring Library Effectiveness: A Symposium.* Syracuse, N.Y.: Syracuse University School of Library Service, 1972.

Dowell, David. "How Would You Rate Joe Benson?" *Southeastern Librarian* 27 (Summer 1977): 71–78.

Dowlin, Kenneth E. "An Employee Evaluation System," *Library Journal Special Report #10: Personnel in Libraries.* New York: R.R. Bowker, 1979.

Duda, Frederick. "Columbia's Two-Track System." *College and Research Libraries* 41 (July 1980): 296–304.

Ellison, John W. and Deborah B. Lazeration. "Personnel Accountability Form for Academic Reference Librarians: A Model." *RQ* 16 (Winter 1976): 142–49.

Evans, G. Edward and Benedict Rugaas. "Another Look at Performance Appraisal in Libraries." *Journal of Library Administration* 3 (Summer 1982): 61–69.

F. Fournies and Associates. *Performance Appraisal Design Manual.* Bridgewater, N.J.: F. Fournies and Associates, 1983. Looseleaf.

Fast, Elizabeth T. "In-Service Staff Development As a Logical Part of Performance Evaluation." *School Media Quarterly* 3 (Fall 1974): 35–41.

Ford, Robert C. and Kenneth M. Jennings. "How to Make Performance Appraisals More Effective." *Personnel* 54 (March-April 1977): 51–56.

Gardner, Jeffrey J. "Performance Evaluation in Libraries." In *Personnel Development in Libraries,* R. Kay Maloney, ed. New Brunswick, N.J.: Bureau of Library and Information Science Research, Rutgers University Graduate School of Library Service, 1976.

Gibson, Strickland. *Some Oxford Libraries.* London: Oxford University Press, 1914.

Hackman, J. Richard et al. "A New Strategy for Job Enrichment," *California Management Review* 17 (October 1970): 57–71.

Hall, Mary A. "A Funny Thing Happened On the Way to . . . a Performance Appraisal Forum." *Public Libraries* 171 (Spring 1978): 13–14.

Hannabus, Stuart. "The Concept of Performance: A Semantic Review." *ASLIB Proceedings* 39 (May 1987): 149–58.

Hayashikawa, Doris et al. "Library Faculty Evaluation: The Texas A & M Case." *Texas Library Journal* 51 (Summer 1975): 68–71.

Haynes, Marion G. "Developing An Appraisal Program." *Personnel Journal* 57 (January 1978): 14–19.

Hewitt Associates. *Employment Coordinator*. Section 14,051. New York Research Institute of America, 1984, looseleaf.

Hiatt, Peter. "Should Professionals Be Managers?" *Journal of Library Administration* 4 (Spring 1983): 21–39.

Hilton, Robert C. "Performance Evaluation of Library Personnel." *Special Libraries* 69 (November 1978): 429–34.

Hodge, Stanley P. "Performance Appraisals: Developing a Social Legal and Managerial Systems." *College and Research Libraries* 44 (July 1983): 235–44.

Holleman, Peggy. "Evaluating Community College Faculty Librarians." *Community and Junior College Libraries* 2 (Fall 1983): 63–72.

Holley, William H. and Hubert S. Feild. "Performance Appraisal and the Law." *Labor Law Journal* 26 (July 1975): 423–30.

Jacobs, Arturo A. "What's Wrong With Performance Evaluation Programs?" *Supervisory Management* 22 (July 1977): 10–14.

Jaffe, Martin Elliott and Sheila Ives. "They Shoot Supervisors, Don't They?" *Library Journal* 112 (15 February 1987): 116–18.

Johnson, Marjorie. "Performance Appraisal of Librarians—A Survey." *College and Research Libraries* 33 (September 1972): 359–67.

Kane, Jeffrey S. and Kimberley A. Freeman. "MBO and Performance Appraisal: A Mixture That Is Not a Solution, Part 2." *Personnel* 64 (February 1987): 26–32.

Kaske, Neal K. "Personnel and Employment: Performance Appraisal." In *ALA Yearbook 1978: Review of Library Events, 1977*. Chicago: American Library Association, 1978.

Kearney, William J. "The Value of Behaviorally-Based Performance Appraisals." *Business Horizons* 19 (June 1976): 75–83.

Kellogg, Marion S. *What to Do About Performance Appraisal*. New York: American Management Association, 1965.

Kendall, Alva F. and James Gatza. "Positive Program for Performance Appraisal." *Harvard Business Review* 41 (November-December 1963): 153–66.

Kim, Jay S. and W. Clay Hammer. "Effect of Performance Feedback and Goal Setting on Productivity and Satisfaction in an Organizational Setting." *Journal of Applied Psychology* 61 (February 1976): 48–57.

Krull, Jeffrey R. "A Merit Pay Plan for Public Libraries." *Library Journal* 112 (15 June 1987): 34–37.

Lancaster, F.W. "The Evaluation of Library and Information Services." In Lancaster, F.W., and C.W. Cleverdon, *Evaluation and Scientific Management of Libraries and Information Centers*. Leyden: Noordhoff, 1977.

Lee, M. Blaine and William L. Zwerman. "Designing a Motivating and Team Building Employee Appraisal System." *Personnel Journal* 55 (July 1976): 354–57.

Levinson, Harry. "Appraisal of What Performance?" *Harvard Business Review* 54 (July-August 1976): 30–46, 160.

Lewis, Martha. "Management by Objectives: Review, Application, and Relationships with Job Satisfaction and Performance." *Journal of Academic Librarianship* 5 (January 1980): 329–34.

Library Selection Project. *Selection Systems Design for Entry Level Librarians* Phase II. Sacramento, Calif.: Selection Consulting Center, 1978.

Lindsey, Jonathan A. *Performance Evaluation: A Management Basic for Libraries*. Phoenix: Oryx Press, 1986.

Linkins, Germaine C. "Department Head Evaluations: The Virginia Tech Library Experience." *Journal of Library Administration* 5 (Winter 1984): 53–60.

Locher, Alan H., and Kenneth S. Teel. "Performance Appraisal—A Survey of Current Practices." *Personnel Journal* 56 (May 1977): 245–54.

Lubben, Gary L., Duane E. Thompson, and Charles R. Klasson. "Performance Appraisal: The Legal Implications of Title VII." *Personnel* 57 (May-June 1980): 11–15.

Lynch, Beverly. "Supervisory Training in Libraries: Performance Appraisal, Communication, Decision Making, and Motivation." *Journal of Library Administration* 1 (Fall 1980): 33–41.

McAnally, Arthur A. "Privileges and Obligations of Academic Status." *College and Research Libraries* 24 (March 1963): 102–108.

McClure, Charles R. "Library Managers: Can They Manage? Will They Lead?" *Library Journal* 105 (15 November 1980): 2388–91.

McEvoy, Glenn M. and Paul F. Buller. "User Acceptance of Peer Appraisals in an Industrial Setting." *Personnel Psychology* 40 (1987): 785–86.

MacGregor, Douglas. "An Uneasy Look at Performance Appraisal." *Harvard Business Review* 50 (September-October 1972): 133–38.

McGuire, Peter J. "Why Performance Appraisals Fail." *Personnel Journal* 59 (September 1980): 744–62.

McMillan, John D. and Hoyt W. Doyel. "Performance Appraisal: Match the Tool to the Task." *Personnel* 57 (July-August 1980): 12–20.

Maier, Norman R.F. *The Appraisal Interview: Three Basic Approaches*. La Jolla, Calif.: University Associates, 1976.

Mali, Paul. "Developing and Using a Personnel Evaluation System." In *Personnel Evaluation Institute, Proceedings Held at Eastern Illinois University, Charleston, Illinois, October 24-26, 1975*, ed. Frances M. Pollard, ed. Charleston, Ill.: Eastern Illinois University Department of Library Science, 1976.

Martin, Jess A. "Staff Evaluation of Supervisors." *Special Libraries* 70 (January 1979): 26–29.

Mayer, Richard J. "Keys to Effective Appraisal." *Management Review* 69 (June 1980): 60–62.

Messenger, Michale. "Professional Staff Assessment: The Shropshire Pattern." *Library Association Record* 77 (January 1957): 2–4.

Metz, Paul. "The Role of the Academic Library Director." *Journal of Academic Librarianship* 5 (July 1979): 148–52.

Meyer, Herver H., Emanuel Kay, and John R.P. French, Jr. "Split Roles in

Performance Appraisal." *Harvard Business Review* 43 (January-February 1965): 123–29.

Michalko, James. "Management by Objectives and the Academic Library: A Critical Overview." *Library Quarterly* 45 (July 1975): 235–52.

Michalree, Paul Kevin. "Subjectivity in Appraisal—The Supervisor's Role." *Training and Development Journal* 33 (February 1979): 48–51.

Miner, John B. *Personnel and Industrial Relations: A Managerial Approach.* London: Macmillan, 1969.

Mollenhoff, David V. "How to Measure Work by Professionals." *Management Review* 66 (November 1977): 39–43.

National Library of Medicine. *Employee Performance Management System Reference Section EPMS Elements—Calendar Year 1987*, pp. 110–56. Bethesda, Md: n.d.

Odiorne, George S. *Guide to Successful Goal Setting.* Westfield, Mass.: MBO, Inc., 1980.

Patz, Alan L. "Performance Appraisal: Useful But Still Resisted." *Harvard Business Review* 53 (May-June 1975): 74–80.

Peele, David. "Performance Ratings and Librarians' Rights." *American Libraries* 1 (June 1970): 595–600.

Person, Roland. "Library Faculty Evaluation: An Idea Whose Time Continues to Come." *Journal of Academic Librarianship* 5 (July 1979): 142–47.

Peterson, Lorna. "The Pecking Order Reversed: A Description of Administrative Review at the William Robert Parks and Eleu Sorge Parks Library." *Journal of Educational Media and Library Sciences* 22 (Spring 1985): 231–41.

Pfister, Fred C. "Competencies Essential for School Media Specialists." *Journal of Education for Librarianship* 23 (Summer 1982): 29–42.

Pfister, Fred C. and Nelson Towle. "A Practical Model for Developmental Appraisal Program for School Library Media Specialists." *School Library Media Quarterly* 11 (Winter 1983): 111–21.

Pigors, Paul and Charles A. Myers. *Personnel Administration: A Point of View and a Method,* 8th ed. New York: McGraw-Hill, 1977.

Price, Cheryl A. "What Professional Librarians Expect from Administrators: One Librarian's View." *College and Research Libraries* 48 (September 1987): 408–12.

Renfro, Kathryn R. "Raters and Rating." *Mountain Plains Library Quarterly* 16 (November 1971): 3–12.

Rizzo, John R. *Management for Librarians: Fundamentals and Issues.* Westport, Conn.: Greenwood Press, 1980.

Rothstein, Samuel. "Professional Staff in Canadian University Libraries." *Library Journal* 111 (1 November 1986): 31–34.

Schneier, Craig Eric. "Multiple Rater Groups and Performance Appraisal," *Public Personnel Management* 6 (January-February 1977): 13–20.

Schneier, Craig Eric and Richard W. Beatty. "Combining BARS and MBO: Using an Appraisal System to Diagnose Performance Problems." *Personnel Administrator* 24 (September 1979): 51–60.

———. "Developing Behaviorally-Anchored Rating Scales (BARS)." *Personnel Administrator* 24 (August 1979): 59–68.

————. *Personnel Administration Today: Readings and Commentary*. Reading, Mass.: Addison-Wesley, 1978.

Schneier, Dena B. "The Impact of EEO Legislation on Performance Appraisal." *Personnel* 55 (July-August 1978): 24–34.

Schwab, Donald P. and L.L. Cummings. "Theories of Performance and Satisfaction: A Review." *Industrial Relations* 9 (October 1970): 408–30.

Schwartz, Diane G. and Dottie Eakin. "Reference Standards, Performance Criteria, and Evaluation." *Journal of Academic Librarianship* 12 (March 1986): 4–8.

Sing, Marjorie B. "Merit Rating." *PNLA Quarterly* 20 (October 1955): 40–42.

"Six Broadly Defined Selector Characteristics Central to Quality Subject Selection with Lists of What an Excellent Collection Developer Does." Phoenix Public Library, Phoenix, Arizona, typewritten, n.d.

Smith, Howard P., with the assistance of Paul J. Brouwer. *Performance Appraisal and Human Development: A Practical Guide to Effective Managing*. Reading, Mass: Addison-Wesley, 1977.

Sparks, David G.E. "Academic Librarianship: Professional Strivings and Political Reality." *College and Research Libraries* 41 (September 1980): 408–21.

"Standards for Faculty Status for College and University Librarians." *College and Research Library News* 8 (September 1972): 210–12.

Starratt, Joseph A. and Thomas A. Tollman. "Upward Evaluation of Library Middle Managers." Material distributed at ALA Poster Session, Chicago, 1985.

Stevenson, Sally. *Performance Appraisal for Librarians: A Guided Self Study Approach*. Albany, N.Y.: State University of New York, 1984. ED234-084.

Stinson, John and John Stokes. "How to Multi-Appraise." *Management Today* (June 1980): 45–53.

Teel, Kenneth S. "Performance Appraisal: Current Trends, Persistent Progress." *Personnel Journal* 59 (April 1980): 296–316.

————. "Self-Appraising Revisited." *Personnel Journal* 57 (July 1978): 364–67.

Thayer, Fred C. "Civil Service Reform and Performance Appraisal: A Policy Disaster." *Public Personnel Management Journal* 10 (1980): 20–28.

Thompson, Paul H. and Gene W. Dalton. "Performance Appraisal: Managers Beware." *Harvard Business Review* 98 (January-February 1970): 149–57.

Turner, Anne M. "Why Do Department Heads Take Longer Coffee Breaks?—A Public Library Evaluates Itself." *American Libraries* 9 (April 1978): 213–15.

U.S. Office of Personnel Management. *Guide for Improving Performance Appraisal: A Handbook,* prepared by Priscilla Levinson. Washington, D.C.: OPM. Revised June, 1980.

University of Illinois at Urbana-Champaign. *Visiting Committee Procedures: Evaluation of Job Performance of Departmental Library Services Faculty*. Appendix B, typewritten, n.d.

Van Zant, Nancy Patton, ed. *Personnel Policies in Libraries*. New York: Neal-Schuman, 1980.

Veenstra, Joyce D. *Performance Standards for Librarians: Are They Coming or Not?* Paper presented at the American Library Association Annual Conference, New York, 1974. ED 096 956.

Vincelette, Joyce P. and Fred C. Pfister. "Improving Performance Appraisal in Libraries." *LISR* 6 (1984): 191–203.

Walford, Bess P. "The Evaluation of Special Librarians." *Special Libraries* 65 (December 1974): 489–92.

Wallace, Patricia M. "Performance Evaluation: The Use of a Single Instrument for University Librarians and Teaching Faculty." *Journal of Academic Librarianship* 12 (November 1986): 284–90.

Weech, Terry L. "Who's Giving All Those Wrong Answers? Direct Service and Reference Personnel Evaluation." *Reference Librarian* 11 (Fall/Winter 1984): 109–22.

Weingand, Darlen E. and Noel Ryan. "Managerial Competencies and Skills: A Joint Study in the United States and Canada." *Journal of Library Administration* 6 (Spring 1985): 23–44.

Whisler, Thomas L., and Shirley F. Harper, eds. *Performance Appraisal Research and Practice*. New York: Holt, Rinehart, and Winston, 1962.

Wilson, Thomas B. "Making Negative Feedback Work." *Personnel Journal* 57 (December 1978): 680–81.

Winstanely, N.B. "Legal and Ethical Issues in Performance Appraisals." *Harvard Business Review* 58 (November-December 1980): 186–92.

Yarbrough, Larry. "Performance Appraisal in Academic and Research Libraries." *Association of Research Libraries Management Supplement* 3 (May 1975): 1–5.

Yeh, Thomas Yen-Ran. "Library Peer Evaluation: A Blessing or Nuisance?" *PNLA Quarterly* 42 (Fall 1977): 10–14.

———. "Library Peer Evaluation for Promotion and Merit Increase: How It Works." *College and Research Libraries* 34 (July 1973): 270–74.

Yoder, Dale. *Personnel Principles and Policies: Modern Manpower Management,* 2nd ed. Englewood Cliffs: N.J.: Prentice Hall, 1959.

Young, William F. "Methods for Evaluating Reference Desk Performance." *RQ* 25 (Fall 1985): 69–75.

Zawacki, Robert A. and Robert L. Taylor. "A View of Performance Appraisal from Organizations Using It." *Personnel Journal* 55 (June 1976): 290-99.

8
Compensation Management
Frederick Duda

The social and technological revolutions of the past twenty years have caused profound changes in how librarians function and have enabled some academic librarians, for example, to obtain the status and recognition formerly held only by their faculty colleagues. In some instances, academic librarians have exceeded faculty in salary compensation. All of this has come about during a period of great fiscal constraint.

Librarians of the mid-1960s were underpaid, still bound by the routines and traditions of the late 19th century, and subservient to the power and influence of boards of trustees, faculty, and civil service commissions. We've come a long way, but we rightly continue to despair over our image and role in society, our inability to recruit the best and brightest of college graduates, and our alleged meager financial rewards.

We continue to debate the nature of librarianship and its professional status. Writing just before the outbreak of World War I, Justice Brandeis defined a profession as:

> . . . an occupation for which the necessary preliminary training is intellectual in character, involving knowledge and to some extent learnings, as distinguished from mere skill; which is largely pursued for others, and not merely for one's self; and in which the financial return is not the accepted measure of success.[1]

Whether or not one accepts the Justice's definition, the assumption is that librarianship is a profession and that, like other professions, it is pursued largely for others, whether these others be society as a whole or the clientele of parent institutions.

As a service profession librarianship is ranked low, like teaching, nursing, and social work. Our society is such that librarians will never attain the salaries and the prestige of lawyers, doctors, or corporate executives, but they have in many cases surpassed the compensation levels of the teaching and nursing professions. Societal needs are beginning to rectify the compensation problems of teachers and nurses, and school librarians may well benefit from improvements in the salaries of teachers. Academic librarians, who have benefited from improvements in faculty salaries, will continue to seek higher compensation by capitalizing on their role as information specialists in the electronic age, regardless of their success in meeting either institutional or societal needs.

Our success as a profession depends on the nature and quality of the services we provide and, as it has become increasingly apparent, on cost effectiveness. We should continue to value the nonfinancial rewards of librarianship for, after all, they are what motivated us to become members of the profession. It is equally important, however, to bear in mind that a measure of success must entail appropriate remuneration. We do the profession and ourselves a disservice if we do not make an effort to understand the many factors involved in compensation and utilize them to develop appropriate programs.

THE NATURE OF COMPENSATION PROGRAMS

Compensation programs are based on a number of complex factors internal and external to an organization. These include status and governance, the nature of compensation of faculty and other professionals within the institution, the general cost of living in the area, salary equity and comparable worth considerations, and unionization.

As Milton Rock has stated, compensation is one of the great challenges to management, requiring the creation of "an environment which stimulates people in their jobs."[2] As important as compensation is in recruiting, maintaining, and motivating staff, it is not the sine qua non in an organization. Job content, developmental opportunities, and performance appraisals are all important parts of the total reward system. In addition, the management style of an organization is becoming an increasingly more important factor in the total reward system. As Rock has pointed out:

> . . . compensation is more than pay. It is a total reward system involving incentives and noncash benefits, performance appraisal, and work force development as well as base wages and salaries. Thus, in addition to providing for material needs, the compensation administrator must consider the employee's need for self-realization—the need to feel that he or she is having a real impact on the organization. While money, in one form or another, is a major source of satisfaction and motivation, other factors can be equally important to employee morale. These include the nature of the work, the

organizational environment and style of management, and the company's past performance and its outlook for the future.[3]

OBJECTIVES OF COMPENSATION MANAGEMENT

Compensation management is a specialization that developed in business and civil service in response to the growth in the size and complexity of organizations. As a specialization within the personnel area, it is one that gets scant attention in library administration courses. Library directors and library personnel administrators must therefore learn how to deal with compensation as they must learn how to deal with other aspects of library management, whether it be budget planning or fund raising. Because libraries are part of larger entities, they rely on staff in central administration offices to provide expertise on compensation. This often presents serious disadvantages because of the lack of understanding of the function and duties of librarians, a problem compounded by the dramatic changes in librarianship during the past two decades.

Those who have responsibility for administering compensation programs must educate the specialists in their central personnel offices by presenting them with facts on the nature of library work, particularly that of the professional. The director has an even more important role: educating the administration of the institution and obtaining funds.

Stated succinctly, compensation is what employees get in exchange for their work. The adequacy of the compensation has great impact on the ability of an organization to meet its goals. Inadequate compensation leads to poor performance, absenteeism, excessive turnover, grievances, and strikes. Although such problems will never completely disappear, morale can be positively affected if an organization has formulated and disseminated its compensation objectives.

The objectives of compensation programs are quite practical:

1. *Recruitment:* Compensation needs to be competitive to attract qualified applicants. It also needs to respond to the supply and demand of workers.
2. *Retention:* Competitive compensation prevents excessive turnover.
3. *Equity.* Internal equity requires that pay be related to the relative worth of jobs. That is, similar jobs get similar pay. External equity involves paying workers at a rate equal to the pay that similar workers receive in other companies.
4. *Reward desired behavior.* Compensation should reinforce desired behaviors and act as an incentive for those behaviors to occur in the future.
5. *Control costs.* A sound compensation program helps an organization to obtain and retain its work force at a reasonable cost. Without a systematic

wage and salary structure the organization could overpay or underpay its employees.

6. *Comply with legal regulations.* As with other aspects of personnel management, wage and salary administration faces legal constraints. A sound pay program considers these constraints and ensures compliance with all government regulations that affect employee compensation.

7. *Further administrative efficiency.* In pursuing the other objectives of compensation management, wage and salary specialists try to design the program so that it can be efficiently administered. Administrative efficiency, however, should be a secondary consideration compared with other objectives.[4]

JOB EVALUATION OR CLASSIFICATION

A method of evaluating or classifying employee duties is needed to determine what to pay them in exchange for their work. As O. Glenn Stahl pointed out, this need was recognized by the Senate some 150 years ago:

> On the insistence of a number of government clerks urging equal pay for equal work in 1838, the United States Senate was moved to pass a resolution instructing department heads to prepare a "classification of the clerks" . . . in reference to the charter of the labor to be performed, the care and responsibility imposed, the qualifications required, and the relative values to the public of the services of each class as compared with the others.[5]

Despite this recognition of problems in the federal service, Congress did not take comprehensive action to establish classification systems until 1923.

It is the rare exception now to find an organization that does not have some system of organizing positions or functions, along with salary schedules outlining compensation levels. There are a variety of job evaluation systems in effect in libraries. The most common are based on systems developed in business and industry: job ranking, job grading, factor comparison, and point systems. Many academic libraries have ranking systems for professional positions, generally based on the model of teaching faculty (in institutions where librarians have faculty status, faculty titles are frequently used). An interesting variation on the standard practices in academic libraries is Columbia University Libraries' system which combines both traditional position classification and faculty ranking systems.[6]

The most common job evaluation systems are covered in detail by Sheila Creth in Chapter 4. All such systems involve some degree of subjectivity and, as Donald Treiman and Heidi Hartman have observed, have come under careful scrutiny because of concerns involving pay equity:

> It is important to recognize that job evaluation ultimately rests on judgments. Jobs are described in terms of their tasks, duties, and responsibilities, and these descriptions are rated or ranked with respect to some set of factors. The factor ratings are seldom based on objective information; rather, they represent judgments about such amorphous features of jobs as the responsibility entailed or the experience required. The nature of job evaluation makes it possible for bias to enter at two points: in the writing of the job descriptions and in the evaluation of the descriptions with respect to a set of factors.[7]

Despite the problems inherent in job classification systems, Treiman and Hartman recognize that job evaluation systems do "provide a systematic method of comparing jobs to determine whether they are fairly compensated."[8] They also recognize the possibility of improving them.[9]

Because of the importance job evaluation systems have in compensation, some mention should be made of the Hay System, the best-known point-system method of job evaluation, which was developed by Edward N. Hay and Dale Purves in 1951. It has been applied in some library settings, but has not gained wide acceptance in academic librarianship. This may be due to the real or imagined problems academic library administrators see in assigning points to management functions and to the functions of so-called knowledge workers, that is, librarians engaged primarily in collection development, reference, bibliographic control, and library instruction. However, this is not necessarily the case. In updating the classification scheme for librarian positions at Columbia in 1985, the professional classification task force recognized certain drawbacks to position-grading systems, which "can lead to inequities and to an eventual erosion of the scheme."[10] To compensate for this, a set of principles or point factors were developed to provide "a more consistent approach in the overall assessment of positions."[11]

There are difficulties in evaluating professional and managerial positions. As Paul Pigors and Charles Myers have noted, it is a problem found in all professions:

> [Professional jobs] are much more difficult to describe and analyze in terms of the job content and job factors. Job assignments to many professional people are given on the basis of their individual professional qualifications, and only in large organizations is it possible to describe broad categories of engineering or scientific jobs. This has been called the "generic" approach, which is used in place of either the individual approach or the "career-curve" approach based on professional degrees and years of service. In the latter, the

more advanced professional degrees a person has and the longer the service, the higher the salary. Public school teachers are often paid on this basis.

Some authorities believe that managerial positions at the higher levels are difficult to evaluate because the work of the job is so much a function of the individual in it. As one management consultant has said, "It is pointless to talk about evaluating an executive job, when the real evaluation relates to what an individual has made of his job, compared with what others have made of their jobs. In the final analysis, an executive is 'worth' what his supervisors believe he is worth." He might have added, "and what other firms might pay him if he left."[12]

The quality and success of a job classification scheme will depend to a large extent on the process used in its design and implementation. Since it is impossible for one person to have all the knowledge and understanding necessary to evaluate all jobs in an organization, a job classification committee plays a critical role in the development of a scheme. The committee should be comprised of appropriate representatives from the organization and conduct its work openly. The latter is particularly important because the more open the scheme is to review by employees whose jobs are affected, the better the likelihood that the scheme will be accepted.[13]

DESIGNING A COMPENSATION PROGRAM

The authority of the library director in the design and implementation of compensation programs varies considerably, depending on the organizational structure of the institution, the status of the librarians in the institution, and governance. The authority of directors in libraries with collective bargaining agreements and those in the public sector is often limited, and at times they face seemingly insurmountable obstacle. Academic library directors in private institutions, on the other hand, often have considerable discretion in these areas.

Regardless of local constraints, directors have the most important role to play in establishing and modifying compensation programs. As chief administrators of the library, they are responsible for meeting the service objectives of the institution. Their success in this effort depends on their ability to recruit, motivate, and retain high quality staff. Although they rely on their library personnel administrators to provide the data and expertise to support their arguments, they must also understand the dimensions of salary compensation and the factors common to all organizations and to libraries specifically.

Three factors common to all organizations should be considered carefully in any effort to design or modify a compensation program:[14]

1. The quality of employees the organization needs for effective operation.
2. The compensation among other organizations for employees of this quality.
3. The ability of the organization to pay levels of wages and salaries that will attract and hold the people it needs.

Reviewing Existing Policy

An important initial step in designing or modifying a salary program involves a review of existing policy, both institutional and library. Institutional policies generally include the following factors:[15]

1. Minimum and maximum levels of pay (taking into consideration ability and willingness to pay, government regulations, union influences, and market pressures).
2. The general relationships among levels of pay (between nonexempt and exempt senior management and operating management, operatives and supervisors).
3. The division of the total compensation dollar (i.e., what portion goes into base pay, what portion into benefits, what portion into merit pay or pay-for-performance programs).

Within these general guidelines, the following determinations then have to be made:

1. What is the lowest rate of pay that can be offered for a job that will entice the quality of employees the organization desires to have as its members?
2. What is the rate of pay that must be offered to incumbents to ensure that they remain with the organization?
3. Is it wise or necessary to offer more than one rate of pay to employees performing either identical or similar work?
4. What is considered to be a sufficient difference in base rates of pay among jobs in a class-series that require varying levels of knowledge and skills and responsibilities and duties?
5. Does the organization wish to recognize dangerous and distressing working conditions within the base pay schedule?
6. Should there be a difference in changes in base-pay progression opportunities among jobs of varying worth?
7. Do employees have a significant opportunity to profess to higher-level jobs? If so, what should be the relationship between promotion to a higher job and changes in base pay?
8. Will policies and regulations permit incumbents to earn rates of pay higher than established maximums and lower than established minimums? What would be the reasons for allowing such deviations?
9. How will the pay structure accommodate across-the-board, cost-of-living, or other adjustments not related to employee tenure, performance, or responsibility and duty changes?[16]

Conducting Salary Surveys

Salary surveys are an essential step in designing or modifying a salary program. They involve several steps:

1. *Selection of area or industry, and firms or organizations to be included in the survey.* This is frequently a point of difference with unions, since the inclusion of low-wage, nonunion firms in the sample will usually cause a particular firm's wage level to compare "favorably" with the community or industry.
2. *Listing key jobs and positions common to most firms in the survey.* Detailed descriptions of these jobs [are needed], so that valid comparisons can be made.
3. *Making a schedule of information to be obtained,* e.g., hourly rates or earnings, weekly earnings or salaries, hours worked, shift premiums, other wage and salary supplements, and methods of wage payment. These data are necessary since the meaning of "wages" and "salaries" often varies in different organizations.
4. *Collection of accurate wage and salary data* on jobs that are essentially similar, by questionnaires, or preferably interviews, in each firm.
5. *Compilation of the wage and salary data for each job,* showing the mean or arithmetical average, the median, the range of rates paid, and supplementary wage and salary data. The data may also be reported by companies or organizations, labeled A, B, C, etc.
6. *Finally, presentation of results and recommendations* to management.[17]

Salary surveys may be taken before or during the actual design of a salary structure and are generally considered the most helpful tools in compensation management. They should not be undertaken without a thorough review of survey techniques and methodology.

A critical aspect of any salary survey is identifying *key* or *benchmark* positions. Simply identifying job keys by title does not provide sufficient information. For example, the scope of responsibilities of an interlibrary loan librarian may vary considerably from one library to another. To avoid this pitfall, a *thumbnail sketch,* or job summary, should be developed, consisting of a clear summary of the job description, which provides information on both the general and specific responsibilities of the position.[18]

Fortunately, the library profession has access to important salary data. For many years, academic librarians have relied on the annual salary surveys of the Association of Research Libraries (ARL), which in recent years has been expanded to provide data on ranks and minority status. Another important source is the ALA Survey of Librarian Salaries, first published in 1982 and expanded in 1984 to include ARL members.

There are a variety of informal regional and similar-interest salary surveys in academic librarianship, such as those conducted by the Big Ten, the Gnomes (Chicago, Columbia, Cornell, Harvard, MIT, Princeton, Stanford, Yale), and the ACRL Personnel Officers Discussion Group. In addition, libraries interested in salary information on specific specialist positions can contract with ARL for the manipulation of their data base.

Salary surveys involve a number of complexities that cannot be mastered without considerable study and the expertise of specialists. They have to be approached with careful consideration of institutional policies and guidelines. There is much at stake here because the final product carries great weight. It tells employees what value the organization places on jobs, the job and compensation advancement opportunities available, and how competitive the pay practices are with other organizations.

Although librarians might seem to be at a disadvantage when faced with the technical aspects of compensation design, the fact that libraries are components of larger institutions or governmental bodies means that compensation specialists should be available to provide the necessary expertise.

A brief summary of some of the technical aspects involved in designing a pay structure provides an indication of the complexity involved.

1. *Determining a Pay Policy Line.* A pay policy line is one that best represents the middle pay value of jobs that have been evaluated or classified to have particular worth. It is arrived at through various mathematical formulas.
2. *Deciding on the Need for More Than One Pay Structure.* Since there are different forces at play for different occupational groups, different pay structures are required for clerical workers, unskilled workers, and professionals and administrators.
3. *Identifying Lowest and Highest Rates of Pay.* Consideration here must be given to legal issues, such as the Fair Labor Standards Act, as well as to the ability of the organization to pay.
4. *Developing Pay Grades.* Pay grades are basically convenient groupings of a wide variety of jobs or classes similar in work difficulty and responsibility requirements. They provide a link between the evaluation and classification process and the assignment of pay to a particular job or class.[19]

After the technical aspects of design have been completed, compensation experts need to review the program to insure that there is an orderly and logical progression in the structure. This is necessary to insure that:

1. All jobs have been analyzed and described.

2. Jobs have either been classified or evaluated so that an internally equitable ordering of jobs can be established.
3. Jobs have been located on a scatter diagram and clusters of jobs have been identified so that a first attempt can be made at a potentially acceptable grouping of jobs for classification or grading purposes.
4. One or more benchmark (key) jobs have been identified for each potential pay grade.
5. A survey has been completed in which actual rates of pay and pay range data have been collected. (This is a huge assumption as many surveys are not designed to collect actual rate of pay.)
6. Pay survey data have been analyzed and a summary of the data includes mean, and median (50th percentile) rates of pay for each job; 10th, 25th, 75th, and 90th percentile data; lowest and highest rates of pay reported for each job; average established range maximums and minimums for each job; and highest maximum and lowest minimum or reported established ranges.[20]

Establishing Hiring Salaries

There seems to be reasonable consistency in establishing salaries for recent recipients of the M.L.S. Although some upward adjustment in compensation might be made in recognition of relevant preprofessional experience, such as an internship, beginning librarians are generally hired at the minimum salary. Complications arise when an individual has had substantial experience in another profession, particularly if it is in the teaching or computer fields. It is both reasonable and defensible to compensate an individual for such experience, provided there is consistency in assessing the experience and guidelines for determining compensation. A similar problem involves assessing nonprofessional library experience.

Establishing hiring salaries for experienced librarians is not as straightforward as it might seem because of the great variation in compensation policies and programs throughout the country. Many institutions are limited in their ability to negotiate individual salaries because of collective bargaining agreements, salary equity requirements, or budgetary constraints.

It is just as important to establish compensation policies on hiring from outside the organization as it is on promotions from within. It is also important to insure that external candidates understand the general salary range of the position before they commit themselves to an interview for the position. Since job advertisements often list wide salary ranges, an employer would be wise to indicate the hiring point aimed at.

Circled Salaries

Minimum and maximum salaries are common features of compensation programs, but are often modified. For example, some collective bargaining agreements state that new employees are to be hired below the minimum salary, usually until the completion of the probationary period. This can also occur if there are limits on a promotional increase. An employee who is promoted several grades above his or her original position may be paid below the minimum of the new grade for some time. The term *green circle* is used to describe the salary of an employee below the minimum.[21]

Red circle rates are more common. An employee's salary is red circled when it is above the maximum. This generally occurs when an employee's position is downgraded, usually as the result of organizational changes. Some compensation programs limit the amount of the red circle to a fixed percentage above the maximum.

Silver and *gold circle* salaries refer to provisions made for employees with "superseniority."[22] A silver circle refers to a fixed increase above the maximum. If provisions are made for merit beyond the fixed increase, a gold circle situation exists.

EXTERNAL INFLUENCES ON COMPENSATION

The British Parliament passed a minimum wage act in 1562,[23] but it was not until some hundred years after the beginning of the Industrial Revolution that society began recognizing the inhumane aspects of working conditions. Although President Martin Van Buren issued an executive order establishing a ten-hour day for workers on government contracts in 1840, it was not until after the Civil War that efforts began to reduce working hours and increase wages in the United States.[24] Modern legislation dealing with employment and compensation began in the 1930s.

The major acts relating to compensation practices may be categorized under the broad headings of wage and hour legislation, income protection legislation, and antidiscrimination legislation:[25]

Wage and Hour Legislation

The *Davis-Bacon Act* of 1931 was the first national legislation on minimum wages. It required construction contractors and subcontractors receiving federal funds in excess of $2,000 to pay at least the prevailing wages in the area.

The *National Industrial Recovery Act* (NIRA) of 1933 was an attempt to establish a national minimum wage. It was declared unconstitutional by the Supreme Court in 1935.

The *National Labor Relations Act* of 1935 gave employees the right to bargain collectively for wages, benefits, and working conditions.

The *Walsh-Healy Public Contracts Act* of 1936 was another attempt of the federal government to deal with minimum wages. It required that prevailing wages be paid in all government-sponsored contract work exceeding $10,000 and time-and-a-half for work exceeding eight hours a day and forty hours a week.

The *Fair Labor Standards Act* (FLSA) of 1938 enabled the "federal government to become deeply involved in regulating minimum wages for all employees engaged in interstate or foreign commerce or in the production of goods for such commerce, and for all employees in certain enterprises."[26] It also established wage requirements and defined specific occupations. The Fair Labor Standards Act, as amended, has had considerable impact on wages and hours, including the establishment of the minimum hourly rate.

Income Protection Legislation

Both federal and state governments have become increasingly involved in providing economic protection for employee compensation, beginning with the enactment of Worker's Compensation in 1911.[27] Other landmark laws are the Social Security Act of 1935 and Unemployment Compensation (Title IX of the Social Security Act of 1935).

Laws relating to pensions are the most recent in the income protection area. The primary ones are the Welfare and Pension Plan Disclosure Act of 1959 and the Employee Retirement Income Security Act (ERISA) of 1974.

Antidiscrimination Legislation and Compensation

Starting in the 1960s a number of laws and executive orders, based on the Bill of Rights, have been passed bringing civil rights into the workplace. Those relating most directly to compensation are:

The *Equal Pay Act* of 1963, an amendment to the Fair Labor Standards Act. It is the first federal antidiscrimination law relating directly to women requiring equal pay for equal work for men and women; it defines equal work as that which requires equal skill, effort, and responsibility under similar working conditions. Under the Equal Pay Act employers can only establish different wage rates on the basis of a seniority system, a merit system, a system that measures earnings by quantity and quality of production, and a differential based on any factor other than sex. All four exceptions must apply equally to men and women.[28]

Title VII of the Civil Rights Act of 1964, known also as the Equal Opportunity Employment Opportunity Act. It prohibits unlawful employment practices, including failure to hire, failure to provide employment, or failure to promote because of a person's race, color, religion, sex, or national origin.[29]

Equal Pay and Comparable Worth

The concept of equal pay for work of comparable value is commonly known as comparable worth and pay equity. Although the terms are sometimes used interchangeably, there are important distinctions. Both the Equal Pay Act and Title VII address discrimination in compensation, which is why both acts are considered in cases involving sex discrimination in compensation.

Title VII came into play in discrimination cases because the Equal Pay Act is limited to situations in which men and women do the same or similar work as described in the standards of the Act, namely, that the jobs require equal skill, effort, and responsibility. Although the standard for comparing jobs is the same under Title VII as under the Equal Pay Act, the prohibition against discrimination in compensation in Title VII is stated more broadly than in the Equal Pay Act, implying that there may be a broader base of recovery under Title VII. For example:

> An individual seeking to redress sex-based wage differentials under the Equal Pay Act must demonstrate that persons of the opposite sex working for the same single establishment are paid higher wages for substantially equal work. Title VII, however, does not contain a "single establishment" requirement. In a Title VII sex-based wage discrimination suit, a bias claimant may properly present to the court evidence that employees of the opposite sex working at separate establishments maintained by the employer receive higher wages for substantially equal work.[30]

Comparable worth is fundamentally an approach to expanding coverage of sex discrimination in compensation under Title VII of the Civil Rights Act of 1964. Although there have been more than one hundred state and local government initiatives on comparable worth since the late 1970s, no federal legislation has been enacted which identifies and defines a method for determining comparable worth. Recent initiatives dealing with equal pay and comparable worth range from a pay equity study in New York State to the appropriation in Minnesota of $21.7 million in the spring of 1983 for pay equity increases over a two-year period. (In the spring of 1985, the Minnesota legislator allocated an additional $11.7 million to complete pay equity implementation for state employees by 1987.)[31]

Treiman and Hartman recognize that there are no simple answers to the questions raised by comparable worth. They are convinced, however, that bias does exist:

> Our economy is structured so that some jobs will inevitably pay less than others, and the fact that many such jobs are disproportionately filled by women and minorities may reflect differences in qualifications, interests, traditional roles, and similar factors; or it may reflect exclusionary practices with regard to hiring and promotion; or it may reflect a combination of both. However, several types of evidence support our judgment that it is also true in many instances that jobs held mainly by women and minorities pay less at least in part *because* they are held mainly by women and minorities. First, the differentials in average pay for jobs held mainly by women and those held mainly by men persists when the characteristics of jobs thought to affect their value and the characteristics of workers thought to affect their productivity are held constant. Second, prior to the legislation of the past two decades, differentials in pay for men and women and for minorities and nonminorities were often acceptable and were, in fact, prevalent. The tradition embodied in such practices was built into wage structures, and its effects continue to influence these structures. Finally, at the level of the specific firm, several studies show that women's jobs are paid less on the average than men's jobs with the same scores derived from job evaluation plans. The evidence is not complete or conclusive, but the consistency of the results in many different job categories and in several different types of studies, the size of the pay differentials (even after worker and job characteristics have been taken into account) and the lack of evidence for alternative explanations strongly suggest that wage discrimination is widespread.[32]

Equal pay and comparable worth issues will be the primary area of focus in compensation for some time. In view of the different approaches under way in states such as Minnesota, California, and Washington, it seems that a variety of different methods will be used to resolve salary inequities.[33] (As of this writing, the Federal Employee Compensation Equity Act of 1987 [S.552] is meeting some resistance in the Senate. No serious opposition is expected to the Federal Equitable Pay Practices Act of 1987 [H.R. 387]).

Other External Influences

The American Library Association (ALA), representing a profession dominated by women, has been active in supporting the concepts of equal pay and comparable worth and is represented on the board of directors of the National Committee on Pay Equity. Through its Office for Library Personnel Resources, ALA provides a variety of information sources on pay equity and is committed to educating members through programs such as the pay equity institute held at its annual conference in 1986.[34] ALA's Office of Library Personnel Resources published *Pay Equity: An Action Manual for Library Workers* in the fall of 1988. The manual provides techniques for documenting pay inequities and establishing strategies for obtaining appropriate compensation.

Although there has been a decline in union influence since the 1970s, unions continue to have a strong influence on compensation. Moreover, minorities and women are becoming more active in the union movement, which makes issues of equal pay and comparable worth of particular interest in organizing campaigns and collective bargaining. Unions were in the forefront in making progress in Connecticut, Washington, and Minnesota. They will continue to be actively involved in issues of equal pay and comparable worth.

MERIT OR PERFORMANCE-BASED REWARD SYSTEMS

Financial incentive systems supplement salary and should be addressed in the design of a compensation program.[35] A variety of incentive systems are common in business and industry—production bonuses, profit-sharing, incentive programs, commissions—but not relevant in the library environment. Others, such as overtime and shift differentials, generally apply only to individuals in nonexempt classifications.

Merit Systems

The most common financial incentive system found in libraries is merit, often referred to in business and industry as "performance-based reward programs." Merit systems are found in a variety of libraries, including those covered by collective bargaining agreements and civil service. There is great variety in merit pay programs and each organization should consider the variables that apply to its situation when designing or implementing such a program. Among the variables that are particularly applicable to libraries are:

1. Ability to specify quality and quantity of good service.
2. Employee needs, perceptions, and demands.
3. External environmental pressures, including consumers of goods or services, market demand for goods or services, legal requirements, and society in general.[36]

The Equal Pay Act permits employers to administer merit raises without concern that a differential that may result can be found to be unlawful under the Act.[37]

Performance Standards

The success of a merit system depends to a great degree on standards, which are scrutinized and analyzed by those affected. All work-related standards, whether they apply to evaluating jobs, establishing pay rates, or assessing work performance, should meet two criteria:

1. *Consistency*. Standards must be consistent; that is, a standard must recognize similar employee inputs by providing similar employer output. (If job knowledge, responsibility requirements, and working conditions are similar, base rates should likewise be similar. Similar work effort by employees having similar skills and motivation should result in comparable piece rate earnings or performance appraisal ratings.)
2. *Fairness*. Standards must be fair. Whatever the final purpose of the standard, those persons working under its rules must accept it as just and reasonable.[38]

A major problem with performance standards is, of course, interpretation. Individual biases in the form of differing expectations come into play which require continual discussion and review to insure equity and consistent application. Normally the responsibility for interpreting and assessing performance standards rests with management, namely the chief librarian and the personnel administrator. The personnel administrator, however, should not have the final say in such matters.

Performance Appraisal Programs

Implicit in any merit system is an ongoing performance appraisal program which may be similar or different from the program used for merit raises. In addition to their function in merit, performance appraisals are important in promotional opportunities within an organization and in identifying developmental opportunities for future advancement. As such, they are an integral aspect of an organization's compensation program.

Responsibility for Merit Adjustments

Line managers clearly have responsibility for getting effective results and should be concerned with the wages and salaries paid to those they supervise. Personnel administrators have an important function to perform in the development, implementation, and interpretation of performance standards; but they should not overrule the line. Any disputes between the personnel administrator and a line manager should be referred to the head librarian, who can resolve the matter with the appropriate senior administrator.

BENEFITS AND SERVICES

Fringe benefits have been the focus of considerable attention in the 1980s because of increased employee needs and the escalation of costs to the employer. It is not uncommon to find employers cutting back on fringe benefits, eliminating some programs completely, or requiring employees to carry a portion of the cost.

An average of 35 percent of payroll costs have been allocated to benefits in the 1980s. This, of course, is on top of salary. It is predicted that this figure will increase to 50 percent by 1990.[39]

There are several reasons for the importance of fringe benefits in the compensation package:

1. The imposition of wage ceilings during World War II forced organizations to offer more and greater benefits in place of wage increases to attract new employees and to keep current workers.
2. With the increasing unacceptability of autocratic management and the decline of paternalism, instead of using threats or a variety of protective procedures, organizations have used benefits to gain employee compliance and loyalty, which has resulted in a more acceptable form of paternalism.
3. Possibly the most important reason has been the rise of union influence and the steady increase of wages to the point where they now satisfy the basic needs of the employees they represent. In turn, this has led to increased interest and bargaining for more and greater benefits.
4. In the 1970s inflation, rising wage levels, and heavier income tax burdens aroused interest in tax shelters at lower levels in the organizational structure. Many employers are now providing an even greater array of benefits that employees consider valuable. This approach reduces the tax burden of the employer and, at the same time, increases the disposable income available to employees by providing benefits and services they would otherwise have to purchase with after-tax dollars.
5. More recent changes in public policy to shift the cost burden from the federal government to private-sector employers regarding health-care services and protection and continuing public concern over the long-term viability of Social Security have placed even greater pressure on employers to provide more protection in these already costly areas.[40]

We will continue to see efforts to restrict the percentage of the payroll that goes to benefits. Many institutions and organizations have recognized the need for cost containment and have either renegotiated their benefits coverage with their usual carriers or contracted with new carriers. The advent of employee spending accounts and flexible benefit plans are the results of efforts of the federal government to bring the rapidly escalating costs of benefits—particularly health-care benefits—under control.

Employee services, which vary greatly, are also part of the total compensation program. The two major elements of employee services are pay for time not worked, such as holidays, vacation, jury duty, and income equivalent payments (education subsidies, child care, subsidized housing) and reimbursements for incurred expenses (moving expenses, travel reimbursement).

Although benefits and services are sometimes viewed as the forgotten stepchild of the total compensation package, they have become increasingly important in the recruitment and retention of staff. They are complicated by the variety of components and options available, legal requirements, and financial implications.

Although benefits present many complexities, it is incumbent upon compensation and personnel administrators to develop a fundamental understanding of benefits so that they can work with the specialists in efforts to provide the best coverage for available dollars.

COMPENSATION ADMINISTRATION

A compensation program is not complete until procedures and processes are in place to insure timely and proper administration. This includes taking steps to insure that employees understand the nature of the program. Employees should not have to search for answers to such basic questions as:[41]

1. When is the next pay day?
2. When is the first increase possible?
3. What are the criteria for raises?
4. What are the eligibility requirements for vacations?
5. How long is the first vacation?
6. How many paid holidays are there? What are they? Are there eligibility requirements?
7. What are the criteria for promotions?
8. Are cost-of-living adjustments provided?
9. How are overtime opportunities determined?
10. Is an employee's pay ever reduced?

A great amount of time and money is expended in developing or modifying a compensation program. Its success should not be endangered by a failure to apprise employees of the nature of the program or to take steps to insure that all payroll transactions are processed in a timely fashion. The latter is often a serious flaw in salary administration. Delays in processing payroll transactions can seriously damage the credibility of the personnel office. Regardless of where the snags develop—within the library or in some central institutional office—the library personnel staff should resolve the problem.

Pay Structure Adjustments

Most organizations make annual adjustments to the structure of their salary program. In organizations covered by collective bargaining agreements or civil service, the adjustments are often known several years in advance, and the function of the library personnel administrator is limited to processing payroll adjustments. In organizations where there is more flexibility it is not uncommon for library directors to take an active part in determining changes in the salary structure, not only for professional librarians but for all staff.

Merit Guidelines

When merit increases are a part of a salary program many libraries follow guidelines to determine adjustments and to assure that salary differentials are based on demonstrated performance. Although merit guidelines vary, they have certain basic characteristics:

Maximum:
- Performs in a superior manner for sustained period of time ("Superior" or "Distinguished").
- Performs in a commendable manner; consistently exceeds fully satisfactory levels of performance for extended periods of time ("Commendable" or "Fully Satisfactory").

Midpoint:
- Consistently performs all responsibilities in a fully satisfactory manner; is fully trained and normally has from 2 to 4 years' experience on the job ("Satisfactory" or "Competent").
- Performs responsibilities between a marginal and a satisfactory level. Incumbent is still in a learning stage and has not performed all responsibilities at a fully proficient level for a reasonable period (e.g., 6 months).

Minimum:
- Performs responsibilities at a marginal or less level. If in this pay bracket for more than 24 months, should be assigned or terminated ("Unacceptable").
- Probationary range.[42]

Since words like "distinguished," "superior," and "competent" are loaded and have different meanings to different people, descriptive terms are avoided in some organizations.

Merit Pay Distribution Schedules

Certain aspects of merit pay distribution seem particularly appealing in the academic environment because of the constraints of available funds. These include a policy for paying different rates of pay to individuals receiving identical merit ratings.[43] This generally means that individuals in the upper ranges receive a smaller percentage increase than those in the lower ranges. It is an effective way of rewarding and encouraging less-senior staff members.

Forced-distribution rating systems are sometimes used, which require distributing percentage increases according to a predetermined mix and limiting the number of superior ratings.[44] Forced distribution systems present certain psychological constraints and can create inequities and morale problems if applied too narrowly.

Merit pay distribution schedules based on actual percentages, on the other hand, can be helpful tools in budget planning. The following is an example of such a schedule:

Merit Pay Distribution Schedule[45]
(based on actual percentages)

Performance Rating	Distribution	Merit Range Increase
Superior	Top 5 to 10%	10 to 20%
Commendable	Next to 15%	8 to 12%
Satisfactory	Middle 60 to 75%	6 to 10%
Marginal	Next 5 to 10%	0 to 5%
Unacceptable	Bottom 0 to 5%	0%

If there is a relatively consistent interpretation of performance standards in an organization, the distribution schedule often remains relatively the same over several years.

Other Compensation Administration Issues

Some mention should be made of other aspects of compensation administration because of their role in the overall program.

Pay Plan Analysis: Compa-ratio is one method of analysis which enables management to assess a compensation program.[46] It involves analyzing pay grades or salary ranges which cannot be done unless midpoints are set and jobs are assigned to pay grades. The compa-ratio enables an organization to determine its competitiveness and can be used to analyze the pay treatment of specific groups of employees by such factors as gender, race, or age group.

Guidelines for Promotion and Demotion: Although there is wide variation in compensation policies on promotion and demotion, a rule of thumb is to increase (or decrease) an individual's salary by the difference in the minimum between the old and new job grades. To insure equity it is important to have written guidelines.

Premium Rates and Market Considerations: Major problems for compensation administrators occur when there is a considerable shortage of workers with particular knowledge or skill (computer specialists, for example). Equally problematic are efforts to accommodate so-called "superstars." Such practices are not uncommon in academia where institutions make compensation concessions to attract high-level teaching and research staff. Individual salary negotiations are common for directorships, as they are for chief executive positions in business and industry.

Although many libraries permit some flexibility in negotiating individual salaries for all levels of professional positions, the practice can create morale problems and lead to salary inequities. It is important, therefore, to document the rationale for all salary offers that exceed general hiring guidelines and to insure that exceptions are in line with the affirmative action and salary equity policies of the parent institution.

Salary Equity Analysis

The Equal Pay Act of 1963 and pending legislation on pay equity and comparable work, as well as affirmative action requirements, clearly underline the importance of avoiding salary discrimination by reasons of sex or ethnicity. Many institutions require an annual salary equity analysis to identify discriminatory compensation practices. Such an analysis should be incorporated in the administration of a compensation program even if there is no institutional requirement.

In planning a salary equity analysis it is important to note that under the Equal Pay Act, employers can only establish different wage rates on the basis of a seniority system, a merit system, a system that measures earnings by quantity or quality of production, and a differential based on any factor other than sex. (These conditions are often referred to as the four affirmative defenses of the Equal Pay Act.) All four exemptions must apply equally to men and women.[47]

Example of a Salary Equity Analysis

Background: As part of its affirmative action analysis for the federal government, University X is required to undertake a salary equity analysis to determine whether and the extent to which women and minorities have been subjected to salary discrimination by reason of their sex or ethnicity.

With respect to professional librarians, the examination will be conducted through a four-step analysis:

Step 1: Determination of Counterparts. The analysis will begin by identifying, for each female and minority person, one or more white male counterparts, determined on the basis of objective factors to be developed in consultation with the university librarian. If one or more of the males match the female or minority person with respect to all of the objective factors, those white males will be considered counterparts of the female or minority person.

The librarians at University X are not unionized and have academic status. The counterparts for librarians are determined initially by rank:
—Librarian Instructor (Rank I)
—Assistant Librarian (Rank II)
—Associate Librarian (Rank III)
—Librarian (Rank IV)

Step 2: Mechanical Screening. As of May 1, 1988 the salary of the female or minority person (averaged with the salaries of other female or minority persons who are also counterparts, if any) will be compared with the mean (average) and the median of the white male counterparts. If it is more than five percent below either, the case will be considered a situation that warrants further scrutiny and will be analyzed in detail under Step 3. If there is no counterpart for the female or minority person, no further analysis will be conducted.

Step 3: Analysis of Nondiscriminatory Factors. Every case identified for further scrutiny will first be examined to determine whether that person's relative salary position is attributable to certain nondiscriminatory factors, which will be examined for their relative impact.

Where discrepancies remain unexplained by objective factors, the analysis will turn to judgmental factors.

Throughout this analysis, differences of 5 percent or less will be considered *de minimis.*

Step 4: Determination of Appropriate Salary Adjustments. Where a salary discrepancy is not fully explained by the analysis of factors in Step 3, each situation will be reviewed to determine an appropriate salary in light of the analysis in Steps 2 and 3. A salary adjustment will be made after consultation with the appropriate dean or other administrative officer.[48]

Simply stated, the relevancy of two factors are critical in determining if any discriminatory compensation practices exist:

• Non-discriminatory *objective factors* that justify a salary differential among counterparts.
• *Judgmental factors* that justify a salary differential among counterparts.

The Computer and Compensation

Payroll was one of the earliest processes to benefit from computerization, and automated personnel-information systems now provide a vast variety of information on payroll, benefits, and other elements of compensation. Libraries often find a need for information not always readily available from the institution's personnel information system. The advent of personal computers with an array of spread-sheet and database systems available at reasonable costs enable the staff in the library personnel office to supplement the institution's system to meet specific library needs in areas as diverse as budget planning and administration and monitoring performance appraisal schedules and applicant flow data.

RESPONSIBILITIES IN COMPENSATION MANAGEMENT

As the primary staff representative of the chief librarian in all aspects of human resources, personnel administrators have major responsibilities in the development, modification, and administration of a compensation program. Line managers also have an important role to play, but this role is too often overlooked. After all, it is the line managers who have the responsibility for accomplishing organizational objectives; they should have input into the compensation program.

The advice of both personnel administrators and line managers may be limited in the public sector and in institutions covered by collective bargaining agreements, but it should always be sought. Regardless of the constraints within the organization, chief librarians should actively seek advice on compensation from their management team and actively seek appropriate changes. The ultimate responsibility for a library's compensation program rests with the chief librarian.

References

1. Justice Louis Brandeis, *Business: A Profession* (Boston: Small, Maynard and Company, 1914), p. 2.
2. Milton L. Rock, ed., *Handbook of Wage and Salary Administration,* 2nd ed. (New York: McGraw-Hill, 1984), p. xix.
3. Ibid.
4. William B. Werther, Jr., and Keith Davis, *Personnel Management and Human Resources,* 2nd ed. (New York: McGraw-Hill, 1985), p. 318.
5. O. Glenn Stahl, *Public Personnel Administration,* 5th ed. (New York: Harper & Row, 1962), p. 148.
6. Frederick Duda, "Columbia's Two-Track System," *College & Research Libraries* 41 (July 1980): 295–304.
7. Donald J. Treiman and Heidi I. Hartman, eds., *Women, Work, and Wages: Equal Pay for Jobs of Equal Value,* Report of the Commission on Occupational Classification and Analysis, National Research Council, National Academy of Sciences (Washington, D.C.: Academy Press, 1981), p. 77.
8. Ibid., p. 81.
9. Ibid.
10. Columbia University Libraries, "The System of Professional Position Categories," in *Handbook for Librarians,* Professional Classification Task Force, 18 November 1985, p. II-17.
11. Ibid.
12. Paul Pigors and Charles A. Myers, *Personnel Administration: A Point of View and a Method,* 8th ed. (New York: McGraw-Hill, 1977), p. 348.
13. Richard I. Henderson, *Compensation Management: Rewarding Performance,* 4th ed. (Reston, Va.: Reston Publishing, 1985), pp. 268–69.
14. Pigors and Myers, pp. 334–35.
15. Henderson, p. 379.
16. Ibid., pp. 379–80.
17. Pigors and Myers, pp. 335–36.
18. Henderson, p. 343.
19. Ibid., pp. 381–424.
20. Ibid., pp. 418–19.
21. Henderson, p. 411.
22. Ibid.
23. Ibid., p. 64.
24. Ibid., p. 65.
25. Ibid., pp. 67–68.
26. Ibid., p. 68.
27. Ibid., pp. 71–79.
28. Ibid., p. 80.
29. Ibid., p. 81.
30. Commerce Clearing House, "Harassment and Pay Discrimination," p. 25.
31. American Library Association, Office for Library Personnel Resources, T.I.P. Kit #9 (Topics in Personnel), Item 1a, "History of Pay Equity in Minnesota," n.d.
32. Treiman and Hartman, p. 93.

33. Ibid., pp. 69–90. See also T.I.P. Kit #9 cited in footnote 31.
34. ALA, Office for Library Personnel Resources, T.I.P. Kit #9.
35. Werther and Davis, pp. 333–38.
36. Henderson, p. 488.
37. Commerce Clearing House, p. 20.
38. Henderson, p. 489.
39. Ibid., p. 432.
40. Ibid., pp. 432–33.
41. Ibid., p. 582.
42. Ibid., p. 595.
43. Ibid., p. 596.
44. Ibid., pp. 594–96.
45. Ibid., p. 596.
46. Ibid., pp. 603–04.
47. Henderson, p. 80.
48. Columbia University, "Salary Equity Analysis," 4 August 1978. The "Example of a Salary Equity Analysis" is based on the methodology described in this report.

Bibliography

American Library Association, Office for Library Personnel Resources, T.I.P. Kit #9 (Topics in Personnel), Item 1a. "History of Pay Equity in Minnesota." n.d. Mimeographed.
American Library Association, Office for Library Personnel Resources. T.I.P. Kit #9 (Topics in Personnel). "Pay Equity: A Selected Bibliography." May 1986. Mimeographed.
Brandeis, Louis. *Business: A Profession*. Boston: Small, Maynard and Company, 1914.
Columbia University. "Salary Equity Analysis." 4 August 1978.
Columbia University Libraries. "The System of Professional Position Categories," in *Handbook for Librarians,* Professional Classification Task Force, 18 November 1985.
Commerce Clearing House. *Harassment and Pay Discrimination in the Workplace.* CCH Editorial Staff Publication. Chicago: Commerce Clearing House, 1986.
Creth, Sheila D. "Personnel Planning and Utilization." In *Personnel Administration in Libraries,* edited by Sheila D. Creth and Frederick Duda. New York: Neal-Schuman, 1981.
Duda, Frederick. "Columbia's Two-Track System." *College and Research Libraries* 41 (July 1980): 295–304.
Henderson, Richard I. *Compensation Management: Rewarding Performance.* 4th ed. Reston, Va.: Reston, 1985.
Lynch, Mary Jo, "ALA Salary Survey 1986: Figures Managers Need for Setting Competitive Salaries." *American Libraries* 17 (October 1986): 680.

Pigors, Paul and Charles A. Myers. *Personnel Administration: A Point of View and a Method.* 8th ed. New York: McGraw-Hill, 1977.

Rock, Milton L., ed. *Handbook of Wage and Salary Administration.* 2nd ed. New York: McGraw-Hill, 1984.

Stahl, O. Glenn. *Public Personnel Administration.* 5th ed. New York: Harper & Row, 1956.

Treiman, Donald J. *Job Evaluation: An Analytic Review.* Interim Report to the Equal Employment Opportunity Commission. Committee on Occupational Classification and Analysis, Assembly of Behavioral and Social Sciences, National Research Council. Washington, D.C.: National Academy of Sciences Press, 1979.

Treiman, Donald J. and Heidi I. Hartmann, eds. *Women, Work, and Wages: Equal Pay for Jobs of Equal Value.* Committee on Occupational Classification and Analysis, Assembly of Behavioral and Social Sciences/National Research Council. Washington, D.C.: National Academy of Sciences Press, 1981.

Werther, William B., Jr., and Keith Davis. *Personnel Management and Human Resources.* 2nd ed. New York: McGraw-Hill, 1985.

9
Labor Relations
Frederick Duda

The union movement has a longer history in public libraries than in
other types of libraries. As Theodore L. Guyton and others have pointed
out, professionals in college and university libraries are still not as
extensively unionized as those in public libraries.[1] In characterizing the
nature of institutions of higher education that have professional unions,
Gwendolyn Cruzat has noted that these unions are dominant in community colleges and four-year state and municipal colleges.[2] Although the
type of library and the composition of the bargaining unit are significant
in labor relations, the problems encountered and the steps to be taken to
resolve them are similar in all libraries and bargaining units. Similarly,
grievances submitted by members of the supporting staff may differ
substantially from those submitted by professionals, but the proper
methods of dealing with them remain the same regardless of the
category of staff or type of library.

REASONS FOR UNIONIZATION

Many unionists cite unsatisfactory wages, poor working conditions,
favoritism by the employer, and other failings of management as factors
that lead to collective bargaining. Those who have served as managers
during the organizing period point out that outside professional agita-
tors and internal malcontents help bring in the union. Both viewpoints
may seem extreme, but each offers insight into factors that generally
determine the success or failure of a union movement.

The history of the labor movement in the United States during the
first half of this century clearly indicates that unionists made major
contributions by improving the lot of the average worker, raising the
standard of living, and controlling the abuses of captains of industry. E.
Wight Bakke's description of a union as an employer-regulating device

"which seeks to regulate the discretion of employers,"[3] though stated in 1946, continues to be quoted often by authorities writing on contemporary industrial relations. The implication that employers were the abusers of power and that unions were the champions of the common worker was outdated even at the time of Bakke's statement.

In reaction to the considerable gains made in industry by unions following the enactment of the National Labor Relations Act of 1935 (Wagner Act) and the public reaction to strikes during World War II, the Labor Management Relations Act of 1947 (Taft-Hartley Act) was passed; it included a number of provisions to curb the unions' powers. Subsequent legislation was more favorable to unions.

As C. Wilson Randle and Max S. Wortman, Jr., point out, "Labor laws can be examined meaningfully only within the context of their origin—within the prevailing economic and social setting."[4] The context of the economic and social setting *and* the nature of the occupation are important factors to consider in examining the reasons for unionization in libraries, particularly among professionals. Too often, the observers of unionization in libraries fail to make important distinctions between the nature of work in libraries and in industry. The predictions made so often in the late 1960s that unions would make dramatic inroads in libraries have not materialized because organizers have not adapted techniques that historically proved successful in industry. For example, in 1976, we find Dennis Chamot using the following reasoning to attract librarians to unionism:

> The individual professional has lost, or is in danger of losing, all control of the job, the nature of the work assignment, methods, pace, etc. The organization removes his or her control or so dilutes it that the individual contribution is small relative to the job and the total enterprise. Too often, the individual's advancement becomes dependent more on favoritism or politics than on professional achievement.[5]

Such reasoning ignores the considerable impact, beginning in the early 1970s, of participative management and affirmative action in all types of libraries. It also ignores the generally high level of educational attainment of individuals employed in supporting staff, specialist, and professional positions.

This does not mean that findings in industry bear no relation to situations and attitudes found in libraries. The reasons given by many careful observers of union organization in industry indicate that employees join unions for a number of reasons:

Desire for Better Economic and Working Conditions
Most people want to increase their income—even in top-paying companies.

Seldom do we find a man who is convinced that the economic returns and physical satisfactions provided by his job are perfect and quite beyond improvement. In the United States, the greatest growth period of unions [the 1940s] coincided with a rapidly rising income level for workers. Whether the unions have really obtained higher wages and better pension, insurance, and other benefits for their members, or whether these would have come anyway through normal economic and social pressures, is not the point. The point is that an impressive number of employees *believe* that unions are responsible for improving their economic lot.

Desire for Control Over Benefits
In our society, many employees are unhappy when they are completely dependent on someone else for the satisfaction of their needs. Even when that "someone else" is very good, as many managements have been, and even provides good wages, steady employment, and desirable working conditions, workers tend to be uneasy when they have no power to control the benefits received. In fact, management makes matters worse by emphasizing how much it has "given" its employees (that is, benefits provided at the discretion of the company, not offered because they *had* to be). In telling people that they should be thankful for what has been voluntarily given them, a company is also saying that what it has given can also be taken away.

Even in organizations where employees have always been treated with complete fairness and justice, stories circulate that John Jones over in Department 16 has been severely penalized for something he didn't do because a supervisor "had it in for him." In any situation where we lack power to control what happens to us, we are more than ready to believe these "atrocity" stories and think "Next time that could happen to us." The truth or falsity of the rumor may be unimportant.

Furthermore, in a large company where top management is many levels removed from the individual employee, the individual's sense of dependency and lack of control over what happens to him is magnified.

Desire for Self-Expression and Communication with Higher Management
Many an employee feels that, as far as his company is concerned, he is nothing more than a time-clock number. Though many would not want the responsibility of management, they would like greater opportunity to express themselves. In part, this is just the desire to complain when hurt. But more importantly, as individuals we all have a need to express our point of view—not to "get more" for ourselves, but to enjoy the feeling of being a whole person instead of a pair of hired hands.

Without a union, most employees feel they have no means of "safely" going over the head of their boss with a problem. After all, they must rely on this man to do many things for them. There are a hundred and one ways in which a supervisor can make their working life unpleasant and unrewarding. Discretion is frequently the better part of valor; when the supervisor says "No," most employees accept it as the final word.

The feeling of helplessness is particularly acute when the immediate supervisor is unsympathetic to their demands, either because he has no

decision-making authority of his own, or because he has a natural unwillingness to reverse his own decisions. If only they can gain access to higher levels
in the organization, employees reason, they may find someone with the
authority to satisfy their requests.

The union promises the worker an opportunity to protest inequities, to
believe that if something goes wrong he will have a chance to be heard. The
union offers a direct road to participate, for its leaders have access to the top
decision-making levels of the organization.[6]

Other reasons often cited for unionization in industry include feelings that it will lead to more democracy in the workplace, increase unity
and morale, and provide job security. As William F. Glueck has stated,
"It is probable that most persons join unions as much for protection,
security, and self-respect as to increase their economic status."[7]

Joel Seidman, Jack London, and Bernard Karsh conducted a classic
study among members of a midwest local of the United Steelworkers of
America, identifying a wide variety of reasons to explain why workers
became union members. Of the 114 workers involved in the research
project not one identified economic reasons as a motivating factor. The
reasons most often cited for joining the union were family background
(generally, the father was a union member), earlier work or union
experience (either the individual had previously worked in a union
environment or had been sympathetic to attempts to unionize), experience within the plant (unpleasant experiences with previous or current
employers), and peer pressure.[8]

Observers of unionization in libraries find similar as well as different reasons to explain why library employees unionize. However, when
we look at working conditions in libraries, we find something quite
different from those in industry. For example, safety has been an
integral aspect of contract negotiations in steel mills while library
workers rarely perform comparable hazardous duties. Until recently,
improved working conditions to a library employee generally has meant
benefits such as coffee breaks, sick leave, and early release during heat
waves. A combination of technology, environmental consciousness, and
societal changes has had its impact in library land. Employees are
concerned with such important issues affecting working conditions as
the health hazards from video-display terminals and the asbestos that
insulates many library facilities.

Factors other than working conditions are considered more important for a successful unionization effort in libraries. In a study of the
pattern or organization in public libraries where unions have been most
successful, Guyton identifies disenchantment with library administrators and detachment from administrators as key underlying causes for
successful organization.[9] (This is not unlike the "unpleasant work

experiences" cited in the Seidman study above.) According to Guyton, the major concerns of public librarians in unions involve a desire for a greater voice in personnel policies affecting them, a desire for more control over professional issues, and a desire for closer contact and more communications with the library administration.[10]

As Guyton and others point out, certain external factors must exist for successful organization—enabling legislation, proximity to organized employees, and availability to unions. The ingredient which Guyton describes as the key internal factor for successful organization is the reaction to the "diminution of daily interactions" between administrators and the staff.[11] This occurs either because of hierarchical structures of bureaucratization or through administrative policy. In other words, either the layers or levels of the organization inhibit meaningful interaction between management and staff, or management, consciously or unconsciously, excludes staff from involvement in the decision-making process.

The lack of staff involvement in decision making and poor communication were apparently key factors in the successful organization of the nonsupervisory librarians at the Boston University Library in 1978. The primary issues involved in negotiating their first contract seemed to be professional development and communications. The first contract contained a clause that "provides that the library director meet with the librarians at least six times a year, which should ease the communication problem."[12]

Unionization undoubtedly increases communication among employees and management. Management cannot ignore employee complaints and problems once it has agreed to a grievance procedure that generally includes arbitration for the final resolution of problems and disputes. Experienced contract administrators know well that more communication does not necessarily mean improved communication, nor does it guarantee that employees will have a more meaningful role in the decision-making process. The adversary nature of labor relations clearly implies that both unions and management need to maintain a clear line of control, which means that the actions of individual union members and managers are limited.

Richard DeGennaro's observations on the emergence of unionization and participative management in libraries in the early 1970s provide a balanced perspective on the realities of both movements and are particularly interesting from a perspective of some 15 years:

> While it is difficult to predict whether unionization or participative management will emerge as the dominant trend in libraries in the next decade, it is clear that these two ideas are basically incompatible. Those idealistic librarians, and there are many, who espouse both unionism and

participation will be forced to make a choice when these two ideas clash as they inevitably must. Whatever the choice, there is likely to be considerable disillusionment, for the disadvantages of unionism are sometimes underestimated while the promise of participative management are frequently exaggerated.[13]

Some impressive gains have been made by unions in libraries in the 1980s. These include the advent of collective bargaining for both professional and supporting staff on the nine campuses of the University of California system; the unionization of the supporting staff of the Yale University Library, which involved a bitter ten-week strike in the fall of 1984; and the unionization of Harvard's supporting staff in the spring of 1988.

Participative management is not the panacea that many hoped it would be, but it seems to have maintained some dominance in the troublesome 1980s, particularly in academic libraries where peer review and the delegation of problem solving to committees and task forces have become accepted practices. But neither unionization nor participative management have been dominant in libraries in the 1980s. The profession has been more concerned with technology, diminished financial resources, the nature of the profession itself, and a floundering leadership. Governance issues have been put "on indefinite hold."

Regardless of how we characterize the reasons for unionization, they inevitably involve two concerns: salaries and working conditions. Although many observers of unionism consider "salaries and working conditions" as one concern and discuss other reasons for unionization under a variety of different headings, "working conditions" are really a separate area that encompass a number of different problems relating to the nature of the work being performed and the category of staff involved. Archie Kleingartner makes a distinction between two levels of goals in his writings. The first he identifies as concerns for satisfactory salaries and working conditions. The second is the concern of salaried professionals: autonomy, occupational integrity and identification, individual satisfaction and career development, and noneconomic security.[14] Employers who fail to provide some level of satisfaction in either of these areas are likely to be unsuccessful in their efforts to avoid unionization.

The fact that library work provides satisfaction in noneconomic areas undoubtedly has had an important effect on the failure of unions to gain a dominant role in libraries in the last two decades. Other factors stemming the growth of unionism include the impact of participative management, which has at least provided employees with some semblance of involvement in the decision-making process, and the failure of the union movement to develop strategies to attract white-collar workers.

The decline in the union movement in the period since World War II has undoubtedly stemmed the growth of unions in libraries. The proportion of nonagricultural workers who are unionized has fallen from more than 30 percent in the mid-1950s to less than 20 percent in the mid-1980s.[15] Scholars of the labor movement attribute this phenomenon to various factors: a decline of the political left; unions pricing themselves out of jobs by undercutting management profits with high wages (the crises in the American steel and automotive industries are obvious examples); the failure of unions to attract new groups of workers such as blacks, women, and Hispanics; and the lack of flexibility to adapt to changing economic conditions.[16]

This does not mean that library administrators can view the decline of the union movement as an assurance of the status quo. The relationships that exist within a library among managers and the staff are not stagnant. We are still in the midst of a technological revolution that is dramatically altering the role and nature of libraries in society and the role of the professional. If we accept Alvin Toffler's argument that we are on the threshold of a "Third Wave Civilization," we will find a different kind of expectation from workers in the years ahead:

> . . . individuals will vary more vividly tomorrow than they do today. More of them are likely to grow up sooner, to show responsibility at an earlier age, to be more adaptable and to evince greater individuality. They are more likely than their parents to question authority. They will want money and will work for it—but, except under conditions of extreme privation, they will resist working for money alone.[17]

These elements perhaps present a greater challenge to library administrators today than enabling legislation did in the 1960s and 1970s. Undoubtedly, the qualities that Arthur M. McAnally and Robert B. Downs emphasized for a model director in the 1970s will continue to remain critical: flexibility and adaptability, a stable and equal temperament, endurance, and exceptional persuasiveness.[18] Those who do not meet the challenges and who do not have or develop the qualities for leadership may, indeed, be confronted with unionization and the constraints and inflexibility that are too often inherent in collective bargaining.

COLLECTIVE BARGAINING LAW

Although a category of staff in a library can unionize without enabling legislation provided the employer is willing to engage in

254 PERSONNEL ADMINISTRATION

collective bargaining, an employer is not compelled to recognize a union until mandated by state or federal law. Without enabling legislation, large unions are generally reluctant to embark on efforts to organize which might fail if the employer is able to withstand the pressures and disruptions of an organization drive.

The applicability of collective bargaining law differs depending on whether the employer is in the private or public sector. As Andrew M. Kramer has noted, "For many years library personnel were in the no-man's-land of labor relations, outside the reach of any statutory framework to guide them in their dealings with the employer."[19]

The first broad legislation was the National Labor Relations Act of 1935 (Wagner Act), which was enacted to promote collective bargaining and industrial peace. The Wagner Act related only to employees in the private sector and did not cover professionals. The Labor Management Reporting Act of 1947 (Taft-Hartley Act) did include professionals. The National Labor Relations Board, however, excluded private, nonprofit, educational institutions from collective bargaining until it reversed a 1951 decision involving the support staff of Columbia University by ruling in 1970 that Cornell University could be required to bargain with its nonacademic staff.[20]

The Supreme Court's ruling in early 1980 that the faculty of Yeshiva University are not covered by federal labor law will have important implications not only for faculty in private institutions. The Yeshiva ruling clearly indicates that faculty collective bargaining might never advance beyond the eighty private institutions with contracts in effect at the time of the decision.[21] Some colleges and universities with contracts will undoubtedly try to disassociate themselves from future bargaining. The concept of "maturity" introduced in the Yeshiva decision is critical in deciding if teaching faculty are managerial staff. In writing the majority decision, Associate Justice Powell provided some guidance to determine the maturity of the relationship between the faculty and the administration. The factors to be considered include the degree of faculty involvement in hiring, tenure, and curriculum.[22]

The issue of the status of academic librarians will undoubtedly stimulate interesting arguments for and against applying the maturity-of-relationship concept (as of this writing it is an argument being used by Rutgers University to exclude a number of key library positions from coverage under its collective bargaining agreement with the AAUP). Librarians with faculty status might well argue that their relationship with the administration is less mature than the faculty's, therefore, they should be able to engage in collective bargaining. Conversely, arguments could be made by librarians with academic status that their relationship with the administration is quite similar to the faculty's because, for example, they have representation in the Senate or other policy-making body, are governed by a peer-review process for promotion, and are involved in the decision-making process through participative management.

In the first edition, the writer assumed that some controversy would exist among academic librarians in private institutions as a result of the Yeshiva ruling, which might result in modifications of the statement on collective bargaining of the Association of College and Research Libraries (ACRL), which has been in effect since the early 1970s. This did not occur and ACRL's policy continues to be to include academic librarians with their faculty colleagues in units for collective bargaining and to use as a guide the *Joint Statement on Faculty Status of College and University Librarians.*[23]

Perhaps ACRL's members will recognize eventually that faculty status has been and will continue to be rejected by many academic librarians who prefer to concentrate on improving their status and role as distinct groups of professionals within the academic community. The issue of collective bargaining is not necessarily related to faculty status. John Weatherford is not the first to observe "that the universities with the fifty largest libraries have not been fertile soil for unions so far unless they are scooped up by bureaucratic multicampus systems."[24] This tradition does not mean that librarians in these institutions may not be moved to unionize, although in the private sector such efforts may be complicated by the Yeshiva ruling. The faculty status movement per se should be abandoned not because it has failed to attain parity for librarians in many areas, but because it illustrates the inability of members of ACRL to deal realistically with the functional and historical differences between faculty and academic librarians.

The right to bargain is more complex in the public sector, since public employees do not fall under the jurisdiction of the NLRB, and not all states have enacted collective bargaining legislation. There is also a lack of uniformity among the states that have enacted such legislation. The 1960s, which earned a place in labor relations history as the decade of the public employee, witnessed the dawn of the modern era of public sector bargaining. The impetus was the issuance of Executive Order 10988 by President Kennedy in January 1962. E.O. 10988 for the first time entitled federal employees to elect an "employee organization" to negotiate on matters "concerning grievances, personnel policies and practices, or other matters affecting the general working conditions of employees in the unit."[25] As Harold W. Davey has pointed out:

> E.O. 10988 had a catalytic impact far beyond the confines of the federal establishment. It was of great value in stimulating the drive for unionization among employees of state, municipal, and county agencies. Union growth in these areas has been nothing short of spectacular in the period since 1962.

The ferment of unionism has produced a rash of state legislation, ranging from complete and fairly sophisticated treatment with full-time administrative agencies in charge (as in New York and New Jersey) to simple legislative affirmations of the right to organize and to bargain collectively, but with no implementation provisions.[26]

A number of flaws in E.O. 10988 were remedied by President Nixon's Executive Order 11491, which became effective January 1, 1970. These remedies include the establishment of the Federal Labor Relations Council to "administer and interpret" provisions of the order, the establishment of the Federal Service Impasses Panel to resolve disputes, and six federal agency management unfair labor practices and six labor organization unfair labor practices.[27] Although E.O. 11491 provides the framework for effective bargaining for federal employees, there are many problems yet to be resolved in the public sector. The most complex concerns are the almost universal statutory prohibition against strikes and the source of revenues of government. Although public employee strikes occur despite the prohibitions, the issues present a special problem not found in the private sector. California's Proposition 13 and similar taxpayers' revolts have become major factors in public bargaining in the 1980s and cause government to take strong positions in negotiations.

Some observers contend that only federal legislation can resolve the problems and establish the guidelines necessary for effective labor relations. Although bargaining in the public sector is plagued by many difficulties, Davey points out that there are models in a number of jurisdictions that are worthy of study and emulation, including New York City's Office of Collective Bargaining.[28] The reasons for Davey's qualified optimism for improvements in the public sector continue to be open to challenge because of economics and the need for tax relief:

> One reason for qualified optimism as to the future of public-sector labor relations is the nonprofit, service nature of government employment. This factor should contribute to *a sense of shared responsibility* on the part of *all* government employees for *maintaining and improving the quality of services rendered.*
>
> The business of government in a very literal sense is everyone's business. This fact is known and appreciated by government employees. Therefore, *the obligation of bargaining to finality in peaceful fashion* is one that should be strongly felt by both management and employers.
>
> It is also vitally important that no government agency be permitted to maintain an intransigent stance in any situation by wearing the cloak of sovereignty. In an age of constitutionalism there is no room for using an outmoded political theory to justify denial of employee rights.[29]

It will be interesting to see whether public opinion will encourage or discourage a hard line from government in its negotiations with public employees during the fiscal constraints we can expect to face in the foreseeable future.

THE ORGANIZING PERIOD

Organizing begins when a group of employees seek union representation by inviting organizers to the place of employment to solicit membership. Since unions are in business to increase membership to expand their revenue sources, which come primarily from dues and employers' contributions to welfare and pension plans, it would be unusual for a union to accept an invitation to organize without some prior assessment of its ability to conduct a successful campaign.

The goal of union organizers is to convince a category or categories of employees to sign authorization cards indicating that they agree to have the union function as their bargaining agent. Once 30 percent of the employees have signed authorization cards the union can call for an election through the National Labor Relations Board (NLRB) or its regional offices. Four general requirements must be met before the NLRB can act on a petition for certification or decertification of a union.[30] First, the employer's business must fall under the interstate commerce requirements spelled out in the National Labor Relations Act. Second, the union must claim recognition as the bargaining unit of the employees involved. The third requirement involves the presentation of evidence indicating that 30 percent of the employees favor the certification or decertification. The fourth requirement involves a determination of the NLRB on the appropriateness of the bargaining unit. This is a complex process involving hearings with representatives of both the employer and the union and can take months to resolve depending on the category of employees involved and the existence or lack therefore of relevant precedents.

Assuming that all four requirements are met, the NLRB notifies the employer and the union of the date of the election. Upon notification the employer is required to post NLRB Form 666, which informs the employees of their rights to organize and gives examples of conduct that interferes with the rights of employees and may result in the setting aside of the election. Since NLRB Form 666 reflects key provisions of the National Labor Relations Act and its amendments, it is quoted in full:

Employee Rights:
• To self-organization

- To form, join, or assist labor organizations
- To bargain collectively through representatives of your own choosing
- To act together for the purpose of collective bargaining or other mutual aid or protection
- To refuse to do any or all of these things unless the union and employer, in a state where such agreements are permitted, enter into a lawful union

Examples of Conduct Which Interferes with the Rights of Employees and May Result in the Setting Aside of the Election:
- Threatening loss of jobs or benefits by an Employer or a Union
- Misstating important facts by a Union or an Employer where the other party does not have a fair chance to reply
- Promising or granting promotions, pay raises, or other benefits, to influence an employee's vote by a party capable of carrying out such promises
- An Employer firing employees to discourage or encourage union activity or a Union causing them to be fired to encourage union activity
- Making campaign speeches to assembled groups of employees on company time within the 24-hour period before the election
- Incitement by either an Employer or a Union of racial or religious prejudice by inflammatory appeals
- Threatening physical force or violence to employees by a Union or an Employer to influence their votes.[31]

Although an employer is legally prohibited from engaging in a number of actions and activities during the organizing period, it is important that management actively inform both the employees and the managers of the facts of unionization, the nature of collective bargaining, and the actions that a manager or administrator can and cannot engage in during a union organizing drive. Literature disseminated by Columbia University when a union embarked on an effort to represent nonunion clerical workers at the university serves as an example of the kind of information that management is legally entitled to and should utilize during a union organizing drive.[32] (It is important to note that there are differences in labor legislation among the states and that the following is in compliance with New York State law.)

What Administrators Can and Cannot Do in a Union Organizing Drive:
   In the near future University employees will have to decide whether they wish to be represented by District 65, Distributive Workers of America. While the decision must be made by the employees, the conduct of University Officials will have significant impact on the outcome of the election.
   As a member of management, an administrator's or department head's attitude, actions, and opinion in the areas of unionism and labor-management relations are of major significance. The National Labor Relations Board (NLRB) and the courts have held that a university is legally responsible for the administrator's actions. It is especially important, therefore, for you to

know what you CAN and CANNOT do under the Labor-Management Relations Act.

Below you will find a list of DO'S and DON'TS based on the findings of the NLRB with respect to supervisory conduct during a union organizing drive.

What Administrators CAN DO

1. Keep outside organizers off the premises.
2. Inform employees of the advantages and disadvantages of belonging to District 65 or any union in such areas as dues, fines, assessments, strikes, strike benefits, and organizational structure of the unions in general.
3. Tell employees that those who are opposed to the union are as free to speak and campaign against it as its supporters are to speak and campaign for it. However, no employee should neglect her or his work or interfere with the work of others.
4. Inform employees of any untrue or misleading statements made by a union organizer. You may give employees the facts.
5. Explain University policies and working conditions. To avoid misinforming employees, check with the Personnel Office with regard to policies on which you are uncertain.
6. Urge all eligible employees to vote: this is critical since it is a majority of the people who do vote that makes the decision which will bind everyone. For example, approximately 900 employees are eligible to vote in this election. If only 100 employees vote, 51 employees will decide the fate of all 900 eligible employees.
7. Tell employees that the election will be conducted by secret ballot and that no one will know how an individual has voted.
8. Tell employees that the signing of a union authorization card does not bind them to vote for the union. The National Labor Relations Act guarantees employees the right to vote for or against whomever they please, regardless of what they might have signed.
9. Tell employees that they are free to join or not to join any organization. If employees should ask, you can tell them that we think it is most beneficial to the employees and to the administrator to continue to work together in an effort to solve our problems and to accomplish Columbia's academic mission without the imposition of a third party with different interests.
10. Insist that any solicitation for membership or discussion of union affairs be conducted outside of working time.
11. Administer University rules and policies impartially according to customary practices and without regard to the employee's membership in or activities on behalf of a union.
12. Explain to employees that while a union can make promises, it can deliver only what the University agrees to.

What Administrators CANNOT DO

1. Tell employees that the University will fire or punish them if they engage in union activity.

2. Ask employees about confidential union matters, meetings, etc. (Some employees may, of their own accord, walk up and tell of such matters. *It is not unfair practice to listen and to discuss these matters,* but you must not ask questions to obtain additional information.)
3. Ask employees how they intend to vote or whether they have signed authorization cards.
4. Promise benefits to employees if they reject the union involved.
5. Start a petition or circulate against the union or encourage or take part in its circulation if started by employees.
6. Attend any union meeting or engage in any surveillance or any activity which would indicate that the employees are being kept under surveillance to determine who is and who is not participating in union activities.
7. Bar an employee union representative from soliciting employee memberships during nonworking hours when the soliciting does not interfere with the work of others.
8. Prevent employees from wearing union buttons.
9. Call any employee into an office to discuss the Union or election. If the employee comes in on his own and wants to discuss these things, that is fine. (The best place to talk to employees about these things is in their work areas or in public areas where other employees are present.)
10. Discriminate against employees with respect to wages, hours, or any other terms or conditions of employment based on their support or opposition to the union.
11. Ask employees what they think about the union or any of the union's representatives.
12. Ask an applicant for employment during a job interview about his affiliation with, or position on, labor unions.
13. Ask employees about the identification of the leader of employees favoring the union.
14. Say that if the union becomes the bargaining agent, there will be more layoffs.
15. Say that if the union becomes the bargaining agent, the University will take away vacation or other benefits and privileges presently enjoyed.
16. Say that you or the University will not deal with the union.
17. Urge employees to try improperly to induce others to oppose or support the union.
18. Visit the homes of employees to urge them to reject the union.
19. Make speeches to massed assemblies of employees on University time in the 24-hour period before the election.

Another document issued by Columbia University during the organizing drive dealt with facts that the University felt were important to provide to the staff:

Promises versus Reality
In this memorandum, we would like to discuss WHAT THE UNION HAS

NOT TOLD YOU concerning the campaign "promises" of District 65 and the reality of how collective bargaining actually functions.

During their attempt to influence the vote in the upcoming National Labor Relations Board election, District 65 has continually made all kinds of "promises" that if it were to win the election it would guarantee more money and benefits for the voters. The Union would have you believe that all they have to do is make demands and that Columbia University will automatically agree to them. NOTHING COULD BE FURTHER FROM THE TRUTH: DO NOT BE MISLED BY SUCH FALSE AND IRRESPONSIBLE PROMISES.

Under the law, if District 65 were to win the election then it merely means that the union has the right to propose contract demands to the University. The legal obligation of the University in such an *adversarial relationship* is to listen to such demands and to discuss them in good faith in an effort to reach agreement with the Union. The University also makes contract demands of the Union. There is absolutely no obligation on the part of the employer to agree to the union's demands if such demands are not realistic or financially feasible.

In any event, negotiations with the union could end in agreement or disagreement. Joining a union is not a one-sided affair. When the University and the union start to negotiate a contract, there are two sides to be considered. The University must only sign a contract *if* it, as the employer, and the union can agree to the terms. The law does not compel the University to give a salary increase, fringe benefits or anything else. If the University cannot agree to the union's demands because of economic or other reasons, it does not have to sign a contract. If the University and District 65 could not reach an agreement, District 65, if it desired, could call a strike.

When a union calls a strike, work is disrupted and there is also a loss of income to employees. Such a disruption would be difficult for the University in attempting to continue its education and research goals. There are often stories about strikes in the newspapers and other media. We are all familiar with relatives, friends, or neighbors who have suffered from strikes. No one gains in such situations. No matter what the outcome of a strike might be, employees are usually hard put to make up the money lost while they are out of work. Financial and social problems are created for the employee and for his or her family as well as for the employer.

To put it simply, *strikes are costly to all*. Did the employees of the Metropolitan Museum of Art ever make up the lost salary that resulted from their 52-day strike? Did the employees at Concord Fabrics ever make up the lost wages that resulted from the 19-month strike? Remember, the union representing employees at these institutions was the same one that is attempting to organize you here—District 65 of the Distributive Workers of America. The strike history of District 65 is known to the employees at Columbia. Every employee who is eligible to vote in the coming election should carefully consider the problems that can be created in such strike situations. Strikes are a reality in unionized work environments.

Look at the record. District 65 has been unsuccessful in attaining representational status at all other major universities which it has attempted to organize. It represents fewer than 400 university employees throughout the nation. Campaign promises are nothing more than that: the past record of District 65 should be reviewed to determine its ability to "deliver" in university settings or even in industrial settings for that matter. In the contract negotiations just completed in January 1976 at the Museum of Modern Art here in New York, District 65 agreed to a freeze on wages for seven months for its 160 clerical employees.

Before you cast your ballot in the February 18th election here on campus, ask yourself:

Do you wish to place your future in the hands of the few individuals who are organizing for District 65?

Please weigh all of the issues before casting your vote—dues, assessments, initiation fees, possible strikes, etc. When all of these matters are considered and weighed, we feel certain that you will wish to *cast your secret ballot for "No Union"* in the upcoming NLRB election.[33]

Other documents that management can issue during an organizing drive cover such items as costs of membership (initiation fees, dues assessments for unexpected expenses), obligations of union membership (attendance at meetings, picketing during strikes), and eligibility for unemployment benefits during a strike. It is also legal for management to remind employees of the nature and extent of their benefits, as well as improvements made in fringe benefits, prior to the start of the union organizing drive.

The outcome of an election may not be known for some time if there are a large number of votes challenged by either of the parties. Challenges generally are made when one of the parties considers an individual employee or a category of job titles ineligible for membership in the bargaining unit agreed to by the NLRB. The NLRB holds hearings in order to determine whether the challenged votes should be included or excluded from the final tally. This can be a crucial phase of the process, and it is not uncommon to find that the final decision on the challenged votes determines the outcome of the election. Another factor that may delay the determination of the election concerns the "representative" nature of the voters. Although a union must poll a majority of all the votes cast in an election, it does not need to win the approval of a majority of all the employees who were eligible to vote. It must, however, win a majority of a representative number of the eligible voters. Interpretations of what is a "representative" number have varied: "In one case, a turn-out of around 31 percent of all eligible voters was held to be 'representative'; in another, a vote of 21 percent was labeled 'nonrepresentative.' In the latter case, however, there was some evidence that eligible voters had attempted to cast ballots after the closing hour."[34]

If the union wins the election, the process of contract negotiation begins. If the union loses, it may not embark on another organizing drive with the employer for a period of one year.

CONTRACT NEGOTIATIONS

Once a union has been certified as the collective bargaining agent for a group of employees, both the union and the employer are legally bound to bargain. The legal basis is found in Section 8(d) of the NLRA:

> . . . to bargain collectively is the performance of the mutual obligation of the employer and the representative of the employees to meet at reasonable times and confer in good faith with respect to wages, hours, and other terms and conditions of employment or the negotiation of an agreement, or any question arising thereunder, and the execution of a written contract incorporating any agreement reached if requested by either party, but such obligation does not compel either party to agree to a proposal or require the making of a concession.[35]

Collective bargaining is inevitably concerned with the economic issues of wages and benefits. The types of items included in the noneconomic area of working conditions vary depending on the nature of the work being performed and the category of staff in the bargaining unit. Dissatisfaction with past practices or conditions within a particular library often lead to the inclusion of special items aimed at improving the general working conditions of the employees. Typical times included in the negotiation of the first contract include basic provisions for contract management, recognition of the bargaining agent, composition of the bargaining unit, duration of the contract, no strike/no lock-out clause, dues check-off, and grievance procedures.[36] Two areas involving considerable controversy in the negotiation of the first contract—union security and management rights—are covered in some detail in this section.

Randle and Wortman have pointed out that "in collective bargaining, only the negotiation process is more important than the preparations that must be made for it."[37] The problems encountered in negotiating the first contract clearly underline the importance of thoughtful preparation. Managers who fail to plan adequately for negotiations may find that they have given away important prerogatives that may take years to regain.

The extent of the preparations depend on the nature of the bargaining unit and the reporting relationship of the library. Libraries are normally components of larger entities—school systems, municipal governments, companies, universities. The library representative on the management negotiation committee should therefore have access to centralized personnel or labor relations expertise.

This expertise can provide the library with considerable assistance in determining management's response to the union's demands in the key economic areas of rates of pay and fringe benefits. On the other hand, unless the library representative is assertive in setting forth the special needs of the library to the central office, the central office might agree to certain noneconomic demands from the union that could seriously impede the service or operational needs of the library. This is most likely to occur when the bargaining unit consists of several quite different categories of staff (for example, library supporting staff and clerical staff in other units of an institution, or professional librarians and nonsupervisory staff in units other than the library). Regardless of the willingness of the central office or other components in the bargaining unit to concede to specific union demands, the library management's representative must persistently articulate all special needs and interests of the library.

Management's Preparations

The summary of techniques and procedures that follows is adapted from Davey.[38] It is not intended to be all-inclusive, and certain techniques and procedures may not be relevant in all situations.

1. Thorough study of the current contract to determine if any sections or language need modification. (If it is the first contract, obtain copies of contracts previously agreed to by the union and contracts from libraries which have unions.)
2. Systematic analysis of prior grievances and arbitrations to identify any defective or unworkable contract language. Such analysis could also provide indications of probable union demands.
3. Frequent conferences with line supervisors for the dual purpose of better training of supervision in contract administration and receipt of information on how the contract is working out in practice.
4. Conferences with other employers who have contracts with the union to exchange viewpoints and anticipate the union's demands. (This is especially important when preparing for the first contract since it will provide information on the nature of items agreed to by the union.)
5. Informal conferences with local union leaders (shop stewards, delegates) to discuss the operation effectiveness of the contract and to send up trial balloons on management changes at the next negotiations. (This is recommended only for experienced labor relations administrators because of the sensitivity of unions to actions that could be viewed as collusion with management.)
6. Systematic use of a commercial reporting service on labor relations for the

purpose of keeping abreast of developments that may affect forthcoming contract negotiations. (This function is generally performed by the central office.)

7. Collection and analysis of economic data on matters of importance in the next negotiations. (Generally, the central office collects and analyzes data on wages and fringe benefits. The library is usually concerned with items such as absenteeism, turnover, and average wages for specific job classifications.)

8. Participation with the union in prenegotiation conferences to reach agreement on ground rules for upcoming negotiations. (This is generally the function of the central office.)

Maintaining good communications with line supervisors before and during contract negotiations is very important. Since they are the ones who have or will have responsibility for administering the contract on a daily basis, they are in the best position to identify problem areas in old contracts or items that should be incorporated into a new contract.

During the initial years of unionization, library personnel administrators are likely to find that supervising librarians are reluctant to contribute to the contract negotiation process or view it as outside of their area of responsibility. This may be due in part to the feelings of intimidation that management is often prone to following the union's victory in an election. It also is due to the lack of emphasis on management courses in library schools and the limited training in supervision that librarians obtain on the job.

Although advice often is not forthcoming from line supervisors, they will expect to be kept informed of the progress of the negotiations. The library personnel administrator should solicit their input, regardless of the lack of response.

Periodic reports from the library personnel administrator are important, not only to counterbalance the effects of rumors, but to communicate to the line supervisors that they are an integral part of the management team. The efforts made by the library personnel administrator during the initial years of unionization cannot guarantee productive relationships among staff and line officers, but they can help provide a solid foundation for ongoing labor relations.

Union's Preparations

Davey notes that few empirical studies have been done on how employers and unions prepare for negotiations. One study by "informed neutrals" confirms the general opinion that management is giving increased attention to careful preparations for negotiations.[39] Although unions vary considerably in their preparations, they often follow the same techniques and procedures used by management. Critical considerations for the union are internal needs and requirements and the goals or demands of a particular group of employees in a local bargaining unit. Regional or national goals of the union may conflict with local demands. The resolution of the conflict will depend to a considerable degree on the extent of democratic governance within the union. Since union officials are elected, to insure reelection they must either satisfy the demands of a majority of the membership or be able to convince the majority that union needs must take precedence over local demands. Two critical considerations for the union in its preparations are an assessment of the ability of management to withstand the effects of a strike and the skill and experience of the management negotiation team, including management's reaction to a possible strike or other form of work action.

Key Issues in the First Contract

The hostility that generally exists during the negotiation of the first contract is understandable since the conflicting objectives of the two sides have been tested since the onset of the union organizing drive. The adversary relationship is unavoidable. Davey has observed that the atmosphere ranges from one of uncertainty to outright hostility, owing to a number of factors:

1. The union has to make a good showing. This is a political necessity in dealing with a recently unionized employer.
2. Management generally is determined to give as little as possible.
3. The negotiators probably do not know one another. They do not know each other's strengths and weaknesses. Suspicion, if not outright distrust of the other party, is usually present.
4. The parties often lack experience in negotiation.
5. The local union committee may attempt to convert the negotiations into a complaint session over an accumulation of past grievances. Such a tactic can hamper negotiation of the basic contract.
6. When the company is one of the last to be organized in its industry or area, the pressure to achieve at one stroke the gains accrued in years of bargaining with other firms may seriously complicate the agreement-making process.[40]

The items negotiated in the first contract are critical to both sides for different reasons, which can be explained both by the nature of the items dealt with and the implications that they have for future negotiations and for administering the contract after it has been signed. Glueck identifies five categories of items typically included in the negotiation of the first contract:

1. *Compensation and Working Conditions.* This includes direct compensation

rates, benefits, and hours of work. Issues such as voluntary overtime, cost-of-living adjustments, and newer benefits such as dental care are examples. Unions bargain not only about the payments for pensions but also about the details of early retirement provisions, for example.

2. *Employee Security.* (Especially with regard to seniority.) Unions feel that seniority should be the determining factor in promotions, layoffs, and recalls. Management contends it is their right to make these decisions on the basis of job performance, or efficiency will suffer. The clause that many contracts have usually stipulates that in cases of promotion and layoff, when efficiency and ability are substantially equal, the most senior employee shall be favored. Seniority is continuous service in a work unit, plant, or organization.

3. *Union Security.* Unions wish to have as much influence over members as possible, so they try to write in a requirement for a union shop. A union shop is an employment location at which all employees must join the union after a brief introductory period. Failing this, the union tries to get a modified union shop: all employees except a few exempted groups must join the union. If the union shop clause cannot be won, an agency shop may be acceptable to the union. In this, those who do not join must pay the equivalent of union dues to the union. [The closed shop, which requires membership in the union before a job applicant can be employed, was abolished by Section 8(a)(3) of the National Labor Relations Act.]

4. *Management Rights.* Management lists certain areas or decisions as management rights or prerogatives which are thus excluded from bargaining. Management tries to make these lists long, and unions have chipped away at them. Recently, the United Auto workers argued that handling health and safety problems should be a joint management right. It also disputes a foreman's right to suspend a worker without pay over issues other than violence, drunkenness, and illegal refusal to work.

5. *Contract Durations.* Companies tend to prefer longer contracts so as to have less turmoil. Over 90 percent of the U.S. contracts now cover two- or three-year periods.[41]

Despite the importance of wages and other money items in all contract negotiations, union security and management rights require special attention during the negotiation of the first contract because of the significance they have on future working relationships with the union.

Union Security

Randle and Wortman state that union security is one of the most controversial and least understood issues in labor relations today.[42] They point out that this state of affairs may be due more to emotion than to reason. Davey notes that the issue has always had an "explosive character."[43]

Before exploring the reasons for the controversy surrounding this issue, a distinction should be made between union security and employee security:

> When demands are made for pensions, welfare plans of various types, supplemental unemployment benefits, illness and disability plans or insurance programs, the union is thinking primarily of employee economic security. It is the individual member who profits directly from these demands. On the other hand, when the union profits directly from such demands as the union shop, agency shop, maintenance-of-membership, the check-off, and, to some extent, seniority, it is primarily seeking security for the union organization as such. In these areas, unionism as an institution profits directly. In almost every collective bargaining session, some demands are made primarily in the interest of the employees and some primarily in the interest of the union. In their secondary effects, it must be admitted that these demands are difficult to separate, for what benefits the individual member may also benefit the organization. In terms of primary benefit, however, a general line of demarcation may be drawn between union and employee demands.[44]

The so-called "right to work" laws, which prohibit any form of union security clause, have been sanctioned by Section 14b of the NLRA.[45] They are a primary target of unions. Davey, who states in his preface that he "has felt (in fact, obligated) to state my policy stance on controversial matters,"[46] clearly has little tolerance for proponents of the "right to work" laws:

> The term "right to work" is a misnomer. *There is no unqualified "right to work" anywhere, anytime, for whomever one chooses.* The right to work is a *qualified* right as are most other "rights" in labor relations (and in society). The right to strike and the right to lock out employees are qualified by a considerable body of federal and state legislation and court decisions. The right to bargain collectively is a conditioned right. Even First Amendment constitutional use of "free speech" by employers and union leaders is not unqualified in a labor relations context. Its constitutional force is subject to Taft-Hartley limitations. The Act prohibits both unions and employers from interfering with, restraining or coercing employees in the exercise of *their* rights.
>
> Looked at in this kind of perspective, a union clause provides one more qualification on an always-qualified right to work as related to any particular employer. When the contract requires union membership, it is one more "condition of employment" the prospective employee must consider in deciding whether to accept a job with a particular concern.[47]

Randle and Wortman point out that the light in which one views the pros and cons of union security depends on one's philosophy, background, and inclinations.[48] An adaptation of their arguments for and against union security follows:

Arguments for Union Security:
1. *Elimination of the "Free Rider."* It is difficult to disagree with the union argument that workers who enjoy most of the benefits of unionism should take on the responsibilities and obligations of union membership.
2. *Power in Bargaining.* The union's ability to gain concessions in bargaining derives from the strength of its membership.
3. *Fear of the Employer.* The union's concept of collective bargaining and management's concept of its prerogatives create conflicts that motivate unions to achieve maximum security.
4. *Fear of Being Undermined.* Under less than union shop security, unions fear being undermined by employees outside the union and by competing unions.
5. *Improved Labor Relations.* Advantages found by employers in union security include elimination of strife between union and nonunion employees. Regional or industrywide union shops tend to stabilize wages and thus eliminate labor costs as a competitive factor. Union security tends to free employers from jurisdictional disputes, and troublesome interruptions, and improve discipline among employees.

Arguments Against Union Security:
1. *Violation of Freedom of Economic Choice.* The argument here is that an employee should not be compelled to become a union member to obtain or hold a job and that such a requirement is contrary to the free enterprise system. Other arguments are that union security creates monopolies, which are contrary to the American way, and that union security puts the employer in a false position of upholding the union's membership and indirectly its prestige by forcing the employer to fire workers who are not union members in "good standing."
2. *Violation of Individual Rights.* This concern comes from employees with no desire to join unions. A related concern is the argument that an employee may be placed in economic jeopardy because comparatively little is known about union admission requirements, initiation fees, and the internal operation of unions.
3. *Interference with Operations and Efficiency.* Employers often argue that union security forces them to hire only union members or those willing to join unions rather than the most capable job applicants. Other inefficiencies cited are decreases in productivity due to an inability to reward exceptional performance by merit increases and a general lowering of productivity due to the employee's primary allegiance to the union rather than to the employer.[49]

Regardless of one's personal views, union security is generally accepted as a primary requirement by unions negotiating a first contract and agreed to by most employers. A skilled management negotiator, however, generally does not accept the inevitability of a union security clause before receiving assurances from the union that key management items will also be included in the contract.

Management Rights

The management rights clause, which has been defined as one that "expressly reserves to management certain rights and specifies that the exercise of these rights shall not be subject to the grievance procedure or arbitration,"[50] is equally as controversial an issue as union security. The rights of management generally include the following:

1. To direct and control its work force
2. To determine the means, processes, materials, and schedules of production
3. To utilize fully its work force and machines
4. And to maintain employee discipline and production efficiency[51]

Although such clauses are found in most contracts, "exclusive management functions—impregnable for all time—have yet to be defined."[52] This situation is due in part to the modi vivendi worked out by unions and management through years of contract negotiation and administration and, in part, to the expanded scope of negotiable items that have arisen since World War II.

The controversy over management rights stems from the principal theories on management authority. Randel and Wortman, who note that these theories are not mutually exclusive, provide the basis for the following summary of the principal theories of management authority:

1. The *absolute* concept of management rights contends that there are areas in which the union has no voice and should not be allowed to bargain. Under this concept, management believes that certain functions are clearly managerial prerogatives—functions such as work schedules, work assignment, type of product to be made, production methods and processes, employee selection, product pricing, and location of the plant. This approach emphasizes that management should take a firm stand against union penetration.
2. The *limited management* theory assumes that administrative initiation for any function or action rests with management, but that it is subject to challenge through the grievance procedure. Issues that arise under this theory are promotion, demotion, layoff, and recall procedures; discipline by discharge, suspension, or warning; rules covering seniority; and establishment of wage rates under various job evaluation methods. Sound management principles dictate that authority and responsibility be placed in the hands of the management team. However, the union processes grievances on violation of the contract or actions that it feels are contrary to the spirit of the contract.

3. The *residual theory* provides that the employer has all the rights or prerogatives he would have had in the absence of a union except those that the employer specifically has granted to the union through negotiations. This theory views the evolution of collective bargaining as a continually advancing encroachment upon the employer's right to direct operations. Managerial authority has been circumscribed by the advances of unionism. Management retains all of its former rights and privileges, however, if they are not abridged or limited by the contract. This theory would support an employer who advocated the policy of containment. Through such a policy, management would be able to retain as many of its rights and privileges as its economic power would sustain. Under this concept, the contract is envisioned as a flag of truce rather than a treaty that would encourage cooperation for mutual advancement from both parties. Unions frequently attempt to combat the residual rights theory by the principle of implied limitations. Although the contract may not say anything about certain issues, the union contends that certain provisions, such as seniority, wages, and the recognition clause, really make the employer maintain the status quo. The union feels that if it did not follow precedent as well as the spirit of the contract, many benefits and rights that had been negotiated would not be available to the membership. Thus management, despite its residual rights, cannot do anything contrary to the spirit of the contract or the union membership would not realize the rewards of the contract.
4. The *trusteeship theory* states that the primary responsibilities of management are to its investors, its customers, its employees, and its community. Under the trusteeship theory, there are no sacred management functions. In this approach, the union is looked upon as a partner in production, and collective bargaining is looked upon as a valuable managerial tool to gain the enthusiastic support of the employees in production. Normally, the trusteeship would be employed in a cooperative or accommodation atmosphere so that labor and management could aid each other in the improvement of the firm's competitive position.[53]

Although various aspects of all four theories on management authority may dominate different phases of an organization's relationship with a union, in collective bargaining in the United States management generally leans towards the residual or reserved rights theory, while unions operate more under the limited management theory. Arthur J. Goldberg contends that management seldom should have the initiative to act without union concurrence, a position that Randle and Wortman identify as the most extreme form of the union prerogative argument.[54]

In explaining his point of view, Goldberg states that labor's rights are often regulated to a lower level than management's because arbitrators often give more weight to management's arguments that it took certain actions, which it considered reasonable, because of the need for efficiency. Few would disagree that arbitrators should give equal consideration to reasonable justifications for actions taken by both union and management. In arguments such as the one cited below, Goldberg would lead us to believe that unions are too often the victims of a management bias in the arbitration process:[55]

> Somehow a company motivated by a desire for greater efficiency is aligned on the side of the angels, but a union motivated by a desire to retain conditions which please the workers is playing politics for failing to live up to its responsibilities. How often do we hear these sentiments? Yet what do they represent but the belief that the parties to the agreement are not equal and the desires of one are weighty but the desires of the other are frivolous.

Even a superficial review of arbitration decisions will demonstrate the flaws in Goldberg's point of view.

Inclusion or Exclusion of a Management Rights Clause. If there were no other reason to include a management rights clause in the first contract than to give a boost to the morale of the managers and supervisors, this would be more than sufficient justification. The conflicts throughout the various stages of unionization create major morale problems for managers because they are too often unable to maintain a reasonable degree of productivity, owing to the disruptions and challenges of union activists. The inclusion of a management rights clause in the contract will not insure an easy transition into contract administration, but it provides a tool that enables management to regain operational controls that might have been lost or weakened under the state of siege of the organizing drive.

Although there are arguments for and against the inclusion of a management rights clause that relate to the various theories on management authority, these arguments should not dissuade management from insisting on such a clause. If it is not included in the first contract, it may be impossible to obtain union acceptance in future negotiations without making major concessions to the union in other significant areas or without being willing to withstand the consequences of a strike.

Randle and Wortman provide a succinct summary of the arguments on a management rights clause:

Arguments for Including a Management Rights Clause:
1. It prevents the union from further encroachment. [For example, scheduling, work performance, attendance standards, managerial appointments.]
2. It indicates the rights not limited to the agreement. [For example, automation and other operational changes.]
3. It tends to reduce possible disputes. [If, for example, the right to schedule is stated in the management rights clause, management will be able to maintain its position in a grievance and in arbitration, provided that it administered the policy in a reasonable and consistent manner.]

Arguments Against Including a Management Rights Clause
1. Damage to management may result if the clause is not complete and does not spell out all of its reserved rights. [In view of the general understanding and acceptance of the basic reserved rights of management, this is not a compelling argument.]
2. Specific definitions of management rights might be interpreted as limiting management. [Again, this is not a compelling argument in view of the acceptance of the basic reserved rights of management in labor relations in the United States.][56]

The Negotiations

Contract negotiations generally involve four distinct stages:

1. *Each side presents its demands.* Usually, the two parties are far apart on some issues.
2. *Reduction of demands.* After postures have been taken, each side trades off some of the demands they were not serious about. These demands were included for trading purposes. Pressure is received from the public, customers, union demands, and others regarding the bargaining terms.
3. *Subcommittee studies.* Getting down to business, the two parties form joint subcommittees, which try to work out reasonable alternatives.
4. *Informal settlement.* The two sides go back to their reference groups. The management team determines if top management will accept the terms and union leaders take soundings of the memberships to see their reaction. If management is agreeable, the process develops into the formal settlement stage.[57]

Each of the four stages can present a variety of different problems depending on, for example, the experience of the chief negotiators, whether the negotiation involves a first contract, and the degree of democracy within the union. Impasses can be reached at any stage. The reduction of demands is often an involved process, especially when a specific demand carries more meaning for one component of the bargaining unit than it does for another. The use of subcommittees occurs more frequently during the negotiation of early contracts because of the variety of different issues on the table. Serious complications can arise at the final stages of negotiations either because of poor communication or because union issues differ from employee issues.

Davey provides a useful list of common-sense guidelines on general procedures that should be considered for constructive negotiations:

1. Both the union and the management negotiating teams should be reasonably small. If the union or company committee is too large and everyone insists on participating, much time will be consumed, tempers will become

frayed, and much irrelevant material may be introduced. [When commit-tees are too large, individual grievances often impede the resolution of important issues.]

2. One person must be in charge of conducting the negotiations for each side. Division of authority in negotiation is fatal to orderly procedure and usually impedes the agreement-making process. [Experienced negotiators, howev-er, do not decide which issues to drop without discussion with the appropri-ate negotiating committee.]

3. The parties should agree in advance on the time of day and desired length of bargaining sessions. Each side can then make its plans accordingly. [To expedite negotiations, management should insure that they occur after working hours.]

4. Careful preparation for negotiations should include exchange of demands or proposals for study before actual bargaining begins. A frequent source of trouble is the springing of a complicated new proposal during negotiations. [Although this is highly undesirable, unions often take the position that new items can be introduced at any time prior to the settlement of the total package.]

5. Advance agreement on procedures will eliminate such unnecessary argu-ments as whether subject X is "in order at this time."

6. Negotiators should have authority to make decisive commitments in the course of negotiations. Company negotiators generally have the power to bind their principals. In most unions the negotiated terms are subject to ratification or rejection by the membership. Membership rejection can be a serious problem.

7. Negotiations should begin with a well-planned agenda that includes a complete statement of all disputed issues together with a listing of propos-als and counterproposals on the disputed points.

8. If possible, an agreed statement of relevant economic data should be employed. This can be done when the parties have made effective use of the prenegotiation conference.

9. The negotiators should first resolve the less controversial issues and reduce their agreement to writing before proceeding to the tougher issues.

10. The difficult issues can be divided into those that involve money outlays and noneconomic demands.

11. Many noneconomic issues can be negotiated individually in terms of their intrinsic merit rather than in terms of the bargaining strength of the principles. This generalization would clearly not apply, however, to union demands relating to such "noneconomic" matters as union security or seniority.

12. Finally, and of critical importance in most negotiations, a decision must be made as to whether to bargain out the demands involving money outlays one by one or to negotiate on an economic package basis.[58]

Bargaining techniques encompass the entire spectrum of human behavior, ranging from fist pounding by representatives on one side to civility and good humor on both sides. Much depends on the nature of the previous bargaining relationship, as well as on the issues currently on the table and the state of the economy. There are techniques that can be utilized to decrease the animosity that often characterizes negotiations and to increase the possibility of a timely and mutually acceptable settlement.

Randle and Wortman recommend various techniques that have proved valuable in reaching timely settlements:

1. Learn the value of a change in the subject. When it becomes apparent that no agreement can be reached at the time, table the issue and move on to less controversial matters. Often the solution to the tabled issue appears as negotiations proceed.
2. Be a good listener. Psychologically it is a good technique to let each speaker finish talking. There will be time enough to offer a counterproposal or issue a denial after the facts have been obtained.
3. Do not hurry the negotiation. If there are attempts to guide the discussion, one party may become irritated and the bargaining atmosphere may deteriorate. If negotiations slow down, call for a recess.
4. Learn to identify the techniques giving the best results. Discard those which irritate the other party. Use the techniques which minimize the existing differences.
5. Question the evidence offered. Through questions, the group may obtain insights into the other group's point of view and perhaps get an indication of the arguments which they may use. Questions may also expose weaknesses in the other party's position.
6. Use data and "facts" only after they are thoroughly verified. Be honest and know the information, for erroneous or false statements can seriously affect negotiations.
7. Hold statistical materials in reserve and carefully prepare an opening for their use. If used too early, before their implications are fully apparent or before a favorable atmosphere has been created for them, they will lose their impact. Graphical data are more convincing than raw figures, since the latter generally are distrusted and confusing rather than convincing.
8. If there are "blue-sky" or unrealistic demands during negotiations, sidetrack them carefully without ridicule, for the other party may be looking for an opportunity to become angry.
9. Be factual rather than emotional. Think through the arguments, issues, and problems.
10. Occasionally bring up matters of common interest and agreement.
11. Beware of arguments of "principle." Negotiators feel more emotional about principles than they do about specifics.
12. Proper language assists bargaining. Bargainers should avoid inflammatory remarks questioning the sincerity or good faith of the other party. Do not refer to personalities or use red-flag words, such as "management prerogatives," "anti-union," "arbitrary," "union racketeer," and "discharge," since they only excite emotions of the parties.
13. Avoid taking a stand publicly through releases or advertisements in ad-

vance of or during negotiations. A publicized position makes concessions difficult and may stall the negotiations.

14. Do not take unfair advantage of the other party. Constructive collective bargaining takes place in an atmosphere of confidence and trust, not in one of suspicion and doubt.

15. Do not threaten to strike or lock out at the bargaining table. The implied threat is already present and gratuitous strike or lockout threats destroy the confidence of one party in the other during negotiations.[59]

Although these techniques may prove valuable in reaching timely settlements, they are often ineffective because of the very nature of the collective bargaining process and the makeup of the parties. As Davey points out, ideal negotiators are a rare breed:

> Negotiating is a demanding, wearing kind of business. It requires a rather unusual personal chemistry, an abundance of physical and mental vigor and specialized know-how. The model negotiator lives only on the printed page. Few, if any, mortals satisfy all criteria in the required amounts. Although each party tries to maintain a favorable light during the course of negotiations, each may use tactics to further its best interests.[60]

There are a number of tactics used exclusively by unions to further their best interests and to gain advantages over management:

1. *The union attempts a show of strength.* This may occur because the union feels that management does not believe that the membership is behind the demands of the union. Since solidarity is an important factor for any union involved in negotiations, the union rarely has difficulty demonstrating the support of the membership.
2. *The union resorts to the threat of sanctions.* This takes the form of a strike vote from the membership, which is normally obtained early in the negotiations.
3. *Demonstrations, slowdowns, and coercion.* Demonstrations are common actions used by unions to emphasize the needs of the membership. They are permissible provided that they do not interfere with the normal activities of the organization. Slowdowns, which are prohibited by the NLRA, do occur nonetheless. The union position is not to sanction slowdowns which it considers individual rather than group actions. Coercion, which is also prohibited by the NLRA, is also considered spontaneous by the union. When actions take place that are in violation of the NLRA, management can seek an injunction if it has sufficient documentation.
4. *Support from other unions.* Such support generally comes from other unions within the area or organization. During a strike, it is not uncommon for other unions to go out in sympathy with the striking union.[61]

Tactics used by management during negotiations are more in the line of defensive measures taken in response to union actions. In response to the union's show of strength and solidarity through obtaining a strike vote from the membership, management negotiators consult with top management to obtain their vote of confidence. The usual outcome of competing shows of strength is a neutralization of the two positions. Under Section 301 of the Taft-Hartley Act, management has the right to prosecute the union for any financial damages to property or any threats to cause irreparable damage. To obtain compensation requires clear evidence of union involvement, which is difficult to prove. During a strike, a common tactic employed by management is to maintain essential services and operations by the utilization of nonunion staff. In a library, this generally involves assigning all technical services staff to key service and processing functions (one of the key elements of a library strike contingency plan is to identify the essential services to be maintained).

A common tactic used by management to further its best interests should not be overlooked, namely, to set the expiration of a contract at a period of time that will do it least harm in the event of a strike. In certain industries the goal is to set an expiration date that will coincide with the slack season. The implication here for libraries is to avoid contract expirations that come close to peak user periods. Academic, public, and school libraries should avoid expiration dates that are just near the commencement of classes.

Conciliation, Arbitration, and Mediation

Davey notes that the overall record on labor peace is a reasonably good one, and he does not consider the use of economic force a problem of unusually serious magnitude. He points out, however, that the increased strike activity in the public sector during the late 1960s indicates that we should "pause before we speak glibly of the decline and fall of the strike."[62] Strikes, which are the ultimate result of negotiation disputes, can have serious and far-reaching consequences for both parties, either or both of whom may be willing to endure if disputed issues are of major significance.

As Randle and Wortman point out, "The bargaining parties possess a duty to themselves, to their organizations, *and to the public*. From all three points of view, there exists a strong obligation to continue the bargaining—to walk the extra mile."[63] When both parties have reached an impasse in negotiations, several alternatives remain open that can prevent a strike:

1. *Conciliation.* Originally, conciliation consisted of having a third party intervene in negotiations to attempt to get the parties together and keep them at

the negotiating table. The conciliator offers no solution for the dispute or deadlocked negotiations.

2. *Mediation.* Mediation brings in a third party who actively proposes solutions to the two parties and attempts to keep them negotiating over the deadlocked issues.

3. *Arbitration.* This involves having a third party decide the disposition of the disputed issues for labor and management. Although the bargainers may be understandably reluctant to call for a third party, a fresh point of view sometimes encourages agreement. An opportunity also may be provided for the parties to get together on the basis of a suggestion by the third party without losing face. Mediation is much more effective if used before a shutdown.[64]

Since arbitration presents risks for both sides, it is the less desirable alternative to use to resolve deadlocks. Mediation is the preferred alternative because it allows both sides to use a third party to agree to compromises with which they both can live.

RESPONSIBILITIES FOR LABOR RELATIONS

Regardless of an organization's structure, one office or individual within the library should be responsible for administering labor relations. A large university or public library usually has a centralized personnel or labor relations office which generally has responsibility for heading the contract negotiation committee and administering the last internal step of the grievance procedure. The library personnel administrator works closely with the central unit. Another way to organize responsibility for labor relations is assigning a labor relations administrator from the central personnel office to the library.

The key reason for establishing responsibility for labor relations is to insure consistency in the interpretation of the contract and in the administration of grievances and disciplinary actions. A failure to maintain a reasonable degree of consistency can lead to the loss of rights gained through negotiations or preferential treatment of individual employees due to a supervisor's inexperience, feelings of independence, or timidity. Inconsistent administration of the contract inevitably results in decisions favoring the union when grievances are referred to the central personnel office or to arbitration. When one individual or office is responsible, the likelihood of inconsistencies diminishes dramatically, provided that the line and staff function as a team. As Randle and Wortman point out, teamwork is critical in labor relations:

Teamwork among all management personnel having anything to do with labor relations is very important. It is obvious that in order for the teamwork to be effective, the staff and the line must understand and empathize with the other's goals and objectives. Through this mutual aid, both parties are able to accomplish their tasks in labor relations. . . . Without cooperation between the line and the staff, company policies may deteriorate subtly, with little or no discussion of their rationale.[65]

The Importance of Training

To avoid irreparable harm to organizational objectives, both the library personnel administrator and the managers need training for their responsibilities in labor relations. In a medium-sized public library, the head librarian may arrange for staff from the central personnel office to head a seminar on contract and grievance administration. If the supervisory staff is large, the training program has to be extensive, reflecting the problems and issues that are typical in larger organizations. Although the nature of the training program will vary depending on the size and complexity of the organization, it is important to include managers and administrators in the program even though they may not have direct responsibility for unionized staff. This will insure that they have an understanding of the problems and constraints that line supervisors must deal with in labor relations.

The responsibility for developing training programs belongs with the personnel office staff. If there is a central training office or staff member within the library with such responsibilities, the labor relations administrator should work closely with the training staff in designing the programs. When a library has no formal training program, the responsibility for insuring that supervisors and managers understand the requirements and constraints of collective bargaining must fall on the shoulders of the managerial and personnel staff. Although this kind of informal training is bound to be less effective than a formal program, it can convey the importance of sound labor relations practices to line supervisors.

Library administrators can contract with outside trainers, depending on the availability of funds, the priorities of the staff, and the urgency of the need for training. A number of state schools of industrial or labor relations offer such programs, which can be modified to meet local needs and which are less expensive than those offered by private management and personnel associations. Training should not end after the first years of unionization; there will always be supervisors joining the staff who need to be trained.

CONTRACT ADMINISTRATION

Contract administration is a daily responsibility. In the early years of unionization, contract administration is complicated by the need to modify or develop policies and procedures to insure compliance with the contract and to establish ground rules with the union to insure that management rights are not compromised either because of the aggressiveness of the union or the reluctance of supervisors to fulfill their responsibilities as members of the management team.

To begin the process of adapting to a union, the personnel administrator should distribute copies of the contract to all managerial and supervisory staff and hold meetings to review and explain the meaning and intent of key clauses. If there is a delay in publishing the first contract, the key clauses should be summarized in writing and distributed.

Problems often arise in introducing the supervisory staff to the contract. For instance, ambiguities may be noticed by the supervisors that were overlooked by the management negotiation team. These usually can be clarified by the personnel administrator through discussions with the central personnel office or the management labor counsel. Another problem involves disagreements between management and the union on the intent of the language in specific contract clauses. When such disagreements cannot be resolved, they are referred to arbitration.

The introduction of the contract is the preliminary step in training supervisors to function effectively in a union environment. One simple technique requiring a minimum of time and effort is to schedule periodic meetings to review and discuss problems and questions relating to the administration of the contract. Such meetings help the personnel administrator determine if supervisors are adhering to the contract and, in addition, provide ideas for items to include in the list of management demands for the negotiation of the next contract.

One of the most troublesome problems is the reluctance of supervisors to resolve conflicts and grievances at an early stage. (A number of library personnel administrators attribute this reluctance to the profession's continued failure to address the functional responsibilities of the librarian as manager and administrator. We neither recruit into the professional the types of individuals who are attracted to careers as managers, nor do we provide the education and training librarians need to meet the challenges of management.) When supervisors fail to take the initiative to resolve problems at any early stage, grievances increase at the intermediate or personnel office level.

Personnel administrators have to be careful to avoid ruling against supervisors who do not seek resolutions to grievances at the department level. They must also avoid the pitfalls of pressure tactics from the union. Unions often deluge the system with grievances to gain concessions that they failed to achieve in negotiations or to demonstrate to the employees that they are indeed able to control management. It is just as important for a personnel administrator to work with supervisors to help them overcome their reluctance to function constructively and aggressively as members of the management team as it is to avoid reacting to pressure tactics by compromising organizational objectives.

Pressure Tactics

Randle and Wortman have pointed out that pressure tactics are most common during the early years of unionization and are used by employees to gain objectives during the life of the contract.[66] Although the increased use of arbitration to resolve management and labor conflicts diminishes the incidence of pressure tactics, they are still realities of the collective bargaining phenomenon. This aspect of contract administration is often overlooked because pressure tactics can appear to be unrelated to the position of the union leadership and may occur with little or no formal organization.[67]

Union members tend to use pressure tactics when they feel that management is vulnerable. Randle and Wortman identify two stages: the period of organization and the development of the contract. In both stages the union feels that force is the only language that management understands.[68] A third stage occurs after the contract has been negotiated and centers on the development of daily working relationships between management and the union. Management generally has more resources to combat such tactics once the contract has been signed because there are specific clauses to prohibit slowdowns, work stoppages, and strikes. The most common pressure tactics are:[69]

1. *Wildcat strikes,* which are illegal and in violation of the contract. The mere threat of a strike is also a pressure tactic.
2. *Slowdowns,* which also violate the contract, are quite common and generally occur when there is an impasse in negotiations. Waste and various types of vandalism are closely related in their objectives.
3. *Flooding of the grievance procedure,* which is a common tactic during the period that a contract is running out.

Although slowdowns and flooding of the grievance machinery may on the surface seem to be minor annoyances, they interfere with the staff's ability to function. An intangible effect noted by Randle and Wortman involves the loss of authority and prestige of management through the declining importance of disciplinary policy.[70]

Management faces a dilemma when confronted with pressure tactics. It can take disciplinary action against a group of employees, but it faces real difficulties in obtaining evidence that will hold up in arbitration. This is not to say that management rarely invokes group disciplinary action; however, it generally is reluctant to do so during the initial years of unionization. If management continues to fail to take appropriate disciplinary action under such circumstances, the employees will continue to use such methods whenever they seem appropriate to their cause.

The Nature of Grievances

In a classic study of employee complaints, three types were identified according to content.[71] The first type involves sensory experiences relating to sight and touch and could easily be verified (a piece of equipment is malfunctioning, the library paste doesn't adhere). The second type also involves sensory experience, but of the type that cannot easily be agreed upon ("It's too hot in the stacks." "There's too much work to be done."). The third type of complaint relates to the hopes and fears of the employee ("The supervisor plays favorites." "I'm not appreciated for my ability.").

The first type of complaint is relatively easy to resolve because there is little area for disagreement—either the equipment works or it doesn't. The second type does present problems because of the different reactions individuals have to variations in temperature and work loads. The third type of complaint is the most prevalent and the most difficult to resolve, since it generally combines elements of fact with subjective sentiments.

In the early years of unionization all complaints tend to be initiated through the formal channels of the grievance machinery regardless of their substance. In later years, minor problems or dissatisfactions are most likely to be resolved informally. Although there are legitimate distinctions to be made between complaints and grievances, since the latter should involve some violation of the contract, it is common for management to respond to both minor complaints and alleged violations of the contract as if both fell within the purview of the grievance machinery. A purist might tell the union that management will not consider issues that are not alleged violations of specific clauses in the contract, but a pragmatist would consider all complaints as subject to the grievance machinery if for no other reason than to demonstrate to the union and the employees that management is interested in attempting to resolve all problems affecting the staff.

Record Keeping

To insure fair treatment of employees and consistent interpretations of policies, the personnel office should maintain records of precedents and past practices whether or not the employees are unionized. With unionization the records become critical because management will be subject to repeated challenges by the union regardless of the validity of the complaint or grievance. During the initial years of unionization, pressures from the union may be such that the personnel staff might lose sight of the importance of maintaining a grievance log. This oversight can lead to inconsistencies in contract administration that can result in arbitration decisions favorable to the union and detrimental to organizational objectives.

A grievance log provides management with information that can be used in planning for renegotiation of the contract by helping to identify ambiguities that can be added to the list of management "demands." An analysis of the grievance log also helps management identify areas of employee dissatisfaction and components of the library system that might have a disproportionate number of grievances because of poor or improper supervision. If the analysis indicates significant areas of dissatisfaction among employees, management might consider changes that could lead to improvements in morale and productivity. Although management might conclude through an analysis of grievances that serious problems exist because of improper supervision in certain units, such conclusions should not be drawn without full knowledge of the situation. Pigors and Myers have pointed out the dangers of hasty assumptions:

> No one can tell *what* is indicated by the number of complaints unless he takes into account *the rate* at which they are being expressed and understands the situation well enough to know how closely complaints correspond to facts. The rate is significant. A large number of complaints within a short time may be a healthy sign, for example, if it indicates that hitherto suppressed dissatisfactions have suddenly been released.[72]

On the other hand, a unit with a minimal number of grievances may have significant problems that cannot be identified through an analysis of the grievance log. Such problems may be manifested by high levels of absenteeism or staff turnover.

The Grievance Procedure

The size and nature of the bargaining unit generally determines the number of steps in the grievance procedure, the formality of the various steps, the step at which the grievance is reduced to writing, and the number and level of union and management representatives present at a grievance hearing. The following summary of a typical grievance procedure has been adapted from Randall and Wortman[73] and modified to reflect library terminology and organization:

First Step:

Management Representatives	*Union Representatives*
	Aggrieved employee (Normally a union representative does not participate.)

First step of a grievance generally involves an informal meeting. During the initial years of unionization, the immediate supervisor may ask that another management representative or the personnel administrator be present at the meeting if the union brings a representative. Responses to first step grievances are usually not in writing.

Second Step:

Immediate supervisor and the library personnel or labor relations officer	*Aggrieved employee and a representative of the union*

The grievance is usually presented and responded to in writing at the second step. The grievance is to be submitted within a reasonable period of time following the first step response. Some contracts specify the number of days that an employee has to appeal the first step response to the second step. Once the grievance has been reduced to writing, there is usually a specified time period for a written response.

Third Step:

Immediate supervisor, library personnel officer and personnel or labor relations representative from the central office	*Aggrieved employee and at least one representative of the union*

The grievance and the response are in writing and time periods are specified for submission and response. In addition to the local union delegate or steward, an official of the union usually participates.

Arbitration: The management and union representatives and the aggrieved employee participate in the arbitration hearing. Other relevant witnesses may participate at the request of either side. Many libraries utilize labor counsels as spokespersons at arbitrations.

Defining the Scope of a Grievance

Although many contracts contain statements defining grievances as disputes arising between the two parties on the interpretation or application of the contract, experience indicates that grievances often involve areas not covered in specific clauses of the contract. Line and staff officers in a recently unionized library may make concerted efforts to reduce the number of grievances by insisting on strict interpretation of what is under the terms of the contract. The union and the employees, on the other hand, may insist that all employee dissatisfactions legitimately fall under the terms of the contract because they relate to working conditions.

Accusations by the union of "arbitrary and capricious" actions on the part of management will only intensify union-management conflicts. This is not to say that one should not draw the line somewhere. The question management should ask is "When?" The response may well depend on the union's willingness to work cooperatively in administering the contract. Davey's advice in this area places the burden squarely on management:

> All employees and unions should endorse the psychological proposition that *a grievance exists whenever an employee feels aggrieved*, whether or not the source of his grievance is contractual. If an employee or some employees feel, rightly or wrongly, that they are being unjustly treated, a human relations problem exists that merits the attention of both management and the union.[74]

Contract administration involves a willingness on both sides to compromise and to make concessions. The personnel administrator or supervisor who fails to make some reasonable concessions or who makes too many will eventually become ineffective. There is a delicate balance to be maintained to avoid giving too little or too much. The personnel administrator who errs in either extreme will face real conflicts with the line and may seriously impede the organizational objectives of the library.

Principles of Resolving Grievances

The personnel administrator plays an important role in establishing the framework for viable labor relations by insuring that supervisors observe certain basic principles or guidelines in attempting to resolve grievances:

1. *Define the grievance.* As simple as this may seem and often is, it can be complex when emotional issues are involved.
2. *Be a good listener.* The right of the employee to a fair hearing dictates that the supervisor and the personnel administrator listen. This does not mean that the hearing officer must listen to endless harangues or excessive irrelevancies. A comment to the effect that the grievant is straying from the point at issue should get the meeting in order. It is not unusual for an experienced union representative to make such a comment.
3. *Investigate the facts carefully.* This often requires research and consultations with other representatives of the union or management.
4. *Put the employee at ease.* Regardless of one's preconceptions, it is important to make the employee feel at ease. Despite the presence of the union, many employees still feel threatened by the authority symbolized by a management representative.
5. *Avoid arguing.* The tone of the hearing should be businesslike and along the line of a mutual discussion of a problem. There will be times when tempers flare, but management should avoid fighting fire with fire whenever possible.
6. *Avoid snap judgments.* The response to a grievance need not be given on the spot. Management should avoid openly siding with either the employee or the supervisor. Too quick a decision creates unfavorable reactions even if favorable to the grievant. If the decision is positive, the grievant might feel that management was aware of and had been condoning the situation. If negative, the grievant might well feel that the supervisor's or hearing officer's mind was made up in advance.
7. *Factors to consider in making a decision.* The relation of the grievance to the contract and to existing policy should be weighed carefully. Compromise may be appealing, but consider the implications, including the precedents that might be established.
8. *Timely responses.* It is important to adhere to the time elements specified in the contract in responding to grievances. If the issue is complex and requires additional time to resolve, inform the union of the reasons for the delay. Repeated failures of management to respond to grievances in a timely manner may provide the union with justification for arbitration.

The length of a written response to a grievance will vary depending on the issues involved. Generally, verbatim summaries of extraneous points or issues should not be included in responses. The response should include a concise summary of the issues, the main arguments put forth by both sides, and the reasons for granting or denying the grievance. During the early years of unionization, management is more likely to provide lengthy explanations for actions taken, since it feels it must justify its position to both the union and the line supervisors. This approach may well be the only course of action to follow when the union is aggressively pursuing its point of view and when the line supervisors need assurances that management is on their side.

It is particularly important during the early years of unionization for management to realize that its relationship with the union changes dramatically once a contract has been negotiated. It changes because both parties have reached an agreement through a legally binding document. As parties to a contract, management and the union have a peer relationship with a commitment to resolve disputes and grievances affecting the employees in the bargaining unit. Representatives of both parties often fail to realize that they must bury old antagonisms and begin to work constructively in order to make the contract work for both parties and for the employees.

Discipline and Discharge

In labor relations, it is generally understood that discipline involves the entire scope of collective bargaining in which management sets standards to which the employees must conform and in which the union challenges management's use of its authority and attempts to discipline management.

The days of unilateral firings by management have long since passed, primarily because of the impact of collective bargaining. Max S. Wortman, Jr., and George C. Witteried state that policies on discipline have changed more than any other aspect of collective bargaining because of the following developments:

1. The establishment of standards so that employees know what is expected from them.
2. The development of reasonable rules and regulations for employee conduct on the job.
3. The uniform application of established standards.
4. The discipline of employees on a "just cause" basis (fact, not emotion).
5. The improvement of methods of discipline.
6. The use of constructive rather than arbitrary discipline.
7. A continual examination of the employer's personnel policies.[75]

Disciplinary action is initiated by management primarily to resolve employee problems relating to unsatisfactory work performance, excessive tardiness and absenteeism, violation of work rules, and insubordination. The term most commonly used in labor relations to describe current approaches to these problems is "progressive discipline" (also, "corrective" or "constructive discipline"). Progressive discipline generally involves the following sequence of actions and penalties:

1. *Oral warning.* An oral warning is given to an employee by the immediate supervisor when the employee fails to maintain certain standards or has broken a rule or policy. The supervisor warns the employee that a repetition

may result in more serious discipline, and the supervisor should offer to help the employee work out ways to avoid repetition.

2. *Written warning.* The first formal step involves a written warning. Although a written warning may not differ much from an oral warning, it does become part of the employee's official personnel record and is used as evidence should the matter be grieved.

3. *Suspension* (sometimes called "disciplinary layoff"). There may be more than one written warning before an employee is placed on suspension without pay. Suspensions vary in length depending on the nature and severity of the offense. The purpose of a suspension is to demonstrate to the employee that the seriousness of the offense is significant enough to result in a loss of pay. The number of days is based on action previously taken for similar infractions by other employees. Usually, a first suspension is for two or three days. The second suspension should be progressively longer (e.g., five days). If the union can demonstrate that management has not been consistent in its application of discipline, the suspension may be reduced in one of the steps of the grievance procedure or in arbitration. A record or log of suspensions should be maintained by the personnel office to insure a consistent application of discipline.

4. *Discharge.* This should be administered only when all other efforts to correct the problem have failed. It is not uncommon to administer two suspensions before proceeding to a discharge. In view of the possibility of arbitration, management's chances of sustaining a discharge are increased if the employee was suspended twice before being discharged.

The time taken between the four steps in progressive discipline varies according to the nature of the problem and the efforts made by the employee to correct it. Too much time between steps can be interpreted as an indication that management does not view the problem as serious or significant. Too little time between steps can also provide problems for management because it can be argued that the employee was not given sufficient time to demonstrate corrective action.

Although some labor relations administrators contend that a written warning remains in effect for a year, it is unwise to proceed from a written warning that is a year old to a suspension without prior action, either in the form of a second written warning or a documented discussion with the employee. Timing is important in progressive discipline, and it would be difficult to convince an arbitrator that management was justified in moving to the next step of discipline if either there was too little or too much time between steps.

Establishing a program of progressive discipline in a library that had no program prior to unionization will present problems to the personnel administrator. These problems can be overcome if the program is introduced gradually and if the personnel administrator demonstrates that it is aimed at correcting actions or behavior that are preventing the library from realizing its organizational objectives. The union may well protest any efforts to institute a program of discipline; management has the right, however, to establish reasonable rules of conduct and performance.

It is unwise to develop such a program without prior discussions with union representatives and with the central personnel office. If the program is sound and if management can provide reasonable documentation to demonstrate the need for the program, it will be accepted by the employees. Most employees would agree that reasonable standards are necessary to insure that some employees are not taking advantage of basic rules and regulations.

The personnel administrator also may encounter resistance from line supervisors, who may resent interference from the staff or may be reluctant to assume their required role in labor relations. These and other forms of resistance can be overcome once the personnel administrator demonstrates to top management that the program is sound and necessary. The personnel administrator should utilize both participative management techniques and the view of behavioral science to promote an acceptance of the program. In using this approach, Pigors and Myers state that disciplinary programs can only play a part in the kind of mutually responsible behavior that contributes to peak efficiency if it meets the following specifications:

1. Starts with an effort to foster mutual understanding and an organization-centered view.
2. Is fair.
3. Is demonstrably consistent with sound principles of human relations (including "due process" and the right of appeal).
4. Is in accord with a policy statement on discipline which is clear and well known to all.
5. Implements ideas that have been worked out by conferring with representatives of those who are subject to discipline.
6. Takes account of any extenuating features in each situation where someone feels that discipline is called for.[76]

It is common to find contract clauses specifying management's right to bypass the normal disciplinary procedures for a variety of serious infractions—drunkenness, assault, drug abuse, serious disruptive conduct, gross insubordination, and conduct that jeopardizes the health and safety of others. It is important that immediate action be taken when an employee engages in such activities. The employee should be placed on immediate suspension pending a disciplinary hearing to determine if discharge is justified.

THE ARBITRATION PROCESS

Arbitration is a "method of deciding a controversy under which the parties to the controversy have agreed in advance to accept the award of a third party," and is the predominant method used for the final resolution of disputes in labor relations.[77] The American Arbitration Association was founded in 1926 "to foster the study of arbitration in all its aspects, to perfect its techniques and procedures under law, and to advance generally the science of arbitration."[78]

The growth and development of arbitration in the United States followed the growth of collective bargaining. Randle and Wortman point out that arbitration became an accepted technique of resolving conflicts in industries that had the longest records of collective bargaining: printing trades, glass-bottle blowing, local transportation, and photoengraving.[79] The sources of the arbitration process, however, predate the beginnings of English common law. As the Elkouris note, King Solomon was an arbitrator who followed procedures similar to those used by arbitrators today.[80]

There are four basic steps in the arbitration process: referral, formulation and submission of the issues, hearing, and the award and opinion. Mutual consent to arbitration is rare in collective bargaining agreements. Most contracts allow either party to refer an issue to arbitration. The language quoted below from the contract of The New York Public Library is typical of arbitration referral clauses:

> Appeals from an unsatisfactory decision at Step 4 may be brought by the grievant to impartial arbitration within fifteen (15) working days of receipt of the decision by referring the grievance to the American Arbitration Association. In this arbitration step, the entire case, in all its aspects, both procedural and substantive, shall be before the arbitrator. The cost of such arbitration shall be borne equally by the grievant and/or his or her representative and the Library. The decision of the arbitrator shall be final and binding.[81]

Some contracts require that the parties submit a joint statement of the issue to be arbitrated, but it is not uncommon for each party to prepare its own statement indicating how it views the issue. The critical step in the process is the hearing, which may be formal or informal depending on the wishes of the parties, and the arbitrator, the nature of the issue, and the importance of the dispute. Formal hearings follow legal or courtroom conduct and usually have the following characteristics:

1. The parties are represented by legal counsel.
2. A verbatim transcript is made of the hearing.
3. The parties submit written briefs.

4. Witnesses are sworn in, examined, and may be cross-examined by the other party.
5. Objections are raised to undocumented or hearsay evidence.[82]

Informal hearings are more common and have the following characteristics:

1. The representatives of the parties are usually at the local level, though they may be supplemented with other officials.
2. Counsel is rarely seen.
3. Arguments are presented orally.
4. No written record of proceedings is kept, although the arbitrator and the other participants make such notes as they need.
5. Witnesses are used less frequently than in the formal procedure, if at all. If used, they are not formally sworn in.
6. Few if any legal rules are observed.[83]

Whether the hearing is formal or informal, it is important to plan and prepare for the meeting. Both parties have to bear in mind that the arbitrator will not be familiar with the issue and that inadequate preparation by one party may be advantageous to the other.

Although Randel and Wortman state that "compromise has no place in arbitration,"[84] arbitrators often propose a compromise solution, which if accepted by both parties, releases the arbitrator from the commitment to make an award and opinion. The parties might accept the compromise suggested rather than take a chance on a less favorable award following the hearing. Compromise often occurs in arbitrations involving discharges, which normally include a demand from the union that the employee be reinstated with full back pay. Management might agree to a compromise that involves reinstatement without back pay or back pay without reinstatement.

If no compromise is possible, the arbitrator is required to provide a written award, which "shall be rendered promptly by the Arbitrator and, unless otherwise agreed by the parties, or specified by the law, not later than thirty days from the date of closing the hearings, or if oral hearings have been waived, then from the date of transmitting the final statements and proofs to the Arbitrator."[85] The arbitrator's decision generally includes a statement of the issues, the positions of both parties, and the reasons for the award and opinion. The justification for the award of the arbitrator is important because it affects the future actions and positions of both parties and is incorporated into their methods of operation in the future. The personnel administrator should communicate in general terms the outcome of an arbitration so that line supervisors will be aware of the implications.

Both parties should make every effort to resolve disputes without using arbitration, not only because of the time involved, but also because of some of the liabilities involved. As Davey points out, these liabilities involve the following types of problems:

1. Some relationships continue to be marred by "excessive" arbitration for a variety of reasons, including poor screening, friction between the parties, and inability or unwillingness on the union's part to educate its membership on the point that everyone with a grievance does not have a constitutional right to arbitration.
2. Continuing "immaturity" in some relationships, as evidenced by unjustified blacklisting of arbitrators on such sophomoric bases as "box scores."
3. A continuing failure in some relationships to recognize the economics to be achieved by careful preparation and presentation of cases.
4. The continued resort to "brinkmanship" in contract administration (that is, failing to adjust or withdraw the case until just before the hearing).
5. A tendency in many relationships to make too much of a production out of arbitration by insisting on posthearing briefs, transcripts, citations of decisions of other arbitrators under the contracts, and so forth. Such practices increase the delays, costs, and formalism of arbitration. They are contrary to the spirit and rationale of the process as originally conceived.
6. Reluctance to make use of qualified new arbitrators for either or both of two reasons: (a) the new arbitrator has had a prior professional affiliation solely with management or union; or (b) the new arbitrator has no direct case experience. He is therefore rejected, no matter how good he may look on paper.[86]

These liabilities are not inherent in the process, but they are the consequences of the actions or points of view of those involved in contract administration. The advantages of arbitration, as Davey summarizes them, are not to be overlooked:

1. Continued acceptance of arbitration as the terminal step in the contract's grievance procedure, combined with more intelligent and sparing use of arbitration as an integral element in contract administration.
2. Improved contract language for defining grievance and arbitration procedures and stating the limits of the arbitrator's authority and jurisdiction.
3. Growth of the practice of naming a permanent arbitrator or a panel of arbitrators in the contract to minimize the delays and uncertainties that often occur in ad hoc selection procedures.
4. Visible improvement (in many relationships) in reducing the arbitration caseload to manageable proportions by more rigorous screening on the part of both management and union.
5. Growing sophistication in treating the problem of acceptability of arbitrators, that is, an apparent decline in "blacklisting" and the related practice of "shopping around" for new arbitrators.
6. Improved understanding of the need for firm agreement between the parties as to the proper function of arbitration under the contract.

7. A clear majority preference for the "judicial" conception of the arbitrator's task and a corresponding decline in the use of arbitration for additional bargaining or problem-solving.
8. Increasing competence of management and union representatives in case preparation and presentation.[87]

The consensus is that arbitration is definitely an asset in labor relations, but there are two problems relating to the process that should be mentioned. The first involves the question of the limits of an arbitrator's authority in resolving a dispute. The overwhelming number of arbitration decisions are honored, but there are instances wherein one of the parties has gone to court to compel enforcement of a decision or to obtain an exception to it. This might happen because one of the parties contends that the arbitrator's decision went beyond the limits of the issue.[88]

The second problem involves timeliness. Although contracts usually specify that a grievance must be submitted to arbitration within a certain number of days, it is not uncommon to find a union taking an issue to arbitration long after the expiration date. This practice presents serious problems for management, since management tends to assume that an issue has been resolved once the expiration date passes. The problem is compounded when a termination is involved because of the possibility of reinstatement into a position that undoubtedly has been filled. Unfortunately, there is little that management can do to avoid such situations, since most contracts allow either party to take a grievance to arbitration. The timeliness question should be a key argument when management presents its case to the arbitrator since it may influence important aspects of the arbitrator's award. The frequency of such occurrences is often related to the political pressure put on the union by the membership, or the standing of the aggrieved employee among the rank and file.

IMPLICATIONS OF COLLECTIVE BARGAINING

The standard texts on collective bargaining and labor relations in business and industry generally include discussions of the advantages and disadvantages of unionization in relation to organizational objectives and product or service costs. Library literature on labor relations does not place much emphasis on these two important areas, but seems to be more concerned with the impact of unionization on professionalism, participative management, and systems of governance. Since concerns for organizational objectives and service costs are indicative of an orientation in management theory and practice, the lack of emphasis on these topics in library literature seems to be related to the generally accepted contention that library educators and practitioners have yet to come to grips with the importance of management per se. Margaret Beckman's comments on this problem and her recommendations for action to be taken are in the context of academic librarianship, but they are applicable to any library with a staff sufficiently large to interest a union:

> . . . I am convinced that if academic library administrators had realized at any point within the past ten years that library management is a unique and demanding scientific discipline and had borrowed some of the techniques and methodologies being practiced in the business community, they could have been in a position of bargaining from strength rather than from weakness. . . . There are still steps which library administrators can take to ensure that their libraries will be in a relatively strong position in relationship to a union. The implications of collective bargaining for academic libraries are identifiable and positive. They are that we must achieve, in as short a time as possible, effective consultative (or participatory) library management systems, using the principles of library management so well defined by the Management Studies Office of the Association of Research Libraries (ARL).[89]

Perhaps the problem is not that library administrators and educators have failed to realize the significance of management techniques and methodologies, but that too many practitioners either have been unwilling because of temperament or philosophy or unable because of inadequate preparation to assume the full range of responsibilities inherent in management. It may be unfortunate, but too often collective bargaining has a positive effect on a library because it forces the staff to assume its managerial functions and responsibilities.

Positive Implications

As George Strauss and Leonard B. Sayles indicate, "there is little question that the introduction of a union may prove a traumatic experience for management."[90] The trauma is generally most acute during the early years of unionization, when both parties are fighting for what they consider their rights, and it is not uncommon for a spirit of detente to develop after the first three or four years of unionization. Until this occurs, management may be hard pressed to find any positive implications of unionization.

Collective bargaining provides opportunities for improving human relations: a peaceful means for resolving conflicts resulting from the needs of the individual and the needs of the organization, constructive recommendations for improving work flow and productivity, and mechanisms for introducing change through prior consultation with union representatives and officials.

Among the positive implications of unionization noted by Beckman are improved communication; increased understanding by both parties of the nature and goals of the institution or organization; standardization of administrative policies and procedures; increased level of compensation; guarantees of employee rights; improvement for women and minorities through equal pay schedules; and standardization of performance evaluation, recruitment, and promotion policies.[91]

There is some disagreement on the effectiveness of unions in increasing compensation levels, especially in a period of restricted funding. Guyton, among others, indicates the difficulty of correlating salaries with unionization in public libraries.[92] Cruzat points out that an examination of contracts of four-year institutions of higher education has shown that while there are indications that professional librarians' salaries have improved, librarians have generally not obtained parity with teaching faculty "in areas of most significance—salary, reappointment, tenure, and promotions."[93] My own experience with a clerical union for a period of some fifteen years was that the union did not make meaningful changes in the salary levels and this led to exceptionally high turnover among union members.

Negative Implications

Strauss and Sayles refer to several noneconomic negative implications of unionization which seem particularly relevant to libraries: challenges to management decisions, competition for loyalty, continual review of personnel policies, threats to efficiency, and withdrawal of line authority in personnel areas.[94] A library that is well managed should not be reluctant to deal with challenges to its decisions or policies, and the need to withdraw authority in the personnel area from line supervisors for the sake of consistency should not create irreparable problems for line and staff. Competition for the loyalty of employees may seem paternalistic, but it is a fact of organizational life and often causes greater problems for union members than for management. It is not uncommon for union members to seek advice from management when they are confronted with the realities of a job action or strike. Many managers also find it difficult to adjust to a working environment in which an employee's first allegiance is to a union that generally keeps a low profile except during negotiations. The change in the relationship between management and the employee is dramatic and adversely affects productivity to some extent.

In discussing the negative aspects of collective bargaining, Davey comments on the low level of professionalism that exists in some important union-management relationships.[95] In such situations, either side may be responsible for preventing the development of a viable union-management relationship, which can lead to unnecessary slowdowns, strikes, excessive grievances, or confusing contract language.

One aspect of this problem, however, may be attributable to the realities of unions as organizations. Union officials are elected, and they must be reasonably successful in satisfying the needs of the majority of their constituents if they are to remain in office. The demands placed on union organizers and representatives are great and require considerable stamina and political know-how. Such pressures, coupled with limited opportunities for advancement within the union hierarchy, lead to high rates of turnover among union officials. This in turn affects the union's ability to maintain continuity in contract negotiation and administration and can provide a relatively stable management team with considerable advantages as well as disadvantages. An experienced personnel administrator may be unable to resist the opportunity to take advantage of a novice union representative despite the fact that it might be detrimental to the best interests of the employee. Such temptations should be resisted. On the other hand, the turnover problem among union representatives may lead to inordinate delays in resolving grievances and damage progress made in the past in developing viable union-management relationships.

Regardless of one's personal reactions to the advantages and disadvantages of unionization, to the pressures of power tactics that can adversely affect large numbers of staff, and to the inherent adversary nature of collective bargaining, many managers in unionized libraries find satisfaction in fulfilling their responsibilities. One can get considerable satisfaction from helping to resolve seemingly irresolvable conflicts, from helping both sides to see the importance of working together to meet organizational objectives, and from being secure enough to admit that neither side is always right.

BUILDING BRIDGES

Unionization can create bitter conflicts that seriously disrupt an organization and demoralize those managers who are strongly committed to the goals and objectives of the library. Strauss and Sayles contend that unionization provides opportunities for improved labor relations, which can be capitalized on once management recognizes that "its own actions and policies have a major impact on union behavior."[96] The development of sound relationships requires initiative from management and the willingness to explore new techniques. The burden of responsibility rests on the shoulders of the line and staff, who must have the support and understanding of top management. If management does not make the effort to build bridges with the union, it will never meet its primary obligation of providing service to its clientele with any degree of distinction.

References

1. Theodore L. Guyton, *Unionization: The Viewpoint of Librarians* (Chicago: American Library Association, 1975), p. 2.
2. Gwendolyn Cruzat, "Issues and Strategies for Academic Librarians," *Collective Bargaining in Higher Education: Its Implications for Governance and Faculty Status for Librarians,* ed. Millicent D. Abell, ACRL Publications in Librarianship, no. 38 (Chicago: American Library Association, 1976), p. 99.
3. E. Wight Bakke, *Mutual Survival: The Goal of Unions and Management* (New Haven: Labor and Management Center, Yale University, 1946), p. 7.
4. C. Wilson Randle and Max S. Wortman, Jr., *Collective Bargaining Principles and Practices* (Boston: Houghton Mifflin, 1966), p. 41.
5. Dennis Chamot, "The Effect of Collective Bargaining on the Employee-Management Relationship," in *Employee Organizations and Collective Bargaining in Libraries,* Margaret A. Chaplan ed., *Library Trends* 25, no. 2 (Urbana-Champaign; University of Illinois Graduate School of Library Science, October 1976), p. 489.
6. George Strauss and Leonard R. Sayles, *Personnel: The Human Problems of Management,* 2nd ed. (Englewood Cliffs, N.J.: Prentice-Hall, 1967), pp. 106–07.
7. William F. Glueck, *Personnel: A Diagnostic Approach* (Dallas: Business Publications, 1974), p. 571.
8. Joel Seidman, Jack London, and Bernard Karsh, "Why Workers Join Unions," *Annals of the American Academy of Political and Social Science* 274 (March 1951): 76–79.
9. Guyton, p. 130.
10. Ibid.
11. Ibid., p. 156.
12. "Boston University Librarians Win First Labor Contract," *American Libraries* 10 (November 1979): 575.
13. Richard DeGennaro, "Participative Management or Unionization?," *College & Research Libraries* 33 (May 1972): 174.
14. Archie Kleingartner and Jean B. Kennelly, "Employee Relations in Libraries: The Current Scene," in *Collective Bargaining in Libraries,* ed. Frederick A. Schlipf, Allerton Park Institute, 20 (Urbana-Champaign: University of Illinois Graduate School of Library Science, 1975), pp. 16–17.
15. Karen J. Winkler, "Precipitous Decline of American Unions Fuels Growing Interest Among Scholars," *The Chronicle of Higher Education,* 12 November 1986, p. 5.

16. Ibid., p. 16.
17. Alvin Toffler, "A New Kind of Man in the Making," *The New York Times Magazine,* 9 March 1980, sec. 6, p. 30.
18. Arthur M. McAnally and Robert B. Downs, "The Changing Role of Directors of University Libraries," *College & Research Libraries* 34 (March 1973): 122–23.
19. Andrew M. Kramer, "The Legal Environment," in *Collective Bargaining in Libraries,* ed. Frederick A. Schlipf, Allerton Park Institute, no. 20 (Urbana-Champaign: University of Illinois Graduate School of Library Science, 1975), p. 30.
20. Cruzat, p. 92.
21. Edward B. Fiske, "Unions May Be Out of Luck at 'Mature' Private Colleges," *The New York Times,* 24 February 1980, sec. E, p. 7.
22. Gene I. Maeroff, "End of Unionization at Colleges Is Seen," *The New York Times,* 21 February 1980, sec. A, p. 21.
23. American Library Association, Association of College and Research Libraries, *Statement on Collective Bargaining,* approved by the Board of Directors of the Association of College and Research Libraries on 3 July 1975.
24. John Weatherford, "Collective Bargaining and the Academic Libraries: 1976-1979," *Library Journal* 107 (15 February 1980): 482.
25. U.S., President, "Employee-Management Cooperation in the Federal Service," Executive Order 10988, *Federal Register* 28 (January 19, 1962): 551.
26. Harold W. Davey, *Contemporary Collective Bargaining,* 3rd ed. (Englewood Cliffs, N.J.: Prentice-Hall, 1972), p. 342.
27. U.S. President, "Labor-Management Relations in the Federal Service," *Executive Order* 11491, Federal Register 34 (October 31, 1969): 17605.
28. Davey, p. 365.
29. Ibid., p. 366.
30. Commerce Clearing House, *1980 Guidebook to Labor Relations,* 19th ed. (Chicago: Commerce Clearing House, 1979), pp. 74–78.
31. National Labor Relations Board, *Form NLRB 666: Notice to Employees from the National Labor Relations Board* (Washington, D.C.: U.S. Government Printing Office, July 1972).
32. Ross Rimicci, Columbia University in the City of New York, "Fact Sheets on Upcoming Union Organizing Drive," 10 February 1976.
33. Ibid., 11 February 1976.
34. Commerce Clearing House, p. 95.
35. Ibid., p. 286.
36. Russell A. Smith, "Legal Principles of Public Sector Bargaining," in *Collective Bargaining in Higher Education: Its Implications for Governance and Faculty Status for Librarians,* ed. Millicent D. Abell, ACRL Publications in Librarianship, no. 38 (Chicago: American Library Association, 1976), Appendix I, pp. 134–44.
37. Randle and Wortman, p. 145.
38. Davey, p. 121.
39. Ibid.
40. Ibid., p. 139.
41. Glueck, pp. 582–84.

42. Randle and Wortman, p. 454.
43. Davey, p. 69.
44. Randle and Wortman, p. 454.
45. Commerce Clearing House, p. 65.
46. Davey p. viii.
47. Ibid., p. 70.
48. Randle and Wortman, p. 455.
49. Ibid., pp. 456–58.
50. Bureau of National Affairs, *Primer of Labor Relations,* 20th ed. (Washington, D.C.: Bureau of National Affairs, 1975), p. 131.
51. Randle and Wortman, p. 524.
52. Ibid.
53. Randle and Wortman, pp. 525–26.
54. Ibid., p. 533.
55. Arthur J. Goldberg, "Management's Reserved Rights: A Labor View," in *Unions, Management, and the Public,* 3rd ed., eds. E. Wight Bakke, Clark Kerr, and Charles W. Anrod (New York: Harcourt, Brace & World, 1967), p. 239.
56. Randle and Wortman, pp. 528–30.
57. Glueck, p. 586.
58. Davey, p. 129.
59. Randle and Wortman, pp. 193–94.
60. Davey, p. 134.
61. Randle and Wortman, p. 195.
62. Davey, pp. 193–94.
63. Randle and Wortman, p. 203.
64. Ibid., pp. 203–07.
65. Randle and Wortman, p. 128.
66. Ibid., p. 220.
67. Ibid.
68. Ibid.
69. Ibid., pp. 221–22.
70. Ibid., p. 222.
71. F.J. Roethlisberger, William J. Dickson, and Harold A. Wight, *Management and the Worker: An Account of a Research Program Conducted by the Western Electric Company, Hawthorne Works, Chicago* (Cambridge, Mass.: Harvard University Press, 1947), p. 258.
72. Paul Pigors and Charles A. Myers, *Personnel Administration: A Point of View and a Method,* 7th ed. (New York: McGraw-Hill, 1973), pp. 231–32.
73. Randle and Wortman, p. 233.
74. Davey, p. 144.
75. Max S. Wortman, Jr., and George C. Witteried, *Labor Relations Collective Bargaining Text and Cases* (Boston: Allyn and Bacon, 1969), pp. 335–36.
76. Pigors and Myers, 8th ed., pp. 301–02.
77. Bureau of National Affairs, *Primer of Labor Relations,* 20th ed. (Washington, D.C.: Bureau of National Affairs, 1975), p. 124.
78. American Arbitration Association, *Why Unions & Companies Use AAA*

Labor Arbitration Services (New York: The Association, November 1978), p. 9.

79. Randle and Wortman, p. 253.
80. Frank Elkouri and Edna Asper Elkouri, *How Arbitration Works,* 3rd ed. (Washington, D.C.: Bureau of National Affairs, 1978), p. 2.
81. The New York Public Library and Local 1930, p. 10.
82. Randle and Wortman, p. 267.
83. Ibid., p. 268.
84. Ibid., p. 270.
85. American Arbitration Association, *Voluntary Labor Arbitration Rules* (New York: The Association, April 1979), p. 6.
86. Davey, p. 160.
87. Ibid., pp. 159–60.
88. Ibid., 170ff.
89. Margaret Beckman, "Implications for Academic Libraries," in *Collective Bargaining in Libraries,* ed. Frederick A. Schlipf, Allerton Park Institute, no. 20 (Urbana-Champaign: University of Illinois Graduate School of Library Science, 1975), p. 122.
90. Strauss and Sayles, p. 119.
91. Beckman, pp. 130–31.
92. Guyton, pp. 94–121.
93. Cruzat, p. 106.
94. Strauss and Sayles, pp. 117–19.
95. Davey, p. 384.
96. Strauss and Sayles, p. 119.

Bibliography

American Arbitration Association. *Voluntary Labor Arbitration Rules.* New York: The Association, April 1979.
———. *Why Unions and Companies Use AAA Labor Arbitration Services.* New York: The Association, November 1978.
American Library Association, Association of College and Research Libraries. "Joint Statement on Faculty Status of College and University Librarians." *College & Research Libraries News* (February 1974).
———. "Standards for Faculty Status for College and University Librarians." *College & Research Libraries* (May 1974).
———. "Statement on Collective Bargaining." Mimeographed. Chicago: The Association, 21 January 1970.
Baer, Walter E. *Discipline and Discharge Under the Labor Agreement.* New York: American Management Association, 1972.
Bakke, E. Wight. *Mutual Survival: The Goal of Unions and Management.* New Haven: Labor and Management Center, Yale University, 1946.
Beckman, Margaret. "Implications for Academic Libraries." In *Collective Bar-*

gaining in Libraries, edited by Frederick A. Schlipf. Allerton Park Institute no. 20. Urbana-Champaign: Graduate School of Library Science, University of Illinois, 1975.

Black, James Menzies. Positive Discipline. New York: American Management Association, 1970.

Bok, Derek, C. and John T. Dunlop. Labor and the American Community. New York: Simon and Schuster, 1970.

"Boston University Librarians Win First Labor Contract." American Libraries 10 (November 1979): 575.

Bureau of National Affairs. Primer of Labor Relations. 20th ed. Washington, D.C.: Bureau of National Affairs, 1975.

Chamberlain, Neil W. "Public vs. Private Sector Bargaining." In Collective Bargaining in Government: Readings and Cases, Englewood Cliffs, N.J.: Prentice-Hall, 1972.

Chamot, Dennis. "The Effect of Collective Bargaining on the Employee-Management Relationship." In Employee Organizations and Collective Bargaining in Libraries, edited by Margaret A. Chaplan. Library Trends 25, no. 2. Urbana-Champaign: Graduate School of Library Science, University of Illinois, October 1976.

Columbia University in the City of New York. "Fact Sheets on Upcoming Union Organizing Drive." 10 and 11 February 1976. Mimeographed.

Commerce Clearing House. 1980 Guidebook to Labor Relations. 19th ed. Chicago: Commerce Clearing House, 1979.

Cottam, Keith M. "Unionization Is Not Inevitable." Library Journal 93 (1 November 1968): 4105–06.

Cruzat, Gwendolyn. "Issues and Strategies for Academic Librarians." In Collective Bargaining in Higher Education: Its Implications for Governance and Faculty Status for Librarians, edited by Millicent D. Abell. ACRL Publications in Librarianship no. 38. Chicago: American Library Association, 1976.

Davey, Harold W. Contemporary Collective Bargaining. 3rd ed. Englewood Cliffs: N.J.: Prentice-Hall, 1972.

DeGennaro, Richard. "Participative Management or Unionization?" College & Research Libraries 33 (May 1972): 173–74.

Drucker, Peter F. The Practice of Management. New York: Harper & Row, 1954.

Elkouri, Frank and Edna Asper Elkouri. How Arbitration Works. 3rd ed. Washington, D.C.: Bureau of National Affairs, 1978.

Fiske, Edward B. "Unions May Be Out of Luck at 'Mature' Private Colleges." The New York Times, 24 February 1980, sec. E., p. 7.

Garbarino, Joseph W. "Faculty Unionism: The First Ten Years." Annals of the American Academy of Political and Social Science 448 (March 1980): 74–85.

Glueck, William F. Personnel: A Diagnostic Approach. Dallas: Business Publications, Inc., 1974.

Goldberg, Arthur J. "Management's Reserved Rights: A Labor View." In Unions, Management, and the Public, edited by E. Wight Bakke, Clark Kerr, and Charles W. Anrod. 3rd ed. New York: Harcourt, Brace & World, 1967.

Guyton, Theodore L. Unionization: The Viewpoint of Librarians. Chicago: American Library Association, 1975.

McAnally, Arthur M. and Robert B. Downs. "The Changing Role of Directors of University Libraries." *College & Research Libraries* 34 (March 1973): 103–25.

Maeroff, Gene I. "End of Unionization at Colleges Is Seen." *The New York Times,* 21 February 1980, sec. A. p. 21.

National Labor Relations Board. *Form NLRB 666: Notice to Employees from the National Labor Relations Board.* Washington, D.C.: U.S. Government Printing Office, July 1972.

New York Public Library Local 1930, District Council 37, AFSCME, AFL-CIO. "Union Contract: July 1, 1978-June 30, 1980." Mimeographed. New York: n.d.

Oberg, Marilyn, Mary Blackburn, and Joan Dible. "Unionization: Costs and Benefits to the Individual Library." In *Employee Organizations and Collective Bargaining in Libraries,* edited by Margaret A. Chaplan. Library Trends 25, no. 2. Urbana-Champaign: Graduate School of Library Science, University of Illinois, October 1976.

Phelps, Orme W. *Discipline and Discharge in the Unionized Firm.* Berkeley and Los Angeles: University of California Press, 1959.

Pigors, Paul and Charles A. Myers. *Personnel Administration: A Point of View and a Method.* 7th ed. New York: McGraw-Hill, 1973.

———. *Personnel Administration: A Point of View and a Method.* 8th ed. New York: McGraw-Hill, 1977.

Randle, C. Wilson and Max S. Wortman, Jr. *Collective Bargaining Principles and Practices.* Boston: Houghton Mifflin, 1966.

Robinson, James W. and Roger W. Walker. *Labor Economics and Labor Relations.* New York: Roland Press, 1973.

Roethlisberger, F.J., William J. Dickson, and Harold A. Wight. *Management and the Worker: An Account of a Research Program Conducted by the Western Electric Company, Hawthorne Works, Chicago.* Cambridge, Mass.: Harvard University Press, 1947.

Rogers, Rutherford D. and David C. Weber. *University Library Administration.* New York: H.W. Wilson, 1971.

Sayles, Leonard. *Managerial Behavior: Administration in Complex Organizations.* New York: McGraw-Hill, 1964.

Schlacter, Gail A. "Professionalism vs. Unionism." In *Employee Organizations and Collective Bargaining in Libraries,* edited by Margaret A. Chaplan. Library Trends 25, no. 2. Urbana-Champaign: Graduate School of Library Science, University of Illinois, October 1976.

Seidman, Joel, Jack London, and Bernard Karsh. "Why Workers Join Unions." *Annals of the American Academy of Political and Social Science* 274 (March 1951): 75–84.

Smith, Russell A. "Legal Principles of Public Sector Bargaining." In *Collective Bargaining in Higher Education: Its Implications for Governance and Faculty Status for Librarians,* edited by Millicent D. Abell, ACRL Publications in Librarianship, no. 38. Chicago: American Library Association, 1976.

Strauss, George and Leonard R. Sayles. *Personnel: The Human Problems of Management.* 2nd ed. Englewood Cliffs, N.J.: Prentice-Hall, 1967.

Toffler, Alvin. "A New Kind of Man in the Making." *The New York Times Magazine,* 9 March 1980, sec. 6, p. 244.

U.S. President. Executive Order 10988. "Employee-Management Cooperation in the Federal Service." *Federal Register* 27 (19 January 1962): 551.

————. Executive Order 11491. "Labor-Management Relations in the Federal Service." *Federal Register* 34 (31 October 1969): 17605.

Weatherford, John. *Collective Bargaining and the Academic Librarian.* Metuchen, N.J.: Scarecrow Press, 1976.

————. "Collective Bargaining and the Academic Librarian: 1976-1979." *Library Journal* 107 (15 February 1980): 481–82.

Winkler, Karen J. "Precipitous Decline of American Unions Fuels Growing Interest Among Scholars." *The Chronicle of Higher Education* (12 November 1986): 5, 16, 17.

Wortman, Max S., Jr., and Witteried, George C. *Labor Relations Collective Bargaining Text and Cases.* Boston: Allyn and Bacon, 1969.

Appendix
Resources for Library Personnel Administrators
Jeniece Guy

The introduction to the first edition characterized personnel as a rapidly changing field and noted the challenges it presents to both new and experienced library personnel administrators. That observation is even more true today. The pace of change has accelerated, and new issues must be faced, some of which were barely on the horizon in the early eighties: AIDS in the workplace, substance abuse, and child and elder care are just a few. Regulation of personnel practices by government agencies encompasses almost every aspect of the personnel function. Clearly, a complex field has become more complex.

The multidisciplinary nature of personnel administration means that resources can sometimes be fragmented. For example, personnel and employee relations draw on economics, actuarial science, business, law, psychology, sociology, adult education, and other behavioral and social sciences. The literature and organizations of these disciplines therefore yield valuable resources to personnel administrators.

Mastering such a complex, diverse subject can seem a formidable challenge. This appendix is intended as a guide to the major organizations and publications covering various aspects of personnel administration. It is designed to be illustrative rather than definitive.

ORGANIZATIONS

Organizations that offer resources for the personnel administrator are divided into: professional and trade associations in personnel and related fields; professional associations in the library field; research or advocacy organizations; U.S. government agencies; state and local governments; community agencies; and educational institutions and libraries.

Associations in Personnel and Related Fields

One of the most important resources for the library personnel administrator is membership in a personnel-related professional association. The many services provided by a professional association in the field of personnel include information clearing houses, continuing education opportunities, newsletters, access to specialized libraries, journal subscriptions, annual conferences, accreditation or certification, contact with others in the field, and assistance with special problems.

Acquiring access to so many services makes membership in a professional association a bargain and is perhaps the easiest and most basic way to keep abreast of developments in the field.

Following is a selected list of general and specialized professional associations in the field of personnel.

American Society for Personnel Administration (ASPA)
606 N. Washington St, Alexandria, VA 22314
703-548-3440

ASPA has been a leader in promoting the concept of personnel management as a profession. It provides all the services of a professional association listed in the description, above. One of ASPA's most noteworthy services is a legislative update that tracks the status of pending federal legislation affecting the personnel profession. ASPA was also a leader in developing an accreditation program for personnel practitioners, founding the ASPA Accreditation Institute, now the Personnel Accreditation Institute. Personnel managers can be accredited in the field if they meet the requisite qualifications of experience and education and pass the examinations to qualify as PHR (Professional in Human Resources) or SPHR (Senior Professional in Human Resources).

Members of ASPA receive its journal, *The Personnel Administrator*.

International Personnel Management Association (IPMA)
1617 Duke St, Alexandria, VA 22314
703-549-7100

IPMA membership is primarily personnel managers in the public sector. Members receive *Public Personnel Management Magazine* and *IPMA Newsletter,* reduced rates at IPMA conferences and seminars, and a discount on IPMA publications.

American Arbitration Association
140 W. 51 St, New York, NY
212-484-4000

American Compensation Association (ACA)
6619 N. Scottsdale Rd, Scottsdale, AZ 85253
602-951-9191

Industrial Relations Research Association (IRRA)
7226 Social Science Bldg, University of Wisconsin, Madison, WI 53706
608-262-2762

Employment Management Association (EMA)
Five W. Hargett St, Suite 1100, Raleigh, NC 27601
919-828-6614

Human Resource Planning Society
Box 2553, Grand Central Sta., New York, NY 10163
212-490-6387

American Society for Training and Development (ASTD)
Box 1443, 1630 Duke St, Alexandria, VA 22313
703-683-8100

International Association for Personnel Women
5820 Wilshire Blvd, Suite 500, Los Angeles, CA 90036
213-937-9000

Personnel Services of Library Associations

Although professional personnel and industrial relations associations provide essential services for the personnel administrator, library associations also have personnel-related services that will supplement the services of a professional library association. The services are similar to those provided by professional personnel associations but usually on a smaller scale. Personnel-related services of library associations include workshops and seminars, consultant services, publications, and salary data. Many library associations offer placement services, which will be an important recruiting source for the library personnel administrator. Library associations with personnel-related services include:

American Library Association
50 E. Huron, Chicago, IL 60611
312-944-6780
Many ALA divisions, such as the Association of College and Re-

search Libraries (ACRL) and the American Association of School Librarians (AASL), provide personnel-related services of interest to members of that division.

The unit within ALA that specializes in library personnel management is the Personnel Administration Section (PAS) of the Library Administration and Management Association (LAMA). Membership in LAMA-PAS will acquaint the library personnel administrator with colleagues who are also working in the field. In addition to providing a support system, LAMA-PAS also does extensive programming in the personnel field at annual conferences, and has sponsored several publications on library personnel management. Current committees include Staff Development, Economic Status, Welfare and Fringe Benefits, and two ad hoc committees, Union Relations for Supervisors and Personnel Dynamics for Supervisors.

ALA also has an office that provides staff services in the area of personnel, the Office for Library Personnel Resources (OLPR). OLPR operates the placement service at the Annual Conference and Midwinter Meeting, provides individual consultation in the field of library personnel, and will answer personnel-related questions by mail or telephone. OLPR has several publications including a newsletter, *Library Personnel News* and the series *Topics in Personnel*. (Full citations for both publications appear in the Current Awareness Service section of this appendix.)

Association of Research Libraries
1527 New Hampshire Ave, NW, Washington, DC 20036
202-232-2466

Libraries that are members of the Association of Research Libraries and libraries that are participants in the Academic Library Management Program may take advantage of the programs of ARL's Office of Management Studies. ARL also offers workshops, which are open to the public, in the area of management. Many of the Systems Procedures and Exchange Center (SPEC) publications are devoted to personnel topics such as performance evaluation or position classification.

Medical Library Association (MLA)
919 N. Michigan Ave, Suite 3208, Chicago, IL 60611
312-266-2456

MLA provides a year-round placement service and an expanded placement service at conferences. Training programs, which consist of one- or two-day workshops in all aspects of library practices, are provided upon request. MLA also has a voluntary certification program with mandatory recertification.

Special Libraries Association
1700 18 St, NW, Washington, DC 20009
202-234-4700

SLA has a placement service that consists of a monthly newsletter with expanded service at conferences. Local chapters also have their own placement service; however, the type of service varies from chapter to chapter. SLA has a continuing education program for SLA members that is open to nonmembers.

Although they are not listed individually, state, local, and regional library associations, state library agencies, and library networks and systems can also be important resources in the area of library personnel. Many of these organizations have placement services, including job hotlines. Many sponsor workshops, seminars, and continuing education programs. Consultant services are frequently available.

Other Professional and Trade Organizations

Several types of organizations produce special reports, newsletters, and other publications that are of interest to personnel administrators. Policy research organizations, often nicknamed think tanks, study social and political issues as well as issues that are directly related to human resources. Frequently these groups publish material not available elsewhere. Advocacy or special interest groups such as the American Federation of Labor are useful for learning the point of view of the sponsoring organization and its constituents. Other trade and professional associations such as the American Management Association, while not exclusively a personnel related association, often cover personnel topics in their publications, workshops, and seminars. Below is a list of some organizations that fall in the category of policy research, advocacy, or other professional and trade organizations:

American Enterprise Institute for Public Policy Research
    1150 17 St, NW, Washington, DC 20036
American Federation of Labor–Congress of Industrial Organizations
    815 16 St, NW, Washington, DC 20002
American Management Association
    135 W. 50 St, New York, NY 10020
Brookings Institute
    1775 Massachusetts Ave, NW, Washington, DC 20036
Catalyst
    14 E. 60 St, New York, NY 10022
Chamber of Commerce of the United States of America
    1615 H St, NW, Washington, DC 20062

The Conference Board, Inc.
  845 Third Ave, New York, NY 10022
Employee Benefit Research Institute
  2121 K St, NW, Washington, DC 20037-2121
National Commission of Working Women
  1221 Connecticut Ave, NW, Washington, DC 20036
New Ways to Work
  149 Ninth St, San Francisco, CA 94103
Urban Institute
  2100 M St, NW, Washington, DC 20037

Government Agencies

There are several governmental departments and agencies concerned with personnel administration, usually because they have regulatory and enforcement powers over specific personnel practices. State and local governments also have laws and regulations that affect personnel practices, so the library personnel administrator must be aware of state and local regulations as well as federal ones. There are often state government departments and agencies with functions similar to the federal ones; and these local agencies, such as a state department of labor or a state fair employment practices commission, will also be important. In the public sector, labor relations and union activity, if regulated, will be regulated by a state or local agency rather than the federal National Labor Relations Board, since jurisdiction over public sector labor relations in state and local governments is left to the states by the federal regulations governing labor relations, union activity, and collective bargaining. Similarly, other legal regulations may not apply in the same manner to libraries in the public sector and those libraries in private institutions.

U.S. Department of Labor
  This department administers federal labor laws pertaining to safe and healthful working conditions, minimum wages and overtime pay, employment discrimination, unemployment and workers compensation, and pension plans. It also collects statistics on the labor force and labor economics and issues many publications about current labor market trends. Its most notable publication is the *Monthly Labor Review* (see: Journals: A Basic List).
  Department of Labor agencies that will affect libraries the most are:

Bureau of Labor Statistics—issues many of the publications of the Department.
Occupational Safety and Health Administration—administers health and safety laws for private sector employers only.

Office of Federal Contract Compliance—administers affirmative action regulations for federal contractors or organizations receiving federal funds.

Employment Standards—administers wage and hour laws.

Employment and Training Administration—administers unemployment compensation.

Women's Bureau—statistics and publications about women in the labor force.

U.S. Equal Employment Opportunity Commission

This agency enforces equal employment opportunity laws that prevent discrimination on the basis of race, color, religion, sex, national origin, age, or handicap. Employees with a complaint of discrimination may file with this agency.

Federal Mediation and Conciliation Service

This agency, which has regional offices, has a very important service. It will provide a neutral third-party federal mediator to assist when collective bargaining negotiations between employer and union are at an impasse. With the recent growth in public sector unionism, FMCS commissioners now find that their services are frequently utilized in the public sector. Library personnel managers faced with a strike or with negotiations that are at an impasse may want to consider a mediator from FMCS. The emphasis of FMCS is on bringing the two parties together, thus this is not binding arbitration but nonbinding mediation.

National Labor Relations Board

Those libraries in the private sector that are subject to the Wagner and Taft-Hartley Acts and other federal labor laws will find both their labor relations activities and the unions regulated by this agency. Libraries that fall under the jurisdiction of this agency include those in large private universities and many that are private research institutions.

U.S. Office of Personnel Management

Although not a regulatory or enforcement agency, OPM is an important resource for library personnel administrators because of the large number of publications and training materials it issues. The OPM is the personnel department for the federal government. It has assumed many of the activities and programs of the former U.S. Civil Service Commission, and is primarily responsible for providing personnel services to government employees, government managers, and applicants for positions in the federal government. In addition to being an important source of publications, audiovisual materials, and other training materials, the OPM has an extensive library, which is open to the public, on personnel administration. The index *Personnel Literature* cited in the section Indexes and Computerized Data Bases is published by OPM and is a compilation of material received by the OPM library. Information on OPM publications can be had from the Publications Unit, Office of Intergovernmental Personnel Programs, OPM, P.O. Box 14184, Washington, DC 20044. Information on audiovisual material produced by the OPM can be obtained from the Office of Public Affairs of the OPM.

Continuing and Formal Educational

There are many seminars and workshops available in the field of personnel. Commercial organizations, consulting firms, professional organizations, and university extension or continuing education divisions are among the sponsors of this type of educational opportunity. Seminars and workshops are frequently advertised by direct mail and by ads in the professional personnel literature. Finding out about the many seminars and workshops available is not a problem, choosing which ones to attend is. Training and development specialist Dugan Laird offers several suggestions for evaluating seminars and workshops. Among the questions he suggests are

1. Does the brochure publish learning objectives or expected outcomes?
2. Are those outcomes stated in behavioral terms and are the behaviors observable, reasonable, and measurable?
3. Is a topical outline on the announcement?
4. Does the brochure specify what types of employees should register? (nature of position, level of position, etc.)
5. Is there time for questions and answers?
6. Is there provision for process feedback?
7. Does the brochure describe the type of learning methods which will be employed? Do these methods involve "action training," that is, practical experience for the trainees?
8. Are the workshop leaders known to people in the field, have they published on their subject, and have they worked in or consulted for corporate and bureaucratic organizations?[1]

If most of these questions do not rate a yes answer, Laird suggests further investigation. Inquire into the background of the sponsoring organization and inquire of those who have participated in the workshops.

Library personnel administrators may feel the need for a more formal educational background in the field. It may be one or two courses in specific functional areas, such as compensation management, affirmative action programming, or organizational behavior, or he or she may decide to pursue a second master's in the field of personnel and industrial relations. There are several colleges and universities that have both graduate and undergraduate programs in personnel and industrial relations. A complete list of academic programs will be found in the appendix of Vol. 8 of the *ASPA Handbook.*[2]

Specialized Libraries

There are many specialized libraries in the field of personnel and industrial relations. They are usually under the auspices of a professional association in the field of personnel or a school of personnel and industrial relations affiliated with a major university. Both ASPA and IPMA maintain libraries for the use of their members. Examples of specialized libraries associated with schools of personnel and industrial relations are the Martin P. Catherwood Library at the New York State School of Industrial and Labor Relations at Cornell University. A complete list of university personnel and industrial relations research units and libraries can be found in the appendix of Vol. 8 of the *ASPA Handbook.*[3]

Many of the organizations listed above have libraries. The Business and Professional Women's Foundation and Catalyst libraries are open to the public; the American Society for Personnel Administration library is restricted to members only.

Mailing Lists

Many organizations have mailing lists, and having your name on them can be a source of useful information. Among these organizations are commercial firms—particularly consultants and firms that sell packaged training materials or conduct workshops and seminars— local and federal governmental agencies, associations, and unions and labor organizations. It is also possible to get on mailing lists by writing a request, by attending a professional conference or seminar, by joining a personnel-related professional organization, by subscribing to a personnel-related journal, or by filling out product information cards requesting information on a specific product or line of products. While having your name on a mailing list may be a source of useful information, it may also be somewhat a curse in that you may be inundated with mail, much of which may not be useful to you. Be selective about the mailing lists you request your name added to, and have your name removed from those lists that are totally useless to you.

Community Resources

Community resources can be useful in all aspects of personnel from recruiting to affirmative action, to training and development. These resources will vary from community to community, but some that may be available are: local institutions such as colleges and universities which may be sources for recruiting; local minority organizations, which are always good for affirmative action recruiting; businesses or corporations in the area, which may provide speakers, films, or other resources useful in training programs; local firms or associations, which may sponsor salary surveys that provide information on local compensation practices; and the parent institution of a library, whether it is a college or university or municipality, which is an important local resource and may have personnel, affirmative action, and training departments that can play an important role in the library's personnel program.

Using Consultants

When to call in a consultant and when to do it yourself is a key question for the personnel administrator, whether in a library or industry. Consultants can be used in almost any aspect of the personnel program from recruitment to labor relations; the most common use for personnel consultants in the library world, however, seems to be in developing position classification and compensation systems and planning and developing training programs, particularly management training programs.

Consultants are an important resource and the use of qualified consultants can enhance the personnel program; the effective use of consultants, however, requires careful decision making. Leonard R. Brice in the chapter "Professional Services for PAIR," Vol. 8, *ASPA Handbook,* gives the following suggestions: careful definition of the problem, careful selection of the consultant, agreement on mutual obligations, proper supervision and support of the consultant's work, implementation of recommendations (instead of the file and forget syndrome), and measurement of results.[4]

Marvin Weisbord, organization development consultant and author, suggests three points for the negotiation of a successful client-consultant contract: what each expects to get from the relationship; how much time each will invest and at what cost; the ground rules under which the parties will operate. Names of consultants in the field of personnel can be found in ads in professional journals (personnel and industrial and related journals). Professional conferences and seminars in the personnel area are also a good place to find the names of consultants. Many consultants exhibit at the national conferences of ASPA and other professional societies. Referral by colleagues in the field is another way to locate consultants.

It is never wise, however, to rely exclusively on ads, word of mouth referral, or any similar source in selecting a consultant. In all cases, you should evaluate the consultant's background yourself, first by checking references, and then by asking the consultant carefully designed questions to insure that there is mutual agreement on philosophy and goals and objectives.[5]

PUBLICATIONS

Indexes and Computerized Data Bases

There is no one periodical index that provides comprehensive coverage of personnel and industrial relations literature, but several of the most important are:

Work Related Abstracts covers many journals in such diverse topics as psychology, economics, management, and personnel and industrial relations. Topics are indexed under broad categories with more specific subtopics. No author index.

Business Periodicals Index, the leading index to business journals, does cover personnel and industrial relations topics but does not have author listings.

Psychological Abstracts includes coverage of the field of industrial psychology and will thus be of interest to personnel practitioners. It includes abstracts of books, journal articles, and other publications in the field of psychology.

Personnel Literature, a monthly publication of the U.S. Office of Personnel Management, indexes only those items received by the Office's library, but because the library collection is quite extensive, *Personnel Literature* does give fairly complete coverage of the field.

Personnel Management Abstracts, published quarterly by the Graduate School of Business Administration of the University of Michigan, has an author, title, and subject index and abstracts both books and journal articles. The abstracts for books are lengthier than the abstracts of journal articles.

Databases

There is now a database devoted exclusively to personnel and more will no doubt be developed as the human resource function assumes a more strategic role for employers. Databases covering business topics will also cover personnel.

Personnel and Industrial Relations Database
Human Resources Information Network
9585 Valpariso Ct, Indianapolis, IN 46268

Other Databases with Personnel Coverage
ABI/Inform indexes many of the same journals as *Business Periodicals Index*. Includes coverage of several personnel and industrial relations topics such as labor relations and employee benefits. Further information is available from ABI/Inform, Article Retrieval Service, 620 S. Fifth St, Louisville, KY 40202.
Psychological Abstracts is a computerized version of the American Psychological Association-sponsored publication. Available through private vendors or from the American Psychological Association, 1200 17 St, NW, Washington, DC 20036.
Management Contents Data Base, the computerized version of the publication by the same name, does include personnel topics. For further information: 11 Davis Dr, Belmont, CA 94002.

Journals: A Basic List

An excellent way to stay current is to read or glance through several journals on a regular basis. Personnel and industrial relations journals were once divided between practitioner oriented and scholarly journals. In recent years this distinction has become less rigid. Many scholarly journals now publish articles aimed at the practitioner and many popular journals print research based articles. Following is a selective list:

Compensation Review. American Management Association Subscription Services, Box 319, Saranac Lake, NY 12983. Articles on compensation and benefits, also abstracts of compensation articles appearing in other journals and of books.
Employee Benefit Plan Review. Charles D. Spencer and Associates, Inc., 222 W. Adams St, Chicago, IL 60606. Short articles on all areas of employee benefit administration. Contains a directory of benefit administrators and consultants.
Employee Benefits Journal. International Foundation of Employee Benefit Plans, 1871 W. Bluemont Rd, Box 69, Brookfield WI 53005. Covers all aspects of benefit administration, contains articles on communicating benefits to employees. Gives reviews and coverage of other publications in the field.
Employee Relations Law Journal. Executive Enterprises Publications Co., Inc., 33 W. 60 St, New York, NY 10023. Especially good in its coverage of equal employment opportunity. Also covers OSHA (safety) and National Labor Relations Board decisions.
Employee Services Management. National Employee Services and Recreational Association, 20 N. Wacker Dr, Chicago, IL 60606. Covers the area of fitness, wellness, and employee recreational programs.

Employment Relations Today. Executive Enterprise Publications Co., Inc., 22 W. 21 St, New York, NY 10010. Covers fair employment practices in the areas of selection, training, promotion, compensation, and termination, and key court decisions.

Human Resource Management. John Wiley and Sons, 605 Third Ave, New York, NY 10158. Formerly published by the University of Michigan Graduate School of Business, and still edited by them, HRM is aimed at both the scholar and the practitioner and emphasizes strategy and theory.

Human Resource Planning. Human Resource Planning Society, Box 2553, Grand Central Sta, New York, NY 10163. Covers staffing, career development and managerial succession. Good coverage of the use of computers in human resource planning and career development.

Journal of Applied Psychology. American Psychological Association, Subscription Section, 1400 N. Uhle St, Arlington, VA 22201. Scholarly publication useful for the practitioner. Good coverage of behavioral areas including job satisfaction, stress, and morale.

Journal of Organizational Behavior Management. The Haworth Press, 28 E. 22 St, New York, NY 10010. Focuses on productivity improvement and behavior modification.

Labor Law Journal. Commerce Clearing House, Inc., 4025 W. Peterson Ave, Chicago, IL 60646. Coverage of the whole field of personnel law, not just laws pertaining to union organization and collective bargaining. Covers court decisions, regulations, and arbitration decisions.

Management. Superintendent of Documents, U.S. Government Printing Office, Washington, DC 20402. Published by the U.S. Office of Personnel Management, articles are written by federal staff members and cover a wide range of personnel topics.

Monthly Labor Review. Superintendent of Documents, U.S. Government Printing Office, Washington, DC 20402. Published by the U.S. Bureau of Labor Statistics, this is an important source of information about today's labor market. Gives good coverage of labor statistics, current trends in the labor market, and significant court and administrative decisions in labor cases.

Personnel. American Management Association, Subscription Services, Box 319, Saranac Lake, NY 12983. Emphasis on short, practical articles in all aspects of personnel management.

The Personnel Administrator. American Society for Personnel Administration, 606 N. Washington St, Arlington, VA 22314. Official journal of the society. Each issue has a theme such as EEO, training, or staffing. A frequent feature is the Research Roundup column which contains new developments in the field.

Personnel Journal. A.A. Crofts, Inc., 245 Fischer Ave, B2 Costa Mesa, CA 92626. Covers all aspects of personnel management and is oriented toward the practitioner. Many articles review successful personnel programs in private and public sector organizations. The regular column Resource Market Place is an excellent source of new training aids, films, and other products.

Personnel Psychology. Order from Personnel Psychology, Inc., Box 6965, College Station, Durham, NC 27708. Covers the latest research in personnel psychology but is directed more toward the practitioner than are many psychological publications. Good coverage of new books and publications.

Public Personnel Management. International Personnel Management Association, 1850 K St, NW, Suite 870, Washington, DC 20006. Personnel and labor relations issues in the public sector.

Review of Public Personnel Administration. Bureau of Governmental Research and Service. University of South Carolina, Columbia, SC 29208. Covers public personnel management and is more scholarly than *Public Personnel Management.*

Supervision. Supervision Subscription Department, 424 N. Third St, Burlington, IA 52601. Practical tips for the first line supervisor.

Supervisory Management. American Management Association, Subscription Services, Box 319, Saranac Lake, NY 12983. Oriented toward the first line supervisor with a case study in each issue.

Training. Lakewood Publications, 731 Hennepin Ave, Minneapolis, MN 55403. Good source of information on training, and available hardware and software.

Training and Development Journal. American Society for Training and Development, Subscription Department, Suite 305, 600 Maryland Ave, SW, Washington, DC 20024. Official journal of the Society, it prints articles on training and human resources development. Covers both theory and practice and emphasizes both the latest developments in the field and the basics in training and development.

Current Awareness Publications

Newsletters, loose-leaf reporting services, and government publications are probably the best way to keep up with new legislation, court decisions, administrative regulations, and other legal developments. This category of publications can also be a good source of information about current research and personnel practices in both the public and private sector.

Newsletters are usually published by an agency or organization as a means of distributing timely information to clients. Loose-leaf publications are current awareness publications designed for continuous updating. Most of them are in ring-binder form and are sold by subscription. As new pages are issued, they must be interfiled, and obsolete pages deleted. These publications are usually the most current source of information on personnel topics.

Although loose-leaf publications provide an excellent current awareness service, subscriptions are quite expensive. Ideally, the library personnel office should have its own subscription to a general series such as the BNA or Prentice Hall series; if this is not financially possible, however, subscriptions to partial sets are available. Personnel administrators whose libraries subscribe to some of the services on this list may be able to arrange to have new pages routed before they are interfiled in binders.

The oldest and largest publishers of loose-leaf services in the personnel and industrial relations area are Bureau of National Affairs, Inc., 1231 25 St, NW, Washington, DC 20037; Commerce Clearing House, Inc., 4025 W. Peterson Ave, Chicago, IL 60646; and Prentice-Hall, Inc., Englewood Cliffs, NJ 07632.

Loose-leaf Publications: A Select List
Arbitration in the Schools. American Arbitration Association, 140 W. 51 St, New York, NY 10020. Covers arbitration and fact-finding awards in all levels of education. Gives summaries of the awards only, but full text is available at additional cost.
BNA Policy and Practice Series. Bureau of National Affairs, Inc., 1231 25 St, NW, Washington, DC 20037. Nine volumes covering six different areas of personnel practice: Compensation, Fair Employment Practices, Job Safety and Health, Labor Relations, Personnel Management, and Wages and Hours. Subscriptions can be for the entire series or individual topics. A subscription also includes two newsletters, *Bulletin to Management* and *Fair Employment Practices.*
Collective Bargaining Negotiations and Contracts. Bureau of National Affairs, Inc., 1231 25 St, NW, Washington, DC 20037. Covers all aspects of private sector collective bargaining, including current bargaining proposals and counter-proposals, and contract settlements. Gives texts of collective bargaining agreements that are representative of industry patterns and also contains full texts of many collective bargaining clauses. Subscription includes the newsletter: *What's New in Collective Bargaining Negotiations and Contracts.*
Daily Labor Report. Bureau of National Affairs, Inc., 1231 25 St, NW, Washington, DC 20037. Gives in-depth coverage of current events in labor relations, for example, legislation, regulations, court decisions, and union events, including conventions and policy meetings.
Educators Negotiating Service. Educational Service Bureau, Inc., 1835 K Street, NW, Washington, DC 20006. Covers collective bargaining in education, current events, legislation, and court decisions. Also gives the texts of major contract agreements.

EEOC Compliance Manual. Bureau of National Affairs, Inc., 1231 25 St, NW, Washington, DC 20037. Texts of EEOC publications and guidelines.

EEOC Compliance Manual. Commerce Clearing House, Inc., 4025 W. Peterson Ave, Chicago, IL 60646. Similar to above entry in coverage but includes case table.

Employment and Training Reporter. Bureau of National Affairs, Inc., 1231 25 St, NW, Washington, DC 20037. Specializes in sources of government funding in the employment and training area. Extensive coverage of CETA (Comprehensive Employment and Training Act).

Employment Coordinator. Research Institute of America, 589 Fifth Ave, New York, NY 10017. Easy to use, covers laws and regulations applying to the personnel function.

Employee Benefits Compliance Coordinator. Research Institute of America, 589 Fifth Ave, New York, NY 10017. Specializes in coverage of ERISA (Employee Retirement Income Security Act); however does include coverage of many types of benefit plans.

Employment Safety and Health Guide. Commerce Clearing House, Inc., 4025 W. Peterson Ave, Chicago, IL 60646. Coverage of OSHA (Occupational Safety and Health Act), including decisions of the Occupational Safety and Health Commission.

Government Employee Relations Report. Bureau of National Affairs, Inc., 1231 25 St, NW, Washington, DC 20037. Covers labor relations and collective bargaining on the federal, state, and local level. A good source of information on state labor laws. Also gives examples of existing contract agreements in the public sector and public sector arbitration awards.

Labor Law Reports and Labor Law Library. Commerce Clearing House, Inc., 4025 W. Peterson Ave, Chicago, IL 60646. Gives decisions and arbitration awards. Among the separate volumes are *Employment Practices Guide; Labor Relations; State Labor Law;* and *Wages-Hours.*

Labor Relations Reporter. Bureau of National Affairs, Inc., 1231 25 St, NW, Washington, DC 20037. Among the individual volumes are *Analysis; News and Background Information; Fair Employment Practices; Labor Arbitration Reports; Labor-Management Relations; Labor Relations Expediter; Labor Relations Yearbook; State Labor Laws;* and *Wages and Hours.*

National Public Employment Reporter. Labor Relations Press, Box 579, Highland Office Center, Fort Washington, PA 19034. Coverage of public sector labor relations, including decisions and orders of boards and commissions.

Personnel Management Program. Prentice-Hall, Inc., Englewood Cliffs, NJ 07632. Comparable to BNA's *Policy and Practice* series, this series has eight volumes that cover seven different areas of personnel management. As with the BNA set, subscriptions are available either for the entire set or for specific topical areas. Topical volumes include *Communications; Compensation; Industrial Relations Guide; Labor Relations Guide.*

Public Personnel Administration Series. Prentice-Hall, Inc., Englewood Cliffs, NJ 07632. Comparable to BNA's *Policy and Practice* series and the Prentice-Hall *Personnel Management Program,* this series covers public sector personnel management. Individual volumes offer the following topical areas: *Public Personnel Administration; Labor-Management Relations and Public Personnel Administration; Policies and Practices for Personnel.*

Public Sector Arbitration Awards. Labor Relations Press, Box 579, Highland Office Center, Fort Washington, PA 19034. Gives both texts and summaries of labor arbitration awards in the public sector.

Summary of Labor Arbitration Awards. American Arbitration Association, 140 W. 51 St, New York, NY 10020. Coverage is limited to arbitration awards in the private sector. Gives summaries of the awards only; full texts are available at an additional cost.

Newsletters and Miscellaneous Publications

Academe. American Association of University Professors, One Du Pont Circle, Washington, DC 20036. Subscription free with membership in AAUP. Covers collective bargaining in colleges and universities.

Arbitration Commentary. Labor Relations Press, Box 579, Highland Office Center, Fort Washington, PA 19034. Commentary by Morris Stone, retired vice president of the American Arbitration on current developments in labor arbitration.

Assessment and Development. Development Dimensions, Inc., 250 Mt. Lebanon Blvd, Pittsburgh, PA 15234. Covers staffing, the assessment center as a performance evaluation technique.

Behavioral Sciences Newsletter. 60 Glen Ave, Glen Rock, NJ 07542. Covers the areas of training, motivation, staffing, job design, and staffing.

Bulletin on Training. BNA Communications, Inc., 9401 Decoverly Hall Rd, Rockville, MD 20850. Covers the area of training, features case studies and interviews with notable people in the field.

Career Development Bulletin. Columbia University, Center for Research in Career Development, Graduate School of Business, New York, NY 10027. Abstracts of research projects in the field of career development. Also covers current practices in corporations. Covers management selection and development as well.

Discipline and Grievances. National Foremen's Institute, 24 Rope Ferry Rd, Waterford, CT 06386. Case studies of grievances that have been brought to arbitration.

Dynamic Supervision. National Foremen's Institute, 24 Rope Ferry Rd, Waterford, CT 06386. Work improvement methods and personnel management tips for supervisors. Two separate editions, one directed at blue collar supervisors, one at supervisors of white collar clerical workers.

The EEO Report. Institute for Management, IFM Bldg, Old Saybrook, CT 06375. Reports current changes in the law and suggests how managers can ensure compliance.

The EEO Review. Executive Enterprises Publications Co., 22 W. 21 St, New York, NY 10010. Aimed at the first-line supervisor, or department manager, this letter emphasizes preventing discrimination complaints or resolving them at the local level.

Employee Benefit News. Enterprise Communications, 1483 Chain Bridge Rd, Suite 202, McLean, VA 22101. Short newspaper style articles on employee benefits.

Employment Relations Report. National Information Bureau, 930 F St, NW, Suite 807, Washington, DC 20004. Covers the field of labor relations. Includes legal developments.

Equal Employment Opportunity Forum. 1201 S. Washington Blvd, Venice, CA 90291. Covers equal employment and affirmative action issues with emphasis on the point of view of minorities and women. This newsletter contains job listings, so it is a potential recruiting source.

Fair Employment Compliance: A Confidential Letter to Management. Management Resources, Inc., 757 Third Ave, New York, NY 10017. Covers the field of fair employment compliance. Supplements give detailed coverage of specific issues.

From the State Capitals (series of newsletters). Bethune Jones, 321 Sunset Ave, Asbury Park, NJ 07712. The newsletters in the series are *Labor Relations Report; Personnel Management Report; Unemployment Compensation Report; Wage-Hour Regulation; Workmen's Compensation Report.* They cover state laws, regulations, and development in the topical areas described above.

Guide to Library Placement Sources. American Library Association, Office for Library Personnel Resources, 50 E. Huron, Chicago, IL 60611. This reprint from the Bowker Annual is a very comprehensive guide to all sources of listings for library job openings, including periodicals with ads, hotlines, and placement services. Although directed at the librarian who is job hunting, it is also a valuable source of recruiting information for the library personnel administrator.

The Government Manager. Bureau of National Affairs, Inc., 1231 25 St, NW, Washington, DC 20037. Directed at public sector supervisors; gives tips on people management.

Human Resource Executive. Axon Group, 1035 Camphill Rd, Fort Washington, PA 19034. Features innovative company programs.

Industrial Relations News. Enterprise Publications, 20 N. Wacker Dr, Chicago, IL 60606. Although the title emphasizes industrial relations, this publication actually covers general personnel topics. It has two monthly supplements, one featuring news items about people in the field, including promotions and transfers of prominent personnel executives, and the other giving in-depth coverage of selected issues. Access to an information service, IRN Hotline, also comes with a subscription.

In the Public Service. AFL-CIO, Public Employee Department, 815 16 St, NW, Washington, DC 20006. Covers public sector unionism and collective bargaining.

Interface. Council of AFL-CIO Unions for Professional Employees, 81 16 St, NW, Washington, DC 20006. Covers union issues of interest to professional union members.

International Council for the Quality of Working Life Newsletter. London Graduate School of Business Studies, International Council for the Quality of Working Life, Regents Park, London, England, NW1 4SA. International coverage of programs to improve the quality of working life.

IPMA News. International Personnel Management Association, 1850 K St, NW, Washington, DC 20006. Subscription free to IPMA members. Association newsletter.

IRRA Newsletter. Industrial Relations Research Association, 7226 Social Science Bldg, University of Wisconsin, Madison, WI 53706. News of the Association.

Job Safety and Health Report. Business Publishers, Inc., P.O. Box 1067, Blair Station, Silver Spring, MD 20910. Covers federal and state job safety and health legislation and current developments.

Labor Relations in Education. Capitol Publications, Inc., 2430 Pennsylvania Ave, NW, Washington, DC 20005. Covers trends in unionism and collective bargaining in schools and colleges.

Library Personnel News. American Library Association, Office for Library Personnel Resources, 50 E. Huron, Chicago, IL 60611. Newsletter devoted to personnel issues that affect libraries. Gives information on personnel practices in libraries based on the results of canvasses and surveys. Covers trends, laws, and new developments in personnel.

Midwest Monitor: A Digest of Current Literature and Developments in Public Sector Labor Relations. Indiana University, School of Public and Environmental Affairs, 400 E. Seventh St, Bloomington, IN 47401. Published by the Midwest Center for Public Sector Labor Relations. Gives good coverage of trends and developments in labor relations and collective bargaining in the public sector.

National Center for the Study of Collective Bargaining in Higher Education Newsletter. City University of New York, Baruch College, 155 E. 24 St, New York, NY 10010. National Center for the Study of Collective Bargaining in Higher Education, 17 Lexington Ave, New York, NY 10010. Covers collective bargaining in colleges and universities. Good discussion of contract provisions.

Newsletter for Industry: Affirmative Action for Handicapped People. Harold Russel Associates, 304 Cambridge Rd, Woburn, MA 01801. Covers legislation and current development. Also gives case studies from industry.

OSHA Up to Date. National Safety Council, 425 N Michigan Ave, Chicago, IL 60611. Coverage of health and safety issues in the workplace.

Personnel Advisory Bulletin. Bureau of Business Practice, 24 Rope Ferry Rd, Waterford, CT 06386. General personnel topics with emphasis on staffing.

Personnel Management Week. Executives Research Council, 666 E. Ocean Blvd, Long Beach, CA 90802. General personnel management newsletter.

Personnel Manager's Legal Reporter. Bureau of Law and Business, Box 7-601, West Hartford, CT 06107. Covers legal developments in all areas that affect the field of personnel management. Suggestions for compliance with the laws.

Personnel Materials and Resources. Available through the American Library Association, OLPR American Library Association, 50 E. Huron St, Chicago, IL 60611. A compilation of all personnel-related publications of the American Library Association, including nonprint material.

SPEC (Systems Procedures Exchange Center) Kits. Association of Research Libraries, 1527 N. Hampshire Ave, NW, Washington, DC 20036. Packets of materials usually consisting of forms, policy statements, or other types of materials that illustrate current practices in member libraries. Many deal with personnel, including kits on position classification and performance evaluation.

Successful Supervisor. Dartnell Corporation, 4660 Ravenswood Ave, Chicago, IL 60640. Aimed at helping the supervisor, gives problem-solving ideas and self-evaluation check lists.

The Supervisor's EEO Review. Executive Enterprises Publications Co., Inc., 33 W. 60 St, New York, NY 10016. Aimed at the first-line supervisor.

Topics in Personnel (T.I.P. Kits). American Library Association, Office for Library Personnel Resources, 50 E. Huron, Chicago, IL 60611. Series of kits containing reprints, original articles, forms, and other material covering writing job descriptions, hiring, pay equity, performance appraisal, and employee assistance programs. OLPR usually issues two new kits each year.

Select List of Government Publications

If a library personnel administrator needs the original text of a law or regulation governing an aspect of personnel practice, the following sources should be consulted. For those who do not need the original text but simply wish to keep abreast of current developments, subscribing to relevant loose-leaf publications or newsletters listed in previous sections is a more efficient way of keeping up with legal developments. These loose-leaf and newsletter services also have the advantage of covering court decisions as well as federal regulations.

Although it is not possible to list all of the government publications in the field of personnel, a select list is given here to provide examples of available material.

Black News Digest. U.S. Department of Labor, Office of Information, Publications and Reports, Washington, DC 20210. Statistics and news of employment and training opportunities and other government programs which are of interest to blacks.

Casehandling Manual National Labor Relations Board. U.S. Government Printing Office, Washington, DC 20402. A compliance manual for labor relations matters coming under the jurisdiction of the National Labor Relations Board.

Court Decisions Relating to the National Labor Relations Board. Texts of court decisions involving the National Labor Relations Board.

Decisions and Orders of the National Labor Relations Board. Texts of National Labor Relations Board decisions.

Employment Standards Digest. U.S. Department of Labor, Employment Standards Administration, Washington, DC 20210. News of the employment standards administration.

Federal Personnel Manual System. U.S. Government Printing Office, Washington, DC 20402. Formerly issued by the U.S. Civil Service Commission, this publication is now issued by the Office of Planning and Evaluation. Covers the federal personnel system.

Intergovernmental Personnel Notes. Office of Intergovernmental Programs, U.S. Office of Personnel Management, Box 14184, Washington, DC 20044. Covers items of interest to public sector personnel managers.

Labor Management Relations Issues in State and Local Governments. Office of Intergovernmental Programs, U.S. Office of Personnel Management, Box 14184, Washington, DC 20044. Because individual issues give in-depth coverage of specific topics, this is an excellent introduction to labor relations in the public sector for both library personnel officers and library supervisors.

Women and Work. U.S. Department of Labor, Office of Information Publications and Reports, Washington, DC 20210. Statistics on women in the labor force; also news of government programs of interest to women.

Code of Federal Regulations. Office of the Federal Register. National Archives and Records Service. General Services Administration. U.S. Government Printing Office, Washington, DC 20402. The CFR is a codification of the general and permanent rules published in the Federal Register by the Executive departments and agencies of the federal government. The code is divided into fifty titles that represent broad areas subject to federal regulation.

Federal Register. Office of the Federal Register. National Archives and Records Service. General Services Administration. U.S. Government Printing Office, Washington, DC 20402. Gives current regulations as soon as they are issued.

U.S. Statutes at Large. Published by the Authority of Congress under the Direction of the Secretary of State. U.S. Government Printing Office, Washington, DC 20402. Contains the laws that form the basis of federal regulations.

SOURCES OF STATISTICAL INFORMATION

The two most common types of statistical information needed by library personnel administrators are demographic statistics on the race, gender, and ethnicity of the work force and statistics on compensation and salary. The most complete source of demographic information is the U.S. Census. Many state departments of labor abstract the information on the work force for their local area. Whenever these compilations are available, they are much easier to use than the Census as a whole. Information on librarians is available in: American Library Association. Academic and Public Librarians: *Data by Race, Ethnicity and Sex.* Chicago: American Library Association, Office for Library Personnel Resources, 1986.

Compensation and Salary Data

The salary surveys given in this section are all conducted regularly. Many are annual; others biannual or of other frequency.

Learmont, Carol L. and Van Houten, Stephen. "Placements and Salaries." *Library Journal.* Annual article in Library Journal, usually in the fall.

Lynch, Mary Jo and Margaret Myers. *ALA Survey of Librarian Salaries.* Chicago: American Library Association. Biannual.

Association of Research Libraries. *ARL Annual Salary Survey.* Washington, D.C.: ARL. Annual.

College and University Personnel Association. *Administration Compensation Survey Report*. Washington, D.C.: CUPA. Annual.

American Library Association. *Public Library Data Statistical Report*. Chicago: PLA. Annual.

International City Management Association. "Salaries of Municipal Officials" in *Municipal Year Book*. Washington, D.C. ICMA. Annual.

Educational Research Service, Inc. *National Survey of Salaries and Wages in Public Schools*. Arlington, VA: ERS. Annual.

HBW Associates, Inc. *Public Library Work Benefits Survey*. Dallas, TX: HBW, 1988.

The U.S. Department of Labor, Bureau of Labor Statistics. *Area Wage Surveys*. Surveys of over 80 standard metropolitan areas conducted on an annual basis. Covers primarily clerical and manual labor. Also covers benefits.
U.S. Department of Labor, Bureau of Labor Statistics. *National Survey of Professional Administrative, Technical and Clerical Pay*, March, 1987 (S/N-029-001-02936-5). Available as Bulletin 2243. $5 from the Superintendent of Documents, GPO, Washington, D.C. 20402.
The Administrative Management Society, 4622 Street Road, Trevose, PA, 19047 conducts a survey of clerical, data processing, and middle management jobs.

For a list of salary surveys in special libraries, state libraries, medical and law libraries, and library schools, see Appendix A, *ALA Survey of Librarian Salaries* cited above.

BOOKS

General Books

Beatty, R.W. and C.E. Schneier, *Personnel Administration: An Experiential Skill Building Approach,* rev. ed., 5th ed. Reading, Mass.: Addison-Wesley, 1981.
French, Wendell. *The Personnel Management Process,* 5th ed. Boston: Houghton Mifflin, 1982.
McCormick, Ernest J. *Job Analysis: Methods and Applications*. New York: American Management Association, 1979.

Miner, John B., and Miner, Mary G. *Personnel and Industrial Relations: A Managerial Approach,* 4th ed. New York: Macmillan, 1985.

Yoder, Dale, *Personnel Management and Industrial Relations,* 6th ed. Englewood Cliffs, NJ: Prentice-Hall, 1970.

————, and H.G. Heneman, eds. *Administration and Organization,* ASPA Handbook of Personnel and Industrial Relations, Vol. 6, Washington, DC: Bureau of National Affairs, 1977.

————. *Planning and Auditing PAIR,* ASPA Handbook of Personnel and Industrial Relations, Vol. 4. Washington, DC: Bureau of National Affairs, 1976.

————. *PAIR Policy and Program Management,* ASPA Handbook of Personnel and Industrial Relations, Vol. 7. Washington, DC: Bureau of National Affairs, 1977.

Employee Selection, EEO/Affirmative Action, and Human Resources Planning

Anderson, Howard J. *Major Employment Law Principles Established by the EEOC, the OFCCP and the Courts.* Washington, DC: Bureau of National Affairs, 1980.

Dunnette, Marvin and Edwin Fleishman, eds. *Human Capability Assessment.* Hinsdale, NJ: Erlbaum Assoc., 1982.

Burack, Elmer H. *Creative Human Resource Planning: A Strategic Approach.* Englewood Cliffs, NJ: Prentice-Hall, 1988.

Manager's Guide to EEO. New York: Executive Enterprises Publishers, 1977.

Yoder, Dale, and H.G. Heneman, Jr., eds. *Staffing Policies and Strategies,* ASPA Handbook of Personnel and Industrial Relations, Vol. 1. Washington, DC: Bureau of National Affairs, 1974.

Labor/Employee Relations

Belcher, David and Thos. J. Alchisen, *Compensation Administration.* 2nd ed. Englewood Cliffs, NJ: Prentice-Hall, 1987.

Cummings, L.L. and Donald P. Schwab, *Performance in Organizations: Determinants and Appraisal.* Glenview, Ill.: Scott Foresman, 1978.

Yoder, Dale and H.G. Heneman, Jr., eds. *Motivation and Commitment,* ASPA Handbook of Personnel and Industrial Relations, Vol. 2. Washington, DC: Bureau of National Affairs, 1975.

Davey, Harold W. *Contemporary Collective Bargaining,* 4th ed. Englewood Cliffs, NJ: Prentice-Hall, 1982.

Elkouri, Frank and Edna A. Elkouri, *How Arbitration Works,* 4th ed. Washington, DC: Bureau of National Affairs, 1985.

Grievance Guide, 6th ed. BNA Editorial Staff, Washington, DC: Bureau of National Affairs, 1982.

Richardson, Reed C. *Collective Bargaining by Objectives: A Positive Approach,* 2nd ed. Englewood Cliffs, NJ: Prentice-Hall, 1985.

Weatherford, John W. *Collective Bargaining and the Academic Librarian.* Metuchen, NJ: Scarecrow, 1976.

Yoder, Dale and H.G. Heneman, Jr., eds. *Employee and Labor Relations,* ASPA Handbook of Personnel and Industrial Relations, Vol. 3. Washington, DC: Bureau of National Affairs, 1975.

Training and Human Resources Development

Creth, Sheila. *Effective on the Job Training.* Chicago, ALA, 1986.

Davis, Larry N. and McCallon, Earl. *Planning, Conducting, Evaluating Workshops: A Practitioner's Guide to Adult Education.* Austin, Tex.: Learning Concepts Publishing Co., 1974.

Fordyce, Jack K. and Raymond Weil. *Managing with People: A Manager's Handbook of Organization Development Methods,* 2nd ed. Reading, Mass.: Addison-Wesley, 1979.

French, Wendell L. and Cecil H. Bell, Jr. *Organization Development: Behavioral Science Interventions for Organization Development,* 3rd ed. Englewood Cliffs, NJ: Prentice-Hall, 1984.

Kellogg, M.S. *What To Do About Performance Appraisal,* rev. ed. New York: American Management Association, 1975.

Laird, Dugan, *Approaches to Training and Development,* 2nd ed. Reading, Mass.: Addison-Wesley, 1985.

Nadler, Leonard. *Corporate Human Resource Development.* New York: Van Nos Reinhold Co., 1980.

Yoder, D. and H.G. Heneman, Jr., eds. *Training and Development,* ASPA Handbook of Personnel and Industrial Relations, Vol. 5. Washington, D.C.: Bureau of National Affairs, 1977.

Background Reading

Campbell, J.P. et al. *Managerial Behavior, Performance and Effectiveness.* New York: McGraw-Hill, 1970.

Carlzon, Jan. *Moments of Truth.* Cambridge, Mass.: Ballinger Publ., 1987.

Landy, Frank J. and Don A. Trumbo. *Psychology of Work Behavior,* 3rd ed. Homewood, Ill.: Dorsey Press, 1985.

Luthans, Fred. *Organizational Behavior.* 4th ed. New York: McGraw-Hill, 1985.

———, and R. Kreitner. *Organizational Behavior Modification and Beyond.* 2nd ed. Glenview, Ill.: Scott Foresman, 1985.

McCormick, Ernest J. and David Glen. *Industrial and Organizational Psychology,* 8th ed. Englewood Cliffs, N.J.: Prentice-Hall, 1985.

Porter, Lynman W. *Behavior in Organizations.* New York: McGraw-Hill, 1975.

Tarkenton, Fran. *How to Motivate People.* New York: Harper & Row.

ASPA Book Awards

Fear, Richard A. *The Evaluation Interview.* New York: McGraw-Hill, 1973. Year Award Given: 1974

Glueck, William F. *Personnel: A Diagnostic Approach.* Dallas, Tex.: Business Publ. Inc., 1974. Year Award Given: 1975

Luthans, Fred. *Organizational Behavior Modification.* Glenview, Ill.: Scott Foresman & Co., 1975. Year Award Given: 1976

Killian, Ray A., AEP. *Human Resources Management: An ROI Approach.* New York: AMACOM, 1976. Year Award Given: 1977

Beatty, Richard W. and Craig Eric Schneier. *Personnel Administration: An Experiential Skill-Building Approach.* Reading, Mass.: Addison-Wesley, 1977. Year Award Given: 1978

Cohen, Allen R. and Herman Gadon. *Alternative Work Schedules.* Reading, Mass.: Addison-Wesley, 1978. Year Award Given: 1979

Erdlen, John D. and Donald H. Sweet. *Job Hunting for the College Graduate.* Lexington, Mass.: Heath & Co., 1979. Year Award Given: 1980

Walker, James W. *Human Resource Planning.* New York: McGraw-Hill, 1980. Year Award Given: 1981

Meyer, Mary Coeli, Jeanenne Oestriech, Frederick J. Collins, and Inge Berchtold. *Sexual Harassment.* New York: Petrocelli Books Inc., 1981. Year Award Given: 1982

Kirkpatrick, Donald L. *How to Improve Performance Through Appraisal and Coaching.* New York: AMACOM, 1982. Year Award Given: 1983

Henderson, Richard I. *Practical Guide to Performance Appraisal.* Reston, VA: Reston Publ. Co., 1984. Year Award Given: 1985

Kirkpatrick, Donald. *How to Manage Change Effectively.* San Francisco, CA.: Jossey-Bass Publ. Co., 1985. Year Award Given: 1986

Bellman, Geoffrey M. *Quest for Staff Leadership.* Glenview, Ill.: Scott Foresman & Co., 1986. Year Award Given: 1987

Block, Peter. *The Empowered Manager: Positive Political Skills at Work.* San Francisco, CA.: Jossey-Bass Publ. Co., 1987. Year Award Given: 1988

NONPRINT MATERIALS

Nonprint materials in the human resources field are primarily used in training and development. There is no one source or bibliography that lists available nonprint materials. The best way to become acquainted with nonprint materials is to regularly scan journals in the area of training and development listed in this Appendix's Basic and Supplementary Journals sections. Practitioner-oriented journals, such as *Personnel Journal* with its Resource Market Place column, are a good way to become aware of the resources available. In addition to columns that feature reviews, many nonprint training materials are advertised in these journals. It goes without saying that ads alone are not sufficient, and the library personnel administrator should preview and carefully evaluate advertised materials.

Perhaps one area of nonprint material, the management training film, deserves special attention. Individual film titles will not be listed here because the training needs vary widely from organization to organization. There are, however, several commercial film companies that have many excellent management training and personnel-related films. Names of the most prominent are listed below, and administrators may consider ordering catalogs from these companies. Most films are available for preview, although there is often a fee.

BNA Communications Inc., 9401 Decoverly Hall Rd, Rockville, MD 20850. 301-948-0540. BNA has several training films in the personnel and industrial relations area, including films on union grievance procedures and arbitration, and EEO/Affirmative Action. BNA often holds previews in major urban areas, so it can be useful to be on their mailing list.

CRM McGraw-Hill Films, Box 60164, Del Mar, CA 92014. 800-421-0833. Films on all aspects of management, including time management. Strong in such aspects of human resources development as motivation and communication.

Roundtable Films, 113 N. San Vicente Blvd, Beverly Hills, CA 90211. 213-675-1402. Films on all aspects of management and on several human resources topics. This company also has several films on organization development.

Salenger Educational Media, 1635 12 St, Santa Monica, CA 90404. 213-450-1300. Films on management, human resources development, organization development, and health and safety.

References

1. Dugan Laird, *Approaches to Training and Development.* (Reading, Mass.: Addison-Wesley, 1978), pp. 68, 69.
2. Georgianna Herman and Gwendolyn Lloyd, "PAIR Literature: Keeping Up to Date," *ASPA Handbook of Personnel and Industrial Relations,* Vol. 8 *Professional PAIR,* ed. by Dale Yoder & Herbert G. Heneman, Jr. (Washington, D.C.: Bureau of National Affairs), 1979, p. 8–243.
3. Ibid.
4. Leonard R. Brice, "Professional Services for PAIR: Associations and Consultants," *ASPA Handbook of Personnel and Industrial Relations, vol. 8, Professional PAIR,* ed. by Dale Yoder & Herbert G. Heneman, Jr. (Washington, D.C.: Bureau of National Affairs), 1979, p. 8-69, 8-63.
5. Marvin Weisbord, "The Organization Development Consultant," *Organization Development, Theory, Practice, Research,* ed. Wendell L. French, et al. (Dallas: Business Publications, 1978), p. 321.

Index

ACRL. *See* Association of College and Research Libraries.

AIDS virus tests, laws on, 29, 30

ALA. *See* American Library Association

Ability, as staff development goal, 131

Absolute concept of management, 270

Academic institutions, unions for librarians at, 23, 24

Academic libraries staffing
  changes occurring in, 55
  standards for, 48–49

Access to personnel records, rights of employees, 28–30

Accountability, role of in job factors, 92

Advertising, relation to recruitment, 106

Advisory committees, for staff development, 123

Affirmative action, 19–23
  court decisions on, 22–23
  drafting plans for, 21–22
  relation to recruitment, 106

Age discrimination, laws on, 18

Age Discrimination in Employment Act, 18

Alcohol tests, laws on, 29–30

American Library Association

(ALA), role of in compensation regulation, 234–235

Analysis of personnel administration activities, 66

Antidiscrimination,
  executive orders on, 19
  laws on 232–233

Appraisal systems. *See* Performance appraisal

Arbitration (with unions), 278, 290–293

Arbitrators, role of, 290–293

Arizona Board of Regents, role of in salary allocation, 163

Arizona State University Libraries
  behavior patterns, 182
  multiple raters, 194
  performance appraisal, 165

Art libraries, standards for staffing, 51

Association of College and Research Libraries (ACRL)
  peer evaluation requirements, 189
  staffing percentages, 42
  unionization policies of, 255

Automation. *See* Computerization

BARS. *See Behaviorally-Anchored Rating Scales*

Behavior patterns, use of in

performance appraisal, 181–182, 183

Behavioral science research, 4

Behaviorally-Anchored Rating Scales (BARS), 171, 175, 181–182

Benchmark jobs, 84

Benefits and services, 237–238

Books for personnel administrators, 327–330

Boston University Library, unionization of, 251

COLT. *See* Council on Library/Media Technical Assistants

Career ladders, effects of on staffing, 58

Case study techniques, for staff development trainers, 139

Case Western Reserve University Library, job analysis, 89–91

Center for Research Libraries, performance standards, 176

Characteristics and qualifications for personnel administrators, 8–10

Checklists for orientation projects, 125

Choices among people technique, use of in performance appraisal, 175–176

Circled salaries, 231

Circular A-76 (Office of Personnel Management), 51

Civil Rights Act of 1964 (Title VII), 14–15, 17, 25–26, 33, 167, 233

Civil Service Reform Act of 1978, 179, 180–181

Clerical workers. *See* Support staff

Cognitive resources, role of in job factors, 92

Collection development, staffing, changes occurring in, 53–54

Collective bargaining, 23–24
effects of on recruitment, 68–69

implications of, 293–296
laws on, 253–257
New York City regulation of, 256–257
See also Contract negotiations with unions

College libraries, staffing, standards for, 49

Columbia University, literature distributed by during union organizing, 258, 260–262

Columbia University Libraries
peer evaluation system, 190–191
performance standards, 179
unionization of, 254

Comparable worth and equal pay, 233–234

Comparison of employees, use of in performance appraisal, 178

Compensation
computerization of, 243
external influences on, 231–235
laws on, 17–18, 231–235

Compensation management, 221–246
objectives of, 223–224
responsibilities in, 243

Compensation programs
design of, 226–231
nature of, 222–223

Computerization
effects of on library staffing, 56
effects of on personnel administration, 65

Computerized records, privacy of, laws on, 29

Computers, role of in compensation management, 243

Conciliation (with unions), 277–278

Continuing education, 144–148
factors in, 146
funding of, 147

Contract administration, 280–289
discipline and discharge, 287–289
early stages of, 280–281
grievances, 282, 283–287

pressure tactics, 281–282
record keeping, 283
Contract negotiations with unions,
   263–278
   arbitration, 279, 290–293
   collective bargaining implications,
      293–296
   conciliation, 277–278
   first contract issues, 266–267
   management preparations for,
      264–265
   management rights, 270–273
   mediation, 278
   stages of, 273
   union preparations for, 264–265
   union security, 267–270
Cornell University Library,
   unionization of, 254
Council on Library/Media Technical
   Assistants (COLT), roles for
   paraprofessionals set by, 47
Court decisions on affirmative action
   plans, 22–23

Davis-Bacon Act of 1931,
   231
Demonstration techniques for staff
   development trainers, 138
Demotion, guidelines for, 241
Disability insurance for income
   maintenance, 33–34
Discharge of employees, 287–289
Disciplinary action, role of
   performance appraisal in,
   165–167
Discipline (in collective bargaining),
   287–289
Discrimination against the
   handicapped, laws on, 18–19
Discussion techniques for staff
   development trainers, 138–
   139
Drug tests, laws on, 29–30
Dupage Library System,
   performance appraisal, 203

EEOC. See Equal Employment
   Opportunity Commission
EPA. See Equal Pay Act of
   1963
ERISA. See Employee Retirement
   Income Security Act
Elections on unionization
   legal and illegal activities,
      258–260
   literature concerning,
      260–262
   significance of, 262–263
Employee benefits, laws on, 30–34
Employee comparisons, use of in
   performance appraisal, 178
Employee Retirement Income
   Security Act (ERISA) of 1974,
   32, 232
Employee security, 267, 268
Employees
   access of to personnel records, 28–
      30
   background information on, 71–
      72
Employment in education, laws on,
   18
Equal Educational Opportunity Act
   of 1972, 18
Equal employment opportunity, laws
   on, 14–19
Equal Employment Opportunity Act,
   233
Equal Employment Opportunity
   Commission (EEOC), 14, 16–
   17, 21–22
Equal Pay Act of 1963 (EPA), 235,
   17, 33, 232, 241
Equal pay and comparable worth,
   233–234
Evaluation of employees. See
   Performance appraisal
Evaluation of staff development,
   140–143
Evaluators of performance, 186–193
Executive Order 10988, 255–256
Executive Order 11491, 256
Executive orders, relation to
   antidiscrimination, 19

FLSA. *See* Fair Labor Standards Act of 1938

Factor-comparison system, use of in job evaluation, 84

Faculty status
effects of on staffing, 58
effects of on unionization, 24
outlook for, 255

Faculty unions, librarians in, 23

Fair Labor Standards Act (FLSA) of 1938, 25, 232

Federal Employee Compensation Equity Act of 1987, 234

Federal Equitable Pay Practices Act of 1987, 234

Federal Fair Credit Reporting Act, 29

Federal Labor Relations Council, 256

Federal libraries, staffing, standards for, 51

Federal Service Impasses Panel, 256

Finances, effects of on staffing, 57

Forced-choice technique, use of in performance appraisal, 175–176

Fringe benefits, 237–238

Funding
for continuing education, 147
for staff development, 137, 144

Funerals, leaves of absence for, 34

Goal-based systems, use of in performance appraisal, 182, 184–186

Gold circle salaries, 231

Green circle salaries, 231

Grievances
nature of, 282
procedures for, 283–287
process of, 94
resolution of, 285–287
scope of, 285
tactics involving, 281

Griggs v. *Duke Power*, 25–26

Group insurance, laws on, 33–34

Gulf Oil Corporation, multiple raters, 193

HMOs. *See* Health maintenance organizations

Handicapped, discrimination against, 18–19

Harvard University Library, unionization of, 252

Hay System, 225

Health and safety, laws on, 27

Health maintenance organizations (HMOs), laws on, 33

Health sciences libraries, staffing, standards for, 50

Hiring criteria, role of the MLS degree in, 25–27

Hiring goals, affirmative action programs for, 21

Hiring salaries, establishment of, 230

Holiday leave, laws on, 34

Hostile work environment, 16

Hours and wages, laws on, 231–232

Hours of work, laws on, 25

Human relations, relation to job analysis, 93–96

Human resources approach to personnel management, 6

ILTAP. *See* Illinois Task Analysis Project

Illegal aliens, laws on, 27–28

Illinois Personnel Records Statute, 29

Illinois project for job analysis, 87–88

Illinois Task Analysis Project (ILTAP), 43

Immediate supervisors, role of as performance evaluators, 186

Immigration Reform and Control
  Act, 27–28
Improvements of performance, role
  of performance appraisal in,
  157–161
Income protection, laws on, 232
International standards for staffing,
  52
Interpersonal resources, role of in
  job factors, 92
Interviewing of job applicants, 108,
  112–114
  techniques of, 112–114
Interviews
  use of in job analysis, 75, 77–78
  use of in staff development, 133–
  135

Job analysis, 72–80
  human relations aspects of, 93–
  96
  in libraries, 85–91
  methodology for, 75
  planning of, 73–75
Job analysis data, maintenance of,
  95–96
Job applicants
  final selection of, 114–115
  interviewing of, 108, 112–114
  screening of, 107–112
  testing of, 115
Job classification. See Job evaluation
Job descriptions, contents of, 75–77
Job evaluation, 80–85, 224–226
  human relations aspects of, 93–
  96
  in libraries, 85–91
  systems for, 81–85
Job factors, 91–93
  categories of, 91
Job grading, use of in job
  evaluation, 82
Job training
  orientation aspects of, 126–129
  planning of, 128–129
Jury duty, laws on, 34

Kent State University, salary
  allocation, 164
Know-how, role of in job factors, 92
Knowledge, role of as staff
  development goal, 131

Labor Management Relations Act of
  1947, 248, 254
Labor relations, 247–303
  laws on, 23–25
  opportunities for improving, 296–
  297
  responsibilities for, 278–279
  training aspects, 279
Labor unions. See Contract
  negotiations with unions;
  Unionization
Laws and regulations
  effects of on personnel
  administration, 13–39
  effects of on staffing, 57
Leaves of absence, laws on, 34
Lecture techniques for staff
  development trainers, 138
Legal environment of personnel
  administration, 13–39
Librarians
  duties of, 43–44
  in faculty unions, 23
  recruitment of, 101–107
Library administrators, staff
  development role of, 122–123
Library assistants, duties of, 46–47
Library degrees, relation to hiring
  criteria, 25–27
Library of Congress, performance
  standards, 176
Library selection project
  (California), 181
Lie detector tests, laws on, 29–30
Limited concept of management, 270
Line and staff relationships,
  concepts of, 6–8
Line managers, role of in
  performance appraisal, 156
Logs, use of in job analysis, 79

MBO. *See* Management by objective

MLS degree, relation to hiring criteria, 25–27

Management, concepts of, 2–4

Management approach to personnel management, 6

Management by objective (MBO), 168, 171, 184, 193

Management rights (with unions), 258–260, 270

Mandatory testing, laws on, 29–30

Maternity leave, laws on, 15, 34

McGill University Libraries, performance appraisal, 157, 158

Measures of output, use of in performance appraisal, 176

Media centers staffing standards for, 49–50 variations in patterns for, 52–53

Mediation (with unions), 278

Merit guidelines, 239

Merit pay, distribution schedules for, 240

Merit systems for compensation, 235–236 evaluation of, 71 responsibility for, 236–237

Meritor Savings Bank v. *Vincent,* 16–17

Merwine v. *Board of Trustees of State Institutions for Higher Learning,* 26

Multiple raters, use of in performance appraisal, 193–195

NIRA. *See* National Industrial Recovery Act of 1933

NLRB. *See* National Labor Relations Board

National Industrial Recovery Act (NIRA) of 1933, 231–232

National Labor Relations Act of 1935, 24, 232, 248, 254

National Labor Relations Board (NLRB), 24, 254 role of in organizing, 257–258

National Library of Medicine performance standards, 176, 179–180

Negotiations. *See* Contract negotiations with unions

Nepotism, prevalence of, 105

New York Public Library, arbitration agreements, 290

Nonprint materials for personnel administrators, 331–332

Nonprofessionals, substitute terminology for, 45

Norris-LaGuardia Act, 23

Northern Colorado University, peer evaluation system, 191–192

OFCCP. *See* Office of Federal Contract Compliance Programs

OSHA. *See* Occupational Safety and Health Administration

Oakland University, rating on a scale technique used, 175

Observation, use of in job analysis, 78

Occupational Safety and Health Act, 27

Occupational Safety and Health Administration (OSHA), 27

Office of Federal Contract Compliance Programs (OFCCP), 20

Omnibus Crime Control and Safe Streets Act, 29

Open-ended essays, use of in performance appraisal, 174–175

Organizational structure, effect of on staffing, 41

Organizations related to personnel administration, 305–315

Organizing (by unions), 257–263

legal and illegal activities during,
258–260
Orientation
checklists for, 125
job training aspects of, 126–129
staff development role in, 124, 126
Outside candidates for positions, 104
Oxford University Library,
performance appraisal, 200

Paraprofessionals, duties of, 45–47
Parental leave, availability of, 15
Part-time employees, performance
appraisal of, 198
Part-time positions, creation of,
105–106
Pay differential, justification for, 17
Pay plan analysis compa-ratio, 240–
241
Pay structure adjustments, 239
Peer evaluations, split system of at
Columbia University
Libraries, 190–191
use of in performance appraisal,
189–193
Performance appraisal
design of system for, 195–196
implementation of system for,
195–198
importance of, 153–156
as line responsibility, 156
methods of measurement used in,
177–186
multiple raters, 193–195
nature of evaluators, 186–193
nature of what is being measured,
173–174
poorly designed system, 196–197
purpose and techniques of, 152–
204
relation to compensation, 236
techniques for measurements,
174–177
types of systems for, 171, 198–
204
use of, 169–171

value of, 203–204
variations in design of, 198–204
Performance standards for
compensation, 236
Personnel administration
current issues in, 56–58
legal environment of, 13–39
nature of, 1–12
objectives of, 5
planning for, 64–66
viewpoints on, 5–6
Personnel administrators
characteristics and qualifications
of, 8–10
directory of resources for, 305–
332
Personnel planning, 64–100
Personnel records, privacy of, 28–29
Phoenix Public Library, performance
appraisal, 202
Physical resources, role of in job
factors, 92
Planning of personnel operations,
64–66
Point system, use of in job
evaluation, 82–84
Polygraph tests, laws on, 29–30
Position classification schemes, 69–
70
Pregnancy, laws on, 15
Premium pay rates, 241
Privacy
of computer records, laws on, 29
of personnel records, 28–30
Privacy Act, 28–29
Proactive approach to personnel
management, 6
Probationary evaluations, role of
performance appraisals in,
169
Problem-solving, role of in job
factors, 92
Professional librarians, performance
appraisal of, 200–203
Professionals
duties of, 43–45
percentages of in libraries, 42
ratio of to support staff, 41–42

Proficiency, use of in performance appraisal, 176–177

Profiling library personnel, 71–72

Programmed instruction techniques for staff development trainers, 139

Promotion from within, pros and cons of, 103–104

Promotion in rank, 70

Promotional systems, 70

Promotions
guidelines for, 241
role of performance appraisal in, 165

Public libraries staffing
percentages of levels, 42
standards for, 50
variations in patterns for, 52

Publications for personnel administrators, 315–326

Questionnaires, use of
in job analysis, 75, 78–79
in staff development, 133–135

Railway Labor Act of 1926, 23

Ratings on a scale, use of in performance appraisal, 175

Recruitment, 67–69
legal aspects of, 68
strategies for, 104–106

Recruitment of librarians, 101–107

Red circle salaries, 95, 231

Reference letters, role of in screening applicants, 110

Reference service, staffing, changes occurring in, 54

Religious practices, accommodations for, 15

Residual concept of management, 271

Resources for personnel administrators, directory of, 305–332

Retirement age, compulsory, 18

Retirement benefits, laws on, 32

Right-to-work laws, 268

Role playing techniques for staff development trainers, 139

Rutgers University Library, unionization of, 254

Safety and health, laws on, 27

Salaries
circled, 231
hiring, 230

Salary adjustments, role of in job analysis, 95

Salary allocation, role of performance appraisal in, 163–165

Salary compensation, 70–71

Salary equity analysis, 17–18, 241
example of, 242–243

Salary surveys, 228–230

School libraries staffing
percentages of levels, 42
standards for, 49–50
variations in patterns for, 52–53

Screening of applicants, 107–112

Search records, retention of, 115

Selection of employees, role of performance appraisal in, 167–168

Selection of job applicants, 114–115

Self-ratings, use of in performance evaluation, 188–189

Services and benefits, 237–238

Sex discrimination, relation to pregnancy and maternity, 15

Sexual harassment, laws on, 15–17

Sick leave, laws on, 34

Silver circle salaries, 231

Simple ranking, use of in job analysis, 81

Sizes of libraries, staffing, changes affected by, 54–56

Skill, role of as staff development goal, 131

Slowdowns, tactics involving, 281

Social security, laws on, 31
Societal changes, effects of on
        staffing, 56
Special libraries, staffing, standards
        for, 50–51
Specialists, duties of, 44–45
Staff, staff development role of, 123
Staff and line relationships,
        concepts of, 6–8
Staff development, 118–144
    advisory committees' role in, 123
    evaluation of, 140–143
    funding for, 137, 144
    interviews used in, 133–135
    library administrators' role in,
        122–123
    materials for, 129–136
    methods used for, 138–140
    orientation aspects of, 124, 126
    planning of, 130
    program components of, 123
    questionnaires used in, 133–135
    resources for, 136–144
    responsibility for, 121–123
    role of performance appraisal in,
        161–163
    role of trainers in, 140–143
    staff members' role in, 123
    supervisors' role in, 121–122
Staffing
    changes in functions occurring,
        53–54
    effect of
        organizational structure on, 41
        career ladders on, 58
        financial factors on, 57
        internal forces on, 57–58
        legal factors on, 57
        societal changes on, 56
        technology on, 56
    future considerations, 58–59
    levels of, 41–43
    size of libraries as a factor in, 54–
        56
    standards for, 48–52
        state level, 51
    utilization of, 66–96
    variations in patterns for, 52–55

Staffing patterns, 40–63
Standards for staffing, 48–52
    international level, 52
    state level, 51
    use of in performance appraisal,
        178–181
Stanford University Libraries,
        performance appraisal, 158
State level standards for staffing, 51
Statements of behavior technique,
        use of in performance
        appraisal, 175–176
Statistical information sources for
        personnel administrators,
        326–327
Strikes
    effects of, 261
    tactics involving, 281–282
Student assistants
    duties of, 47
    percentages of in libraries, 42
Students, performance appraisal of,
        198
Supervisors
    performance appraisal of, 199–
        200
    staff development role of, 121–
        122
Supervisors' supervisors, role of as
        performance evaluators, 187–
        188
Supplementary evaluators, role of as
        performance evaluators, 187
Support staff
    duties of, 45–47
    percentages of in libraries, 42
    performance appraisal of, 198–
        199
    ratio of to professionals, 41–42
Suspensions (for union members),
        288
Systems approach to personnel
        management, 6

Taft Hartley Act, 24, 248, 254

Task inventory, use of in job analysis, 79–80
Technical services, staffing, changes occurring in, 54
Technology, effects of on staffing, 56
Termination, role of performance appraisal in, 165–167
Testing of applicants, 115
Texas A&M University Library, faculty role in performance appraisal, 188
Title VII. See Civil Rights Act of 1964
Trainers for staff development, 140–143
Training methods for staff development trainers, 138
Trait-based systems, use of in performance appraisal, 177–178
Travel, leaves of absence for, 34
Trusteeship concept of management, 271

Unemployment insurance, laws on, 31–32
Uniform Guidelines on Employee Selection Procedures, 14
Union involvement in job analysis, 95
Union organizing, 257–263
Union security, 267–270
Unionization
  contract negotiations. See Contract negotiations with unions
  laws on, 23–25
  reasons for, 247–253
  rights of management in, 258–260
  status of in libraries, 250–253
U.S. Office of Personnel Management, staffing standards (circular A-76), 51
University libraries staffing

standards for, 48–49
variations in patterns for, 52
University of California at Riverside, performance appraisal, 165
University of California system, unionization of, 252
University of Chicago Library, salary allocation, 164
University of Colorado, salary allocation, 164
University of Connecticut Library
  job analysis, 88–89
  performance appraisal, 158
University of Connecticut Professional Employee's Association, salary allocation, 164
University of Illinois at Urbana-Champaign
  design of system for, 195–196
  performance appraisal, 202
University of Iowa Libraries, job analysis, 85–86
University of Michigan Library, job analysis, 86–87
University of Nebraska at Omaha Library, performance appraisal, 203
University of New Mexico, performance appraisal techniques, 199–200
University of Notre Dame Libraries, supplementary evaluators, 187
University of Texas Medical School Library at San Antonio, job analysis, 89–91
Updating of job analysis data, 95–96
Utilization of staff, 66–96

Vacations, laws on, 34
Vesting, laws on, 34
Vietnam-Era Veterans

Readjustment Act of 1974, 18–19

Vocational Rehabilitation Act of 1973, 18–19

Volunteers, duties of, 47–48

Voting, leaves of absence for, laws on, 34

Washington State University, peer evaluation system, 192

Welfare and Pension Plan Disclosure Act of 1959, 232

Wildcat strikes, 281

Workers' compensation, laws on, 32–33

Wages and hours, laws on, 231–232

Wagner Act, 24, 248, 254

Walsh-Healy Public Contracts Act of 1936, 232

Warnings (for union members), 287–288

Yale University Library, unionization of, 252

Yeshiva University
status of librarians, 24
unionization of faculty of, 254